CLARENDON ARISTOTLE SERIES

General Editors
J. L. ACKRILL AND LINDSAY JUDSON

D1446588

ARISTOTLE
Posterior Analytics

*Translated
with a Commentary
by*

JONATHAN BARNES

Second Edition

CLARENDON PRESS · OXFORD

*This book has been printed digitally and produced in a standard specification
in order to ensure its continuing availability*

OXFORD
UNIVERSITY PRESS

Great Clarendon Street, Oxford OX2 6DP

Oxford University Press is a department of the University of Oxford.
It furthers the University's objective of excellence in research, scholarship,
and education by publishing worldwide in

Oxford New York

Auckland Bangkok Buenos Aires Cape Town Chennai
Dar es Salaam Delhi Hong Kong Istanbul Karachi Kolkata
Kuala Lumpur Madrid Melbourne Mexico City Mumbai Nairobi
São Paulo Shanghai Singapore Taipei Tokyo Toronto

with an associated company in Berlin

Oxford is a registered trade mark of Oxford University Press
in the UK and in certain other countries

Published in the United States
by Oxford University Press Inc., New York

ISBN 0-19-824089-9

PREFACE TO THE FIRST EDITION

The major part of this book was written in the autumn of 1972, when I was a visiting member of the Institute for Advanced Study in Princeton. I am deeply grateful to the Institute for offering me ideal conditions in which to work on Greek philosophy. And I thank my College, Oriel, for enabling me to accept the offer by granting me a term's Sabbatical leave.

Many friends and colleagues on both sides of the Atlantic have helped and encouraged me. In Princeton, Professor Harold Cherniss allowed me to draw on his unparalleled knowledge of ancient philosophy; and Willis Doney regularly sustained my spirits with alcohol and advice. Parts of my notes, badly disguised as a paper, were read to groups at Princeton University, at Brooklyn College, at Dartmouth College, and at the University of Massachusetts in Amherst: my audience invariably pounced on my errors and improved my thoughts. Peggy Van Sant produced a beautiful typescript of the translation.

In Oxford I have received valuable aid from Lesley Brown, Christopher Kirwan, Nicholas Measor, and Richard Robinson. Parts of an early draft were gently mauled by the members of the Oxford Aristotelian Society. A paper based on my notes to *A* 3 was read to a seminar in London organized by Professor D. M. Balme. The Librarian, and the Acting Librarian, of Oriel allowed me to browse freely among the books from Sir David Ross's library. Mrs E. Hinkes typed out the notes with her customary care and skill.

My greatest debt is to Professor John Ackrill. As editor of the Clarendon Aristotle series, he has patiently overlooked my procrastinations and has been in constant and kindly attendance at my labours; he annotated a first, stuttering translation; and his detailed and meticulous criticism has brought numerous and substantial improvements to the notes. As my mentor, he first guided my stumbling footsteps along the steep and stony path of Aristotelian studies. I thank him warmly.

JONATHAN BARNES

Oriel College, Oxford

PREFACE TO THE SECOND EDITION

In the Introduction to the first edition of this book I lamented the fact that the *Posterior Analytics* was often misprized, or even ignored, by Aristotelian scholars. The lament was overblown; but it was not groundless. How things have changed. In the same year as my own book, there was published the monumental commentary on Book *A* by Mario Mignucci. A year earlier—but too late for me to consult—there had appeared Wolfgang Kullmann's *Wissenschaft und Methode*; a year later followed Gilles-Gaston Granger's *La Théorie aristotélicienne de la science*; and in 1978 the eighth Symposium Aristotelicum was devoted to the *Posterior Analytics*. Since then there have been over a hundred articles or books dedicated to one aspect or another of the work; and numerous publications on other parts of Aristotle's philosophy have made more than passing reference to the *Posterior Analytics*. Many of these studies have been primarily exegetical in purpose; but there has also been a revival of strictly philosophical interest in the *Posterior Analytics*, and more than one author has urged that Aristotle's philosophy of science is no more antiquated than his ethics or his metaphysics.

Much of this recent stuff is shoddy—such now is the way of things in the learned world. But a part of it has been far from despicable; and amateurs of the *Analytics* may reasonably believe that the object of their love has become both more widely admired and more deeply understood.

The second edition differs from the first in several respects. The translation has been entirely redone. The original version was a creature of its time. Professing a stern fidelity to Aristotle's Greek, it betrayed a profound misconception of that delicate virtue. It was written in a sort of dog English: always inelegant and sometimes barbarous, it appeared here as comic or disgusting and there as merely incomprehensible.[1] The new translation is more faithful to Aristotle. It is also—and by the same token—

---

[1] The translation was justly castigated by reviewers: see e.g. S. Mansion, *Antiquité Classique*, 46 (1977), 627–8; STRIKER (1977); Dorothea Frede, *Philosophical Review*, 87 (1978), 288–91; EBERT (1980). (The list of Supplementary References gives details of works referred to by capitalized name and date.)

less vile in expression. The new Note on the Translation indicates the principles on which it is based.[2]

The notes have not been rewritten in the same thoroughgoing fashion; but they have all been revised. Some of what I wrote still seems to me to be true, and it stands as it was. In other places I no longer believe my original text but have been unable to hit upon anything more satisfactory; and here too the original matter stands. More generally, the style of the commentary is unchanged—it is as abrupt and unattractive as it ever was.[3] None the less, the revisions are extensive: I have corrected (or suppressed) a number of manifest errors; I have come to hold—and hence to express—a different opinion on a number of substantial issues and on very many points of detail; and I have added a certain amount of new matter. Much of all this derives from discussions with friends and colleagues; some of it derives from the publications of other scholars. (And although I do not pretend to have read—let alone to have pondered—everything which has come out in the last fifteen years, I have tried to be a little more generous than before in my bibliographical references.)

The Introduction remains as it was; but I have added a few supplementary notes. The Note on the Translation is new. The Synopsis and the Note on the Commentary are unchanged. Supplementary references have been adjoined to the List of References. An English–Greek Glossary has been added, and the Greek–English Glossary has been appropriately modified.

All in all, about a third of the revised version is new. I think that it warrants the title "second edition". What other titles it warrants, the reader will decide.

I am grateful to the General Editors of the Clarendon Aristotle series, and to the Clarendon Press, for encouraging me to undertake a new edition. And I am indebted to the members of my 1991 Chalet reading party, who made the initial stages of the task far more fun than such things usually are.

JONATHAN BARNES

Les Charmilles
July 1992

---

[2] A lightly amended version of the original translation was published in my revision of the Oxford Translation of Aristotle: *The Complete Works of Aristotle* (Princeton, NJ, 1984).

[3] After some thought, I have decided to leave the various symbolical formulations in the text, although they have distressed several readers (and perhaps helped none). And I have not had the time or the space to add the more general reflections on Aristotle's arguments and theories which several reviewers of the first edition desiderated.

CONTENTS

INTRODUCTION

I

Aristotle's sweet *Analytics* ravished generations of European scholars and scientists. The *Prior Analytics* displayed the pure discipline of logic, well-formed, elegant, seductive; the *Posterior Analytics* beckoned to deeper mysteries, offering a sure path to scientific progress, clear and imperious in its injunctions, delicious in its rigour. If a Bacon or a Locke sternly rejected the ancient pleasures of Aristotelianism, it was only the perverted excesses of scholasticism which fell to their condemnation: the original beauties of the *Analytics* still flashed and excited.

All that has changed. What once was welcomed as a ravishing delight is now reviled as a corruption and a rape: by its meretricious charms (so the accusation reads) the *Analytics* imposed on the learned world a narrow, blinkered, logic, and a stultifying theory of science. Thought was fettered; and if the old thinkers and scientists sang, they sang in chains.

The modern prosecutors generously allow the *Prior Analytics* a little merit for cultivating, with some formality, one small patch of logic; but they do not spare the *Posterior Analytics*: its first book, they allege, presents in the theory of 'demonstration' a barren and pernicious essay in scientific methodology; its second book, on definition, offers a farrago of doctrines about 'essences' and 'real' definitions which should embarrass even the most liberally disposed reader; and the general argument of both books is entangled in a thicket of wrangling, little of which is intelligible and none philosophically interesting.

A historian of ideas, faced by this intemperate charge, might put in a plea of mitigation. After all, a work as influential as the *Posterior Analytics* surely deserves serious and even sympathetic study, however execrable the doctrines it enshrines. Moreover, the *Posterior Analytics* does in a sense provide the framework within which the rest of the Aristotelian corpus, including those parts still generally admired, is arranged and ordered. Modern scholarship has, it is true, repudiated the nineteenth century's efforts to delineate Aristotle's 'system'; the corpus, it is now often claimed, presents no philosophical or scientific system, but offers a series of tentative theses and unresolved puzzles—Aristotle's thought is aporematic, not apodeictic. There are merits in this view, but it is extreme: we may allow that Aristotle's philosophy fails actually to present a grand system, without giving up the conviction that it is potentially and in design systematic; if the Aristotelian corpus is not, as it stands, an Encyclopaedia of Unified Science, it nevertheless forms—or was intended to form—the basis for such a large project. There are hints enough, scattered throughout Aristotle's writings, to show that he had a general conception of the range and classification of human knowledge, and that he saw his own voluminous researches in the light of that conception. And there are hints, less frequent but no less clear, that the theory of the *Posterior Analytics* was meant to provide the proper formal account and presentation of the finished system. In a perfect Aristotelian world, the material gathered in the corpus will be systematically presented; and the logical structure of the system will follow the pattern of the *Posterior Analytics*. If that is so, then any faithful lover of Aristotle will take some pains over the *Posterior Analytics*.

Such a speech might, I think, ensure a charitable sentence for the *Posterior Analytics*; but it will hardly secure a favourable verdict. The prosecution can be more forcibly met: its allegations are false and ill-founded.

First, Book *A* does not contain a theory of scientific methodology. Aristotle does not pretend to be offering guidance to the scientist—or, for that matter, to the historian or the philosopher—on how best to pursue his researches or how most efficiently to uncover new truths; nor, of course, did Aristotle attempt to carry out his own scientific researches in accordance with the canons of the *Analytics*. Book *A* is not a methodology of research; *a fortiori* it is not a barren or a pernicious methodology. Rather, it is concerned with the organization and presentation of the results of research: its aim is to say how we may collect into an intelligible whole the scientist's various discoveries—how we may so arrange the facts that their interrelations, and in particular their explanations, may best be revealed and grasped. In short, the primary purpose of demonstration is to expound and render intelligible what is already discovered, not to discover what is still unknown.[A]

The essential thesis of Book *A* is simple and striking: the sciences are properly expounded in formal axiomatized systems. What Euclid later did, haltingly, for geometry, Aristotle wanted

Supplementary Notes, cued by letters, appear at the end of the Introduction.

INTRODUCTION

done for every branch of human knowledge. The sciences are to
be axiomatized: that is to say, the body of truth that each defines
is to be exhibited as a sequence of theorems inferred from a few
basic postulates or axioms. And the axiomatization is to be for-
malized: that is to say, its sentences are to be formulated within a
well-defined language, and its arguments are to proceed according
to a precisely and explicitly specified set of logical rules. The
notion of formal axiomatization has more than historical value:
the birth and development of that notion are chronicled in the
Posterior Analytics; and if some of Aristotle's speculations are
quaint or antiquated, many remain pertinent to any understanding
of the nature of an axiomatic science.[B]

So much for Book *A*. Book *B*, I think, can also be defended. The
axioms of any science, it supposes, must be (or at least include)
definitions or statements of essence; and its main burden is to ask
how these definitions are to be elicited and exhibited. Unaris-
totelians are inclined to object, with an appealing crudity of
approach, that there are no such things as essences, and that if
there are they are not expressed by definitions. The objection is
wrong on both counts.

Aristotle's essentialism has little in common with its modern
homonym. Aristotelian essences are what John Locke called 'real'
essences: the essence of a kind *K* is that characteristic, or set of
characteristics, of members of *K* upon which any other properties
they have as members of *K* depend. That there are essences of
this sort is at worst a trivial truth (if all the properties of *K* turn
out to be essential), and at best a plausible formulation of one
of the fundamental assumptions of some branches of scientific
inquiry: one of the things a chemist does when he investigates the
nature of a stuff is to seek an explanation of its superficial properties and powers in terms of some underlying structure; one
aim of the psychologist is to explain overt behaviour by means of
covert states or dispositions. There is nothing archaic or 'metaphysical' about the doctrine of real essences: that doctrine merely
supposes that among the properties of substances and stuffs some
are explanatorily basic, others explanatorily derivative. I do not
deny that there are difficulties with such a doctrine (it must at
least answer the old rumblings of Locke); but I leave the reader
to form his own opinion of their relevance and cogency.

The second objection, that *definitions* cannot express real essences, is mere trifling. The suggestion that the word "definition"
be restricted to statements of meaning is purely stipulative: if the

xiii

stipulation is accepted, as a convenient way of avoiding ambiguity, nothing need happen to Aristotle's theory beyond a change of name; and until one is proposed, we may either follow ordinary usage, which surely allows us to apply the word "definition" to statements of essence, or else avail ourselves of the scholastic distinction between 'real' and 'nominal' definition. The whole question is insignificant.

Finally, can anything defend the tangled obscurities through which the two main doctrines of the *Posterior Analytics* fitfully gleam? Whether or not these entanglements are petty and uninteresting I cannot say here: that is a question for piecemeal discussion. It is undeniable, however, that Aristotle's argument is sometimes dark and anfractuous, its course broken by digressions and discontinuities. And such features are plausibly regarded as flaws.

The presence of these infelicities can be explained (and to my mind excused) by reference to two commonplaces of Aristotelian scholarship. First, like all of Aristotle's major treatises, the *Posterior Analytics* was not prepared for publication: we have before us a set of Aristotle's lecture notes, several times reworked. Much of the abruptness, digression, repetition, and inconcinnity which mark and perhaps disfigure Aristotle's argument is, I think, hereby explained; and a commentator's job is, in the most literal sense, to discover in these notes what Aristotle actually said, to write his book for him—to make the dry bones speak.

Secondly, it is plain that the *Posterior Analytics* was first put together when Aristotle was still teaching in Plato's Academy: many of the discussions in the book are evidently tailored to the intellectual controversies current in Plato's circle; and what appears to us allusive or even irrelevant may have been instantaneously intelligible to Aristotle's audience—a thread of argumentation which we have to scrabble for, they will have picked up without a thought.[C]

These brief remarks have, I hope, indicated the lines along which the *Posterior Analytics* can be defended against its modern detractors. Yet I cannot help feeling that there is something vaguely absurd in defending the book at all: it is, on any account, one of the most brilliant, original, and influential works in the history of philosophy; it determined the course of philosophy of science—and to some extent of science itself—for two millennia; it published, developed, and explored the notion of an axiomatic science;

it is stuffed with tight argument. How odd to defend—or to doubt—its accomplishments.

II

The formal logic on which the theory of the *Posterior Analytics* is founded is laid down in the *Prior Analytics*: it is, of course, syllogistic. This commonplace view has, curiously, been the centre of a scholarly controversy: just what is the relation between demonstration and syllogistic? between the *Posterior* and the *Prior Analytics*? The controversy has been carried out in chronological terms. It has been asked whether Aristotle wrote the *Prior* before or after the *Posterior Analytics*; and it has been assumed that the relative proximity of the two works to Platonic notions and theories supplies the key to the problem. Both chronologies—the traditional one, claiming priority for the *Prior Analytics*, and the modern heterodoxy, inverting the order—have been defended and attacked with much ingenuity and scholarship. This is no place to indulge in a detailed assessment of the matter; but I shall venture to suggest two general conclusions which an impartial observer might draw from the debate.

First, the chronological controversy has made it clear that the *Analytics* as they now stand were intended by Aristotle to form some sort of unity—to be twin parts of a single lecture course—and that they were intended to be read in their traditional order: the *Posterior Analytics*, taken as a whole, does indeed presuppose the syllogistic of the *Prior Analytics*.[D]

Secondly, the chronological question, if coarsely posed, assumes that Aristotle either wrote first the *Prior* and then the *Posterior Analytics*, or else vice versa; and this assumption is in all probability false. The two works, as we have them today, represent the latest stage in an uncompleted series of revisions: two sets of notes were worked at, added to, and emended over a period of years; and in the course of their long careers they enjoyed the benefits of a mutual influence. It is plainly silly to say that one treatise was 'written' before or after the other. We can at best hope to show that passage X in treatise A was written, in its present form, after passage Y in treatise B. In so far as such hopes can be fulfilled, they may support a restrained speculation about the development of Aristotle's thought: I am inclined to imagine that Aristotle first conceived his theory of axiomatization, then worked out the formal theory of syllogistic, and finally married the two theories.[E]

Such speculations, however intriguing they may be, should not be allowed to obscure the central fact that the *Posterior Analytics* in the form in which we now read it stands firmly on the logic of the syllogism. And that fact constitutes at once the great glory and the great failing of the *Posterior Analytics*. The glorious aspect is obvious enough; for in his syllogistic Aristotle had limned a logical system of exemplary elegance and rigour, the application of which to the sciences might well be expected to achieve marvels of certainty and exactitude—the comparison with Frege and his *Begriffsschrift* is hackneyed but appropriate. The failing is equally evident: as we all know, syllogistic is only a fragment of logic; it is impossible to force all the arguments of a developed science—or of ordinary discourse—into syllogistic form. This fact indeed shows up in many places in the *Posterior Analytics* itself; for the vocabulary and techniques of syllogistic are time and again applied to refractory matter, and Aristotle's scientific and mathematical examples often sit ill on the schematic theories they are intended to illustrate.[F]

A dash of charity does much to mend the situation: many of Aristotle's philosophical and logical points are not essentially tied to syllogistic, and they can be recast within the framework of a more capacious logic. The old wine can be rebottled. Yet some parts of Aristotle's argument are not so readily modernized; and in certain chapters—I think in particular of *B* 11 and *B* 12— the syllogism is, alas, a positive embarrassment and a bar to understanding.

Whatever attitude he adopts here, a reader of the *Posterior Analytics* must be reasonably at home in syllogistic. Although modern logicians have published several excellent studies of the system of the *Prior Analytics*, there is no settled orthodoxy of interpretation. For that reason I shall now sketch, in a brief and necessarily partial fashion, some fundamentals of syllogistic: my commentary on Aristotle's text will presuppose the interpretation I offer here.

Syllogistic is a theory of the relations that hold between *syllogistic propositions*. A syllogistic proposition is a proposition of the form AxB, where A and B are terms (A the predicate, B the subject) and x is one of the four *syllogistic relations—a, e, i, o*. AaB gives the form of a universal affirmative proposition, "Every B is A" (e.g. "Every man is mortal"); Aristotle normally expresses such propositions by one of the following formulae: "A holds of every B", "A is said of every B", "A is predicated of every B", "A follows every B". AeB is a universal negative, "No B is A". AiB is a particular affirmative ("Some B is A"), and AoB is a particular negative ("Some B is not A").

Certain entailments hold between pairs of syllogistic propositions. The most important of these are the Laws of Conversion ($AeB \dashv\vdash BeA$; $AiB \dashv\vdash BiA$; $AaB \vdash BiA$), and the Laws of Subalternation ($AaB \vdash AiB$; $AeB \vdash AoB$). Both sets of laws underpin Aristotle's development of syllogistic; and the latter bring out, in a starkly explicit way, the fact that universal propositions in syllogistic have 'existential import'.

A *mood* is an ordered sequence of three syllogistic propositions: the first two propositions (the putative premiss pair) have one term, the 'middle', in common; the third proposition (the ostensible conclusion) conjoins the other two terms—the 'extremes'— which appear once each in the premiss pair. Aristotle recognizes three arrangements of premiss pairs which define his three syllogistic *figures*. They are: I AxB, BxC; II MxN, MxX; III PxR, SxR. Evidently, there are $3 \times 4 \times 4 \times 4$, or 192, moods.

In the *Prior Analytics A* 4-6, Aristotle accepts fourteen of these moods as *syllogisms* or valid argument forms. There is considerable controversy over the interpretation of the tie between premiss pair and conclusion in an Aristotelian syllogism. In my view, an Aristotelian syllogism is best regarded as a sequent or argument form—a special case of the argument form P, $Q \vdash R$ (where the turnstile, $\vdash$, can be read as "so").[G] The fourteen syllogisms have traditional names: I—*Barbara, Celarent, Darii, Ferio*; II—*Cesare, Camestres, Festino, Baroco*; III—*Darapti, Felapton, Disamis, Datisi, Bocardo, Ferison*. The names form ingenious mnemonics: it is worth noting here only that the three vowels in each name give in order the three syllogistic relations of the mood. Thus the first syllogism of the first figure goes under the name of *Barbara*, and is represented by the schema: AaB, $BaC \vdash AaC$.

In *A* 8-22 of the *Prior Analytics* Aristotle turns to 'modal' syllogistic, and considers moods at least one of whose component propositions contains one of the modal operators "necessarily" and "possibly". This section of the *Analytics* is desperately difficult and still baffles detailed interpretation. Fortunately, the general thrust of Aristotle's argument is clear enough; and that is all that matters from the point of view of the *Posterior Analytics*.

A *demonstration* is a species of modal syllogism. In a demonstration all the propositions are necessary; and the paradigm demonstrative mood is *Barbara*. Thus if $\square\ P$ represents "Necessarily P", the explicit logical form of a paradigm demonstration will turn out to be: $\Box\, AaB,\ \Box\, BaC \vdash \Box\, AaC$. Aristotle never sets this paradigm out with any clarity or emphasis; and in several passages, whether deliberately or by oversight, he lets the fetters of necessity relax and is even unfaithful to *Barbara*. For all that, it is, I think, surely right to take the syllogism in *Barbara* with necessary components as the model for demonstrative reasoning.[H]

A demonstrative *science* can be displayed as a set of demonstrations. Each premiss of each demonstration in the set is either an axiom (an undemonstrable first principle) or else the conclusion of a prior demonstration. The axioms are finite in number; so, therefore, are the derived conclusions, or theorems: if a science contains n axioms, it has $\frac{1}{2}(n(n-1))$ theorems.

Just as Aristotle sometimes forgets his paradigm demonstration, so he sometimes ignores his model of demonstrative science. Moreover, he fails to realize all the implications, some of them depressingly restrictive, of that model. Aristotle's account of the nature of a demonstrative science is neither as clear nor as constant as we might desire; nor could he share the elation of those modern logicians and scientists who see an infinity of truths flowing from a small stock of axioms. But the theory of demonstration, though it is hampered by the constraints of syllogistic and marred by internal vacillations and confusions, is for all that an admirable and astounding invention.

SUPPLEMENTARY NOTES

A. In an article first published in 1969, I argued that in *APst*[1] "Aristotle was not telling the scientist how to conduct his research: he was giving the pedagogue advice on the most efficient and economic method of bettering his charges. The theory of demonstration offers a formal account of how an achieved body of knowledge should be presented and taught." The negative side of this thesis—that *APst* does not present a theory of scientific method—is, I still think, certainly true; and it has been widely accepted. The positive side—that *APst* was written primarily for pedagogues—has been less well received.[2] There is no doubt that the notion of teaching was closely

---

[1] A list of abbreviations is given in the Notes on the Commentary.

[2] For trenchant criticisms see e.g. KULLMANN (1974), 180–1; BURNYEAT (1981), 115–20; GUARIGLIA (1985), 85–7. There is a survey of opinions in WIANS (1989).

connected, in Aristotle's mind, with the notion of demonstrative understanding: this is shown clearly enough by the various texts which I discussed in my original article.[3] But it is absurd to suggest that *APst* is merely a treatise on teaching methods; and my references to schoolmasters and their charges—to which several critics took exception—were surely malapropos. Rather, and more generally, *APst* is primarily[4] concerned to investigate how the various facts and theories which practising scientists discover or construct should be systematically organized and intelligibly presented. The connection with teaching is this: in so far as a teacher is concerned to transmit a body of scientific knowledge, he will best do so by presenting it in a form in which its organization and explanatory coherence are intelligibly revealed. The paragraph to which this note is annexed still appears to me to represent the best general interpretation of Aristotle's overall aim in *APst*.

There is a second and separate question: What is the relationship between the theory set out in *APst* and Aristotle's own scientific work (in particular, the scientific studies which he records in his various writings on biology and zoology)? It has long been noticed—and this was the starting-point for my 1969 article—that, on the surface at least, there seems to be little or no connection between the scientific writings and *APst*: thus the biological writings contain no explicit *syllogisms*, and they do not appear to exhibit any *axiomatic structure*. Various attempts have been made to explain, or to explain away, this apparent mismatch. Since *APst* does not describe a scientific methodology, it would be misconceived to complain that the methods which Aristotle follows and occasionally describes in the scientific work do not fit the prescriptions of *APst*. Again, in so far as the biological writings do not purport to present a *finished* science, we should not expect them to exhibit the organization and structure which *APst* describes.

None the less, we might well expect to find in the biological works some inklings of the theories expounded in the *Analytics*. And such inklings are indeed to be found.[5] There is a particularly relevant passage near the beginning of the *History of Animals*:

We must first grasp all the actual differences and the items which are incidental to all animals; and then we should attempt to discover their explanations. In this way our method will follow the natural path, once the inquiry about each item is accomplished; for from this will become clear both the items about which our

---

[3] And see further DE GANDT (1975–6).

[4] I do not say that this is the *only* concern which Aristotle has in the work: evidently, many other issues interest him. But his chief and primary concern is with the form of an achieved science.

[5] See especially KULLMANN (1974).

demonstrations must be concerned and the items from which they must proceed. (*A* 6, 491ᵃ9–14)

First, we collect the facts. Secondly, we look for the explanations. Thirdly, we construct the demonstrations. Very roughly speaking, *HA* is given to the first task, *PA* and *GA* to the second. No surviving treatise essays the third task; but the surviving works do in fact proceed with half an eye on that distant goal.

Recent scholarship has thought to discover somewhat more profound and systematic connections between *APst* and the scientific corpus; and in some quarters it is again fashionable to speak, in a carefully qualified fashion, of a *method* promoted in *APst* and practised in the scientific writings. (See e.g. BOLTON (1987), GOTTHELF (1987), LENNOX (1987), CHARLES (1990), on the biological works; and BOLTON (1991) on *Phys.*) Not all these recent suggestions are equally convincing (there are some cool reflections in LLOYD (1990), 29–34); and it is worth noting, in any case, that they tend to refer to the theories of definition discussed in *APst B* rather than to the theories of demonstration discussed in *APst A*. However that may be, it is plain that this is an area in which much work remains to be done.

B. I should not have suggested that *APst* invents the notion of an axiomatized science. Earlier mathematicians had adumbrated the Euclidean project (see esp. Lee, and the classic paper by VON FRITZ (1955); cf. KULLMANN (1974), 134–5); and Plato and his immediate successors in the Academy had given some philosophical attention to the matter (see e.g. KULLMANN (1974), 154–63). Nevertheless, Aristotle was a pioneer: he was the first to produce a full-fledged philosophical theory of axiomatized science; he was the first to investigate, with some attempt at logical rigour, the structure of an axiomatic system and the formal constraints on the components of such a system; he was the first to insist on the independence of the special sciences from one another and to discuss the nature of the axioms which such independent sciences would require. The stuttering practice of the mathematicians, and the grandiose and programmatic notions of the Academy, were replaced by detailed and rigorous philosophical theorizing.

C. Whether or not *APst* was first written or sketched while Aristotle was still a member of the Academy, it remains true that the work—like any other work of Aristotle's—contains frequent references, explicit and implicit, to Academic ideas; and in many cases we have only a shadowy knowledge of what these ideas were. In addition, it should be said that Aristotle was also thoroughly conversant with contemporary scientific practice, and that *APst* also makes frequent reference, explicit and implicit, to this practice. Here too we may find difficulties which Aristotle could not have anticipated; for our knowledge of early Greek science is less than perfect.

D. Note too that the aim of the *Analytics* as a whole is to give an account of demonstration:

> First we must say with what our inquiry is concerned and what it is about: it is concerned with demonstration and about demonstrative understanding. (*APr A* 1, 24ᵃ10–11)

These are the opening words of the work. See BRUNSCHWIG (1981); BARNES (1981), 27–9.

E. In BARNES (1981), I argued in some detail that, first, "apodeictic does not depend essentially on the theory of the syllogism" (p. 33), and secondly—after Solmsen—that the main theory of *APst A* was developed independently of, and indeed before, the syllogistic theory of *APr* (pp. 34–57). More recently, Robin Smith has shown that, even in its present form, *APst* does not presuppose the *full* syllogistic theory of *APr*: those passages which do invoke some feature of syllogistic imply something "decidedly simpler" than the full theory. (For various versions of this view see SMITH (1982*a*), (1982*b*), (1986), (1989), pp. xiii–xv.)

F. That Aristotelian syllogistic is inadequate as a logic for the mathematical sciences was plainly seen and stated by Galen (e.g. *lib prop* xix. 39–40 K), even though Galen's contemporary, Alexander of Aphrodisias, blithely assumed the contrary (see e.g. *in APr* 260. 9–261. 24; 268. 8–269. 25). The issue has been briskly handled by MUELLER (1974); see also KULLMANN (1981).

G. Note, however, that Aristotle's term "*sullogismos*" denotes not an argument-*form* but an argument. *Barbara*, say, is an argument-form; but *Barbara* is not itself an argument or a *sullogismos*: a particular argument or *sullogismos* may be 'in' *Barbara*, that is to say, it may have or exhibit the form *Barbara*. For a more rigorous account see BARNES (1981), 21–5; for a brief account of the theory of the syllogism see BARNES *et al.* (1991), 208–15.

H. It is in fact far from plain that the paradigm logical form for a demonstration is a *modal* syllogism in *Barbara*. Aristotle is indeed clear that all the propositions involved in a paradigm demonstration will be necessary; and it is also true (see e.g. p. 111) that some of his remarks might lead us to think that *modal* syllogistic is the logic of demonstrative reasoning, so that the propositions appearing in a paradigm demonstration will have the form "Necessarily *P*". But Aristotle nowhere says that this is his view, nor do any of his illustrative examples contain an explicit modal operator. (And in so far as his theorizing is done with an eye on actual scientific practice, we should not expect to find such operators in his examples.) Moreover, the propositions involved in a demonstrative science—demonstrative propositions—are what I have called I-predications; that is to say, if *AaB* is a demonstrative proposition, then *A* holds of *B* 'in itself'.

Now it is plain that demonstrative propositions do not *have the form* "*A* holds of every *B* in itself": rather, they have the form "*A* holds of every *B*", and they are demonstrative inasmuch as *A in fact* holds of every *B* in itself. Analogously, then, we must suppose that demonstrative propositions are necessary not in the sense that they are truths of the form "*A* holds necessarily of every *B*" but rather in the sense that they are propositions of the form "*A* holds of every *B*" which are true inasmuch as *A* necessarily holds of every *B*. Modal syllogistic remains acutely relevant to demonstrative science—but it is not the logic of demonstrative science.

NOTE ON THE TRANSLATION

For the Greek I have used the OCT—the Oxford Classical Text—of the *Analytics*.[1] In a few places I have preferred a different reading: these differences are all marked in the footnotes to the translation, and the more significant of them are explained and justified in the commentary.

I have consulted a few earlier translations, occasionally pillaging a phrase or two. I have gained most help from Tredennick's version in the Loeb Classical Library.[2]

Fidelity is the only virtue which a translator need cultivate. But fidelity is a complex virtue, which makes various—and sometimes incompatible—demands. In a translation of a philosophical work intended for philosophical readers it is, I assume, fidelity in the matter of sense which must be paramount. That is to say, each unit in the translation should in principle convey all and only the sense which is conveyed by the corresponding unit in the original text. It is plain that such semantic fidelity is an ideal to which real translations can only approximate.

In recent years, English translators of ancient philosophical texts have shown themselves acutely and honourably conscious of their primary duty. Devotees of semantic fidelity, they have developed a number of devices and conventions which pretend to make their translations ever more faithful and ever more literal. The first version of my translation of the *Posterior Analytics* was an example—I may say, without boasting, a paradigm—of this genre: thus I attempted to put English and Greek words in one–one correspondence; I doggedly translated all Aristotle's logical particles; I sometimes mirrored in English the syntax and even the word-order of Aristotle's Greek.

The genre is noble in aspiration, absurd in reality. It is not merely that it encourages the construction of an argot which is perplexing to all but the initiate. Rather, the goal of semantic fidelity is itself missed—and in at least two ways. First,

---

[1] W. D. Ross and L. Minio-Paluello (eds.), *Aristotelis* Analytica priora et posteriora (Oxford, 1964). I have checked the OCT's *apparatus criticus* against the readings recorded by WILLIAMS (1984).

[2] In H. Tredennick and E. S. Forster (eds.), *Aristotle*: Posterior Analytics *and* Topica (London/Cambridge, Mass., 1960).

practitioners of the genre gaily set down sentences which no writer of English would ever countenance. (I offered my earlier readers the 'sentence': "For relatives are more together.") Such sentences cannot be faithful English versions of anything—for they are not English versions of anything. Secondly, by nicely scrutinizing each individual Greek word, translators have often produced sentences which are wildly unfaithful to the Greek. (I am assured that a Platonic interlocutor's response "*kalōs legeis*" ["You're right"] has been turned by "You are speaking finely".) Such efforts betray a misconception of fidelity, for which the relevant semantic unity is rarely the word.

Well, I am now cured of that malady—and as a result the new translation is (or so I believe) more rather than less faithful to Aristotle's Greek. Of course, I have frequently failed: in some places scholars will find that interpretation sullies the pure water of translation; in other places readers will still find traces of the old distemper. But failure is the unavoidable fortune of the translator.

Not that all the *bêtises* in the new translation—the obscurities, the crabbed phrases, the jargon, the brutally abrupt transitions—are failures. On the contrary, some of them are successes. For Aristotle's Greek, in the *Posterior Analytics*, is not an easy, undulating prose. He is usually rough and craggy. (John Aubrey said of a different ancient philosopher: "He writeth as a boar pisseth—by jerks.") His arguments are rarely smooth and clean. He is sometimes ambiguous. He is frequently obscure. In parts he is downright unintelligible. A hard text requires a hard translation: some, at least, of the oddities and anfractuosities of my English are deliberately chosen—in the name of semantic fidelity—to reflect the anfractuosities and oddities of Aristotle's Greek. (And there is a bonus. Such features of the translation do something—not, alas, very much—to meet a second demand made by fidelity; for they do something to convey the style and tone of Aristotle's writing.)

Three more particular issues ask for a paragraph apiece.

First, certain words occur frequently and thematically in the *Posterior Analytics*. They are not always *technical* terms, or even ordinary words used in a technical sense. (Some of the most significant of them are prepositions: the words *kata*, *dia*, and *ek* all play an important role in Aristotle's philosophical vocabulary—and 'philosophizing by prepositions' was to be a characteristic feature of some parts of later Greek thought.) In many ways it is desirable to signal the occurrence of these words; and translators sometimes make a practice of reserving a single English word (or family of words) for each such Greek word. But the practice is expensive: the cost is an artificiality which often leads to semantic infidelity. I have adopted a bourgeois compromise: for certain terms I have in principle aimed at one–one correspondence; but I have followed the principle only 'for the most part', relaxing my practice where fidelity and tolerable English demand. The Greek–English Glossary lists the main correspondences—and also notes the more significant relaxations.

Secondly, there is the problem set by certain characteristically Aristotelian terms for which a particular translation is already entrenched in the secondary literature. Thus "syllogism" is the entrenched version of *sullogismos*, and "cause" is the entrenched version of *aitia*. If a translator believes that one of these entrenched versions is a bad version (or that in the course of time it has become a bad version), then he finds himself in a dilemma: if he sticks to the convention, he fails in fidelity; if he offers something heterodox, he will surely seem quirky and he may actually mislead the unwary. On the whole I have chosen the second horn—thus the reader will not find, say, the word "syllogism" in my translation. In the more important cases, a note explains and attempts to justify the unorthodox version; and the Glossaries, again, offer a general guide.

Finally, a point which is usually and easily overlooked. I have followed the traditional division of the *Posterior Analytics* into chapters: this division does not go back beyond the Renaissance. I have subdivided the chapters into sections and paragraphs: such subdivisions (in which I generally follow the OCT) are modern. And the paragraphs /break into sentences: even these divisions are, in a sense, post-Aristotelian; for when Aristotle wrote, it was not usual to employ the devices of punctuation by means of which a modern author will make plain the articulation of his thought and avoid ambiguities. Greekless readers of the translation should bear all this in mind. They are not in a position to meddle with my punctuation; but, if they will, they may change my paragraphing and my capitulation without thereby tampering with Aristotle's text.

BOOK ALPHA

CHAPTER I

All teaching and all learning of an intellectual kind proceed from 71^a pre-existent knowledge. This will be clear if we study all the cases: the mathematical sciences are acquired in this way, and so is each of the other arts. Similarly with arguments, both deductive 5 and inductive: they effect their teaching through what we already know, the former assuming items which we are presumed to grasp, the latter proving something universal by way of the fact that the particular cases are plain. (Rhetorical arguments too persuade in the same way—either through examples, which is 10 induction, or through enthymemes, which is deduction.)

There are two ways in which we must already have knowledge: of some things we must already believe that they are, of others we must grasp what the items spoken about are (and of some things both). E.g. of the fact that everything is either asserted or denied truly, we must believe that it is the case; of the triangle, that it means *this*; and of the unit both (both what it means and 15 that it is). For these items are not all equally plain to us.

It is possible to acquire knowledge when you have acquired knowledge of some items earlier and get knowledge of the others at the very same time (e.g. items which in fact fall under a universal of which you possess knowledge). Thus you already knew that every triangle has angles equal to two right angles; but 20 you got to know that this figure in the semicircle is a triangle at the same time as you were being led to the conclusion. In some cases learning occurs in this way, and the last term does not become known through the middle term—this occurs when the items are in fact particulars and are not said of any underlying subject.

Before you are led to the conclusion, i.e. before you are given a 25 deduction, you should perhaps be said to understand it in one way—but in another way not. If you did not know whether there was such-and-such a thing *simpliciter*, how could you have known that it had two right angles *simpliciter*? Yet it is plain that you do understand it in *this* sense: you understand it universally—but you do not understand it *simpliciter*. (Otherwise the puzzle in the

30 *Meno* will arise: you will learn either nothing or what you already
know.)
    We should not argue in the way in which some who attempt to
solve the problem do. ("Do you or don't you know of every pair
that it is even?"—When you say "Yes", they bring forward some
pair which you did not think existed, and hence which you did
not think was even.) They try to solve the problem by denying that
they know of *every* pair that it is even—rather, they know it only
71ᵇ of everything which they know to be a pair. Yet what they know
is the item to which their demonstration applies and about which
they made their assumptions; and they made their assumptions
not about everything of which they know that it is a triangle or
that it is a number, but about every number or triangle *simpliciter*.
For no propositions of this sort are taken as assumptions (that
5 what you know to be a number . . . , or what you know to be rectilineal . . .): rather, we assume that something holds of every case.
    But surely nothing prevents us from in one sense understanding
and in another being ignorant of what we are learning. What is
absurd is not that you should know in *some* sense what you are
learning, but that you should know it in *this* way, i.e. in the way
and in the sense in which you are learning it.

CHAPTER 2

10 We think we understand something *simpliciter* (and not in the
sophistical way, incidentally) when we think we know of the
explanation because of which the object holds that it is its explanation, and also that it is not possible for it to be otherwise. It
is plain, then, that to understand is something of this sort. And
indeed, people who do not understand think they are in such a
15 condition, and those who do understand actually are. Hence if
there is understanding *simpliciter* of something, it is impossible
for it to be otherwise.

    Whether there is also another type of understanding we shall say
later: here we assert that we do know things through demonstrations. By a demonstration I mean a scientific deduction;
and by scientific I mean a deduction by possessing which we
understand something.
20 If to understand something is what we have posited it to be,
then demonstrative understanding in particular must proceed
from items which are true and primitive and immediate and more

2

familiar than and prior to and explanatory of the conclusions. (In this way the principles will also be appropriate to what is being proved.) There can be a deduction even if these conditions are not met, but there cannot be a demonstration—for it will not 25 bring about understanding.

They must be true because you cannot understand what is not the case—e.g. that the diagonal is commensurate. They must proceed from items which are primitive and indemonstrable because otherwise you will not understand unless you possess a demonstration of these items (to understand something of which there is a demonstration non-incidentally is to possess a demonstration of it). They must be explanatory and more familiar and prior—explanatory because we only understand something when 30 we know its explanation; and prior, if they are explanatory and we already know them not only in the sense of grasping them but also of knowing that they are the case.

Things are prior and more familiar in two ways; for it is not the same to be prior by nature and prior in relation to us, nor to be 72^{a} more familiar and more familiar to us. I call prior and more familiar in relation to us items which are nearer to perception, prior and more familiar *simpliciter* items which are further away. What is most universal is furthest away, and the particulars are 5 nearest—these are opposite to each other.

To proceed from primitives is to proceed from appropriate principles (I call the same things primitives and principles). A principle of a demonstration is an immediate proposition, and a proposition is immediate if there is no other proposition prior to it. A proposition is one part of a contradictory pair,[1] one thing said of one. It is dialectical if it assumes either part indifferently and demon- 10 strative if it determinately assumes one part because it is true. A statement is one part of a contradictory pair. A contradictory pair is a pair of opposites between which, in their own right, there is nothing. The part of a contradictory pair which says something *of* something is an affirmation; the part which takes something *from* something is a negation.

An immediate deductive principle I call a posit if it cannot be 15 proved but need not be grasped by anyone who is to learn anything. If it must be grasped by anyone who is going to learn anything whatever, I call it an axiom (there are items of this

---

[1] Reading ἀντιφάσεως for the MS reading ἀποφάνσεως.

kind); for it is of this sort of item in particular that we normally use this name. A posit which assumes either of the parts of a
20 contradictory pair—what I mean is that something is or that something is not—I call a supposition. A posit which does not I call a definition. Definitions are posits (arithmeticians posit that a unit is what is quantitatively indivisible), but they are not suppositions (for what a unit is and that a unit is are not the same).

25 Given that you must be convinced about some object and know it in so far as you possess a deduction of the sort we call a demonstration, and given that there is such a deduction in so far as *these* items—the items from which it proceeds—are the case, then you must not only already know the primitives (either all or some of them)—you must actually know them better. For something
30 always holds better of that because of which it holds: e.g. that because of which we love something is better loved. Hence if we know and are convinced of something because of the primitives, then we know and are convinced of them better, since it is because of them that we know and are convinced of the posterior items.

If you neither actually know something nor are more happily disposed towards it than you would be if you actually knew it, then you cannot be better convinced of it than you are of
35 something which you know. But this will arise if someone who is convinced of something because of a demonstration does not already have some knowledge; for he must be better convinced of the principles (either all or some of them) than he is of the conclusion.

Anyone who is going to possess understanding through a demonstration must not only get to know the principles better and be better convinced of them than he is of what is being
72ᵇ proved: in addition, there must be no other item more convincing to him or more familiar among the opposites of the principles from which a deduction of the contrary error may proceed—given that anyone who understands anything *simpliciter* must be incapable of being persuaded to change his mind.

CHAPTER 3

5 Some people think that because you must understand the primitives there is no understanding at all; others that there is, but that

there are demonstrations of everything. Neither of these views is either true or necessary.

The one party, supposing that you cannot understand in any other way,[2] claim that we are led back *ad infinitum* on the ground that we shall not understand the posterior items because of the prior items if there are no primitives. They are right—for it is impossible to survey infinitely many items. And if things come to a stop and there are priniciples, then these, they say, are unknowable since there is no *demonstration* of them and this is the only kind of understanding there is. But if you cannot know the primitives, then you cannot understand what proceeds from them *simpliciter* or properly, but only on the supposition that they are the case.

The other party agrees about understanding, which, they say, arises only through demonstration. But they argue that nothing prevents there being demonstrations of everything; for it is possible for demonstrations to proceed in a circle or reciprocally.

We assert that not all understanding is demonstrative: rather, in the case of immediate items understanding is indemonstrable. And it is clear that this must be so; for if you must understand the items which are prior and from which the demonstration proceeds, and if things come to a stop at some point, then these immediates[3] must be indemonstrable.

We argue in this way; and we also assert that there is not only understanding but also some principle of understanding by which we get to know the definitions.

That it is impossible to demonstrate *simpliciter* in a circle is plain, if demonstrations must proceed from what is prior and more familiar. For it is impossible for the same thing at the same time to be both prior and posterior to something—except in different ways (i.e. one in relation to us and the other *simpliciter*), ways which induction makes familiar. But in that case, knowing *simpliciter* will not have been properly defined. Rather, it will be ambiguous. Or else the one demonstration is not a demonstration *simpliciter* in that it proceeds from what is more familiar to us.

For those who say that demonstrations may proceed in a circle there arises the difficulty which I have just described. In addition, they say nothing more than that this is the case if this is the case—and it is easy to prove everything in this way. It will be

---

[2] Reading ἄλλως, with most MSS, for the OCT's ὅλως.
[3] Placing a comma before rather than after τὰ ἄμεσα, with Schöne.

5

plain that this follows if we posit three terms. (It makes no
difference whether we say that the circle revolves through many
terms or through few—or through few or two.) When if *A* is the
case, of necessity *B* is, and if *B* then *C*, then if *A* is the case *C*
will be the case. Thus given that if *A* is the case it is necessary
73ᵃ that *B* is the case and if *B* is the case that *A* is the case (this is
what it is to proceed in a circle), let *A* be *C*. Hence to say that if
B is the case *A* is the case is to say that *C* is the case; and to say
this is to say that if *A* is the case *C* is the case. But *C* is the same
as *A*. Hence it follows that those who declare that demonstrations
5 may proceed in a circle say nothing more than that if *A* is the
case *A* is the case. And it is easy to prove everything in this way.
  Moreover, even this is only possible for items which follow one
another, as properties do. If a single item is laid down, I have
proved that it is never necessary that anything else be the case
(by a single item I mean that neither if a single term nor if a
10 single posit is posited . . .): two posits are the first and fewest
from which it is possible, if at all,⁴ to deduce something. Now if
A follows *B* and *C*, and these follow one another and *A*, in this
case it is possible to prove all the postulates reciprocally in the
15 first figure, as I have proved in my account of deduction. (I have
also proved that in the other figures either no deduction at all
comes about or else none concerning the assumptions.) But items
which are not counterpredicated cannot ever be proved in a
circle. Hence, since there are few counterpredicated items in
demonstrations, it is clear that it is both empty and impossible to
say that demonstrations may be reciprocal and that because of
20 this there can be demonstrations of everything.

CHAPTER 4

Since it is impossible for that of which there is understanding
simpliciter to be otherwise, what is understandable in virtue of
demonstrative understanding will be necessary. (Understanding
is demonstrative if we possess it inasmuch as we possess a
demonstration.) A demonstration, then, is a deduction which
25 proceeds from necessities. We must see, then, from what items,
i.e. from what kind of items, demonstrations proceed. First let us
define what we mean by "of every case", by "in itself", and
by "universally".

----

⁴ Placing a comma after, as well as before, *εἴπερ*.

I say that something holds of every case if it does not hold of some cases and not of others, nor at some times and not at others. E.g. if animal holds of every man, then if it is true to call 30 this a man, it is true to call him an animal too; and if he is now the former, he is the latter too. Similarly if there is a point in every line. Evidence: this is how we bring objections if asked whether something holds of every case—we object either if it does not hold in some cases or if it does not hold at some time.

Something holds of an item in itself both if it holds of it in what it 35 is—e.g. line of triangles and point of lines (their essence comes from these items, which inhere in the account which says what they are)—and also if what it holds of itself inheres in the account which shows what it is—e.g. straight holds of lines and so does curved, and odd and even of numbers, and also prime and composite, and equilateral and oblong: in all these examples, there 73^b inheres in the account which says what they are in the former cases line and in the latter number. Similarly in other cases too it is such things which I say hold of items in themselves. What holds in neither way I call incidental, e.g. musical or white of animal. 5

Again, certain items are not said of some other underlying subject: e.g. whereas what is walking is something different walking (and similarly for what is white[5]), substances, i.e. whatever means this so-and-so, are not just what they are in virtue of being something different. Well, items which are not said of an underlying subject I call things in themselves, and those which are said of an underlying subject I call incidental.

Again, in another way what holds of something because of 10 itself holds of it in itself, and what does not hold because of itself is incidental. E.g. if there was lightning while he was walking, that was incidental: it was not because of his walking that there was lightning—that, we say, was incidental. But what holds because of itself holds in itself—e.g. if something died while being sacrificed, it died *in* the sacrifice since it died because of 15 being sacrificed, and it was not incidental that it died while being sacrificed.

Thus in the case of what is understandable *simpliciter*, whatever is said to hold of things in themselves in the sense of inhering in what is predicated or of being inhered in, holds of them both because of themselves and from necessity. For it is not possible for them not to hold, either *simpliciter* or as regards the

---

⁵ Omitting the OCT's addition of ⟨λευκόν⟩.

20 opposites—e.g. straight or curved of line, and odd or even of number. For a contrary or privation is a contradictory[6] in the same kind: e.g. even is what is not odd among numbers, in so far as it follows. Hence if it is necessary to assert or deny, then what holds of something in itself necessarily holds of it.

25 Let "of every case" and "in itself" be defined in this way. I call universal what holds of every case and in itself and as such. It is clear, then, that whatever is universal holds of its objects from necessity. (To hold of something in itself and to hold of it as 30 such are the same thing: e.g. point and straight hold of lines in themselves—for they hold of them as lines; and two right angles hold of triangles as triangles—for triangles are in themselves equal to two right angles.)

Something holds universally when it is proved of an arbitrary and primitive case. E.g. having two right angles does not hold 35 universally of figures—you may indeed prove of a figure that it has two right angles, but not of an arbitrary figure, nor can you use an arbitrary figure in proving it; for quadrangles are figures but do not have angles equal to two right angles. An arbitrary isosceles does have angles equal to two right angles—but it is not primitive: triangles are prior. Thus if an arbitrary primitive case is **74^a** proved to have two right angles (or whatever else), then it holds universally of this primitive item, and the demonstration applies to it universally in itself. To the other items it applies in another way, not in themselves—it does not apply to the isosceles universally, but extends further.

CHAPTER 5

5 It must not escape our notice that we often make mistakes—what we are trying to prove does not hold primitively and universally although we think we are proving it universally and primitively. We make this error either when there is nothing higher we can take apart from the particular case, or when there is but it is nameless and covers objects of different forms, or when the proof 10 applies to something which is in fact a partial whole. (Although the demonstration will indeed apply to the items in the part and will hold of every case, it will nevertheless not apply to them primitively and universally. I say that a demonstration applies to

---

[6] Deleting the ἤ before ἀντίφασις.

something primitively and as such when it applies to it primitively and universally.)

If someone were to prove that perpendiculars do not meet, the demonstration might be thought to apply to them because it holds of every perpendicular. But this is not so, if it holds not because they are equal in *this* way but in so far as they are equal in any way at all.

Again, if there were no triangles other than isosceles, then having two right angles would be thought to hold of them as isosceles.

Again, it might be thought that proportion alternates for items as numbers and as lines and as solids and as times. In the past this used to be proved separately, although it is possible to prove it of all cases by a single demonstration: because all these items— numbers, lengths, times, solids—do not constitute a single named item and differ in form from one another, they used to be taken separately. Now, however, it is proved universally: what they suppose to hold of them universally does not hold of them as lines or as numbers but as *this*.

For this reason, even if you prove of each triangle, either by one or by different demonstrations, that each has two right angles— separately of the equilateral and the scalene and the isosceles—, you do not yet know of triangles that they have two right angles, except in the sophistical way; nor do you know it of triangles universally,[7] not even if there are no other triangles apart from these. For you do not know it of triangles as triangles, nor even of every triangle (except in number—not of every triangle as a form, even if there is none of which you do not know it).

So when do you not know universally, and when do you know *simpliciter*? Well, plainly you would know *simpliciter* if it were the same thing to be a triangle and to be equilateral (either for each or for all). But if it is not the same but different, and if something holds of them as triangles, then you do not know it. Does it hold of them as triangles or as isosceles? And when does it hold of something in itself and primitively? And to what does the demonstration apply universally? Plainly, to the first item after the removal of which it does not[8] hold. E.g. two right angles will hold of bronze isosceles triangles—and also when being bronze and being isosceles have been removed. But not when figure or limit have been. But they are not the first. Then what is

---

[7] Reading καθόλου τρίγωνον with most MSS, for the OCT's καθ᾽ ὅλου τριγώνου.
[8] Adding μή before ὑπάρχῃ.

9

first? If triangle, it is in virtue of this that it holds of the other items, and it is to this that the demonstration applies universally.

CHAPTER 6

5 If demonstrative understanding proceeds from necessary principles (since what you understand cannot be otherwise), and if whatever holds of an object in itself is necessary (since either it holds in what it is, or else the object holds of what is predicated of it in what it is and the predicates are opposites one of which 10 necessarily holds), then it is clear that demonstrative deductions will proceed from certain items of this sort; for everything holds either in this way or incidentally, and what is incidental is not necessary.

We must either argue like this or else posit as a principle that demonstration is necessary,[9] i.e. that if something has been 15 demonstrated it cannot be otherwise—the deduction, therefore, must proceed from necessities. For from truths you can deduce *without* demonstrating, but from necessities you cannot deduce without demonstrating—this is precisely the mark of demonstration.

There is evidence that demonstration proceeds from necessities in the way in which we bring objections against those who think 20 they are demonstrating: we say that it is not necessary, if we think, either in general or at least as far as their argument goes, that it is possible for it to be otherwise.

From these considerations it is plain too that those people are naïve who think that they assume their principles correctly if the propositions are reputable and true (e.g. the sophists who assume that to understand is to possess understanding). For it is not what 25 is reputable that we count as a principle, but rather what is primitive in the kind with which the proof is concerned—and not every truth is appropriate.

That the deduction must proceed from necessities is clear from the following consideration too. If, in a case where there is a demonstration, someone who does not possess an account of the reason why does not have understanding, and if it might be that *A* holds of *C* from necessity but that *B*, the middle term through 30 which this was demonstrated, does not hold from necessity, then he does not know the reason why. For the conclusion does not

---

[9] Retaining ἀναγκαῖον with the MSS, for the OCT's ἀναγκαίων.

hold because of the middle term, since it is possible for this not to be the case, whereas the conclusion is necessary.

Again, if someone does not know something now, although he possesses the account and is preserved, and the object is preserved, and he has not forgotten, then he did not know it earlier either. But the middle term might perish if it is not necessary. Hence, being himself preserved and the object being 35 preserved, he will possess the account—and yet he does not have knowledge. Therefore he did not have knowledge earlier either. And if, although the middle term has not perished, it is possible for it to perish, the result *can* occur and is possible; but it is impossible to have knowledge under such conditions. 75^a

When the conclusion holds from necessity, nothing prevents the middle term through which it was proved from being non-necessary. For you can deduce a necessity from non-necessities, just as you can deduce a truth from non-truths. But when the middle term holds from necessity, the conclusion too holds from 5 necessity—just as a conclusion from truths is always true. Let A be said of B from necessity, and B of C: then that A holds of C is also necessary. When the conclusion is not necessary, the middle term cannot be necessary either. Let A hold of C not from 10 necessity, while A holds of B and B of C from necessity: then A will hold of C from necessity; but it was supposed not to.

Since, then, if you understand something demonstratively, it must hold from necessity, it is plain that your demonstration must proceed through a middle term which is necessary. Otherwise you will understand neither the reason why nor that it is necessary for it to be the case: either you will wrongly think that you know 15 it (if you believe to be necessary what is not necessary) or else you will not even think you do (equally whether you know the fact through middle terms or the reason why through immediates).

Of incidentals which do not hold of things in themselves in the way in which "in itself" was defined, there is no demonstrative understanding. You cannot prove the conclusion from necessity, 20 since it is possible for what is incidental not to hold (this is the sort of incidental I am speaking about). Yet one might perhaps wonder what purpose there could be in asking about such items if it is not necessary for the conclusion to be the case—you might as well ask an arbitrary question and then state the conclusion. But 25 we should ask questions not on the grounds that the conclusion will be necessary because of the points proposed in the question but rather because it is necessary for anyone who accepts the proposals to state the conclusion—and to state it truly if they hold truly.

Since in each kind whatever holds of something in itself and as
30 such holds of it from necessity, it is clear that scientific demonstrations are concerned with what holds of things in themselves and that they proceed from such items. For what is incidental is not necessary, so that you do not necessarily know why the conclusion holds—not even if it is the case always but not in itself (e.g. deductions through evidence). For you will not understand in itself something that holds in itself, nor will you understand
35 why it holds. (To understand why is to understand by way of the explanation.) Therefore the middle term must hold of the third term, and the first of the middle, because of itself.

CHAPTER 7

Thus you cannot prove anything by crossing from another kind—e.g. something geometrical by arithmetic. There are three things
40 involved in demonstrations: one, what is being demonstrated, or the conclusion (this is what holds of some kind in itself); one, the axioms (axioms are the items from which the demonstrations
75^b proceed); third, the underlying kind whose attributes—i.e. the items incidental to it in itself—the demonstrations make plain.

Now the items from which the demonstrations proceed may be the same; but where the kinds are different, as with arithmetic and geometry, you cannot attach arithmetical demonstrations to
5 what is incidental to magnitudes—unless magnitudes are numbers. (But I shall explain later how in some cases this is possible.) Arithmetical demonstrations always contain the kind with which the demonstrations are concerned, and so too do all other demonstrations. Hence the kind must be the same, either *simpliciter* or
10 in some respect, if a demonstration is to cross. That it is impossible otherwise is plain; for the extremes and the middle terms must come from the same kind, since if they do not hold in themselves, they will be incidentals.

For this reason you cannot prove by geometry that there is a single science of contraries, nor even that two cubes make a cube. (Nor can you prove by any other science what pertains to a
15 different science, except when they are so related to one another that the one falls under the other—as e.g. optics is related to geometry and harmonics to arithmetic.) Nor indeed anything that holds of lines not as lines and as depending on the principles

proper to them—e.g. whether straight lines are the most beautiful of lines, or whether they are contrarily related to curved lines;
for these things hold of lines not in virtue of their proper kind but 20
rather in virtue of something common.

CHAPTER 8

It is clear too that if the propositions from which a deduction
proceeds are universal, then it is necessary for the conclusion of
such a demonstration, i.e. of a demonstration *simpliciter*, to be
eternal. There is therefore no demonstration of perishable things,
nor any understanding of them *simpliciter* but only incidentally, 25
because nothing holds of them universally[10] but only at some
time and in some way.

When there is such a demonstration, one of the propositions
must be non-universal and perishable—perishable because when
it is the case the conclusion too will be the case, and non-universal
because its subjects will sometimes exist and sometimes not
exist.[11] Hence you cannot deduce that anything holds universally 30
but only that it holds now.

The same goes for definitions too, since a definition is either
a principle of a demonstration or a demonstration differing in
arrangement or a sort of conclusion of a demonstration.

Demonstration and understanding of things that come about
often—e.g. of an eclipse of the moon—plainly hold always in so
far as eclipses are such-and-such,[12] but are particular in so far as 35
they do not occur always. As with eclipses, so in the other cases.

CHAPTER 9

Since it is clear that you cannot demonstrate anything except
from its own principles if what is being proved holds of it as such,
understanding is not simply a matter of proving something from
what is true and indemonstrable and immediate. Otherwise it will 40
be possible to prove things in the way in which Bryson proved
the squaring of the circle. Such arguments prove in virtue of a

---

[10] Reading καθόλου with the MSS for the OCT's καθ' ὅλου.
[11] For the reading see notes.
[12] Reading τοιαιδ' with C for τοιοῦδ' (OCT, with B).

common feature which will also hold of something else; and so
76^a the arguments also attach to other items which are not of a kind
with them. Hence you do not understand the item as such but
only incidentally—otherwise the demonstration would not attach
to another kind as well.

5   We understand something non-incidentally when we know it in
virtue of that in virtue of which it holds and from what are its
principles as such. E.g. we understand that having angles equal to
two right angles holds of something when we know it in virtue of
that of which it holds in itself and from its own principles. Hence
if this too holds in itself of what it holds of, the middle term must
be of the same kind.

10   Otherwise, it will be like proving something in harmonics by
arithmetic. Things of this sort are indeed proved in the same way,
but there is a difference: the fact falls under one science (for the
underlying kind is different), while the reason falls under the
higher science which is concerned with the attributes which hold
of it in itself. Hence from this consideration too it is clear that
you cannot demonstrate anything *simpliciter* except from its own
15 principles. But the principles of these sciences have a common
feature.

If this is clear, it is also clear that you cannot demonstrate the
proper principles of anything. For then there will be principles of
everything, and understanding them will be sovereign over everything. For you understand something better if your knowledge
proceeds from higher explanations—your knowledge proceeds
20 from what is prior when it proceeds from unexplainable explanations. Hence if you know better or best, your understanding
will be better or best. But a demonstration does not attach to
another kind—except that, as I have said, geometrical demonstrations attach to mechanical or optical demonstrations, and
arithmetical demonstrations to harmonical.
25   It is difficult to know whether you know something or not. For
it is difficult to know whether or not our knowledge of something
proceeds from its principles—and this is what it is to know
something. We think we understand something if we possess a
deduction from some true and primitive items. But this is not so:
30 in addition, they must be of a kind with them.[13]

---

[13] Omitting τοῖς πρώτοις with Solmsen.

I call principles in each kind those items of which it is not possible to prove that they are. Now what the primitives and what the items proceeding from them mean is assumed; but that they are must be assumed for the principles and proved for the rest. E.g. we must assume what a unit is or what straight and 35 triangle are, and also that units and magnitudes are; but we must prove everything else.

Of the items used in the demonstrative sciences some are proper to each science and others common—but common by analogy, since they are only useful in so far as they bear on the kind under the science. Proper: e.g. that a line is *such-and-such*, and straight 40 so-and-so. Common: e.g. that if equals are removed from equals, the remainders are equal. It is sufficient to assume each of these in so far as it bears on the kind; for it will produce the same results even if it is assumed as holding not of everything but only 76^b for magnitudes (or, for arithmeticians, for numbers).

Proper too are the items which are assumed to exist and concerning which the science studies what holds of them in themselves—e.g. units in arithmetic, and points and lines in 5 geometry. They assume that there are such items, and that they are *such-and-such*. As for the attributes of these items in themselves, they assume what each means—e.g. arithmetic assumes what odd or even or quadrangle or cube means and geometry what irrational or inflexion or verging means—and they prove 10 that they are, through the common items and from what has been demonstrated. Astronomy proceeds in the same way.

Every demonstrative science is concerned with three things: what it posits to exist (these items constitute the kind of which it studies the attributes which hold of it in itself); the so-called common axioms, i.e. the primitives from which its demonstrations proceed; and thirdly, the attributes, where it assumes what each 15 of them means. There is no reason why some sciences should not ignore some of these items—e.g. they need not suppose that the kind exists, if it is clear that it does (for it is not equally plain that there are numbers and that there is hot and cold), and they need not assume what the attributes mean, if they are plain. In the same way, in the case of the common items, they do not 20 assume what to remove equals from equals means, because this is familiar. None the less *by nature* there are these three things: that about which the science conducts its proofs, what it proves, and the items from which it proves.

What must be the case and must be thought to be the case because of itself is not a supposition or a postulate. (Deductions, and therefore demonstrations, are not addressed to external 25 argument but rather to argument in the soul, since you can always object to external argument, but not always to internal argument.) If you assume something which is provable without proving it yourself, then if it is something which the learner thinks to be the case, you are supposing it (and it is a supposition 30 not *simpliciter* but only in relation to the learner); and if you make the same assumption when the learner has no opinion or actually a contrary opinion on the matter, then you are postulating it. It is in this that suppositions and postulates differ: a postulate is something not in accordance with the opinion of the learner which,[14] though demonstrable, you assume and use without proving it.

35   Terms are not suppositions (they are not said to be or not be anything[15]). Rather, suppositions are found among propositions. Terms need only be grasped; and grasping something is not supposing—unless you are going to say that even hearing something is supposing it. Rather, suppositions are items such that, if they are the case, then by their being the case the conclusion comes about.

40   Geometers do not suppose falsehoods, as some people have asserted. They say that you should not use falsehoods but that geometers speak falsely when they say that a line which is not a foot long is a foot long or that a drawn line which is not straight is 77^a straight. But geometers do not conclude anything from the fact that the lines which they have themselves described are thus and so; rather, they rely on what these lines show.

Again, every postulate and supposition is either universal or particular, and terms are neither of these.

CHAPTER 11

5 There need not be any forms, or some one item apart from the many, in order for there to be demonstrations. It must, however, be true to say that one thing holds of many. For there will be no universals if this is not the case; and if there are no universals

---

[14] Omitting ἤ, with Hayduck.
[15] Reading λέγονται with the MSS for the OCT's λέγεται.

there will be no middle terms, and hence no demonstrations. There must, therefore, be something—one identical item—which holds of several cases non-homonymously.

No demonstration assumes that it is not possible to assert and deny at the same time—unless the conclusion too is to be proved in this form. Then it is proved by assuming that it is true to say the first term of the middle term and not true to deny it. It makes no difference if you assume that the middle term is and is not; and the same holds for the third term. For if you are given something of which it is true to say that it is a man, even if not being a man is also true of it, then provided only that it is true to say that a man is an animal and not not an animal, it will be true to say that Callias, even if not Callias, is nevertheless an animal and not not an animal. The explanation is that the first term is said not only of the middle term but also of something else, because it holds of several cases; so that even if the middle term both is it and is not it, this makes no difference with regard to the conclusion.

Demonstrations by reduction to the impossible assume that everything is asserted or denied. They assume it not always and universally but in so far as is sufficient—and it is sufficient in so far as it bears on the kind. (By on the kind, what I mean is the kind about which you are producing your demonstrations, as I said earlier.)

All the sciences associate with one another in respect of the common items (I call common the items which they use as the basis from which to demonstrate—not those about which they prove nor what they prove); and dialectic associates with them all, and so would any science which attempted to give universal proofs of the common items (e.g. that everything is asserted or denied, or that equals from equals leave equals, or any items of this sort). Dialectic is not concerned with any determined set of things, nor with any one kind. If it were, it would not ask questions; for you cannot ask questions when you are demonstrating because the same thing cannot be proved from opposite assumptions. (I have proved this in my account of deduction.)

10

15

20

25

30

35

CHAPTER 12

If a deductive question and a proposition stating one part of a contradictory pair are the same thing, and if there are propositions in each science from which the deductions in each proceed, then there will be scientific questions from which the deductions appropriate in each science proceed.

40   It is plain, then, that not every question will be geometrical (or medical—and similarly in the other cases), but only those from
77ᵇ which you can prove something with which geometry is concerned or which is proved from the same items as geometry (e.g. something in optics). And similarly in the other cases. For
5   these items you should indeed supply arguments from the principles and conclusions of geometry, whereas for the principles a geometer as geometer should not supply arguments—and similarly in the other sciences. Thus we should not ask each scientist every question, nor should he answer everything he is asked about anything, but only those questions within the scope of his science.

10   If you argue in this way with a geometer as geometer it is clear that you will argue correctly if you prove something from this basis. Otherwise you will argue incorrectly—and it is plain that in this way you will not refute a geometer either, except incidentally. Hence you should not argue about geometry among non-geometers—for those who argue poorly will escape detection.
15   And the same goes for the other sciences.

Since there are geometrical questions, are there also non-geometrical questions? And in each science, with regard to which sort of ignorance are questions, say, geometrical? And are ignor-
20   ant deductions deductions from opposite assumptions (or paralogisms, though geometrical paralogisms)? Or are they deductions drawn from another art? E.g. is a musical question about geometry non-geometrical, whereas thinking that parallels meet is geometrical in one sense and non-geometrical in another way? There is an ambiguity here (as in the case of being non-
25   rhythmical): in one sense, being non-geometrical is not possessing geometrical skill, and in another it is possessing it poorly. It is the latter type of ignorance, i.e. ignorance based on the relevant principles, which is contrary to understanding.

    In mathematics paralogisms do not occur in the same way: the ambiguity is always in the middle term (something is said of all of
30   it and it again is said of all of something else—you do not say "all" of what is predicated), and you can as it were see these things in thought. In arguments, however, they escape notice. Is every circle a shape? If you draw one it is plain. Well, is the epic a circle? It is clear that it is not.

You should not bring an objection against it if the proposition
is inductive. For just as there are no propositions which do not 35
hold of several cases (for otherwise they will not hold of all
cases—and deductions depend on universals), so it is plain that
there are no objections of this type either. For propositions and
objections are the same things: what you bring as an objection
might become a proposition, either demonstrative or dialectical.

It happens that some people argue non-deductively because
they assume something which follows both terms. E.g./ Caeneus
does so when he says that fire consists in multiple proportion; for 78^a
fire, he says, is generated quickly, and so is multiple proportion.
In this way there is no deduction; rather, there is a deduction if
multiple proportion follows fastest proportion and the fastest
changing proportion follows fire.

Sometimes it is not possible to make a deduction from the 5
assumptions; and sometimes it is possible but it is not seen.

If it were impossible to prove truth from falsehood, it would be
easy to make analyses; for then the propositions would convert
from necessity. Let A be something that is the case; and if A is
the case, then *these* things are the case (things which I know to be
the case—call them B). From the latter, then, I shall prove that 10
the former is the case. (In mathematics conversion is more common because mathematicians assume nothing incidental—and in
this too they differ from those who argue dialectically—but only
definitions.)

They increase not through the middle terms but by additional
assumptions—e.g. A of B, this of C, this again of D, and so on 15
ad infinitum; also laterally—e.g. A both of C and of E. E.g. A is
definite (or even indefinite) number; B is definite odd number; C
is odd number: therefore A holds of C. And D is definite even 20
number; E is even number: therefore A holds of E.

CHAPTER 13

Understanding the fact and the reason why differ, first in the
same science—and in two ways. In one way, if the deduction
does not proceed through immediates: in this case the primitive 25
explanation is not assumed, but understanding the reason why
occurs in virtue of the primitive explanation. In a second way,

if, although the deduction does proceed through immediates, it proceeds not through the explanation but through the more familiar of the converting terms. For there is no reason why the non-explanatory counterpredicated term should not sometimes be more familiar, so that the demonstration will proceed through this term.

30   E.g. a demonstration that the planets are near, through their not twinkling. Let *C* be the planets, *B* not twinkling, *A* being near. It is true to say *B* of *C*: the planets do not twinkle. And also to say *A* of *B*: what does not twinkle is near. (Let this be
35 assumed through induction or through perception.) Thus it is necessary that *A* holds of *C*, and it has been demonstrated that the planets are near. Now this deduction gives not the reason why but the fact: it is not because the planets do not twinkle that they are near—rather, because they are near they do not twinkle.

It is also possible to prove the latter through the former, and then the demonstration will give the reason why. E.g. let *C* be
78ᵇ the planets, *B* being near, *A* not twinkling. *B* holds of *C* and *A* of *B*: hence *A* holds of *C*. The deduction gives the reason why, since the primitive explanation has been assumed.

Again, consider the way in which they prove that the moon
5 is spherical through its waxing: if what waxes in this way is spherical, and the moon waxes, it is clear that it is spherical. In this way the deduction gives the fact, whereas if the middle term is posited the other way about the deduction gives the reason why. (It is not because of its waxing that the moon is spherical:
10 rather, because it is spherical it waxes in this way. Moon, *C*; spherical, *B*; waxing, *A*.)

Where the middle terms do not convert and the non-explanatory term is more familiar, the fact is proved but not the reason why.

Again, consider cases in which the middle term has outside position. Here too the demonstration gives the fact and not the
15 reason why; for the explanation is not stated. E.g. why do walls not breathe?—Because they are not animals. If this were explanatory of their not breathing, then being an animal would have to be explanatory of breathing: i.e. if the negation is explanatory of something's not holding, then the affirmation is explanatory of its holding (thus if an imbalance of the hot and cold elements
20 explains not being healthy, their balance explains being healthy); and similarly, if the affirmation explains something's holding, then the negation explains its not holding. But in the example set out above, the condition I have just stated is not satisfied—for

not every animal breathes. A deduction giving an explanation of
this type comes about in the middle figure. E.g. let *A* be animal,
B breathing, *C* wall. *A* holds of every *B* (for everything which 25
breathes is an animal), but of no *C*: hence *B* too holds of no
C—therefore walls do not breathe.

Explanations of this sort resemble extravagant statements (i.e.
when you argue by setting the middle term too far away)—e.g.
Anacharsis' argument that there are no flute-girls among the 30
Scyths since there are no vines.

Thus with regard to the same science—and with regard to the
position of the middle term—there are these differences between
a deduction giving the fact and a deduction giving the reason
why.

The reason why differs from the fact in another way in so far as 35
each is studied by a different science. These are the cases which
are related to each other in such a way that the one falls under
the other, e.g. optics to geometry, mechanics to solid geometry,
harmonics to arithmetic, star-gazing to astronomy. Some of these
sciences bear almost the same name as one another—e.g. mathematical and nautical astronomy, and mathematical and acoustical 79^a
harmonics. Here it is for the empirical scientists to know the fact
and for the mathematical scientists to know the reason why. The
latter possess demonstrations which give the explanations, and
often they do not know the fact—just as people who study 5
universals often do not know some of the particulars through lack
of observation.

The items in question are things which, being something different in their essence, make use of forms. For mathematics is
concerned with forms: its objects are not said of any underlying
subject—for even if geometrical objects *are* said of some underlying subject, still it is not *as* being said of an underlying subject
that they are studied.

Related to optics as optics is related to geometry, there is 10
another science—namely the study of the rainbow. Here it is for
the natural scientists to know the fact and for the students of
optics—either of optics *simpliciter* or of mathematical optics—to
know the reason why. Many sciences which do not fall under
one another are in fact related in this way—e.g. medicine to
geometry: it is for the doctors to know the fact that curved 15
wounds heal more slowly, and for the geometers to know the
reason why.

CHAPTER 14

Of the figures, the first is especially scientific. The mathematical
sciences carry out their demonstrations through it—e.g. arith-
20 metic and geometry and optics—and so do almost all those
sciences which inquire into the reason why. For deductions giving
the reason why are carried out, either in general or for the most
part and in most cases, through this figure. For this reason, then,
it is especially scientific; for study of the reason why has most
importance for knowledge.
25   Next, only through this figure can you hunt for understanding
of what a thing is. In the middle figure there are no positive
deductions; but understanding what a thing is is understanding an
affirmation. In the last figure, although there are positive deductions, they are not universal; and what a thing is is something
universal—it is not in a certain respect that man is a two-footed
animal.
30   Again, this figure has no need of the others; but they are thickened and increased through it until they come to the immediates.
   Thus it is clear that the first figure is most important for
understanding.

CHAPTER 15

Just as it is possible for A to hold of B atomically, so it is also
35 possible for it to not hold atomically. By holding or not holding
atomically I mean that there is no middle term for them; for then
they no longer hold or not hold in virtue of something else.
   When either A or B is in something as in a whole (or both are),
then it is not possible for A to primitively not hold of B. Let A be
in C as in a whole. If B is not in C as in a whole (it is possible
that A is in something as in a whole and B is not in it), then there
79ᵇ will be a deduction that A does not hold of B. For if C holds of
every A and of no B, then A holds of no B. Similarly, if B is in
something as in a whole, e.g. in D: D holds of every B and A of
no D, so that A will hold of no B through a deduction. The proof
5 will be the same if both terms are in something as in a whole.
   It is possible for B not to be in something which A is in as in a
whole, or again for A not to be in something which B is in. This
is clear from chains of terms which do not overlap one another. If
nothing in the chain A, C, D is predicated of anything in B, E, F,
10 and if A is in H as in a whole (H being in the same chain as A),

22

then it is clear that B will not be in H; for otherwise the chains will overlap. Similarly if B is in something as in a whole.

If neither is in anything as in a whole, and if A does not hold of B, then it is necessary for A to atomically not hold of B. For if there is to be a middle term, then one of them must be in 15 something as in a whole. The deduction will be either in the first or in the middle figure. If it is in the first, then B will be in something as in a whole (for the proposition with B as subject must be affirmative); and if it is in the middle, then one or other will be in something as in a whole (for if the privative is assumed with both as subject there is a deduction, although if *both* are 20 negative there will not be one).

Thus it is clear that it is possible for one thing to not hold of another atomically; and we have said when it is possible and how.

CHAPTER 16

Ignorance—what is called ignorance not in virtue of a negation but in virtue of a disposition—is error coming about through deduction. In the case of what holds or does not hold primitively 25 it arises in two ways: either when you believe *simpliciter* that something holds or does not hold, or else when you get the belief through a deduction. For simple belief the error is simple; but when the belief comes about through a deduction there are several types of error.

Let A hold of no B atomically: if you deduce that A holds of B, 30 taking C as a middle term, then you will have erred through a deduction. It is possible for both the propositions to be false, and it is possible for only one of them to be false. If neither A holds of any of the Cs nor C of any of the Bs, and if each proposition 35 has been assumed the other way about, then both will be false. It is possible for C to be so related to A and to B that it neither falls under A nor holds universally of B. For it is impossible for B to be in anything as in a whole (since A was said to not hold of it primitively), and it is not necessary that A hold universally of everything there is: hence both propositions may be false. 40

It is also possible for one proposition to be true—not either of them but only AC. The proposition CB will always be false **80^a** because B is not in anything; but AC may be true, e.g. if A holds atomically both of C and of B—when the same thing is predicated

23

primitively of several items, neither will be in the other. (It
5 makes no difference if it holds non-atomically.)

Error to the effect that something holds comes about by these
means and in this way only; for in no other figure was there a
deduction to the effect that something holds. Error to the effect
that something does not hold comes about both in the first and in
the middle figure.
10   First let us say in how many ways it comes about in the first
figure, i.e. in what conditions the propositions must be. It is
possible when both are false, e.g. if *A* holds atomically both of *C*
and of *B*: if *A* is assumed to hold of no *C* and *C* of every *B*, the
propositions are false. It is also possible when one is false—and
15 either one. It is possible for *AC* to be true and *CB* false—*AC*
true because *A* does not hold of everything there is, and *CB* false
because it is impossible for *C*, of none of which *A* holds, to hold
of *B* (for then the proposition *AC* would no longer be true, and
at the same time if they are *both* true the conclusion too will be
20 true). It is also possible for *CB* to be true while the other
proposition is false, i.e. if *B* is both in *C* and in *A*; for then one of
them must fall under the other, so that if you assume that *A*
holds of no *C* the proposition will be false.
25   Thus it is clear that the deduction may be false both when one
proposition is false and when both are.
   In the middle figure it is not possible for both propositions to
be false as wholes. For when *A* holds of every *B*, you cannot take
30 any term which will hold of all the one and of none of the
other. If there is to be a deduction, then you must assume the
propositions in such a way that something holds of one and does
not hold of the other. Hence if they are false when assumed in
this way, plainly they will be the other way about when assumed
in the contrary way—but this is impossible.
   But there is no reason why each proposition should not be
35 partially false—i.e. *C* might hold both of some *A* and of some *B*.
For if *C* is then assumed to hold of every *A* and of no *B*, both
propositions will be false—not, however, as wholes but partially.
And if the privative is posited the other way about, the same
holds.
   It is possible for one of them—either one—to be false. For
what holds of every *A* also holds of *B*; so if *C* is assumed to hold
80ᵇ of the whole of *A* and not to hold of the whole of *B*, *CA* will be
true and *CB* false. Again, what holds of no *B* will not hold of
every *A*. (If of *A*, then of *B* too—but it was assumed not to hold

of *B*.) So if *C* is assumed to hold of the whole of *A* and of no *B*, 5
the proposition *CB* is true and the other proposition false.

Similarly if the privative is transposed. For what holds of no *A*
will not hold of any *B*; so if *C* is assumed not to hold of the whole
of *A* and to hold of the whole of *B*, the proposition *CA* will be
true and the other proposition false. Again, it is false to assume 10
that what holds of every *B* holds of no *A*. For if it holds of every
B, then it must also hold of some *A*; so if *C* is assumed to hold of
every *B* and of no *A*, *CB* will be true and *CA* false.

Thus it is clear that there may be erroneous deductions in the
case of atomic truths when both the propositions are false and 15
also when only one of them is.

CHAPTER 17

In the case of what holds non-atomically, when the deduction of
the falsehood comes about through the appropriate middle term,
it is not possible for both propositions to be false—rather, only 20
the proposition on the major extreme can be false. (I call a
middle term appropriate if the deduction of the contradictory
comes about through it.) Let *A* hold of *B* through a middle term
C. Since *CB* must be assumed as an affirmative if a deduction is
to come about, it is plain that this will always be true; for it does 25
not convert. And *AC* is false; for it is when this is converted that
the contrary deduction comes about.

Similarly too if the middle term is taken from another chain—
e.g. *D*, if it is both in *A* as in a whole and predicated of every *B*.
Then the proposition *DB* must stand and the other proposition 30
must be converted, so that the former is always true and the
latter always false. This sort of error is much the same as error
through the appropriate middle term.

If it is not through the appropriate middle term that the deduction comes about, then when the middle term falls under *A*
and holds of no *B*, both propositions must be false. For the
propositions must be assumed in a way contrary to how they 35
actually are if there is to be a deduction; and so assumed, both
come out false. I.e. let *A* hold of the whole of *D* and *D* of none
of the *B*s: when they are converted there will be a deduction and
the propositions will both be false.

When the middle term, e.g. *D*, does not fall under *A*, *AD* will **81^a**
be true and *DB* false: *AD* is true because *D* was not in *A*; and
DB is false because if it were true the conclusion too would be
true—but it was false.

25

5   When the error comes about through the middle figure, it is not possible for both propositions to be false as wholes. For when B falls under A it is not possible for anything to hold of all the one and of none of the other, as I said earlier. But it is possible
10 for one—either one—to be false as a whole. Let C hold both of A and of B: if it is assumed to hold of A and not to hold of B, then CA will be true and the other proposition false. Again, if C is assumed to hold of B and of no A, then CB will be true and the other proposition false.

15 If the deduction of the error is privative, we have said when and by what means the error will occur. If it is affirmative, then when it proceeds through the appropriate middle term it is impossible for both propositions to be false. For CB must stand if there is to
20 be a deduction, as I said earlier. Hence AC will always be false; for this is the proposition which converts.
     Similarly if the middle term should be taken from another chain, as I said in the case of privative error. DB must stand and AD convert, and the error is the same as before.
     When the deduction is not through an appropriate middle
25 term, then if D falls under A, this will be true and the other proposition false; for it is possible for A to hold of several things which do not fall under one another. If D does not fall under A, this will plainly always be false (for it is assumed as an affirmative), whereas it is possible for DB both to be true and to
30 be false. For nothing prevents A from holding of no D and D of every B (e.g. animal of knowledge, knowledge of music); nor again A from holding of none of the Ds and D of none of the Bs. Thus it is clear that if the middle term does not fall under A it is possible for both propositions to be false and also for one—but not either—proposition to be false.[16]

35 Thus it is clear in how many ways and by what means errors in virtue of deduction may come about, both for immediates and for what is shown through demonstration.

CHAPTER 18

It is clear too that if some perception is wanting, some understanding must also be wanting—understanding which it is impossible

---

[16] Reading καὶ ⟨τὴν ἑτέραν, οὐ μέντοι⟩ ὁποτέραν ἔτυχεν. The OCT deletes the whole sentence.

to get if we learn either by induction or by demonstration, if
demonstration depends on universals and induction on particu- 81ᵇ
lars, if it is impossible to study universals except through induction (even the items we speak about on the basis of abstraction
can be made familiar through induction, i.e. it can be shown
that certain things hold of each kind—even if they are not
separable—in so far as each is such-and-such), and if it is imposs- 5
ible to make an induction without having perception (for particulars are grasped by perception). It is not possible to get
understanding of these items—neither from universals without
induction nor through induction without perception.

CHAPTER 19

Every deduction proceeds through three terms. One type can 10
prove that A holds of C because it holds of B and B of C; and the
other type is privative, having one proposition to the effect that
one thing holds of another and the other to the effect that
something does not hold. Thus it is clear that the principles and
the so-called suppositions are items of these types; for it is these 15
which we must assume in order to conduct proofs—e.g. that A
holds of C through B, and then that A holds of B through
another middle term, and that B holds of C in the same way.

If you are making deductions with regard to opinion and only
dialectically, then plainly you need only inquire whether the
deduction proceeds from the most reputable propositions poss- 20
ible; so that even if there is not in truth any middle term for AB
but there is thought to be one, anyone who makes a deduction
through it has deduced something dialectically. But with regard
to truth you must inquire from the basis of what actually holds. It
is like this: since there are items which themselves are predicated
of something else non-incidentally—by incidentally I mean this: 25
we sometimes say, e.g., that that white thing is a man, and we do
not then make the same sort of statement as when we say that the
man is white; for whereas it is not the case that the man, being
something different, is white, the white thing is a man because
the man is incidentally a white thing. Well, there are some items
which are predicated of things in themselves.

Then let C be such that it itself no longer holds of anything else 30
and B holds of it primitively (i.e. there is nothing else between
them). Again, let E hold of F in the same way, and F of B. Now
must this come to a stop, or is it possible for it to go on *ad
infinitum*?

Again, if nothing is predicated of A in itself and A holds of H
35 primitively and of nothing prior in between, and H holds of G,
and this of B, must *this* come to a stop, or is it possible for *this*
to go on *ad infinitum*? This differs from the earlier question to
this extent: that question asked if it is possible to begin from
something which holds of nothing else while something else holds
of it and to go on upwards *ad infinitum*; whereas the second
82ᵃ question has us begin from something which is predicated of
something else while nothing is predicated of it and inquire if it is
possible to go on downwards *ad infinitum*.

Again, is it possible for the terms in between to be infinite if
the extremes are determined? I mean e.g. if A holds of C, and B
5 is a middle term for them, and for B and A there are different
middle terms, and for these others, is it possible or impossible for
these to go on *ad infinitum*?

This is the same as to inquire whether demonstrations can
proceed *ad infinitum* and whether there can be demonstrations of
everything, or whether terms are bounded by one another.

10 I say the same in the case of privative deductions and propositions. E.g. if A does not hold of any B, either it does not hold
of B primitively or else there will be something prior in between
of which it does not hold (e.g. G, which holds of every B), and
then another term yet prior to this (e.g. H, which holds of every
G). For in these cases too either the prior terms of which A holds
are infinite or they come to a stop.

15 It is not the same for terms which convert. For among counterpredicated terms there is none of which any is predicated primitively or ultimately (in this respect at least every such term is
related to every other in the same way; and if[17] its predicates are
infinite, then the items we are puzzling over are infinite in both
directions)—unless it is possible that the terms do not convert in
20 the same way, one of them holding as an incidental and the other
as a predicate.

CHAPTER 20

It is plain that the terms in between cannot be infinite if the
predications come to a stop downwards and upwards. (By up-

---

[17] Reading εἴ τ᾽ [with Philoponus] . . . ἐπ᾽ [with two MSS and Philoponus] . . . for
the OCT's εἴτ᾽ . . . εἴτ᾽ . . .

wards I mean toward the more universal and by downwards
toward the particular.) Suppose that, when *A* is predicated of *F*, 25
the terms in between—the *B*s—are infinite. It is plain that it
would be possible both that from *A* downwards one term should
be predicated of another *ad infinitum* (for before *F* is reached the
terms in between are infinite), and also that from *F* upwards
there are infinitely many terms before *A* is reached. Hence if this
is impossible, it is impossible for there to be infinitely many terms 30
between *A* and *F*.

If someone were to say that some of *A*, *B*, *F* are next to one
another so that there are no terms between them, and that
the other terms cannot be taken, this makes no difference. For
whichever of the *B*s I take, the terms in between in the direction
of *A* or in the direction of *F* will either be infinite or not. It
makes no difference which is the first term after which they are
infinite—whether at once or not at once; for the terms after this 35
are infinite.

<h2 style="text-align:center">CHAPTER 21</h2>

It is clear too that privative demonstrations will come to a stop if
affirmative demonstrations come to a stop in both directions.
Suppose that it is not possible either to go on upwards from the
last term *ad infinitum* (I call last the term which itself holds of
nothing else while something else holds of it, e.g. *F*), or to go on 82ᵇ
downwards from the first to the last (I call first the term which
itself is said of another while nothing is said of it). If this is so, it
will come to a stop in the case of negations too.

A term can be proved not to hold of something in three ways.
Either *B* holds of everything of which *C* holds and *A* of nothing 5
of which *B* holds—in the case of *BC*, then, and in general of the
second interval, we must arrive at immediates; for this interval is
positive. And plainly if the other term does not hold of something
else prior, e.g. of *D*, this will have to hold of every *B*; and if
again it does not hold of something else prior to *D*, this will have 10
to hold of every *D*. Hence since the path upwards comes to a
stop, the path to *A* will also come to a stop, and there will be
some first term of which it does not hold.

Again, if *B* holds of every *A* and of no *C*, *A* holds of none of
the *C*s. If you must next prove this, then plainly it will be proved 15
either in the above way or in this way or in the third way. The
first way has been discussed, and the second will now be proved.

If you prove[18] in this way e.g. that[19] *D* holds of every *B* and of no
C, then[20] it is necessary for something to hold of *B*. And next, if
20 this is to not hold of *C*, something else holds of *D* which does not
hold of *C*. So since holding of ever higher terms comes to a stop,
not holding will also come to a stop.

The third way was this: if *A* holds of every *B* and *C* does not
hold of it, *C* does not hold of everything of which *A* holds. Next
this will be proved either in the ways described above or else in
25 the same way. If the former, it comes to a stop; and if the latter,
you will next assume that *B* holds of *E*, of not all of which *C*
holds. And similarly next for *E*. Since we are supposing that
things come to a stop in the downward direction, it is clear that
C's not holding will also come to a stop.

It is clear that even if the proof follows not one path but all of
30 them—sometimes in the first figure, sometimes in the second or
third—that it will come to a stop even so. For the paths are
finite, and necessarily anything finite taken a finite number of
times is finite.

So it is plain that it comes to a stop for privations if it does so
35 for holding. That it comes to a stop in the latter case will be plain
if we study the matter generally as follows.

CHAPTER 22

For items predicated in what something is, the case is plain: if it
is possible to define anything, or if what it is to be something can
be known, and if you cannot survey infinitely many items, then
the items predicated in what something is must be finite.
83^a   We argue universally as follows. You can say truly that the
white thing is walking, and that that large thing is a log, and
again that the log is large and the man is walking. When you
speak in these two ways you make different sorts of statement.
5 When I assert that the white thing is a log, I say that something
which is incidentally white is a log, and not that the white thing is
the underlying subject for the log. For it is not the case that,
being white or just what is some particular white, it came to be a
log—hence it is not a log except incidentally. But when I say that
10 the log is white, I do not say that something different is white and

---

[18] Reading δεικνύῃ with most MSS for the OCT's δεικνύοι.
[19] Reading οἷον ὅτι—the OCT accidentally omits ὅτι.
[20] Omitting εἰ with one MS.

that that is incidentally a log, as when I say that the musical thing is white (I am then saying that the man, who is incidentally musical, is white). Rather, the log is the underlying subject which came to be white not in virtue of being something different from just what is a log or a particular log. If we must legislate, let speaking in the latter way be predicating, and speaking in the 15 former way either not predicating at all or else predicating not *simpliciter* but incidentally. (What is predicated is like the white, that of which it is predicated is like the log.)

Let us suppose that what is predicated is always predicated *simpliciter*, and not incidentally, of what it is predicated of; for 20 this is the way in which demonstrations demonstrate. Hence when one thing is predicated of one, either it is in what the item is or it indicates that it has some quality or quantity or relation or is doing something or undergoing something or is at some place or time.

Again, terms which mean substances mean, of what they are predicated of, just what is that thing or just what is a particular 25 sort of it. Terms which do not mean substances but are said of some other underlying subject which is neither just what is that thing nor just what is a particular sort of it, are incidental. E.g. white of a man: a man is neither just what is white nor just what is some particular white—rather, presumably, animal: a man is 30 just what is an animal. Items which do not mean substances must be predicated of some underlying subject, and there cannot be anything white which is not white in virtue of being something different. (We can say goodbye to the forms. They are nonnynoes; and if there are any, they are irrelevant—for demonstrations are concerned with items of the kind I have described.) 35

Again, if it cannot be that this is a quality of that and that of this—a quality of a quality—, then it is impossible for one thing to be counterpredicated of another in this way: it is possible to make a true statement, but it is not possible to counterpredicate truly.

Either a term will be predicated as a substance, i.e. being 83ᵇ either the kind or the difference of what is predicated—but it has been proved that these terms will not be infinite, either downwards or upwards. (E.g. man is two-footed, this animal, this something else . . . Nor: animal of man, man of Callias, Callias of another item in what it is . . .). You can define every substance of 5 this type, but you cannot survey infinitely many items in thought. Hence the terms are not infinite either upwards or downwards; for you cannot define a substance of which infinitely many terms

are predicated. (Terms will not be counterpredicated of one
10 another as kinds; for then something would itself be just what is
some of itself.) Nor is anything predicated of a quality, or of any
of the other types of item—unless it is predicated incidentally.
For all these items are incidental, and they are predicated of
substances.

They will not be infinite in the upward direction. For of each
item there is predicated something which means either a quality
15 or a quantity or the like, or else one of the items in its substance.
But the latter are finite, and the kinds of predicate are finite—
either quality or quantity or relation or doing or undergoing or
place or time.

We have supposed that one thing is predicated of one thing,
and that items which do not signify what something is are not
predicated of themselves. For these are all incidental (though
20 some hold of things in themselves and some in another way), and
we say that all of them are predicated of an underlying subject,
and that what is incidental is not an underlying subject. (We posit
nothing to be of this type unless it is called what it is called in
virtue of being something different and itself holds of other
items.²¹)

25 Thus one thing will not be said to hold of one thing either in
the upward or in the downward direction: the incidentals are said
of items in the substance of each thing, and these latter are not
infinite; and in the upward direction there are both these items
and the incidentals, neither of which are infinite. There must
therefore be some term of which something is predicated primi-
30 tively, and something else of this; and this must come to a
stop, and there must be items which are no longer predicated of
anything prior and of which nothing else prior is predicated.

This is one way of demonstrating the point. There is also another.
There is demonstration of things of which something prior is
predicated. You cannot be more happily related to things of
35 which there is demonstration than by knowing them, nor can you
know them without a demonstration. Now if one thing is familiar
through others, and if we neither know the latter nor are more
happily related to them than by knowing them, then we shall not
understand what is familiar through them.

Thus if it is possible to know something by way of a

---

²¹ Reading ἄλλοις with the MSS for the OCT's ἄλλου, and deleting καὶ ἄλλ᾽ ἄττα
[τοῦτο, OCT] καθ᾽ ἑτέρου.

demonstration—*simpliciter* and not on the basis of something
else, i.e. on the basis of a supposition—, then the predicates in **84ª**
between must come to a stop. If they do not come to a stop and
there is always something above whatever term has been taken,
then there will be demonstrations of all of them. Hence if it is
not possible to survey infinitely many items, we shall not know
through a demonstration items for which there is a demonstration.
Thus if we are not more happily related to them than by knowing 5
them, we shall be able to understand nothing through demonstration *simpliciter* but only on the basis of a supposition.

In general terms, you might be convinced of what we have said
by these arguments; from an analytical point of view, the following considerations make it clear more concisely that the terms
predicated cannot be infinite either in the upward or in the
downward direction in the demonstrative sciences with which our 10
inquiry is concerned.

Demonstration applies to what holds of the objects in
themselves—in themselves in two ways: both the items which
hold of the objects and inhere in what they are, and also the
items for which the objects of which they hold inhere in what
they are (e.g. odd of number—odd holds of number and number 15
itself inheres in its account; and conversely, plurality, or divisi-
bility, inheres in the account of number). It is not possible for
either of these to be infinite. Not as odd of number: then there
would again be something else holding of odd in which odd
inhered; and if this is prime,²² number will inhere in what holds 20
of it. So if it is not possible for infinitely many such items to
hold in a single item, they will not be infinite in the upward
direction. Moreover, they must all hold of the primitive term,
i.e. of number, and number of them, so that they will convert
and not exceed it. Nor, again, can the terms inhering in what 25
something is be infinite; for then it would not be possible to
define it.

Hence if all the predicated terms are said of things in themselves, and if these are not infinite, then the terms leading
upwards will come to a stop. Hence they will come to a stop in
the downward direction too. And if so, then the terms in between
any two terms will also always be finite. 30

If this is so, it is thereby plain too that demonstrations must
have principles and there cannot be demonstrations of everything

---

²² Placing a comma after rather than before *πρῶτον*.

(which, as we asserted at the beginning, is what some people say). For if there are principles, it is not the case that everything is demonstrable, nor is it possible to continue *ad infinitum*: for either of these things to be the case is simply for there to be no
35 immediate and indivisible intervals but for all of them to be divisible. For it is by interpolating a term internally, and not by assuming an additional term, that what is demonstrated is demonstrated. Hence if it were possible for this to go on *ad infinitum*, it would be possible for there to be infinitely many middle terms between two terms. But this is impossible if the
84ᵇ predicates come to a stop in the upward and the downward directions. And that they do come to a stop we have proved generally earlier and analytically just now.

CHAPTER 23

Now that this has been proved, it is clear that if one and the same term holds of two items—e.g. *A* both of *C* and of *D*—which are
5 not predicated one of the other (either not at all or not of every case), then it will not always hold in virtue of something common. E.g. having angles equal to two right angles holds of isosceles and of scalene in virtue of something common (it holds of them as figures of a certain type and not as different items). But this is
10 not always so. Let *B* be that in virtue of which *A* holds of *C*, *D*. It is plain that *B* too will hold of *C* and of *D* in virtue of some other common item, and this in virtue of another; so that infinitely many terms will fall between two terms. But this is impossible.

Thus when one and the same term holds of several items it need not always do so in virtue of something common, since
15 there are²³ immediate intervals. (The terms must be in the same kind and depend on the same atoms, if the common feature is to be something holding of them in themselves; for we have seen that what is being proved cannot cross from one kind to another.)

20 It is clear too that when *A* holds of *B*, then if there is a middle term you can prove that *A* holds of *B*, and the elements of this are²⁴ as many as the middle terms. (It is the immediate propositions

---

²³ Reading ἐπείπερ, with the MSS, for εἴπερ (OCT), and ἔστιν, against the MSS and the OCT, for ἔσται.
²⁴ Omitting ταῦτα [thus the MSS: ταὐτά, OCT] καί.

which are the elements, either all of them or the universal ones.) But if there is no middle term, then there is no longer a demonstration—rather, this is the path to the principles.

Similarly, if *A* does not hold of *B*, then if there is either a 25 middle or a prior term of which *A* does not hold, there is a demonstration. If not, not—rather, it is a principle. And there are as many elements as terms; for the propositions containing the terms are the principles of the demonstration. And just as there are some indemonstrable principles to the effect that this is this, i.e. that this holds of this, so too there are some to the effect that this is not this, i.e. that this does not hold of this. Thus there 30 will be principles to the effect that something is the case, and others to the effect that something is not the case.

When you have to prove something, you should assume what is predicated primitively of *B*. Let it be *C*; and let *D* be similarly predicated of *C*. If you always continue in this way, no proposition and no term holding outside *A* will ever be assumed in the proof. Rather, the middle terms will always be thickened until they 35 become indivisible and single. They are single when they become immediate, and a single proposition *simpliciter* is an immediate proposition. In other areas the principles are simple, though they are not the same everywhere: in weight, the ounce; in music, the semitone; and other things in other cases. So too in deduction the unit is the immediate proposition, and in demonstration and 85ᵃ understanding it is comprehension.

In deductions which prove that something holds, nothing falls outside. As for privative deductions, in one case nothing falls outside the term which must hold. Suppose e.g. that *A* does not hold of *B* through *C* (when *C* holds of every *B* and *A* of no *C*): if 5 you must next prove that *A* holds of no *C*, you should assume a middle term for *A* and *C*; and it will always proceed in this way.

If you have to prove that *D* does not hold of *E* inasmuch as *C* holds of every *D* and of no *E*, then the middle term will never fall outside *E* (this is the term of which it must hold). 10

In the case of the third way, the middle term will never pass outside either the term of which we must make a privative predication or the term which we must predicate privatively.

CHAPTER 24

Some demonstrations are universal, others particular; and some are positive, others privative. It is disputed which are better. 15

Similarly for demonstrations which are said to demonstrate and those which lead to the impossible. First, let us inquire about universal and particular demonstrations; and when we have made this matter plain, let us speak about demonstrations which are said to prove and those which lead to the impossible.

20 Some people might perhaps think, if they inquire along the following lines, that particular demonstrations are better.

If a demonstration in virtue of which we understand better is a better demonstration (this is what makes something a good demonstration), and if we understand something better when we know it in itself than when we know it in virtue of something 25 else (e.g. we know musical Coriscus better when we know that Coriscus is musical than when we know that a man[25] is musical; and similarly in other cases), and if a universal demonstration shows that something else and not the thing itself is in fact so-and-so (e.g. of the isosceles it shows not that an isosceles but that a triangle is so-and-so), whereas a particular demonstration shows that the thing itself is so-and-so—well, then, if a demonstration of something in itself is better, and if particular demon-30 strations rather than universal demonstrations are of this type, then particular demonstrations will be better.

Again, if universals are not things apart from the particulars; and if a demonstration instils an opinion that the item with regard to which it demonstrates is some thing, i.e. that it occurs as a sort of natural object among the things which exist (e.g. a triangle apart from the individual triangles, a figure apart from the indi-35 vidual figures, a number apart from the individual numbers); and if a demonstration about something which exists is better than one about something which does not exist, and a demonstration by which we will not be led into error is better than one which will lead us into error; and if universal demonstrations are of this latter type (for as they proceed, they produce their proofs as they do in the case of proportion, e.g. that whatever is of such-and-such a type—neither line nor number nor solid nor plane but 85^b something apart from them—will be proportional)—well, then, if it is rather demonstrations of this sort which are universal, and if they are less about something which exists than are particular demonstrations, and if they instil false opinions, then universal demonstrations will be worse than particular ones.

---

[25] Reading ἄνθρωπος with the MSS for the OCT's ἄνθρωπος.

Or, first, does the former argument apply any better to the
universal than to the particular case? For if having two right 5
angles holds of something not as isosceles but as triangle, then if
you know that an isosceles has two right angles, you will know it
less as such than if you know that triangles have two right angles.

In general, if something does not hold of triangles as triangles,
and yet you prove it to hold, this will not be a demonstration;
and if it does, then you know better if you know something as it
holds. Thus if triangle extends further than isosceles (and if there 10
is the same account, i.e. if triangles are not so-called in virtue of
a homonymy), and if having two right angles holds of every
triangle, then it is not the triangle as isosceles but rather the
isosceles as triangle which has such an angle-sum. Hence if you
know something universally, you know it better *as* it holds than if
you know it particularly. Hence universal demonstrations are
better than particular demonstrations.   15

Again, if there is a single account of a universal and it is not
homonymous, then it will be some thing no less than some of
the particulars but actually more so, inasmuch as what is imperishable is found among the universals and it is rather the
particulars which are perishable. Again, there is no need to
believe that a universal is some thing apart from the particulars
on the grounds that it makes one thing plain, any more than in 20
the case of those other items which mean not a substance but
either a quality or a quantity or a relation or a doing. So if the
belief is instilled, then the explanation lies not with the demonstration but with the audience.

Again, if demonstrations are probative deductions which give
the explanation and the reason why, and if universals are more
explanatory (for that of which something holds in itself is it- 25
self explanatory for itself; and universals are primitive: hence
universals are explanatory)—then universal demonstrations are
better. For it is rather they which give the explanation and the
reason why.

Again, we seek the reason why up to a certain point, and we
think we know something when it is not the case that it comes
about or exists because something else does—in this sense the
last term is an end and a limit. E.g. with what purpose did he 30
come? In order to get the money. And that in order to pay back
what he owed; and that in order not to act unjustly. Proceeding
in this way, when it is no longer because of something else or
with some other purpose, we say that it is because of this as an
end that he came (or that it is or that it came about), and that

35 then we best know why he came. Thus if the same goes for
all explanations and for all reasons why, and if in the case of
explanations in terms of purpose we know best in this way, then
in the other cases too we know best when this no longer holds
because something else does. So when we know that the external
angles are equal to four right angles because it is isosceles, it still
86ᵃ remains to ask why an isosceles is so—because it is a triangle,
and this because it is a rectilineal figure. And if this is no longer
so because something else is so, it is then that we know best. It is
then too that it is universal. Hence universal demonstrations are
better.

Again, the more particular a demonstration is, the more it
5 tends to what is infinite, while universal demonstrations tend to
the simple and the limit. But as infinite, things are not understandable, while as finite they are understandable. Hence they
are more understandable as universal than as particular. Hence
universals are more demonstrable. But of more demonstrable
items there is more of a demonstration (for correlative items are
more so-and-so at the same time as one another). Hence a uni-
10 versal demonstration is better since it is more of a demonstration.

Again, if a demonstration in virtue of which you know both
this and something else is preferable to one in virtue of which
you know this alone; and if someone who possesses a universal
demonstration knows the particular fact too, whereas the latter
does not know the universal fact,²⁶ then in this way too universal
demonstrations will be preferable.

Again, thus: to prove something more universally is to prove it
15 through a middle term which is nearer to the principles. Immediates are nearest—indeed they are principles. Thus if a demonstration which proceeds from a principle is more exact than
one which does not proceed from a principle, then a demonstration which proceeds more from a principle is more exact than
one which is less so. But a more universal demonstration is of this
type. Hence universal demonstrations will be superior. E.g. if
20 you had to demonstrate A of D. The middle terms are B, C. B is
higher, so that a demonstration through B is more universal.

Some of these remarks are general. It is most plain that universal demonstrations are more important from the fact that in
grasping the prior of the propositions we know in a sense the pos-
25 terior too, i.e. we grasp it potentially. E.g. if you know that every
triangle has two right angles, you know in a sense of the isosceles

²⁶ Reading τό with most MSS for the OCT's τήν.

too that it has two right angles—you know it potentially—, even if you do not know of the isosceles that it is a triangle. But if you grasp the latter proposition you do not know the universal in any sense, neither potentially nor actually.

Universal demonstrations are objects of thought, particular demonstrations terminate in perception.   30

CHAPTER 25

So much, then, by way of showing that universal demonstrations are better than particular demonstrations. That probative demonstrations are better than privative demonstrations will be plain from what follows.

Let one demonstration be better than another if, other things being equal, it depends on fewer postulates or suppositions or propositions—for if these items are equally familiar, knowledge 35 will come about more quickly in this way, and this is preferable.

The argument for the proposition that a demonstration depending on fewer items is better can be stated universally thus. If the middle terms are familiar and the prior terms are more familiar in the same way in each case, then let one demonstration show that *A* holds of *E* through the middle terms *B*, *C*, *D*, and **86ᵇ** let the other show that *A* holds of *E* through *F*, *G*. Thus that *A* holds of *D* and that *A* holds of *E* are on a level. But that *A* holds of *D* is prior to and more familiar than that *A* holds of *E*; for the latter is demonstrated through the former, and that through 5 which something is demonstrated is more convincing than it. Thus a demonstration through fewer items is better, other things being equal.

Now both affirmative and negative demonstrations prove their conclusions through three terms and two propositions. But the former assume that something is the case, whereas the latter assume both that something is the case and that something is not the case. Hence the latter proceed through more items and are therefore worse.

Again, since we have proved that it is impossible for there 10 to be a deduction when both propositions are privative, and that one proposition must be privative while the other says that something holds, we must assume the latter in addition to the former. As a demonstration increases, the positive propositions necessarily become more numerous, whereas it is impossible for 15 there to be more than one privative proposition in any deduction.

Let *A* hold of none of the *B*s and let *B* hold of every *C*. If we must next increase both propositions, a middle term must be interpolated. Let it be *D* for *AB*, and *E* for *BC*. It is clear that *E*
20 is positive, and that *D* is positive for *B* and privative in relation to *A*. For *D* holds of every *B*, and *A* must hold of none of the *D*s. Thus we get a single privative proposition, *AD*.

The same holds for the other deductions. The middle term for
25 the positive terms is always positive in both directions, while for the privative it must be privative in one direction. Hence we get a single privative proposition, the others being positive.

Now if the item through which something is proved is more familiar and more convincing than it, and if privative demonstrations are proved through positive demonstrations whereas the latter are not proved through the former, then positive demon-
30 strations, being prior and more familiar and more convincing, will be better.

Again, if universal immediate propositions are principles of deductions, and if the universal proposition is affirmative in probative demonstrations and negative in privative demonstrations, and if affirmative propositions are prior to and more familiar than negative propositions (for negations are familiar because of
35 affirmations, and affirmations are prior—just as being the case is prior to not being the case), then the principles of probative demonstrations are better than those of privative demonstrations; and a demonstration which uses better principles is better.

Again, they are more principle-like; for without probative demonstrations there are no privative demonstrations.

CHAPTER 26

87ᵃ Since positive demonstrations are better than privative demonstrations, it is plain that they are also better than demonstrations leading to the impossible. But we must learn how they differ from one another.

Let *A* hold of no *B* and *B* of every *C*: it is necessary for *A* to
5 hold of no *C*. If the assumptions are made in this way, the privative demonstration that *A* does not hold of *C* will be probative. The demonstration leading to the impossible goes like this. If we are to prove that *A* does not hold of *B*, we should assume that it does hold and that *B* holds of *C*—hence it follows that *A* holds of *C*. Let it be familiar and agreed that this is
10 impossible. Then it is not possible for *A* to hold of *B*. Hence if *B* is agreed to hold of *C*, it is impossible for *A* to hold of *B*.

Thus the terms are similarly arranged, and the difference is a matter of which privative proposition is more familiar—that A does not hold of B or that A does not hold of C. When the conclusion (that it is not the case) is more familiar, we get a demonstration to the impossible; and when the proposition in the deduction is more familiar, we get a demonstrative proof. By nature the proposition AB is prior to AC. For the items from which a conclusion proceeds are prior to the conclusion; and that A does not hold of C is a conclusion whereas that A does not hold of B is an item from which the conclusion proceeds. For if it follows that something is rejected, we cannot infer that this is a conclusion and the other items are what it proceeds from. Rather, what a deduction proceeds from is something related as whole to part or part to whole—and the propositions AC and BC are not so related to one another.

Thus if a demonstration which proceeds from what is more familiar and prior is superior, and if in both cases conviction proceeds from something's not being the case but in the one from something prior and in the other from something posterior, then a privative demonstration will be better *simpliciter* than a demonstration to the impossible. Hence positive demonstrations, which are better than privative demonstrations, are plainly also better than demonstrations to the impossible.

CHAPTER 27

One science is more exact than another and prior to it if it is concerned both with the facts and with the reason why and not with the facts separately from the science of the reason why; or if it is not said of an underlying subject and the other is said of an underlying subject (as e.g. arithmetic is more exact than harmonics); or if it proceeds from fewer items and the other from some additional posit (as e.g. arithmetic is more exact than geometry). By from an additional posit I mean e.g. that a unit is a positionless substance and a point a substance having position—the latter proceeds from an additional posit.

CHAPTER 28

A science is one if it is concerned with one kind—with whatever items come from the primitives and are parts or attributes of them in themselves. One science is different from another if their principles come neither from the same items nor those of the one **87^b**

from those of the other. There is evidence for this when you come to the indemonstrables: they must be in the same kind as the items demonstrated. And there is evidence for *this* when the items which are proved through them are in the same kind and of a kind.

CHAPTER 29

5 It is possible for there to be several demonstrations of the same thing not only if you take non-continuous middle terms from the same chain—e.g. *C* and *D* and *F* for *AB*—but also if you take middle terms from different chains. E.g. let *A* be altering, *D* changing, *B* enjoying, and then *G* coming to rest. It is true to
10 predicate *D* of *B* and *A* of *D*: anyone who is enjoying himself is changing, and what is changing is altering. Again, it is true to predicate *A* of *G* and *G* of *B*: everyone who is enjoying himself is coming to rest, and anyone who is coming to rest is altering. Hence the deductions proceed through different middle terms which do not come from the same chain. (But it is not the case
15 that neither of the middle terms is said of the other, since there must be a term of some of which both of them hold.)

Inquire in how many ways it is possible to produce deductions of the same thing in the other figures.

CHAPTER 30

You cannot understand through a demonstration what happens
20 by chance. What happens by chance is neither necessary nor for the most part—it is what happens apart from these—and demonstrations are concerned with items of one or the other of these types. For every deduction proceeds either through necessary propositions or through what holds for the most part. If the propositions are necessary, the conclusion too is necessary; and if
25 they hold for the most part, so too does the conclusion. Hence if what happens by chance is neither for the most part nor necessary, there will be no demonstration of it.

CHAPTER 31

You cannot understand anything through perception. Even if perception is of what is such-and-such, and not of what is a this so-
30 and-so, nevertheless what you perceive must be a this so-and-so

at a place and at a time. It is impossible to perceive what is universal and holds in every case. For no universal is a this, nor is it found at some time: in that case it would not be universal, since it is what is found always and everywhere which we say is universal.

Thus, since demonstrations are universal, and universals cannot be perceived, it is clear that you cannot understand anything through perception. Rather, it is plain that even if we could 35 perceive that triangles have angles equal to two right angles, we would still seek a demonstration and would not, as some people say, already understand it. Particulars must be perceived, whereas we have understanding in so far as[27] we get to know universals.

This is why, if we were on the moon and saw the earth screening it, we would not know the explanation of the eclipse. We would 88^a perceive that it is now eclipsed but not why; for we have seen that there is no perception of universals. Nevertheless, if we observed this happening often and then hunted for the universal, we would possess a demonstration; for it is from many particulars that the universal becomes plain. 5

Universals are valuable because they make the explanations plain. Hence universal demonstrations are more valuable than perception or thought—with regard to items which have an explanation different from themselves. (For the primitives, a different account holds.)

Thus it is clear that it is impossible to understand anything demonstrable by perceiving it—unless you say that possessing 10 understanding through a demonstration is perceiving.

Nevertheless, certain features in problems are referred to want of perception. In some cases if we saw we should not seek—not because we have knowledge by seeing but because we grasp the universal from seeing. E.g. if we saw the glass to be perforated and the light coming through it, it would also be plain why it 15 does—even if[28] we see each piece of glass separately whereas we think at a single time that it is thus in every case.

CHAPTER 32

It is impossible for all deductions to have the same principles. First let us study the matter in general terms.

---

[27] Reading τῷ, with most MSS, for the OCT's τό.
[28] Reading καὶ εἰ for the OCT's καίει (the MSS are divided); and τό, with the MSS, for the OCT's τῷ.

Some deductions are true and some false. Even if it is pos-
20 sible to deduce a truth from falsehoods, this only comes about
once. E.g. suppose that *A* is true of *C*, and that *B*, the middle
term, is false of *C* (*A* does not hold of *B* nor *B* of *C*): if middle
25 terms are taken for these propositions, they will be false because
every false conclusion proceeds from falsehoods, whereas true
conclusions proceed from truths. But truths and falsehoods are
different.

Next, not even falsehoods proceed from the same items as one
another: there are falsehoods which are in fact contrary to one
another and cannot be the case together—e.g. that justice is
30 injustice or cowardice, that a man is a horse or a cow, that what
is equal to something is greater than it or less.

On the basis of what we have laid down, we argue as follows.
Not even all truths have the same principles. The principles of
many truths are different in kind and do not attach to one
another (e.g. units do not attach to points, since the former do
not have position whereas the latter do). But they would have to
35 attach either as middle terms or from above or from below (or
else some of the terms would have to be inside and others
outside).

Nor is it possible to find some of the common principles from
88ᵇ which everything will be proved. (I call common e.g. that everything is asserted or denied.) For existent things belong to different kinds (some items hold of quantities alone and others of
qualities), and it is with the help of them that proofs are conducted through the common items.

Again, the principles are not much fewer than the conclusions;
5 for the propositions are principles, and the propositions are
formed either by assuming an additional term or by interpolating
one.

Again, the conclusions are infinite, the terms finite.

Again, some principles are necessary and other contingent.

Inquiring in this way, it is impossible for the principles to be
10 the same and finite if the conclusions are infinite. If anyone were
to mean the claim in some other sense, e.g. that *these* are the
principles of geometry, *these* of calculation, *these* of medicine, he
will simply be saying that the sciences have principles. And it is
ridiculous to say that the principles are the same because they are
15 the same as themselves—in this sense everything turns out to be
the same.

Nor yet is the claim that anything must be proved from everything the same as seeking the same principles for everything.

This is silly. It does not hold in the clear parts of mathematics, nor is it possible on analysis: the immediate propositions are principles, and a different conclusion is reached when an additional immediate proposition is assumed. And if someone were 20 to say that it is the *primitive* immediate propositions which are principles, then there is one of these in each kind.

If the claim is meant neither in the sense that anything must be proved from all the principles, nor in the sense that they are different in such a way that the principles of each science are different, it remains to consider whether the principles of everything are of a kind even though *this* depends on *these* principles and *this* on *these*. It is clear that this too is not possible; for it has 25 been proved that the principles of things different in kind are themselves different in kind. Principles are of two types, those from which and those about which; and while the former are common, the latter are proper—e.g. number, magnitude.

CHAPTER 33

What is understandable and understanding differ from what is 30 opinable and opinion because understanding is universal and comes through necessities. What is necessary cannot be otherwise, while there are some items which are true and are the case but which can also be otherwise. It is plain that understanding cannot be concerned with these items; for then what can be otherwise could not be otherwise. Nor is comprehension con- 35 cerned with them (by comprehension I mean a principle of understanding), nor indemonstrable understanding (this is belief in an immediate proposition). Now it is comprehension and under- **89ᵃ** standing and opinion (and what is called after them) which are true. Hence it remains that opinion is concerned with what is true or false but can also be otherwise. (Opinion is belief in a proposition which is immediate and not necessary.)

This agrees with how things appear to be. For opinion is 5 unstable, and so too is the nature of the items we are talking about. In addition, no one thinks that he opines something when he thinks that it is impossible for it to be otherwise—he thinks that he understands it. Rather, it is when you think that it is so but that nothing prevents it from being otherwise that you think you opine something—implying that opinion applies to this sort of item and understanding to what is necessary. 10

45

Then how is it possible to opine and understand the same thing? And why will opinion not be understanding if you posit that you can opine everything that you know? A knower and an opiner will follow the same path through the middle terms until they
15 come to the immediates. Hence since the former knows, the opiner knows too. For just as you can opine the fact, so too can you opine the reason why—and this is the middle term.

Or if you believe something which cannot be otherwise in the way in which you grasp[29] the definitions through which demonstrations proceed, will you then not opine but understand it?
20 While if you believe that it is true but not that *these* items hold of their subject in virtue of its essence and in virtue of its form, will you then opine and not truly understand it? Will you opine both the fact and the reason why if your opinion has come through immediates, and only the fact if it has not come through immediates?

But there cannot be opinion and understanding of the same thing in every sense. Rather, just as in a certain way there can be
25 both false and true opinion of the same thing, so there can be both understanding and opinion of the same thing. If there is true and false opinion of the same thing in the way some people say, then it follows that you are committed to absurdities—and in particular to the absurdity that you do not opine what you falsely opine. But since things are called the same in several senses, in one sense it is possible and in another not. To opine truly that the
30 diagonal is commensurate is absurd. But because the diagonal with which the opinions are concerned is the same, in this sense they are of the same thing—although what it is to be each of them in respect of its account is not the same. In the same sense there is both understanding and opinion of the same thing. The former is of animal in such a way that it cannot not be an animal,
35 and the latter in such a way that it can—e.g. if the former is of just what is man and the latter of man but not of just what is man. They are the same because man is the same, but they are not the same in the way they take man.

It is clear from this that it is not possible to opine and to understand the same thing at the same time. For then you would
89ᵇ at the same time have the belief that the same thing can be otherwise and cannot be otherwise—and this is not possible. In different people it is possible for there to be each of these attitudes with regard to the same thing, as I have said. But in the

---

[29] Retaining ἔχει, which is found in most MSS and deleted by the OCT.

same person it is not possible even in this way; for he would at
the same time have a belief, e.g. that a man is just what is an
animal (this is what it is for it not to be possible for a man not to 5
be an animal), and also a belief that a man is not just what is an
animal (let this be what it is for it to be possible).

As for how the remaining items should be distributed among
thought and comprehension and understanding and skill and
prudence and wisdom—this is a matter in part for the study
of nature and in part for moral study.

CHAPTER 34

Acumen is a talent for hitting upon the middle term in an imper- 10
ceptible time. E.g. if someone sees that the moon always has
its bright side toward the sun and quickly sees why this is so—
because it gets its light from the sun; or he knows that someone is
talking to a rich man because he is borrowing from him; or why
they are friends—because they are enemies of the same man.
Seeing the extreme terms he gets to know all the explanatory 15
middle terms.

The bright side's being toward the sun, A; getting light from
the sun, B; the moon, C. B, getting light from the sun, holds of
C, the moon; and A, the bright side's being toward that from
which it gets light, of B: hence A holds of C through B. 20

BOOK BETA

CHAPTER I

The things we seek are equal in number to those we understand.
We seek four things: the fact, the reason why, if something is,
25 what something is.

When we seek whether this or that is the case, setting down a
plurality of terms (e.g. whether the sun is eclipsed or not), we are
seeking the fact. Evidence for this: on finding that it is eclipsed
we stop; and if from the beginning we know that it is eclipsed, we
do not seek whether it is. When we know the fact we seek the
30 reason why (e.g. knowing that it is eclipsed or that the earth
moves, we seek the reason why it is eclipsed or why it moves).

These things we seek in this way; but certain items we seek in
another way—e.g. if a centaur or a god is or is not. (I mean if
one is or is not *simpliciter* and not if one is white or not.) And
having come to know that it is, we seek what it is (e.g.: Then
35 what is a god? or What is a man?).

CHAPTER 2

These and thus many are the things which we seek and which
we find and know. When we seek the fact or if something is
simpliciter, we are seeking whether or not there is a middle term
for it; and when, having come to know either the fact or if it
90ª is—either partially or *simpliciter*—, we seek the reason why or
what it is, we are then seeking what the middle term is. (By the
fact that it is partially and *simpliciter* I mean this: partially—Is
the moon eclipsed? or Is it waxing? In such cases we seek if it is
5 something or is not something. *Simpliciter*: if the moon, or night,
is or is not.)

Thus it results that in all our searches we seek either if there
is a middle term or what the middle term is. For the middle term
is the explanation, and in all cases it is the explanation which is
being sought. Is it eclipsed?—Is there some explanation or not?
After that, having come to know that there is one, we seek
10 what it is. For the explanation of its being not this or that but
simpliciter,[1] or of its being not *simpliciter* but one of the items

---

[1] Omitting τὴν οὐσίαν.

48

which hold of it in itself or incidentally—this is the middle term.
By "is *simpliciter*" I mean the underlying subject (e.g. the moon
or the earth or the sun or a triangle), and by "one of the items"
eclipse, equality, inequality, if it is in the middle or not.

In all these cases it is clear that what it is and why it is are 15
the same. What is an eclipse? Privation of light from the moon by
the screening of the earth. Why is there an eclipse? or Why is the
moon eclipsed? Because the light leaves it when the earth screens
it. What is a harmony? A numerical ratio between high and low.
Why does the high harmonize with the low? Because a numerical 20
ratio holds between the high and the low. Can the high and
the low harmonize?—Is the ratio between them numerical? Assuming that it is, then what is the ratio?

That the search is for the middle term is shown by those cases
in which the middle is perceptible. If we have not perceived the 25
middle term, we seek it: e.g. we seek if there is a middle term for
the eclipse or not. But if we were on the moon we would seek
neither if there is an eclipse nor why there is: rather, these things
would be plain at the same time. By perceiving we would come to
know the universal: perception would tell us that the earth is now
screening it (it is plain that it is now eclipsed); and from this the 30
universal would come about.

So, as we say, to know what something is is the same as to
know why it is—either why it is *simpliciter* and not one of the
items that hold of it, or why it is one of the items which hold of it
(e.g. that it has two right angles, or that it is greater or less).

CHAPTER 3

It is plain, then, that whatever is sought, it is a search for a 35
middle term. Let us now say how we can prove what something
is, and in what way we can effect a reduction, and what definitions are, and what they are of; and first let us go through the
puzzles which these matters raise. Let us begin our remarks in
the way most appropriate to the neighbouring arguments.   90^b

You might puzzle over whether you can know the same thing
in the same respect both by a definition and by a demonstration,
or whether this is impossible.

Definitions are thought to be of what something is, and what
something is is in every case universal and positive; but some de- 5
ductions are privative and some are not universal—e.g. those in

the second figure are all privative and those in the third are not universal.

Next, there are not definitions even for all the positive deductions in the first figure—e.g. that every triangle has angles equal to two right angles. The argument for this is as follows. To understand what is demonstrable is to possess a demonstration of it. Hence, since there are demonstrations of such things, plainly there will not also be definitions of them. For then someone might understand them in virtue of the definition without possessing the demonstration, since there is no reason why he should possess them both at the same time.

An adequate justification can also be got by induction: we have never yet got to know anything by defining it—neither anything holding in itself nor any incidental.

Again, if a definition is the recognition of some essence, it is clear that *such* items are not essences.

So it is plain that there are not definitions of everything of which there are demonstrations.

Well then, is there a demonstration of everything of which there is a definition, or not?

One argument in this case is the same as before. Of one thing, as one, there is one mode of understanding. Hence, if to understand what is demonstrable is to possess a demonstration of it, something impossible will follow: anyone who possesses the definition of something without the demonstration will understand it.

Again, the principles of demonstrations are definitions, and it has been proved earlier that there will not be demonstrations of principles—either the principles will be demonstrable and there will be principles of principles, and this will continue *ad infinitum*, or else the primitives will be indemonstrable definitions.

But if the objects of definitions and of demonstrations are not all the same, are some of them the same? Or is this impossible? There is no demonstration of anything of which there is a definition. For definitions are of what something is, i.e. of its essence; but all demonstrations clearly suppose and assume what a thing is—e.g. mathematical demonstrations assume what a unit is and what odd is; and similarly for other demonstrations.

Again, every demonstration proves something of something, i.e. that it is or is not; but in a definition nothing is predicated of anything else—e.g. neither animal of two-footed nor this of animal, nor indeed figure of plane (for a plane is not a figure nor is a figure a plane).

Again, proving what something is is different from proving that it is. Definitions show what something is, whereas demonstrations 91ª show that this is or is not true of that. And of different items there are different demonstrations—unless one demonstration stands to the other as a part to the whole. (I mean by this that the isosceles has been proved to have two right angles if every triangle has been proved to do so: one is a part and the other a 5 whole.) But these items—that something is and what it is—are not related to one another in this way: neither is part of the other.

It is clear, then, that there are not demonstrations of everything of which there are definitions, nor definitions of everything of which there are demonstrations; nor in general is it possible to have both of the same item. Hence it is plain that definitions and 10 demonstrations are not the same, nor is the one included in the other; for then their underlying subjects would be similarly related.

CHAPTER 4

So much for these puzzles. Then are there deductions and demonstrations of what a thing is, or are there not, as the argument just now supposed?

A deduction proves something of something through the middle 15 term. What a thing is both is proper to it and is predicated in what it is; and such items necessarily convert: if *A* is proper to *C*, plainly it is also proper to *B* and *B* to *C*, so that all are proper to one another. Now if *A* holds of every *B* in what it is, and *B* is said universally of every *C* in what it is, then necessarily *A* is said 20 of *C* in what it is. But if you do not make the assumptions in this double fashion, it will not be necessary for *A* to be predicated of *C* in what it is (if *A* holds of *B* in what it is, but *B* does not hold in what it is of what it is said of). Both will contain what it is; therefore *B* too will hold of *C* in what it is. Now if both contain 25 what it is, i.e. what it is to be it, then what it is to be it will already be there in the middle term. In general, if you can prove what man is, let *C* be man and *A* what man is—whether two-footed animal or anything else. If this is deduced, it is necessary for *A* to be predicated of every *B*, and there will be an 30 intermediate account other than A,[2] so that this too will be what man is. So you assume what you have to prove—for B is[3] what man is.

We must inquire in the case of two propositions and of primitives and immediates; for then what we are saying becomes especially clear.

35   Those people who try to prove through conversion what soul is (or what man is, or anything else which exists) postulate what was set at the beginning. E.g. if someone were to claim that soul is what is itself explanatory of its own being alive, and that this is a number which moves itself: it is necessary to postulate that soul **91ᵇ** is just what is a number which moves itself, in the sense of being the same thing as it.

It is not the case that if A follows B and B follows C, then A will be what it is to be C. Rather, it is true[4] to say only that A will hold of C—even if A is just what is some B and is predicated of 5   every B. For what it is to be an animal is predicated of what it is to be a man (it is true that every case of what it is to be a man is what it is to be an animal, just as every man is an animal), but not in the sense of their being one thing.

If, then, you do not make the assumptions in this way, you will not deduce that A is what it is to be C, i.e. its essence; and if you do make the assumptions in this way, you will already have 10   assumed what it is to be C, namely B,[5] and hence you will not have demonstrated it—for you have assumed what was set at the beginning.

CHAPTER 5

The path through the divisions does not deduce definitions either, as I said in my analysis of the figures. For it nowhere becomes 15   necessary for the object to be such-and-such if *these* items are the case—just as someone who is giving an induction does not demonstrate anything. For you must not ask the conclusion, nor must it be the case simply inasmuch as it is granted. Rather, it must be the case if *those* items are the case, even if the answerer denies it.

---

[2] Retaining τούτου (the OCT emends to τοῦτο).
[3] Retaining ἐστι (the OCT emends to ἔσται).
[4] Reading ἦν after ἀληθές, with most MSS.
[5] Retaining τὸ B, which the OCT deletes.

Is man an animal or inanimate? If[6] you assumed animal, you
have not deduced it. Next, every animal is either terrestrial or
aquatic: you assumed terrestrial. And that man is the whole—a 20
terrestrial animal—is not necessary from what you have said;
rather, you assume this too. It makes no difference whether you
do this in many steps or in few—it is all the same. (Indeed, those
who proceed in this way actually make non-deductive use even
of what can be deduced.) For why should all this not be true of 25
man and yet not show what a man is or what it is to be a man?
Again, what prevents you from positing some additional item, or
from removing something, or from passing over something in its
essence?

These points are ignored. It is possible to solve the difficulties
if you assume everything in what the thing is, make the division
consecutive by postulating what is primitive, and leave nothing 30
out. [This is necessary if everything falls into the division and
nothing is omitted; and this is necessary—for it must be atomic.][7]
Nevertheless, there is no deduction here;[8] rather, the procedure
lets us get to know what the thing is in some other way (if at all).
This is not in the least absurd; for neither, presumably, does
someone who gives an induction demonstrate anything—but he 35
nevertheless shows something. If you state the definition on the
basis of the division, you do not give a deduction. In the case of
conclusions without middle terms, if someone says that if these
items are the case then it is necessary for *this* to be the case, it is
possible to ask why: so too in the case of divisional definitions.
What is a man? An animal, mortal, footed, two-footed, wingless. 92^a
Why? (At each additional posit.) He will say—and prove by
the division, as he thinks—that everything is either mortal or
immortal. But an account of this sort, taken as a whole, is no
longer[9] a definition, so that even if it were demonstrated by the
division, that would not mean that *the definition* was deduced. 5

CHAPTER 6

But can you in fact demonstrate what something is in its essence
by arguing on the basis of a supposition and assuming that what it

---

[6] Reading εἶτ' (with most MSS) for the OCT's εἴτ'.
[7] For the text see notes.
[8] Reading ἔνεστι with most MSS (the OCT has ἔστι).
[9] Reading οὐκέτι with most MSS (the OCT prints οὐκ ἔστιν).

is to be something is the property composed of the items in what it is, that *these* items alone are in what it is, and that the totality of them is proper to the thing? This is what it is to be that thing.

10 Or in this case too have you again assumed what it is to be the thing? For you must prove it by way of the middle term.

Again, just as in a deduction you do not assume what being deduced is (for the proposition on which the deduction depends is always whole or part), so too what it is to be something must not be in the deduction; rather, it must be separate from what

15 has been supposed. Then if anyone disputes that something has been deduced, you may meet him by saying "*This* is what a deduction is"; and if anyone says that what it is to be something has not been deduced, you can say "Yes it has; for we are supposing that *this* is what what it is to be something is". Hence the deduction must be carried through *without* assuming what a deduction is or what what it is to be something is.

20 Suppose you do prove something on the basis of a supposition—e.g. if being bad is being divisible, and if (for items which have a contrary) being something is being contrary to what its contrary is, and if the good is contrary to the bad, and the indivisible to the divisible, then being good is being indivisible.

Here too in the proof you assume what it is to be something,

25 and assume it in order to prove what it is to be something.—"But what it is to be something *different*."—Granted; for in demonstrations too you assume that this is true of that—but not of the *same* item, nor of something which has the same account as it and converts with it.

Moreover, both the deductions—the deduction proving by way of division and the present deduction—face the same puzzle: why

30 will man be a two-footed terrestrial[10] animal and not an animal and terrestrial?[11] For the assumptions do not make it necessary that what is predicated form a unity—rather, it is as if the same man were musical and literate.

CHAPTER 7

Then how will a definer prove the essence of something or what it

35 is? He will not, as in a demonstration, show from items agreed to

---

[10] Reading δίπουν πεζόν with the MSS for the OCT's πεζὸν δίπουν.
[11] Omitting the OCT's καὶ δίπουν.

be the case that if they are the case then necessarily something
else is the case (this is demonstration); nor, as in an induction,
will he show by way of the particulars, which are plain, that
everything is thus-and-so inasmuch as nothing is otherwise (for an
induction does not prove what a thing is, but rather that it is 92ᵇ
or is not). What other way is left? He will hardly prove it by
perception or by pointing his finger.

Again, how will you prove what something is? Anyone who
knows what a man or anything else is must also know that it 5
exists. (Of that which does not exist, no one knows what it is.
You may know what the account or the name means when I say
"goat-stag", but it is impossible to know what a goat-stag is.) But
if you are to prove what something is and also that it exists, how
will you prove them by the same argument? Definitions make a 10
single thing plain, and so do demonstrations; but what a man is
and that men exist are different.

Next, we say that everything which a thing is must be proved
through a demonstration—except its essence. But existence is not
the essence of anything; for the things that exist do not constitute
a kind. There will therefore be a demonstration that the item 15
exists. And this is what the sciences as a matter of fact do: a
geometer assumes what triangle means and proves that triangles
exist. So what will a definer prove if not what a triangle is? But
then he will know by the definition what it is and yet not know if
it exists; and this is impossible.

It is clear too that, in the current methods of definition, definers
do not prove that anything exists. Even if there is something 20
equidistant from the middle, *why* does what has been defined
exist? And why is this a circle?—You could say that it was a
definition of mountain-copper. Definitions do not show that what
they describe is possible, nor that the definitions are of what they
say they are—it is always possible to ask why. 25

Then if a definer proves either what something is or what its
name means, and if there is certainly not a proof of what it is,
then a definition will be an account which means the same as a
name. But this is absurd. First, there will be definitions of non-
substances and of things which do not exist—for you can mean
things which do not exist. Again, all accounts will be definitions; 30
for you can assign a name to any account whatever—and we shall
all talk definitions and the *Iliad* will be a definition. Again, no
demonstration would demonstrate that this name shows *this*—so
definitions do not show this either.

35 From these considerations it appears that definitions and deductions are not the same, and that there cannot be deductions
and definitions of the same thing; and further that definitions
neither demonstrate nor prove anything, and that it is not possible to know what something is either by a definition or by a
demonstration.

CHAPTER 8

93ª We must inquire next which of these points have been correctly
made and which not; and we must ask what a definition is, and
whether there can be demonstrations and definitions of what
something is in some way or in no way at all.

　　As we said, to know what something is and to know the
5 explanation of whether it is are the same; and the account of the
fact that something is is the explanation. This is either the same
as it or something else; and if it is something else, it is either
demonstrable or indemonstrable. If it is something else and it is
possible to demonstrate it, then the explanation must be a middle
term and the proof must be in the first figure; for what is being
proved is both universal and positive.

10　　Thus one way would be the one we have just examined—where
we prove what something is by means of another definition.[12] For
in the case of what something is, the middle term must be what
something is (and in the case of a property, it must be a property).
Hence you will prove the one but you will not prove the other
instance of what it is to be the same object. I have said earlier
15 that this way will not be a demonstration; rather, it is a general
deduction of what the thing is.

　　Let us say in what way a demonstration *is* possible, starting again
from the beginning. Just as we seek the reason why when we
grasp the fact (sometimes indeed these two things become plain
at the same time—but it is not possible to get to know the reason
why *before* the fact), in the same way we plainly cannot grasp
20 what it is to be something without grasping that it exists; for we
cannot know what something is when we do not know whether
it exists. But as to whether it exists, sometimes we grasp this
incidentally, and sometimes by grasping something of the object
itself—e.g. of thunder, that it is a sort of noise in the clouds; of

---

[12] Retaining the MS reading τό (the OCT emends to τοῦ).

an eclipse, that it is a sort of privation of light; of man, that he is a sort of animal; of soul, that it is something which moves itself.

When we know incidentally that something exists, necessarily 25 we have no grasp on what it is; for we do not even know that it exists, and to seek what something is without grasping that it exists is to seek nothing. But when we grasp something of the object, the business is easier. Hence in so far as we grasp that it exists, to that extent we also have some grasp on what it is.

When we grasp something of what a thing is, suppose first that it is like this. Eclipse A, moon C, screening by the earth B. To 30 ask whether it is eclipsed or not is to seek whether B is or not. This is no different from seeking whether there is an account of the eclipse; and if there is, we say that it is eclipsed. (Or: of which of the contradictory pair does the account hold—of its having two right angles or of its not having them?) 35

When we discover it, we know at the same time the fact and the reason why—if we proceed through middle terms.[13] Otherwise we know the fact but not the reason why: moon C, eclipse A, not being able to produce a shadow during full moon although nothing visible is between us and it B. If B, not being able to produce a shadow although nothing visible is between us and it, 93^b holds of C, and A, being eclipsed, holds of B, then it is plain *that* it is eclipsed but not yet *why*; and we know *that* there is an eclipse but we do not know *what* it is.

When it is plain that A holds of C, then to seek why it holds is to seek what B is—whether screening or rotation of the moon or 5 extinction. And this is the account of the one extreme, i.e. in this case of A; for an eclipse is a screening by the earth.

What is thunder? Extinction of fire in cloud. Why does it thunder? Because the fire in the cloud is extinguished. Cloud C, thunder A, extinction of fire B. B holds of C, the cloud (the fire 10 is extinguished in it); and A, noise, holds of B—and B is indeed an account of A, the first extreme. (If there is another middle term for this, it will come from the remaining accounts.)

We have said how what something is is taken and becomes 15 familiar. Although there are no deductions and no demonstrations of what something is, nevertheless what something is is made plain through deductions and through demonstrations. Hence without a demonstration you cannot get to know what something is (in cases where the explanation is something else),

---

[13] Reading διὰ μέσων with most MSS for the OCT's δι' ἀμέσων.

20 and yet there are no demonstrations of what something is (as we
said when we went through the puzzles).

CHAPTER 9

Of some things there is something else which is their explanation,
of others there is not. Hence it is plain that in some cases what
something is is immediate and a principle; and here you must
suppose, or make clear in some other way, both that the thing
exists and what it is. (Arithmeticians do this: they suppose both
25 what a unit is and that there are units.) But in cases where there
is a middle term and something else is explanatory of the essence,
you can—as we have said—show what something is through a
demonstration without demonstrating what it is.

CHAPTER 10

Since a definition is said to be an account of what something is, it
30 is clear that one type will be an account of what its name, or
some other name-like account, means—e.g. what triangle means.
When we grasp that this exists, we seek why it is. But it is
difficult to take anything in this way if we do not know that it
exists. The explanation of the difficulty was given earlier: we do
35 not even know whether it exists or not, except incidentally. (An
account is one in two ways: by connection, like the *Iliad*; and by
showing one thing of one thing, non-incidentally.)

One definition of definition is the one we have just stated.
Another definition is an account which shows why something
94^a exists. Hence the former type means something but does not
prove it, whereas the latter will clearly be like a demonstration
of what something is, differing in arrangement from a demonstration. For there is a difference between saying why it thunders
and what thunder is. In the one case you will say: Because the
5 fire is extinguished in the clouds. But: What is thunder?—A
noise of fire being extinguished in the clouds. Hence the same
account is given in different ways: in one way it is a continuous
demonstration, in the other a definition.

Again, a definition of thunder is noise in the clouds; and this is
a conclusion of the demonstration of what it is.
10   The definition of an immediate item is an indemonstrable positing of what it is.

One type of definition, then, is an indemonstrable account of what something is; another is a deduction of what something is, differing in aspect from a demonstration; a third is a conclusion of the demonstration of what something is.

From what we have said it is clear both in what sense there are demonstrations of what something is and in what sense there are 15 not, and in what cases there are and in what cases there are not; and, further, in how many senses we speak about definitions, and in what sense they prove what something is and in what sense they do not, and in what cases they do and in what cases they do not; and, further, how they are related to demonstrations, and in what sense it is possible for there to be demonstrations and definitions of the same thing and in what sense it is not possible.

CHAPTER II

Since we think that we understand something when we know its 20 explanation, and there are four sorts of explanation (one, what it is to be something; one, that if certain items hold it is necessary for this to hold; another, what initiated the change; and fourth, the purpose), all of them are proved through the middle term.

An explanation of the type 'if something holds it is necessary for this to hold' occurs not when a single proposition is assumed 25 but only when at least two are. This is so when the propositions have a single middle term. Thus when this one item is assumed, it is necessary for the conclusion to hold. The following case makes things plain. Why is the angle in a semicircle a right angle? It is a right angle if *what* holds? Let right be A, half of two rights B, the angle in a semicircle C. B explains why A, right, holds of C, the 30 angle in a semicircle. For B is equal to A and C to B (it is half of two rights). Thus if B, half of two rights, holds, then A holds of C (that is, the angle in a semicircle is a right angle). And this is the same as what it is to be it, in so far as this is what its account 35 means.

The middle term has also been proved to be explanatory of what it is to be something.[14]

Why did the Persian war come upon the Athenians? What is the explanation of the Athenians' being warred upon? Because they attacked Sardis with the Eretrians—this initiated the change. **94^b** War A, being first to attack B, Athenians C. B holds of C (being

---

[14] Reading τοῦ with most MSS (τό OCT), and omitting the OCT's ὄν.

first to attack holds of the Athenians), and A holds of B (men
5 make war on those who have first wronged them). Therefore A
holds of B (being warred upon holds of those who first began),
and this—B—of the Athenians (they first began it). Therefore
here too the explanation, what initiated the change, is a middle
term.

Suppose it is the purpose which is explanatory—e.g. Why does
he walk about?—In order to be healthy. Why is there a house?—
10 In order that his belongings may be kept safe. In the one case
with the purpose of being healthy, in the other with the purpose of keeping them safe. (There is no difference between
'Why should you walk about after dinner?' and 'For what purpose should you do so?') A walk after dinner C, the foodstuffs'
not remaining on the surface B, being healthy A. Suppose that
15 making the foodstuffs not remain on the surface at the mouth of
the stomach holds of walking about after dinner, and that it
is healthy. B, the foodstuffs' not remaining on the surface, is
thought to hold of walking about, C, and A, healthy, of B. Then
what is explanatory—the purpose—for C of A's holding of it?—
It is B, not remaining on the surface. And this is as it were an
20 account of A; for A will be elucidated in this way. Why is B
explanatory for C? Because being in such a state is what being
healthy is. (You should take the accounts instead, and then
everything will be clearer.)

Here the events occur in the opposite order compared to explanations in terms of change: there the middle term must occur
25 first; here C, the last term, occurs first, and the ultimate thing to
occur is the purpose.

The same thing may hold both for some purpose and from
necessity—e.g. light shining through a lantern: the finer body
30 passes through the larger pores from necessity (if light does
permeate in this way), and also for some purpose (in order that
we may not stumble). If something may be the case in this way,
may things also come about thus? E.g. if it thunders because
when the fire is extinguished it is necessary for it to sizzle and
make a noise, and also (if the Pythagoreans are right) for the
purpose of threatening the denizens of Tartarus in order to make
them afraid.
35   There are very many things of this sort, especially among
natural processes and products; for one type of nature makes
them for some purpose and another makes them from necessity.
(There are two types of necessity: one, in accordance with nature

and impulse; the other, by force and[15] contrary to impulse—thus 95ᵃ
a stone travels both upwards and downwards from necessity,
but not because of the same necessity.) Among the products of
thought, some are never found spontaneously—e.g. a house or a
statue—nor from necessity either, but rather for some purpose. 5
Others also occur by chance—e.g. health and safety. It is especially among things which can be both thus and otherwise,
when their occurrence, not being by chance, is such that the end
is good, that things come about for some purpose, and then
either by nature or by skill. No chance items come about for any
purpose.

CHAPTER 12

What explains why something is coming about (and why it has 10
come about, and why it will be) is the same as what explains why
it is the case: it is the middle term which is explanatory. But if
something is the case, the explanatory item is the case; if it is
coming about, it is coming about; if it has come about, it has
come about; and if it will be, it will be.

E.g. why has an eclipse come about?—Because the earth has 15
come to be in the middle. And it is coming about because it is
coming to be there; it will be because it will be in the middle; and
it is because it is. What is ice?—Assume that it is solidified water.
Water C, solidified A; the explanatory middle term is B, complete absence of heat. Thus B holds of C; and being solidified, A,
holds of B. Ice is coming about if B is coming about; it has come 20
about if it has come about; and it will be if it will be.

When an item which is explanatory in this way and the item of
which it is explanatory come about, then they both come about at
the same time; when they are the case, they are the case at the
same time; and similarly for "have come about" and for "will
be". But what of items which do not hold at the same time as one
another? Can it be that, in continuous time, as we think, one 25
such item is explanatory of another? Can the fact that *this* item
has come about be explained by something else which has come
about, the fact that *this* will be by something else which will be,
the fact that this is coming about by something which came about
earlier?

---

[15] Reading καί for ἤ (MSS, OCT).

Deductions start from what has come about later (although the principle in these cases is actually something which has already
30 come about—hence similarly with what is coming about): they do not start from what is earlier (e.g. "Since this has come about, this has come about later"). And similarly for what will be the case. For whether the time is indeterminate or determined it will not be the case that since it is true to say that *this* has come about it is true to say that *this*—the later item—has come about: in the interval, when the one item has already come about, the state-
35 ment will be false. The same account goes for what will be.

Nor can you argue that since *this* has come about, *this* will be. For the middle term must be of the same type: something which came about for what came about, something which will be for what will be, something which is coming about for what is coming about, something which is the case for what is the case. But nothing can be of the same type both as "it has come about" and "it will be".

Again, the intervening time can be neither indeterminate nor
95ᵇ determined: in the interval the statement will be false.

We must inquire what it is that holds things together so that after what *has come* about there are items which *are coming* about. Or is it plain that what is coming about is *not* next to what has come about? What came about is not next to what came about, since
5 these things are limits and atomic: just as points are not next to one another, so items which came about are not—both are indivisible. For the same reason, what is coming about is not next to what has come about. What is coming about is divisible, whereas what has come about is indivisible: what is coming about stands to what has come about as a line stands to a point, and
10 infinitely many items which have come about inhere in what is coming about. (But I must discuss this more clearly in my general account of change.)

Let us make this assumption with regard to the explanatory
15 middle term when events come about consecutively. Here too the middle term and the first term must be immediate. E.g. *A* has come about since *C* has come about (*C* has come about later, *A* earlier; but *C* is the principle since it is nearer to the present moment, which is the principle of time); and *C* has come about if *D* has come about. Thus if *D* has come about, *A* must have come
20 about; and *C* is the explanation—for if *D* has come about, *C*

must have come about, and if C has come about, A must have come about earlier.

If we take middle terms in this way, will they come to a stop somewhere at an immediate, or will something always fall in between them because of the infinity, i.e. because (as I have said) what has come about is not next to what has come about? However that may be, we must *begin* from something which is im- 25 mediate and first from the present moment.

The same goes for "it will be". If it is true to say that D will be, then it must earlier have been true to say that A would be. C is explanatory of this; for if D will be, C will be earlier, and if C will be, A will be earlier. Here too the division is infinite in the 30 same way: things which will be are not next to one another. But here too an immediate principle must be assumed.

In concrete terms it is like this. If a house has come about, stones must have been cut and have come about. Why?—Because a foundation must have come about if a house has come about; and if a foundation has come about, stones must have come 35 about earlier. Again, if there will be a house, in the same way there will be stones earlier. As before, the proof is through the middle term: there will be a foundation earlier.

We observe among events a sort of circular coming about. This can be the case if the middle term and the extremes follow one another: they must convert (as I proved at the beginning) 96^a because the conclusions convert; and this is what being circular is. In concrete terms it looks like this. If the earth has been soaked, necessarily steam came about; if steam, cloud; if cloud, water; and if water came about, it is necessary for the earth to 5 have been soaked. But this was the starting-point, so that things have come round in a circle: if any one item is the case, another is; if that, another; and if that, the first.

Some things come about universally (they either are or come about in this way always and in every case), others not always but for the most part—e.g. not every male man has hair on his chin, 10 but they do for the most part. In such cases the middle term must also hold for the most part. For if A is predicated universally of B and B universally of C, it is necessary for A to be predicated of C always and in every case (this is what it is to be universal—to 15 hold in every case and always). But it was supposed to hold for the most part. Therefore the middle term B must also hold for the most part. For what holds for the most part, then, there will be immediate principles which hold or come about in this way for the most part.

CHAPTER 13

20 I have said earlier how what something is can be elucidated in the terms of a deduction, and in what way there are and are not demonstrations and definitions of what something is. Let us now say how we should hunt out the items predicated in what something is.

Of the items which hold of something always, some extend
25 further than it without going outside its kind. (I say that they extend further if they hold of it universally and also hold of something else.) E.g. there are items which hold of every triplet and also of non-triplets: existence holds of triplets and also of
30 non-numbers; odd holds of every triplet and extends further (it also holds of quintuplets), but it does not go outside its kind—for quintuplets are numbers, and nothing outside number is odd.

We should take items of this type up to the point at which we have first taken just so many that, while each extends further, all of them together do not extend further: this must be the essence
35 of the object. E.g. number holds of every triplet, and so do odd and prime (in both senses—both as not being measured by number and as not being compounded from numbers). This, then, is precisely what a triplet is: a number that is odd, prime, and prime in *this* sense. Each of these items holds of all the odds
96ᵇ as well, and the ultimate item holds of pairs as well; but all of them together hold of nothing apart from triplets.

We have shown above that whatever is predicated in what something is is necessary[16] (and what is universal is necessary), and in the case of triplets—and of anything else for which we take
5 terms in this way—whatever we take is in what the item is: thus triplets will have these features from necessity.

That they constitute the essence is plain from the following consideration. If this is *not* what being a triplet is, then it must be some sort of kind, either named or nameless; but then it will extend further than triplets—take us to be supposing that a kind
10 is the sort of item which potentially extends further. Then if it holds of nothing other than atomic triplets, it will be what being a triplet is—take us, further, to be supposing that the essence of

---

[16] Reading ἀναγκαῖα with the MSS (the OCT emends to καθόλου).

64

something is the last such predication to hold of the atoms.
Hence the same will go for what being so-and-so is in the case of
anything else which we prove in this way.

When you are dealing with some whole, you should divide the 15
kind into what is atomic in form, i.e. into the primitives (e.g.
number into triplet and pair). Then you should try to get definitions of these items (e.g. of straight line and circle and right
angle). After this, having got what the kind is (e.g. whether it is a
quantity or a quality), you should study its proper attributes 20
through the primitive common items. For the characteristics of
the items compounded from the atoms will be plain from the
definitions, because definitions and what is simple are principles
of everything, and it is of the simples alone that the characteristics hold in themselves—they hold of the other items in
virtue of the simples. 25

Divisions made according to differences are useful in this pursuit.
I have said earlier in what way they yield proofs: only in the
following way will they be useful for deducing what something is.
   They might indeed be thought to be of no use at all but to
assume everything straight off—as if you were to make your
assumptions at the beginning without a division. But it makes a 30
difference which of the predicates are predicated first and which
later—e.g. whether you say *animal tame two-footed* or *two-footed
animal tame*. For if every item is made up from two things, and if
animal tame constitutes a single item, and if man (or whatever
the single thing in question may be) is next made up from this
and the difference, then you must make a division before making 35
your postulates.
   Again, only in this way is it possible to ensure that you omit
nothing in what the thing is. For if, when the first kind has been
taken, you then take one of the lower divisions, not everything
will fall into it. E.g. not every animal is either whole-winged or
split-winged—rather, every winged animal is (for it is *this* of
which this is a difference). The first difference of animal is that 97^a
into which every animal falls; and similarly for everything else,
both the kinds outside it and the kinds subordinate to it (e.g. the
first difference of bird is that into which every bird falls, and of
fish into which every fish). If you continue in this way you can 5
know that nothing has been omitted: otherwise you are bound to
omit something without knowing it.
   If you are defining and dividing you do not need to know

everything there is. Yet some people say that it is impossible to
know how one thing differs from another without knowing the
other thing, and that you cannot know this without knowing its
10 differences—for a thing is the same as that from which it does
not differ and different from that from which it does differ.

Now, first, this is false: one thing is not different from another
in virtue of every difference. There are many differences between
things which are the same in form—though not differences in
respect of their essence or in themselves.

Next, if you take the opposites, i.e. the difference, and assume
15 that everything falls here or here, and if you assume that what
you are seeking is in one of them, and you know this one, then it
makes no difference whether you know or do not know the other
things of which the differences are predicated. For it is clear that
if you continue in this way until you come to items of which there
is no longer a difference, you will have the account of the essence.
20 (The claim that everything falls into the division—if they are
opposites which have nothing in between them—is not a postulate; for it is necessary for everything to be in one of them if it
is to be[17] a difference of the object.)

To establish a definition through divisions, you must aim for
three things: you must take what is predicated in what the thing
25 is; you must order these items as first or second; and you must
ensure that these are all there are.

The first of these aims is achieved if you have the ability to
establish things through the kind (just as, for incidentals, you
need the ability to deduce that they hold).

You will order the items as you should if you take the first
term; and you will do this if you take the term which follows all
30 the others but is not followed by them all (there must be some
such term). Once this is taken, the same now goes for the lower
terms: the second term will be the one which is first of the others,
and the third the term which is first of the next group (if the
topmost term is removed, the next will be first of the others).
Similarly in the remaining cases.
35 That these are all the terms there are is clear from the following consideration. At the first term in the division you assume
that every animal is either this or that, and that in fact this holds
of it; next you take the difference of this whole; and you assume
that there is no further difference of the ultimate whole—or

---

[17] Reading ἔσται with most MSS (the OCT prints ἐστί).

rather, that what you get immediately after the ultimate differ- ence no longer differs in form from the complex. For it is plain **97ᵇ** that nothing extra has been posited (all the terms you have taken are in what the thing is) and also that nothing is missing. (If anything were missing, it would have to be either a kind or a difference: now the first term, and also this term taken together with the differences, constitute the kind; and the differences are all grasped—there is no later one left; for then the ultimate term 5 would differ in form, whereas it has been said not to differ.)

You should look at items which are similar and undifferentiated, and first seek what they all have in common. Then do the same again for other items which are in the same kind as the first group and are of the same form as one another but of a different form 10 from the first group. When you have got what all these have in common, you must do the same for the remaining groups (inquiring next whether the items you have taken have anything in common) until you come to a single account: this will be the definition of the object. If you arrive not at a single account but at two or more, then plainly what you are seeking is not one item 15 but several.

I mean, e.g., that if we were seeking what magnanimity is, we should inquire, in the case of some magnanimous men we know, what one feature they have in common as such. E.g. if Alcibiades and[18] Achilles and Ajax are magnanimous, what one feature do they all have in common? Intolerance of insult—one made war, one waxed wroth, one killed himself. Next, take some others, 20 e.g. Lysander and[19] Socrates. If their common feature is being indifferent to good and bad fortune, I take these two items and inquire what indifference to fortune and not brooking dishonour have in common. If they have nothing in common, then there will be two forms of magnanimity. 25

Every definition is always universal: doctors do not say what is healthy for some particular eye, but rather for every eye or else for some determinate form of eye.

It is easier to define the particular than the universal (that is why you should move from the particulars to the universals). For homonymy more often escapes notice among universals than 30 among undifferentiated items.

---

[18] Reading καί for ἤ (MSS, OCT).
[19] Reading καί for ἤ (MSS, OCT).

Just as in demonstrations a deduction must have been made, so in definitions there must be clarity; and this will be achieved if, by way of the particulars which you have mentioned,[20] you give a separate definition for each kind (e.g. if you define similarity not

35 for every case but for colours and shapes, and sharpness for sound); and if you continue in this way up to what is common, taking care not to run into homonymy.

If you should not argue in metaphors, it is plain too that you should neither define by metaphors nor define what is said in metaphors; for then you will necessarily argue in metaphors.

CHAPTER 14

98ᵃ In order to get to grips with problems, you should make excerpts from the anatomies and the divisions. Do this by supposing the kind common to all the items and excerpting—if e.g. it is animals which are being studied—whatever holds of every animal. Having

5 done this, next excerpt whatever follows every instance of the first of the remaining terms (if, e.g., it is bird, whatever follows every bird); and in this way always excerpt whatever follows the nearest term. It is plain that we shall now be in a position to state the reason why whatever follows the items falling under the common kind holds of them—e.g. why they hold of man or of

10 horse. Let A be animal, B what follows every animal, and C, D, E individual animals. It is clear why B holds of D: it does so because of A. Similarly in the other cases. And the same account will go for the lower items.

At present we argue in terms of the common names which have been handed down to us. But we should inquire not only

15 in these cases—rather, if any other common feature has been observed to hold, we should extract it and then inquire what it follows and what follows it. E.g. having a manyplies and not having upper incisors follow having horns. Next, ask what items having horns follows. It is plain why the feature in question will hold of these items: it will hold because they have horns.

20 Again, another method is to excerpt by analogy: you cannot take any one identical thing which pounce and spine and bone should be called; but there will be items which follow these features too, as though there were some single nature of this sort.

---

[20] Reading εἰρημένων with the MSS (the OCT prints εἰλημμένων).

CHAPTER 15

Some problems are the same inasmuch as they have the same
middle term, e.g. because they are all cases of reciprocity. Of 25
these, some are the same in kind—those which differ inasmuch
as they hold of different items or in different ways: e.g. Why does
it echo? or Why is it mirrored? and Why is there a rainbow?
All these problems are the same in kind (they are all cases of
reflection), but different in form.

Other problems differ inasmuch as the one middle term falls 30
under the other: e.g. Why does the Nile flow more abundantly at
the end of the month?—Because the end of the month is more
stormy.—And why is the end more stormy?—Because the moon
is waning. These problems are related to one another in this way.

CHAPTER 16

Of explanations and what they are explanatory of, you might 35
wonder whether when the *explanandum* holds the explanation
also holds. Thus if a plant sheds its leaves or if there is an eclipse,
will the explanation of the eclipse or of the shedding also hold—
if this is e.g. having broad leaves or (for the eclipse) the earth's 98^b
being in the middle? If they do *not* hold, then something else
will be explanatory. And if the explanation holds, does the *explanandum* also hold at the same time? E.g. if the earth is in the
middle, there is an eclipse; or if a plant is broad-leaved, it sheds
its leaves.

If so, they will hold at the same time and will be proved by way 5
of one another. Let shedding leaves be *A*, broad-leaved *B*, vine
C. If *A* holds of *B* (everything broad-leaved sheds its leaves), and
B holds of *C* (every vine is broad-leaved), then *A* holds of *C* and
every vine sheds its leaves. *B*, the middle term, is explanatory. 10
But you can also demonstrate that vines are broad-leaved by way
of the fact that they shed their leaves. Let *D* be broad-leaved, *E*
shedding leaves, *F* vine. *E* holds of *F* (every vine sheds its
leaves), and *D* of *E* (everything which sheds its leaves is broad- 15
leaved); therefore every vine is broad-leaved. Shedding its leaves
is explanatory.

If it is not possible for things to be mutually explanatory (for
an explanation is prior to what it is explanatory of), and if the
earth's being in the middle is explanatory of the eclipse whereas

the eclipse is not explanatory of the earth's being in the middle—
20 if, then, the demonstration through the explanation gives the reason why and the demonstration not through the explanation gives the fact, then you know *that* it is in the middle but you do not know *why* it is. It is clear that the eclipse is not explanatory of the earth's being in the middle but rather the latter of the eclipse; for the earth's being in the middle inheres in the account of the eclipse. Plainly, then, the latter becomes known through the former and not the former through the latter.

25 Or is it possible for there to be several explanations of one thing? If the same thing can be predicated of several items primitively, let A hold of B primitively and also of another term, C, primitively, and let these hold of D, E. Therefore A will hold of D, E; and B is explanatory for D, and C for E. Hence when the
30 explanation holds the object must hold; but when the object holds it is not necessary for everything explanatory to hold—rather, something (but not everything) explanatory must hold.

Or if problems are always universal and the explanation is some whole, then must what it is explanatory of be universal? E.g. shedding leaves is determined to some whole, even if this has forms, and it holds of these items universally (either of plants or of
35 plants of such-and-such a form). Hence in these cases the middle term and what it is explanatory of must be equal and must convert. E.g. why do trees shed their leaves? If it is because of solidification of their moisture, then if a tree sheds its leaves solidification must hold, and if solidification holds—not of anything whatever but of a tree—then the tree must shed its leaves.

CHAPTER 17

99^a Can it or can it not be the case that what is explanatory of some feature is not the same for every item but different for different items? If the conclusions have been demonstrated in themselves, and not in virtue of a sign or incidentally, then perhaps the explanations cannot be different (for the middle term is the account of the extreme); but if they have not been demonstrated in this way, perhaps they can be different?
5   You can inquire incidentally both about what it is explanatory of and about what it is explanatory for—but such things are not thought to count as problems. Otherwise, the middle term will

have a similar character—if the items are homonymous, the middle terms will be homonymous; and if they are in a kind, the middle terms will have a similar character. E.g. why do proportionals alternate? The explanation in the cases of lines and of numbers is different—and also the same: as lines it is different, 10 as having such-and-such a ratio it is the same. And so in all cases. The explanation of a colour's being similar to a colour and a figure to a figure is different for the different cases. Here similarity is homonymous: in the latter case it is presumably having proportional sides and equal angles; in the case of colours it is the fact that perception of them is one and the same (or something 15 else of this sort).

Items which are the same by analogy will have their middle terms the same by analogy too.

An explanation, the feature of which it is explanatory, and the item for which it is explanatory, are interrelated in the following way. If the items are taken severally, then the feature of which it is explanatory extends further than them (e.g. having external angles equal to four right angles extends further than triangle or quadrangle); but if they are taken all together it extends equally 20 (for they are all the items which have external angles equal to four right angles). Similarly for the middle term—and the middle term is an account of the first extreme (which is why all the sciences come about through definitions).

E.g. shedding leaves both follows vine and exceeds it, and it follows fig and exceeds it—but it does not exceed all of them: rather, it is equal to them. If you take the primitive middle term, 25 it is an account of shedding leaves. For there will be first a middle term in the one direction (that all are such-and-such); and then a middle term for this (that the sap solidifies, or something of the sort). What is shedding leaves?—The solidifying of the sap at the connection of the seed.

Schematically the matter will be elucidated in the following way, 30 if you are seeking the interrelations between an explanation and the feature of which it is explanatory. Let *A* hold of every *B* and *B* of each of the *D*s—and let *B* extend further. Thus *B* will apply universally to the *D*s. (I call universal a term with which they do not convert; and I call primitive universal a term such that severally they do not convert with it while all together they convert 35 with and extend alongside it.) Thus *B* is explanatory of *A* for the

*D*s. Therefore *A* must extend alongside²¹ further than *B*: if it does not, why will *B* be explanatory rather than *A*?

If *A* holds of all the *E*s, then all of them together will be some
99ᵇ one thing different from *B*. If not, how can you say that *A* holds of everything of which *E* holds whereas *E* does not hold of everything of which *A* holds? Why will there not be an explanation for them as there is for all the *D*s? (But will the *E*s be some one thing? We must inquire into this. Let it be *C*.)

Thus it is possible for there to be several explanations of the
5 same feature—but not for items of the same form. E.g. the explanation of longevity for quadrupeds is their not having bile, while for birds it is their being dry (or something else).

CHAPTER 18

If the explanations do not at once arrive at what is atomic and if there is not one middle term only but several, then the explanations too are several. But which of the middle terms is explanatory for the particulars—the one which is primitive in the
10 direction of the universal or the one which is primitive in the direction of the particular? Plainly, the one nearest to what it is explanatory for. For this term explains why the primitive term falls under the universal. E.g. *C* is explanatory for *D* of *B*'s holding of it. So *C* is explanatory of *A* for *D*, *B* is explanatory of *A* for *C*, and *B* is explanatory of *A* for itself.

CHAPTER 19

15 As for deductions and demonstrations, it is clear both what each of them is and also how they come about—and so too (which is the same thing) for demonstrative understanding. As for the principles—how they become familiar and what is the state which gets to know them—, this will be plain from what follows, when we have first set out the puzzles.
20   I have said earlier that you cannot understand anything through a demonstration unless you know the primitive immediate principles. As for knowledge of the immediates, one might wonder whether it is the same or not the same, and whether there is or is

---

²¹ Reading παρεκτείνειν, with the MSS (the OCT prints ἐπεκτείνειν).

not[22] understanding in each case, or rather understanding in the
one case and some other kind of knowledge in the other; and also 25
whether the states, not being present in us, come about in us or
rather are present in us without being noticed.

It is absurd to suppose that we possess such states; for then
we should possess pieces of knowledge more exact than demonstration without its being noticed. But if we get them without
possessing them earlier, how could we come to acquire knowledge and to learn except from pre-existing knowledge? This is
impossible, as I said in connection with demonstration. It is clear, 30
then, both that we cannot possess these states and also that they
cannot come about in us when we are ignorant and possess no
state at all. We must therefore possess some sort of capacity—
but not one which will be more valuable than these states in
respect of exactness.

And this is clearly true of all animals: they have a connate 35
discriminatory capacity, which is called perception. Given that
perception is present in them, in some animals the percepts are
retained and in others they are not. If they are not, then the
animal has no knowledge when it is not perceiving (either in
general or with regard to items which are not retained). But some
can still hold the percepts in their soul after perceiving them. 100^a
When this occurs often, there is then a further difference: some
animals come to have an account based on the retention of these
items, and others do not.

Thus from perception there comes memory, as we call it,
and from memory (when it occurs often in connection with the
same item) experience; for memories which are many in number 5
form a single experience. And from experience, or from all the
universal which has come to rest in the soul (the one apart from
the many, i.e. whatever is one and the same in all these items),
there comes a principle of skill or of understanding—of skill if it
deals with how things come about, of understanding if it deals
with how things are.

Thus the states in question neither inhere in us in a deter- 10
minate form nor come about from other states which are more
cognitive; rather, they come about from perception—as in a
battle, when a rout has occurred, first one man makes a stand,
then another does, and then another, until a position of strength
is reached.[23] And the soul is such as to be capable of undergoing
this.

---

[22] Retaining ἢ οὔ, which the OCT deletes.
[23] Reading ἀλκήν for ἀρχήν (MSS, OCT).

15   Let us say again what we have just said but not said clearly. When one of the undifferentiated items makes a stand, there is a primitive universal in the soul; for although you perceive par-

100^b ticulars, perception is of universals,—e.g. of man, not of Callias the man. Next, a stand is made among these items, until something partless and universal makes a stand. E.g. such-and-such an animal makes a stand, until animal does; and with animal a stand is made in the same way. Thus it is plain that we must get to know the primitives by induction; for this is the way in which

5 perception instils universals.

Of the intellectual states by which we grasp truth, some are always true and some admit falsehood (e.g. opinion and calculation do—whereas understanding and comprehension are always true); and no kind apart from comprehension is more exact than understanding. Again, the principles of demonstrations are more

10 familiar, and all understanding involves an account. Hence there will not be understanding of the principles; and since nothing apart from comprehension can be truer than understanding, there will be comprehension of the principles. This emerges both from our present inquiry and also because, just as demonstration is not a principle of demonstration, so understanding is not a principle of understanding. Thus if we have no other true kind apart from

15 understanding, comprehension will be the principle of understanding. And the principle will relate to the principle as understanding as a whole is related to its object as a whole.

SYNOPSIS

BOOK ALPHA

[$A1$] All learning depends on pre-existent knowledge in the learner (71^a1). Some things the learner need not know in advance (71^a17); though in a sense he knows the conclusion in advance (71^a24)—this solves a puzzle others have botched (71^a30).
[$A2$] Understanding requires knowledge of the explanation, and is of what cannot be otherwise (71^b9); hence demonstrative understanding proceeds from principles which are true, primitive, and immediate, and prior to, more familiar than, and explanatory of the conclusions (71^b16). (There are two kinds of priority here: 71^b33.) Some terminology for types of principle (72^a5). The principles must be better known than the conclusions (72^a25). [$A3$] This account of understanding threatens a regress which leads either to scepticism (72^b7) or to the admission of circular proof (72^b15); but in fact there is non-demonstrative understanding of the principles (72^b18). Three arguments against circular proof (72^b25). [$A4$] What is understood must derive from necessary principles (73^a21). Elucidations of what it is for something to hold *of every case* (73^a28), *in itself* (four types: 73^a34)—'in itself' predications of the first two types are necessary (73^b16)—and *universally* (73^b25). [$A5$] Three ways in which you may wrongly think you have proved something universally (74^a4); further elucidation of when it is that we know something to hold universally (74^a25). [$A6$] The principles, being necessary, are 'in itself' predications (74^b5). Four arguments that the principles are necessary (74^b13)—though what is necessary *can* be inferred from what is contingent (75^a1). Thus there is no demonstration of incidental predications (75^a18), but only of 'in itself' predications (75^a28). [$A7$] Hence there can be no 'kind crossing'—principles must be 'appropriate' to their conclusions (75^a38). [$A8$] Nor can there be understanding of perishable things (75^b21)—though there is demonstration of what happens often (75^b33). [$A9$] The principles may not apply to another kind (75^b37), unless that kind is subordinate (76^a4). Hence proper principles cannot be proved (76^a16).
[$A10$] Principles are unprovable (76^a31). Principles are proper or common (76^a37); common principles, subjects, and attributes (76^b3) form the three elements essential to demonstrative sciences (76^b12). Suppositions and postulates (76^b23): terms are not suppositions (76^b35); and geometers do not use false suppositions (76^b39). [$A11$] Demonstration does not presuppose substantial universals (77^a5). The Law of Contradiction is not normally assumed in demonstrations (77^a10); the Law of Excluded Middle is only used in *reductio* proofs (77^a22). The relation between dialectic and the sciences (77^a26).

75

[A12] Not all questions fall within the scope of any science (77^a36); but there are different types of, e.g., non-geometrical questions, associated with different types of error (77^b16)—though paralogism is rare in mathematics (77^b27). Two other types of error (77^b34). Analysis (78^a6). How sciences increase (78^a14).

[A13] The difference between understanding of the fact and of the reason why (78^a22), illustrated (78^a30). One science may prove the reason why of another subordinate science (78^b34). [A14] The first figure is most scientific, as yielding explanations, helping in the hunt for essences, and being self-sufficient (79^a17).

[A15] There are immediate negative propositions (79^a33).

[A16] The varieties of ignorance (79^b23): inferred dispositional ignorance of negative atomic facts (79^b29), of positive atomic facts (80^a6), [A17] of positive derivative facts (80^b17), and of negative derivative facts (81^a15); [A18] negative ignorance, due to failure of sense-perception (81^a38).

[A19] Predications in demonstrations must be true and 'natural' (81^b10). Can there be chains of such immediate predications that are infinite either (i) by having no highest term, or (ii) by having no lowest term, or (iii) while having both a highest and a lowest term (81^b30)? Can there be an infinite series of counterpredicable terms (82^a15)? [A20] If the answers to (i) and (ii) are negative, then so is the answer to (iii) (82^a21). [A21] If the answers to (i) and (ii) are negative for affirmative predication, then they are so for negative predication (82^a36). [A22] (A) Essential predications cannot form infinite chains (82^b37); and since demonstration deals with 'natural' predications (83^a1) and is about substances (83^a24) and there cannot be an infinite chain of non-substantial predications (83^a36), the answers to (i) and (ii) are negative (83^b24). (B) If there is demonstration, there cannot be infinite chains of predications (83^b32). (C) Demonstration deals with 'in itself' predications, and these cannot form infinite chains (84^a7). [A23] Hence attributes holding of different subjects need not do so in virtue of something common (84^b3); and all mediated predications are demonstrable (84^b19).

[A24] Universal demonstration is better than particular: two arguments to the contrary refuted (85^a20); seven arguments for the thesis (85^b23). [A25] Four arguments to show that affirmative demonstration is better than negative (86^a31). [A26] Negative demonstration is distinct from *reductio*, and superior to it (87^a1).

[A27] How one science may be more exact than another (87^a31); [A28] criteria of identity for sciences (87^a38).

[A29] There may be different demonstrations of a single proposition (87^b5).

[A30] Chance connections cannot be demonstrated (87^b19).

[A31] Perception cannot give understanding since it does not grasp the universal (87^b28) nor, therefore, the explanation (87^b39).

[A32] Can all demonstrations have the same principles? Seven arguments for a negative answer (88^{a}18); three unsatisfactory reinterpretations of the question (88^{b}9).

[*A*33] Understanding is of what is necessary, opinion of what can be otherwise (88^{b}30); but in a sense there can be opinion and understanding of the same thing (89^{a}11).

[*A*34] Acumen—the art of hitting on a middle term (89^{b}10).

BOOK BETA

[*B*1] There are four types of question (89^{b}23), which [*B*2] reduce to two: Is there an explanatory middle term? and what is it? (89^{b}36).

[*B*3] Can the same things be known both by demonstration and by definition (90^{a}35)? Four arguments that not everything demonstrable is a definition (90^{b}1); two arguments that not all definables are demonstrable (90^{b}18); three arguments that no definitions are demonstrable (90^{b}28). [*B*4] Any attempt to prove a definition is bound to assume what it tries to prove (91^{a}12); illustrations (91^{a}35). [*B*5] The method of division does not demonstrate definitions (91^{b}12); and [*B*6] attempts at hypothetical proof of definitions fail (92^{a}6). Neither division nor hypothetical proof could explain the unity of the *definiendum* (92^{a}27). [*B*7] There is no way in which definitions can be proved (92^{a}34). Three more arguments against the possibility of demonstrating definitions (92^{b}4). It would be absurd if definitions merely said what terms meant, not what things are (92^{b}26). [*B*8] A new approach to the problem (93^{a}1): we may grasp 'something of the object', and hence know that it is (93^{a}15); and this will enable us to construct a demonstration revealing, though not proving, the definition (93^{a}35).—[*B*9] This of course only holds for mediable predications (93^{b}21).—[*B*10] Four types of definition (93^{b}29).

[*B*11] All four types of explanation can be exhibited in a demonstration (94^{a}20); illustrations (94^{a}24). Necessity and teleological explanation are compatible (94^{b}27), and are especially common among natural phenomena (94^{b}34). [*B*12] Explanation and the types of predicative tie (95^{a}10). Can explanations be separated in time from what they explain (95^{a}22)? and if they are, how can we know or prove them (95^{a}27)? (The continuity of time: 95^{b}1.) And how can such proofs be represented (95^{b}13)? Cyclical processes (95^{b}38). Phenomena occurring 'for the most part' (96^{a}8).

[*B*13] How to discover what a thing is (96^{a}20). How to study 'a whole' (96^{b}15). The utility of divisions in definition (96^{b}25). A definer need not know everything that there is (97^{a}6). Further reflections on the use of division in defining (97^{a}23). Definitions may also be won by abstracting similarities (97^{b}7). Definitions are universal (97^{b}25); what is more specific is easier to define (97^{b}28); definitions should seek clarity (97^{b}31), and shun metaphor (97^{b}37).

[*B*14] How to tackle problems: the use of division (98^{a}1); the importance of observing common features not marked in language (98^a13), and of analogies (98^a20). [*B*15] How problems are connected (98^a24).

[*B*16] Must an explanatory middle term convert with the subject term (98^a35)? Three arguments considered (98^b4). [*B*17] Cases in which there might be different explanations of the same attribute (99^a1). Further considerations of the question (99^a16). [*B*18] Is the highest or the lowest middle term explanatory (99^b7)?

[*B*19] How do we learn the principles? and by what state do we apprehend them (99^b15)? They are not innately known (99^b26). But we have an innate capacity—perception: in favoured cases perception leads to memory, memory to experience, and experience to understanding (99^b34). Thus we learn the principles by 'induction' (100^a14). The state by which we apprehend principles is comprehension (100^b5).

NOTE ON THE COMMENTARY

The *Posterior Analytics* is not an easy work to read, and individual sentences often call for individual elucidation. I take it that the first duty of a commentator is to explain his text: hence my notes contain more detailed paraphrase and exegesis than is customary in the Clarendon series. There is correspondingly less criticism, and less discussion at an abstract level, of the stances Aristotle assumes and the philosophical issues which he broaches. My notes will, I hope, at least put the reader in a better position to do that work for himself.

My comments contain a certain quantity of symbolism; although this is sometimes displeasing to the eye, it seems to me to have the twin advantages of brevity and clarity. And the *Analytics* is, after all, a treatise on logic. Most of the symbols used are standard; all are explained at their first occurrence. The formalization adopted for syllogistic is briefly explained in the Introduction. I might note that genuine quotations from Aristotle are always enclosed in double inverted commas, while paraphrases of Aristotle's sentences get single inverted commas. (Of course, double and single inverted commas are also used in several other standard ways.)

Following the custom of the Clarendon series, I do not often acknowledge my debts to the secondary literature. Those modern works to which I do refer are cited by author's name and page number only: full details can be found in the lists of References and of Supplementary References at the end of the Commentary. All references in the form "p. *n*" are to pages of this volume.

I cite Aristotle's works by title, Greek book letter, chapter number, and then page, column, and line in Bekker's edition (e.g. *APst A* 10, 76^{a}40). References to the *Posterior Analytics* usually dispense with the book title. I use the following abbreviations:

Cat	*Categories*
Int	*de Interpretatione*
APr	*Prior Analytics*
APst	*Posterior Analytics*
Top	*Topics* (*Top I* = *Sophistici Elenchi*)
Phys	*Physics*
Cael	*de Caelo*
GC	*de Generatione et Corruptione*
Metr	*Meteorologica*
An	*de Anima*
Sens	*de Sensu*
Mem	*de Memoria*
Long Vit	*de Longitudine Vitae*
HA	*Historia Animalium*

79

PA	de Partibus Animalium
MA	de Motu Animalium
GA	de Generatione Animalium
[Probl]	Problems (spurious)
Met	Metaphysics
EN	Nicomachean Ethics
EE	Eudemian Ethics
Pol	Politics
Rhet	Rhetoric
[Rhet ad Alex]	Rhetorica ad Alexandrum (spurious)
Poet	Poetics

The titles of some of Plato's works are abbreviated, thus:

Crat	Cratylus
[Def]	Definitions (spurious)
[Epin]	Epinomis (spurious)
Euthyd	Euthydemus
Gorg	Gorgias
Phil	Philebus
Rep	Republic
Soph	Sophist
Theaet	Theaetetus
Tim	Timaeus

Note also:

Alexander, in APr	Commentary on the Prior Analytics
in APst	Commentary on the Posterior Analytics
Galen, lib prop	On My Own Books
Proclus, Comm in Eucl	Commentary on the First Book of Euclid's Elements
Sextus Empiricus, adv Math	Against the Mathematicians
Sextus Empiricus, Pyrrh Hyp	Outlines of Pyrrhonism
Themistins, in APst	Commentary on the Posterior Analytics
Theophrastus, Met	Metaphysics

COMMENTARY

BOOK ALPHA

CHAPTER I

A 1 considers in general terms some of the conditions for the acquisition of knowledge; *A* 2 introduces the special notions of 'scientific' knowledge or understanding, and of demonstration; and the succeeding chapters develop and elucidate these notions.

71ᵃ1: The initial sentence, couched in the grand manner of Aristotelian exordia, expresses the contention that if **a** teaches **b** at *t* that *P*, then before *t* **b** had knowledge of something other than *P* on which his learning that *P* depends (cf. *Top Z* 4, 141ᵃ26–31; *Met A* 9, 992ᵇ24–33; *EN Z* 3, 1139ᵇ26–8). Aristotle is not saying that all coming to know requires pre-existing knowledge but rather that all learning requires pre-existing knowledge. It follows that not all our knowledge can be learned: the implications of this are not disentangled until *B* 19, 99ᵇ26–30.

More precisely, Aristotle is making a claim about 'intellectual' teaching and learning. The adjective "intellectual" (*dianoētikos*) normally indicates either what is 'discursive', as opposed to what is 'intuitive' (*noētikos*), or else what involves thought, as opposed to what is given by perception. The latter sense is the more likely here (see MIGNUCCI (1975), 1–3). Aristotle's claim is not intended as an analytic truth; for he proceeds to offer an inductive argument in its favour.

The structure of the argument is uncertain. Some commentators discern an induction from three cases—the demonstrative sciences (71ᵃ3–4), the dialectical arts (71ᵃ5–9), and rhetoric (71ᵃ9–11). But dialectic and rhetoric are more properly contrasted with teaching than taken as species of it (*Top I* 2, 165ᵃ38–ᵇ11; *Rhet A* 1, 1355ᵃ24–7). It is better to restrict the induction to 71ᵃ3–4 and to start a second argument at 71ᵃ5. This second argument ends at 71ᵃ9, and expands as follows: 'All teaching takes place either by deduction or by induction; but both deduction and induction require pre-existing knowledge in the learner: hence all teaching requires pre-existing knowledge in the learner.' (The first premiss of this argument is thoroughly Aristotelian: see *A* 18, 81ᵃ39–40; *APr B* 23, 68ᵇ13–14; and esp. *EN Z* 3, 1139ᵇ26–31, which expressly refers to the present passage; cf. Patzig, 132.) 71ᵃ9–11, on rhetoric, is parenthetical.

71ᵃ2: "... proceed from pre-existent knowledge": the notion of dependence, or 'proceeding from', is here—and often—expressed by the preposition *ek*. "*P* is *ek Q*" may describe a logical relation, an epistemological relation, or a causal relation: "*P* follows from *Q*", "knowledge that *P* is based on knowledge that *Q*", "the fact that *P* is explained by the fact that *Q*". In scientific knowledge, according to Aristotle, all three relations coexist: my understanding that *P* is based on my knowledge that *Q* inasmuch as I infer *P* from *Q*, and *Q* states the explanation of the fact stated in *P*. (*ek* is also used of a relation between *terms*: e.g. *A* 4, 73^{a}36. Aristotle's discussion of the different uses of *ek* in *Met Δ* 24 passes over these issues.)

71^{a}2: "... from pre-existent knowledge": The principal ingredients in Aristotle's vocabulary of knowledge are the three verbs *eidenai*, *gignōskein*, and *epistasthai*, together with the cognate nouns *gnōsis* and *epistēmē*. Aristotle also uses *gnōrizein* (*gnōrimos*, "familiar", p. 95), *sunienai*, and *echein* (as general as "have" in English, but translated as "grasp" in its epistemological use). *Nous* ("comprehension": see p. 267) should also be mentioned.

In non-philosophical contexts *eidenai*, *gignōskein*, and *epistasthai* may all be translated by "know" without much loss; but in Aristotle, or at least in *APst*, the verbs are not intersubstitutable. A detailed study of Plato's usage of these words concluded that "whereas *eidenai* and *epistasthai*, and *eidenai* and *gignōskein* are frequently and clearly convertible in the text, it is not so clear that *gignōskein* and *epistasthai* are ever convertible; and there are passages where they seem to be in contrast" (Lyons, 177). The same conclusion appears to hold for *APst*. Aristotle offers an explicit definition of *epistasthai* at *A* 2, 71^{b}9–16, which carries with it the implication that *gignōskein* has a different sense. Regularly, but not invariably, he uses *epistasthai* in accordance with this definition; and he tacitly treats *eidenai* as a synonym. There is never any attempt to define *gignōskein*.

My original translation adopted different English terms for each of the different elements in Aristotle's vocabulary for knowledge. But I am no longer convinced that Aristotle intended or felt any semantic differences among these elements—with the exception of *epistēmē*; and my original translations, quite apart from their barbarous nature, insinuated distinctions which are not found in the Greek. Hence the word "know" is now used promiscuously. The case is different with *epistasthai* and *epistēmē*; and for them I retain "understand" and "understanding". It has been powerfully urged that *epistēmē*, at least in *APst*, is in fact close to our own conception of understanding and distinct from our own conception of knowledge, so that my translation happily—and accidentally—hit upon the truth. (See esp. BURNYEAT (1981), 97–108; cf. MORAVCSIK (1975).) This cannot be completely right, if only because "I understand that *P*", in its ordinary use, certainly means something quite different from Aristotle's "*epistamai* that *P*". (See more generally PATZIG (1981), 143 n. 2; IRWIN (1988), 530 n. 24.) None the less, we need some way of signalling occurrences of the Greek word, and I can find nothing less bad than "understand". (See further, below p. 91.)

71^{a}5: "both deductive and inductive": "A deduction (*sullogismos*) is an account in which, certain things being posited, something different from the posits results from necessity by their being the case" (*APr A* 1, 24ᵇ18–20; cf. *Top A* 1, 100ᵃ25–7; *Rhet A* 2, 1356ᵇ16–18; *APst A* 10, 76ᵇ38; *B* 5, 91ᵇ14). This shows that *sullogismoi* include much more than Aristotelian syllogisms (for an explanation of this term see above, p. xvii). As defined, Aristotelian *sullogismoi* do not encompass all valid deductive arguments; but it might none the less seem reasonable to suppose that Aristotle's definition was an attempt to characterize deductive inference as such—hence we should translate by means of "deduction", "deduce", etc. (See further Patzig, 44–5; Barnes, 126–7.) At *APr A* 32, 47ᵃ33–5, however, Aristotle distinguishes between a *sullogismos* and what he calls a 'necessity' (*anagkaion*). And it is in fact his notion of a 'necessity' which corresponds most closely to the modern notion of a deduction, i.e. of a deductively valid argument. A *sullogismos* is a special kind of 'necessity', and hence a special kind of deduction. None the less, "syllogism" is an equally misleading translation of "*sullogismos*"; for Aristotle's claim that all *sullogismoi* can be reduced to his three syllogistic figures is not a trivial truth but a false metalogical claim. On balance, I still prefer "deduction". See further BARNES (1981), 21–7.

"Induction (*epagōgē*) is the passage from the particulars to the universal" (*Top A* 12, 105ᵃ13; cf. *APst B* 6, 92ᵃ37). For a full discussion see Ross, 481–5; and, most recently, CAUJOLLE-ZASLAWSKY (1990). "The particular" (*to kath' hekaston*) is systematically ambiguous in Aristotle between "the individual" and "the specific" (in other words, Aristotle muffs the distinction between universal/singular and general/specific: cf. Zabarella, 664A). The context does not always resolve the ambiguity.

71ᵃ7: "the former assuming items . . .": throughout *APst* Aristotle uses the terminology of the game of dialectic. In that game questioner and answerer pick a problem (*problēma*) for debate; the answerer elects to defend the answer *P*, and it is the questioner's job to refute him (*elenchein*) by proving not-*P*. To do this he must question (*erōtan*) his partner, putting forward (*proteinein*) propositions (*protaseis*) for his acceptance or rejection; from the points which he assumes or takes (*lambanein*) from the answerer, he must then deduce (*sullogizesthai*) not-*P*.

71ᵃ9: "Rhetorical arguments": 'example' (*paradeigma*) and 'enthymeme' (*enthumēmē*) together exhaust rhetorical reasoning (*Rhet A* 2, 1356ᵇ5–9; *B* 20, 1393ᵃ24: but contrast *B* 25, 1402ᵇ13). "Example" is often treated as the name given to inductive arguments in rhetorical contexts (e.g. *Rhet A* 2, 1356ᵃ34–ᵇ11); but it is defined as inference from a particular *to a particular*, and thereby distinguished from induction (*Rhet A* 2, 1357ᵇ25–30; *APr B* 24, 69ᵃ13–19). Enthymemes are deductions used in rhetorical contexts; the modern definition of "enthymeme" as "deduction lacking a premiss" is unaristotelian.

71ᵃ11: The knowledge presupposed by a teacher is of two sorts: it consists of (*a*) knowledge of *propositions*, and (*b*) knowledge of *terms* (cf. *A* 10, 76ᵃ31–6, ᵇ3–22). (Should Aristotle have added (*c*) knowledge of rules of inference?)

Aristotle's statement of this is complicated by two factors. The first turns on the peculiarities of the Greek verb *einai*, "to be" (on which see Kahn). Syntactically, *einai* may appear both absolutely ("*X* is") and with a complement ("*X* is *Y*") (cf. *B* 1, 89ᵇ33, notes). Moreover, the variable in "*X* is" may be replaced either by a proper name ("Homer is") or by a general term ("Units are" or "The unit is") or by an oblique sentence ("That nothing can be affirmed or denied is"). The nearest English equivalents for these sentences use three different locutions: "Homer exists", "There are units", "It is the case that nothing can be affirmed and denied". In my translation barbarisms such as "The unit is" are countenanced only where they seem essential to the understanding of Aristotle's argument; usually "*F* is" becomes "There are *F*s", and "That *P* is" becomes "That *P* is the case" (sometimes "*F*s occur" or "That *P* holds" are used)—the reader who prefers consistent barbarism may supply it for himself.

Secondly, Aristotle is prepared to use all terms autonymously: where we distinguish between "*X* is *Y*" and ""*X*" means *Y*" he will write "*X* is *Y*" and "*X* means *Y*" (see *Top I* 14, 174ᵃ8–9).

Thus instead of (*a*) and (*b*) Aristotle says that the learner must already know, in some cases (*a'*) that *X* is, and in others (*b'*) what *X* means.

For some *X* the learner must already know both (*a'*) and (*b'*); for some *X* he need only know (*b'*). These cases are straightforward. Aristotle also seems to say that for some *X* the learner need only know (*a'*). Philoponus suggests that this is so if "*X*" is replaced by an oblique sentence, since only terms and not sentences have meanings; but this suggestion is refuted by *A* 10, 76ᵇ21 (cf. *Int* 4, 16ᵇ26). Others start from 71ᵃ16 ("For these items are not all equally plain to us"), which has a close parallel at *A* 10, 76ᵇ18; and they imagine that e.g. 'the hot' is one of the things for which the learner need only know (*a'*). But in *A* 10 Aristotle's point is that some things (e.g. the meaning of the common axioms) are so familiar that a teacher need not expressly assume them; and this does not imply that the learner need not know them—on the contrary, it implies that the learner does know them. (But it must be admitted that 71ᵃ16 has no plausible sense, apart from that suggested by 76ᵇ18.) There is no solution to this puzzle—the issue is taken up again, in a refined form, in *B* 8.

71ᵃ13: "E.g. of the fact that . . .": Aristotle has argued that if anyone is to learn anything, he must already know something:

(1) (∀*P*) (if **a** is to learn that *P*, then (∃*Q*) (**a** already knows that *Q*)).

He has not argued that there is something which anyone who is to learn anything must already know:

(2) (∃*Q*) (∀*P*) (if **a** is to learn that *P*, then **a** already knows that *Q*).

But he does maintain something very like (2)—see *A* 2, 72ᵃ16–8, notes

—and his examples here are evidently designed to satisfy something like (2). The first example is a loose formulation of an analogue to the Law of Excluded Middle (see *Met Γ* 7).

(In (1) and (2) I use the universal and existential quantifiers, (∀) and (∃). (∀a) (...a---) may be read as: "Take anything you like, ... it---". (∃a) (...a---) may be read as: "There's something of which it's true that...it---". These devices are purely abbreviatory and are not intended to carry any ontological or metaphysical commitment.)

71ᵃ15: "and of the unit both ...": what does it mean to assume 'that the unit is'? And why must the arithmetician do so? *Met M* 3 gives Aristotle's view on mathematical existence. It seems that 'the unit is'—i.e. there are units—if there are objects which may be taken as single entities; that there are such objects is a trivial truth, and hence suitably taken for an axiom. For other mathematical objects, e.g. triangles, we have to prove that 'they are' (*A* 10, 76ᵃ36). It is usually supposed that such a proof will take the form of a construction. (This fits Euclid's practice: e.g. *Elements* i def. 10 assumes the definition of *right angle*, and i. 11 constructs right angles (cf. i def. 20~i. 1; i def. 22~i. 46 etc.). On the other hand, both the meaning and the constructibility of e.g. circles are taken as axiomatic (i def. 15; post. 3).) There is, however, no direct evidence for this view in Aristotle's text; and it is hard to reconcile with the abstractionist account of mathematical objects in *Met M* 3. *Cael A* 10, 279ᵇ32–280ᵃ10, shows that Aristotle did not believe that mathematical objects exist only if they are actually constructed.

Arithmetic requires that there are units because it infers the properties of units from their essence and only things that are have essences; this reasoning only becomes explicit in Book *B* (cf. e.g. *B* 7, 92ᵇ4–11, notes).

71ᵃ17: With this paragraph compare *APr B* 21, esp. 67ᵃ22–6.

If at *t* I learn that **a** is *F* by inference from the two premisses that **a** is *G* and that everything *G* is *F*, then I must have known before *t* that everything *G* is *F*, but I may learn that **a** is *G* "at the very same time" as I learn that **a** is *F*. (I learn it *hama epagomenon*: 71ᵃ21; cf. *APr B* 21, 67ᵃ23. *Epagein* is used here, and at 71ᵃ24, in its non-technical sense of 'lead on', i.e. 'lead on' to knowledge: see Ross, 506.) It is essential to the argument that the laggard premiss is about a particular (cf. *APr B* 21, 67ᵃ9); **a** is one of the things "under a universal of which you possess knowledge", i.e. **a** falls under *G* of which you know that it is *F*. Aristotle does not say that we may learn one of the premisses at the same time *as we learn the conclusion*: he says that we may learn one of the premisses at the same time *as we are being led to the conclusion*. If my teacher is to instruct me that **a** is *F*, then I must know that every *G* is *F* before I come to the class; but I need not have antecedent knowledge that **a** is *G*. (For a different interpretation, which takes *epagein* here in its technical sense, see MCKIRAHAN (1983).)

Aristotle's illustration has been read as a proof that the angle in a semicircle is a right angle (for attempted reconstructions see Heath (2), 37–9; Ross, 505–6). Nothing as elaborate as this is required, as *APr B* 21, 67ᵃ12–16, shows: the illustration is a straightforward case of the schema I have just described, viz:

(3) Every triangle has 2 R.
(4) This figure in the semicircle is a triangle.

Therefore:

(5) This figure in the semicircle has 2 R.

The theorem in (3), Euclid, i. 32, is one of Aristotle's favourite illustrations; for his proof of it see *Met* Θ 9, 1051ᵃ21–6; cf. Heath (1), i. 317–21.

71ᵃ23: "... and the last term ...": since "the middle" refers to the middle term, *to eschaton* probably means "the last term" (its standard sense in *APr*) rather than "the individual" (which it may also mean). In either case the reference is to "this figure in the semicircle" ("*C*" at 67ᵃ14). When Aristotle says that "in some cases learning occurs in this way", does he mean "in the way in which we learn (4)" or rather "in the way in which we learn (5)"? Most commentators opt for the former interpretation (see MIGNUCCI (1975), 13). There are two difficulties with this: first, the close parallel at *APr B* 21, 67ᵃ24–6, suggests that (5) rather than (4) is the relevant proposition; and secondly, the next clause—"the last term does not become known through the middle term"—sits uneasily with (4). (Aristotle would then imply that in *other* cases the proposition analogous to (4) *is* known through the middle term. This is obscure in itself; and it is puzzling in the context—if Aristotle is thinking of (4), then he should rather observe that in other cases the proposition analogous to (4) *must be known in advance* of the instruction.) But the second interpretation is also difficult, since it appears to affirm that (5) is not known on the basis of (3) and (4). The parallel passage in *APr B* 16 suggests that Aristotle has the following thought in mind: 'Given that you already know (3), then once you grasp (4) you will at once assent to (5)—you do not need to rehearse the argument "(3), and (4): so (5)" to yourself'. Yet, to say the least, our text does not express this thought at all clearly. However that may be, if (5)—or (4)—is *not* learned "through the middle", how is it learned?—We 'see' it: "... some things we know immediately, e.g. that it has angles equal to two right angles when we see that it is a triangle" (*APr B* 21, 67ᵃ24–6). For further references to sight or perception of mathematical objects see *A* 12, 77ᵇ31; *EN Z* 8, 1142ᵃ26–9; more often they are apprehended by a quasi-perceptual thought (*noēsis*) (e.g. *Met Z* 10, 1036ᵃ2–6). This view is closely connected with Aristotle's analysis of mathematical objects (see p. 85).

71ᵃ24: "... and are not said of any underlying subject": "and" (*kai*), as often, has the force of "i.e."; it is individuals which are not said of any subject (cf. e.g. *Cat* 2, 1ᵇ3–9), so that this clause indicates which of the sorts of 'particular' Aristotle intends (see p. 83).

71ª24: Having explained that the learner must already know the premisses, Aristotle now adds that in a sense he also knows the conclusion. The puzzle is a special case of the celebrated dispute over '*petitio principii* and the syllogism' (e.g. Mill, *A System of Logic*, II. iii. 2; Sextus Empiricus, *Pyrrh Hyp* ii. 195); it is set out more clearly at *APr B* 21, 67ª8–16. We take an apparently consistent set of propositions:

(6) **b** knows that everything *G* is *F*;
(7) **a** is *G*;
(8) **b** does not know that there is such a thing as **a**.

From (8) Aristotle invites us to infer:

(9) **b** does not know that **a** is *F*.

("If you did not know ..."); yet from (6) and (7) we can apparently infer the contradictory of (9):

(10) **b** knows that **a** is *F*.

—"so that at the same time you will know and be ignorant of the same thing" (*B* 21, 67ª16).

Aristotle's solution to the puzzle consists, characteristically, in accepting both (9) and (10), and maintaining that since they express different *sorts* of knowledge they are not inconsistent. The knowledge involved in (9) is 'knowledge *simpliciter*' ("*simpliciter*" modifies "know" in 71ª26 and 27, despite the word-order). "*Simpliciter*" translates *haplōs*: "A thing is noble or base *simpliciter* if you will say (sc. truly) without adding any qualification that it is noble or the opposite; e.g. you won't say that sacrificing one's father is noble, but that it is noble for certain people—therefore it is not noble *simpliciter*. But you will say that honouring the gods is noble, without adding any qualification; for it is noble *simpliciter*. Hence whatever seems to be noble or base or anything else, without adding any qualification, is called so *simpliciter*" (*Top B* 10, 115ᵇ29–35). Thus (9) uses "know" in an unqualified way; it expresses an ordinary knowledge claim.

What qualification, then, must be understood with (10) if that too is to be reckoned true? The gloss, "you understand it universally", is expanded a little at *B* 21, 67ª16–21: "For knowing of every triangle that it contains two right angles is not simple, but in one case we know it by having universal knowledge, and in the other by having particular knowledge. So in this way with respect to universal knowledge you know of *C* that it contains two right angles, but you do not know this with respect to particular knowledge; so that you will not have contrary pieces of knowledge." The first sentence of this extract suggests that it is (6) and not (10) which Aristotle has in mind; he seems to be offering two readings of "**b** knows that every *G* is *F*". One of these readings is presumably (6) itself; the other may well be:

(6') If anything is *G*, **b** knows that it is *F*.

The distinction is clearly brought out by symbolization, when (6) and (6') appear as:

(*6) **b** knows that (∀x) (if Gx then Fx);
(*6′) (∀x) (if Gx then **b** knows that Fx).

The same distinction probably reappears at A 5, 74ᵃ30–2; the common Greek idiom for "knowing that X is Y", viz. "knowing of X that it is Y" (cf. Lyons, 107–10), hovers ambiguously between (6) and (6′); and the distinction is just what is needed to solve Aristotle's puzzle. For while (6) and (7) do not entail (10), (6′) and (7) do; and while (6), (7), and (8) are consistent, (6′), (7), and (8) are not. (But (6′) is not quite right. Better:

(6†) Of every G, **b** knows that it is F.

I was alerted to this point by FEREJOHN (1988), 116 n. 12; cf. (1991), 42–3.)

Aristotle, however, does not follow out this line of thought; rather, his remarks return to (10), which, he claims, is true only if "know" is expanded to "know with respect to universal knowledge". A 24, 86ᵃ23–7, elucidates this by means of the notion of potential knowledge (cf. *Met A* 2, 982ᵃ21–3): "**b** knows universally that **a** is G" means "**b** knows potentially that **a** is G, inasmuch as he has actual knowledge of a universal proposition which it falls under". Does this solve Aristotle's puzzle? Aristotle clearly sees that (6) and (7) do *not* entail (10) if (10) is read in the ordinary way; yet his answer does nothing to explain why (6) and (7) might *seem* to yield (10)—for his reading of (10) foists an utterly unnatural sense upon it, and his efforts on (10) blind him to the relevance of (6′).

Aristotle thinks that there is more to be said for his reading of (10): without the distinction it relies upon, "the puzzle in the *Meno* will arise" (71ᵃ29). In Plato's *Meno* Meno, baffled in his search for virtue, asks: "And in what fashion, Socrates, will you seek that of which you do not even know if it exists? For what sort of thing from among those you don't know will you set before you and seek? And even if you actually happen across it, how will you know this is what you did not know?—SOCRATES: I know what you mean, Meno. Do you see how you are spinning out an eristic argument to the effect that it is not possible for a man to seek either what he knows or what he does not know? For he wouldn't seek what he knows—for he knows it, and such a person has no need of a search—nor what he does not know—for he does not know what he will seek" (80ᵈ5–ᵉ5). Plato's problem is this: if someone wants to know what X is, then either (*a*) he already knows what X is—in which case he will learn only what he already knows and his search is inane; or else (*b*) he does not yet know what X is—in which case he cannot seek successfully, for he will know neither what he is looking for nor whether he has found it. Plato in effect accepts the bad argument in limb (*b*) of the dilemma, and rejects the good argument in (*a*) (see *Meno* 80ᵈ–86ᶜ). And Aristotle follows him, maintaining that the seeker does in a sense already know what he is looking for. (The affinity to Plato is explicit in the language of *APr B* 21, 67ᵃ23–4.)

71ᵃ30:   The next stretch of argument leaves the *Meno* and considers an alternative solution to the puzzle in (6)–(10). (There is no evidence as to whose solution this was.) It accepts the validity of the arguments in (6)–(10), and consequently modifies a premiss: instead of (6) we should be content with:

(6″) **b** knows that everything he knows to be *G* is *F*.

In symbols:

(*6″) **b** knows that (∀x) (if **b** knows that *Gx*, then *Fx*).

Plainly (6″) and (7) do not entail (10).

Aristotle's rejoinder, that propositions of the form contained in (6″) simply do not occur in ordinary scientific argument, is inadequate, since the solution is urging that such propositions *should* form the staple of a safe science. Perhaps Aristotle means to indicate, what is certainly true, that the solution will lead to a considerable impoverishment of scientific knowledge. A better reason for rejecting the solution is that it concedes far more than is necessary to the puzzle.

CHAPTER 2

71ᵇ9:   The *definiendum* is understanding *simpliciter* (see p. 87). An example of 'sophistical' understanding is given at *A* 5, 74ᵃ27–32; such knowledge is 'incidental' because it is not of its subject as such. 'Incidental' translates *sumbebēkos*, the past participle of *sumbainein* ("result", "happen", etc.); 'incidentals' of *X* are, generally, predicates of *X*, and, specifically, non-essential predicates of *X* (cf. e.g. *Top A* 5, 104ᵇ2–26). The standard translation of *sumbebēkos* is "accident". On 'incidental' knowledge see also e.g. *A* 2, 71ᵇ28–9; *A* 6, 74ᵇ21–6; *EN Z* 3, 1139ᵇ31–5. It is a mistake to look for a uniform characterization of incidental knowledge (or, in general, of what it is to be incidentally *F*): you know something incidentally if your knowledge fails to satisfy one or another of the various conditions which knowledge *simpliciter* must satisfy. There are several ways to fail, and hence several ways of having only incidental knowledge.

The *definiens* contains two conjuncts, one to do with explanation, the other with necessity. "Explanation" and its cognates render *aitia* and its cognates. As synonyms for *aitia* Aristotle uses *to dioti* and *to dia ti* (literally "the wherefore" and "the because of what"—I translate as "the reason why"). Roughly speaking, to give an *aitia* for something is to say why it is the case, and *X* is an *aitia* of *Y* provided that *Y* is because of *X* (see Bonitz, 177ᵃ50–2). More formally, Aristotle will uses phrases of the form "*X* is *aition* of *Z* for *Y*" (e.g. "Having no bile is *aition* of longevity for quadrupeds": cf. *B* 17, 99ᵇ4–6): i.e. *Y* is *Z* because of *X*. (In the context of *APst* at least, it seems that "because of *X*" can—and must—always be expanded into something of the form "because *P*": e.g. "because they have no bile".) The standard English translation is "cause" (with its cognates); but in many contexts this is false, or at any rate seriously misleading. Sometimes "reason" is the right translation; often "explanation" is best. (See esp. MORAVCSIK (1974), (1975).) In the first edition, I resolved to adhere to a single translation for all occurrences of the word; and I opted for "explanation". This was criticized, usually on the grounds that an explanation, unlike an *aitia*, is a linguistic or a propositional item or else a 'theoretical construction'. (See further FREE-LAND (1991), who argues—to my mind unconvincingly—that Aristotelian *aitiai* should not be construed as explanations.) But—in my version of English, at least—explanations are not necessarily linguistic or proposi-tional items, nor are they in any way tied to *theories*: my pupils are late, and the explanation (quite non-linguistic and theory-free) is that they overslept. There is, I still think, much to be said for keeping a single word for *aitia*; and the least bad single word is "explanation". (Some may feel happier with Moravcsik's "explanatory factor"; but that it too cumbersome for a translator.)

The *first* conjunct of the definition of understanding, then, is:

(1) **a** understands X only if **a** knows that Y is the explanation of X.

For parallels to (1) see e.g. *Phys A* 1, 184ᵃ3 (where the verb for "know" is *gignōskein*); *B* 2, 194ᵇ18 (*eidenai*); *Met A* 3, 983ᵃ25–6 (*eidenai*); *α* 2, 994ᵇ29–30 (*eidenai*). The thesis derives from Plato's celebrated sug-gestion that true opinion becomes knowledge if it is "tied down by calculation of an explanation" (*aitias logismōi*) (*Meno* 98ᵃ3; cf. e.g. *Rep* 534ᵇ; *Gorg* 465ᵃ; *Met A* 1, 981ᵃ28). (1) avoids circularity only if "under-stand" (*epistasthai*) and "know" (here *gignōskein*) are kept apart in sense (see p. 82). And such a distinction in sense is also required if we are to reconcile (1) with Aristotle's repeated affirmation that we seek the reason why *after* we have come to know the fact (see *B* 1, 89ᵇ29, note).

The *second* conjunct of the *definiens* is ambiguously expressed: the clause "that it is not possible . . ." may depend either on "we think" or on "we know", yielding in the first case:

(2a) **a** understands X only if X cannot be otherwise,

and in the second:

(2b) **a** understands X only if **a** knows that X cannot be otherwise.

Syntax perhaps favours (2a); it is easily paralleled (e.g. at *A* 4, 73ᵃ21; *A* 6, 74ᵇ6); and it finds a partial analogy at *A* 33, 89ᵃ6–10. But in favour of (2b) there may be cited first the fact that 71ᵇ15 infers (2a) as a *con-sequence* of the definition; and secondly, that *A* 6, 75ᵃ14, unequivocally indicates (2b) in an apparent reference back to our definition. I plump for (2b). (But see EBERT (1980), 89–90.)

The two necessary conditions for understanding are jointly sufficient; thus we have:

(3) **a** understands $X =$ $_{df}$ **a** knows that Y is the explanation of X and **a** knows that X cannot be otherwise.

In (3) I have used the nondescript variables X and Y: it becomes clear from the rest of A 2 that understanding is, at least principally, a species of propositional knowledge; but Aristotle's definition does not, I think, require this, and later discussions of condition (1) are careless of it.

Aristotle offers a justification for (3). 71^{b}9–13 argue: 'We think understanding to be so-and-so; therefore understanding *is* so-and-so' (cf. *EN Z* 3, 1139^{b}20). Such 'consensus' arguments are common in Aristotle (cf. e.g. *Phys Δ* 11, 218^{b}21–33); and they are implicitly recognized as appropriate to principles such as (3) at *Top A* 2, 101^{a}36–^{b}3. No doubt the consensus is not overt but rather latent in linguistic practice: 'We use the term "understand" thus-and-so; therefore understanding is so-and-so' (cf. *Met A* 3, 983^{a}25). 71^{b}13–15 is normally taken as a repetition of this argument; but in fact it adds the new observation that genuine understanders actually *are* so-and-so. Perhaps this is supposed in some way to confirm the latent consensus (at least, its contradictory would prove the consensus mistaken).

So interpreted, Aristotle's argument for (3) seems to be factually mistaken; for (3) does not represent a correct analysis of the actual use of the Greek term *epistasthai*. Could we take (3) as a 'stipulative' definition, declaring that nothing shall count as genuine scientific knowledge if it does not offer explanations and restrict itself to what cannot be otherwise? The "we think" argument will then refer not to linguistic consensus but rather to the views of Aristotle and his fellows on the proper limits of scientific endeavour. This will hardly do (see EBERT (1980), 89–90; BURNYEAT (1981), 108 n. 23); for Aristotle plainly takes himself to be articulating the common conception of *epistēmē* or knowledge.

Aristotle's definition does not fit, and is surely not intended to fit, every legitimate use of the Greek words *epistēmē* and *epistasthai*—and Aristotle himself frequently and unapologetically employs these words in ways which fall outside his definition. Nor, again, does his definition fit the ordinary use of *epistasthai* rather than the ordinary use of *eidenai* or *gignōskein* (see the passages from *Phys* and *Met* cited above in connection with (1)). Rather, he takes himself—as the qualification at 71^{b}9 indicates—to be delineating "an ideal type of knowledge, knowledge strictly or properly speaking, to which other kinds of knowledge can be seen as approximating". (I take these words from TAYLOR (1990), 122. Taylor's article offers a critical survey of the various strands in Aristotle's thought on epistemological matters.) Note, for example, *EN Z* 3, 1139^{b}18–21: "What understanding is will be clear from the following account—if we are to be exact (*akribologeisthai*) and not deal in similarities: we all suppose that what we know cannot be otherwise." Thus the 'strict' notion of knowledge requires that its objects be necessary; but there are other notions—the 'similarities' or approximations—which do not. (See also Theophrastus, *Met* 8, 9^{a}10, 23–^{b}6—which, however, may rather be concerned with the distinction between understanding theorems and understanding principles.) This high-grade knowledge, Aristotle maintains, is what the sciences characteristically aspire to. It comes in two forms: there is demonstrative knowledge, which forms the main subject of *APst A*, and there is the form of knowledge by which we grasp the first principles. (Both these forms, it should be stressed, fall under the general definition of 71^b10–12.)

Is Aristotle right? And how—a more perplexing question—may we appropriately judge whether or not he is right? To most readers, the definition appears far too strict—hence the idea that Aristotle may be making a stipulation (which might be deemed pointless but which could not be judged straightforwardly false), and hence too the notion (not evidently distinct from the stipulative suggestion) that he may be delineating a conception of 'understanding' which is distinct from any common conception of knowledge. Aristotle himself at times appears to find his definition too tight; for at times he allows that we may have proper *epistēmē* of matters which hold not necessarily but only for the most part (see p. 192). Moreover, many of his own illustrative examples in *APst* concern knowledge of *singular* items—that the moon is now eclipsed, that the Athenians attacked Sardis, . . . But he would not be embarrassed by the objection that we all know any number of purely contingent facts: this knowledge, he would urge, is only knowledge by courtesy and in so far as it approximates to knowledge proper. (For a subtler consideration of these issues see VAN FRAASSEN (1980), 21–8.)

A telling objection, I take it, would be this: the sort of knowledge which the sciences—the central and most reputable of the sciences—aspire to is not, or not in all cases, included in the Aristotelian definition. Thus we might urge that the biological sciences, say, are concerned with contingent truths: their theorems do not have the sort of necessity which we associate with the mathematical sciences. Conversely, we might urge that the mathematical sciences have no interest in explanations: their proofs (as some of the ancients maintained: p. 107) do not pretend to offer explanations of their theorems. (Indeed, we might surmise that Aristotle, observing the importance of necessity to the mathematical sciences and the importance of explanatoriness to the natural sciences, mistakenly concluded that both necessity and explanatoriness must be essential parts of any proper or scientific knowledge.)

These objections would need to be elaborated and developed. But it is clear how Aristotle should attempt to meet them. He should first point out that his notion of necessity is not restricted to what we sometimes call logical or conceptual necessity—it certainly includes 'natural' necessity. (For varieties of necessity in Aristotle see SORABJI (1980), 222–4.) Hence the theorems of biology will indeed be necessary truths, their necessity being underwritten not by any analytical connection among concepts but by the essential natures of their subject-matter. (But why suppose that statements of essence are *necessary*? Thunder is, perhaps, essentially a noise caused by the quenching of fire in the clouds; for I say *what thunder is* (*ti esti*) when I say that it is such a noise. Yet is it necessarily such a noise? For discussion of this issue see SORABJI (1980), ch. 13; (1981), 231–44.)

He should secondly point out that his notion of explanation is also a generous one: his conception of an *aitia* can properly be applied not only in areas, like the biological sciences, where we are happy to speak of causal explanations, but also in mathematics, where the explanations are not, of course, causal in the modern sense.

I do not know how successful this line of defence might be. (See further VAN FRAASSEN (1980); PATZIG (1981), 141–5.)

71ᵇ16: "another type of understanding": the apprehension of the principles (see 72ª25–ᵇ3; *A* 3, 72ᵇ18–24; *A* 9, 76ª16–22 etc.). Aristotle's terminology is not stable: here apprehension of the principles is classed as a sort of understanding (cf. Theophrastus, *Met* 9ᵇ8–16); but *B* 19 contrasts the two states. Other passages vacillate; the point is trifling, as *A* 3, 72ᵇ18–25, perhaps realizes. "Another type" means "a type different from demonstrative understanding" rather than "a type different from that defined in (3)" (Zabarella).

71ᵇ18: "a scientific deduction": for "deduction" see p. 83; "scientific" translates *epistēmonikos*—"productive of understanding" better brings out the connection with *epistasthai*.

71ᵇ19: The characteristics of demonstration are inferred from the definition of understanding; *A* 2 concentrates on the implications of (1), leaving (2b) for *A* 4.

The six characteristics fall into two groups of three, the first group containing absolute features of demonstration, the second relative features; this explains the apparent perversity of listing both primitiveness and priority among the features: a proposition (e.g. Euclid's fifth postulate) might be primitive, i.e. have nothing prior to it, and yet not be prior to a given conclusion (e.g. that vines are deciduous). The three relative features entail a fourth, 'appropriateness'; this is elucidated at *A* 6, 74ᵇ21–6 and in *A* 7 (cf. *GA B* 8, 747ᵇ30–748ª11).

The six features properly characterize the *principles* or axioms of a demonstrative science. But Aristotle's thought contains two irritating imprecisions. First, as I have already observed, the relation of *depending on* (*einai ek*: p. 81) may be either the epistemological relation holding between **a**'s knowledge that *P* and the propositions on which it is based, or the logical relation holding between a demonstrated conclusion and its premisses. Secondly, Aristotle does not distinguish clearly between the principles on which a demonstrated conclusion ultimately depends and the premisses from which it immediately derives. A more rigorous statement of his view is this: **a** has demonstrative understanding that *P* only if **a** has produced a sequence of deductions $D_1, D_2, \ldots, D_n$ such that (i) the conclusion of D_1 is *P*; (ii) the conclusion of each D_i for $i > 1$ is identical with a premiss of some D_j where $j < i$; and (iii) each premiss of each D_i is true, is prior to, more familiar than, and explanatory of the conclusion of D_i, and *either* is primitive and immediate *or else* is the conclusion of some D_k, where $k > i$.

When Aristotle writes "They must be true ... They must proceed from items which are primitive ...", he is expressing himself carelessly; for we should expect either "They [sc. the items from which demonstrative understanding proceeds] must be true ... They must be primitive ...", or else "It [sc. demonstrative understanding] must proceed from what is true ... It must proceed from what is primitive ...". But his carelessness may, as it were, hint at the more rigorous statement which I have just rehearsed. However that may be, he certainly gets closer to rigour at *Top A* 1, 100^{a}27–9: "A deduction is a demonstration if it proceeds from items which are true and primitive or else from items which are ultimately known by way of what is primitive and true" (cf. *APst A* 10, 76^{b}10; *Rhet A* 2, 1357^{a}7: see BARNES (1981), 25–7).

71^{b}25: (A) *Truth.* If "they" in "they must be true" refers to the principles, the argument runs: 'Since, by (3), a demonstrator must know the principles which explain the *demonstrandum*, and what is known must be the case, i.e. be true, it follows that the principles must be true.' Against this interpretation some say, first, that 71^{b}26 declares that one cannot *understand* what is not the case, whereas (3) requires only that the principles be *known*; and secondly, that the example of the incommensurability (of the diagonal of a square with its sides: cf. Heath (2), 22–3; 196–7) regularly illustrates the *conclusion* of an inference, not a principle (e.g. *APr A* 23, 41^{a}23–7; *A* 44, 50^{a}35–8). But these objections are minor ("understand" in 71^{b}26 may have its ordinary sense of "know"); and no alternative construe gives Aristotle a plausible argument.

71^{b}26: (B) *Primitiveness.* The commentators offer a variety of glosses on "primitive"; the least implausible states that "primitive", "indemonstrable", and "immediate" are coextensive; for Aristotle offers only a single argument for these three features, and seems at times (e.g. *A* 15, 79^{a}38) to use the three terms promiscuously. But there is an obvious analysis of "*P* is primitive", viz. "there is no *Q* prior to *P*", i.e. "there is no *Q* from which knowledge of *P* must be derived". Aristotle assumes that if *P* is indemonstrable it is primitive, and thus an argument that principles are indemonstrable proves also that they are primitive.

(C) *Immediacy.* To be 'immediate' (*amesos*) is to lack a middle term: a syllogistic proposition *AxC* is immediate if and only if there is no term *B*, distinct from *A* and *C*, such that *AxB*, *BxC* ⊢ *AxC* is a syllogism (and *AxB*, *BxC* are true). The primary case of immediacy concerns *a*-propositions: *AaC* is immediate if and only if ¬ (∃*B*) (*AaB* & *BaC*). But immediate *e*-propositions are admitted in *A* 15. ("¬" signifies negation.)

At 71^{b}27 "indemonstrable" (*anapodeiktos*) replaces "immediate". Sextus reports: "arguments are called *anapodeiktoi* in two ways—those that have not been demonstrated, and those that have no need of demonstration owing to its being at once patent in their case that they are conclusive" (*adv Math* viii. 223; cf. Diogenes Laertius, vii. 79). *Anapodeiktos* means "undemonstrated" at, e.g., *APr B* 1, 53^{a}32; ^{b}2; *EN Z* 12, 1143^{b}12; and the sense "not needing demonstration" fits some contexts in *APst*. But here *anapodeiktos* contrasts with "that of which there is a demonstration", i.e. "that which is demonstrable". Hence it might be thought to mean "indemonstrable"—and so I have translated it. But according to Aristotle (71^{b}28), if it is demonstrable that *P*, then you can only understand that *P* by way of a demonstration. Hence something is demonstrable if and only if it needs demonstration; and something is indemonstrable if and only if it does not need demonstration.

If *P* is indemonstrable, it does not follow that *P* is immediate, even if *P* is of the form *AxC*; for there may be a valid, but non-demonstrative, syllogism concluding to *P* (cf. *A* 13 etc.). If *P* is immediate, it only follows that *P* is indemonstrable on the false assumption that all demonstrations are syllogisms.

The argument at 71^{b}27–9 is obscure. The *second* sentence, "to understand . . .", amounts to:

(4) If *P* is demonstrable, **a** understands *P* if and only if **a** has a demonstration of *P*.

("Non-incidentally", despite the word-order, goes with "understand": see 71^{b}9.) The *first* sentence, "otherwise you will not . . .", expresses a proposition which follows from (4), viz.:

(5) If a principle *Π* is demonstrable, then if **a** does not have a demonstration of *Π*, **a** does not understand *Π*.

(Thus "understand" is again used of principles.) In order to infer from (5) that no principle is demonstrable, we need two further premisses:

(6) Some principles are understood;
(7) No one has a demonstration of any principle.

Premiss (6) is reaffirmed in *A* 3; and (7) is a truism. Premiss (4) clearly needs argument; it is restated and generalized at *B* 3, 90^{b}10; 20–2 (see notes).

71^{b}29: (D) *Explanatoriness*. If **a** has a demonstration of *P*, then **a** understands *P* and so knows the explanation of *P*. If the only knowledge necessary for having a demonstration of *P* is knowledge of the principles from which *P* is deducible, then the principles must contain the explanation of *P*.

71^{b}31: (E) *Priority*. Aristotle regularly distinguishes several varieties of priority (see esp. *Cat* 12; *Met Δ* 11). He has in mind here not the curious 'explanatory' priority of *Cat* 12, 14^{b}9–23, nor temporal priority (for Aristotelian 'causes' need not precede their 'effects'), but priority '*in knowledge*' (*P* is 'prior in knowledge' to *Q* if knowledge that *Q* requires knowledge that *P*, but not vice versa). See esp. *Met Δ* 11, 1018^{b}30–7.

71^{b}30: (F) *Familiarity*. "*Gnōrimos*" is sometimes translated "knowable" and sometimes "known"; on the whole, the latter is better (see S. Mansion, 139 n. 20; Wieland, 71 n. 2; BURNYEAT (1981), 128 n. 53). "Known", however, does not easily take a comparative form ("more known"); "familiar" does, and is in any case marginally more suitable than "known" in non-comparative contexts.

On occasion Aristotle distinguishes between priority and familiarity (e.g. *APr B* 16, 64^{b}30–3), but 71^{b}33–72^{a}5 seems to show that they are identical here (see notes).

The text at 71^{b}31 is ambiguous. Most interpreters put a semi-colon after "explanatory", and take "and we already know them..." to restate the requirement of familiarity. Now the premisses (or principles) of a demonstration must be "more familiar (*gnōrimōtera*)" than its conclusion, and they must also be *progignōskomena* ("we already know" them). But these two claims are quite distinct (see MIGNUCCI (1975), 26); hence the reference at 71^{b}30 to what we already know cannot restate the familiarity condition. We should therefore repunctuate: remove the colon after "explanatory", and take "we already know..." to provide a second argument for the priority condition. It follows that we shall find no explicit justification of the familiarity condition. (We should not seek one at 72^{a}25–^{b}3. There Aristotle is explicitly concerned, not with what is 'more familiar *by nature*', but with what we must already know better. He argues that, in order to come to know something on the basis of a demonstration, we must already have a grasp of the principles which is better than the grasp which we are about to acquire of the conclusion.) But this should not be surprising; for, in this passage at least, Aristotle plainly treats priority (in the relevant sense) and greater familiarity as one and the same thing. (Hence we should properly speak of five, rather than six, conditions on the premisses or principles of demonstrations.)

But there is a difficulty: Aristotle cites the fact that we must already know the principles as evidence that they are prior. It is plain, from the general considerations advanced at 71^{a}1–17, that we must know the principles of a demonstration before we are led to its conclusion. But Aristotle cannot argue that if I know that *P* before I know that *Q*, then *P* is epistemically prior to *Q*. Such an argument ignores the contrast between what is more familiar by nature and what is more familiar to us, which the next paragraph develops.

71^{b}33:   The distinction explained in this section is common (see *Top Z* 4; *Phys A* 1; cf. *APr B* 23, 68^{b}35–7; *Met Z* 3, 1029^{b}3–12; *EN A* 4, 1095^{b}2–4; cf. MANSION (1984)). What it is to be more familiar 'by nature' or *simpliciter* is explained in *Top Z* 4: the genus and the differentia "are also more familiar than the species; for if the species is apprehended, it is necessary that the genus and the differentia are apprehended too ... but if the genus or the differentia is apprehended, it is not necessary that the species too is apprehended; so that the species is more unfamiliar" (141^{b}29–34). Thus being more familiar by nature is the same as being prior in knowledge.

Aristotle does not explain the notion of 'familiarity in relation to us'. Since "X is more familiar by nature than Y" is compatible with "Y is more familiar to **a** than X", "Y is familiar to **a**" cannot entail "**a** understands that P"—but it does entail "**a** knows that P", in a suitably weak sense of "know". (*Met Z* 3 imagines that I become educated in so far as what is more familiar by nature becomes more familiar to me.) Both terms and propositions can be familiar. B is more familiar to me than A, perhaps, if I am better at recognizing Bs than As; Q is more familiar than P, perhaps, if I am more prone to assent to Q than to P.

The question "What things are most familiar by nature?" is, in a loose sense, conceptual; but the question "What things are most familiar to us?" is empirical, and, as *Top Z* 4, 141^{b}36–142^{a}4, recognizes, it has no unitary answer. Thus when Aristotle says that what is "nearer to perception" is more familiar to us, he must be speaking loosely; he can hardly be *defining* the notion of familiarity to us, despite the "I call". By and large, the untutored mind recognizes instances of perceptible properties more readily than instances of abstract properties, and is more inclined to assent to propositions about the immediately perceptible world than to propositions of a more abstract nature (cf. *Top Θ* 1, 156^{a}6). Aristotle would presumably back the claim that X is more general than Y if it is 'further from perception' than Y by appealing to the theory of concept formation expounded in B 19. The connection between generality and perception is thus at best a contingent one. Generality and familiarity are, however, logically tied in the following way: if P is more familiar by nature than Q then P cannot be less general than Q.

The six characteristics of demonstration call for two final comments. First, it may be useful to set out the logical relations between them: (C) entails (B), and (B) entails (A); (E) is equivalent to (F) and entails (D); further, (D) entails (A) (cf. *APr B* 2, 53^{b}9). Secondly, it should be stressed that Aristotle does not require his principles to be 'self-evident'. They must, it is true, be self-explanatory (cf. *APr B* 16, 64^{b}35; *Top A* 1, 100^{b}1; *Phys B* 1, 193^{a}5), and some of them cannot be disbelieved (*A* 10, 76^{b}23, notes); but the later notion that the axioms of a science must be in some way evidently and patently true is not at all Aristotelian. (For an early example of the view see Speusippus, frag. 30 Lang = frag. 73 Tarán.)

72^{a}5: This section fires off a salvo of explanatory glosses; it is not very well integrated into the chapter.

72^{a}5: "To proceed from primitives . . .": If "X is primitive" is equivalent to "X is a principle", then depending on primitives is depending on appropriate principles only if all principles are appropriate. This condition is satisfied if "principle" is taken as a relative term (cf. e.g. *Phys A* 2, 185^{a}4), so that "X is a principle" is elliptical for "X is a principle *of S*". "Principle" is used in a non-relative sense at 71^{b}23, where it takes an argument to show that principles are appropriate.

72^{a}7: "A principle of a demonstration . . .": "proposition", and not the customary "premiss", is the translation of *protasis*; see the definitions at *Top A* 4, 101ᵇ27–36; *Θ* 2, 158ᵃ14–24; *APr A* 1, 24ᵃ16 (cf. p. 83).

Having glossed "principle" as "immediate proposition", Aristotle proceeds to gloss each part of his gloss. It is strange that he does not give the obvious explanation of "immediate" (p. 94).

72ᵃ9: The MSS define a proposition as "one part of a statement" (*apophanseōs to heteron morion*). The reading has worried many scholars; and it is in fact perfectly impossible (*pace* MIGNUCCI (1975), 32–3): a 'statement' is said to be "one part of a contradictory pair" (72ᵃ11; cf. *Int* 17ᵃ23–6); since a contradictory pair is a pair of the form {*P*, not-*P*}, a statement is anything of the form "*P*" or "not-*P*". Then if—with the MSS—a proposition is "one part of a statement", a proposition must be something like a term (subject or predicate). And this flies in the face of everything Aristotle says about propositions. The change from *apophanseōs* to *antiphaseōs* (cf. *Int* 11, 20ᵇ24), which I discover was made before me by Colli, is surely right. (The same error recurs in Alexander, *in APr* 11. 8; the reverse error is found in most MSS at *APst A* 2, 72ᵃ19.) The only difficulty is with the clause *apophansis . . . morion* (72ᵃ11–12). The presence of this clause in the text is awkward and unmotivated rather than inconsistent; and there are more awkward sentences in *APst*. None the less, I suspect that it was added as a (correct) gloss on the text, after *antiphaseōs* had been corrupted; for the new word *apophanseōs* clearly called for an explanation.

72ᵃ9: "one thing said of one": if this means more than "in subject-predicate form", it may be meant to rule out *equivocal* predication (cf. *Met Γ* 4, 1006ᵃ32) or *multiple* predication (cf. *Top I* 6, 169ᵃ7–12; 30, 181ᵃ36–9; *Int* 8, 18ᵃ18–23), or it may be intended to insist that subject and predicate are metaphysical unities (e.g. *Int* 11, 20ᵇ12–21).

72ᵃ10: "It is dialectical if it assumes . . .": cf. *APr A* 1, 24ᵃ22–5: "Demonstrative propositions differ from dialectical propositions because a demonstrative proposition is the assumption of one part of a contradictory pair . . . while a dialectical proposition is a request for one part of a contradictory pair." The 'dialectical' arguer asks whether *P* is the case and is equally prepared to argue from either possible answer. Aristotle regularly says (e.g. *Top A* 1) that dialectical argument starts from 'reputable' propositions (*endoxa*); that is presumably because the wise answerer will plump for whichever answer is the more 'reputable'. (See further *A* 11, 77ᵃ25, notes.)

72ᵃ12: "A contradictory pair . . .": Aristotle recognizes four sorts of 'opposition' (cf. esp. *Cat* 10). In the *Categories* contradictory opposites are defined by the fact that "in the case of them alone it is necessary always for one of them to be true and one false" (10, 13ᵃ37–ᵇ3). If there is nothing 'between' *P* and *Q* (cf. e.g. *Met Γ* 7, 1011ᵇ23), i.e. no third possibility apart from *P* and *Q*, then one at least of *P* and *Q* must be true (and hence, since they are opposites, the other false). The addition of "in their own right" is perhaps intended to indicate that it is part of the nature of a contradiction, and not just a contingent fact, that there is no third possibility 'between' its parts. ("The sky is blue" and "The sky is clouded" are not *contradictory*, though as a matter of fact one or the other is true.)

72ª13: "... which says something *of* something ...": cf. *Int* 6, 17ª25–6. Aristotle often uses the phrase "something of something" (*ti kata tinos*) for negations as well as affirmations.

72ª14: The classification of principles undertaken in this section is treated again in *A* 10. Aristotle's use of the terminology he introduces here is not consistent; he refers to a customary use of "axiom" (cf. *A* 10, 76ᵇ14—perhaps the custom was mathematical: *Met Γ* 3, 1005ª20; but cf. Einarson, 43–6), but he himself uses this term, and also "posit" and "supposition", in a variety of ways (e.g. Ross, 510–11; Bonitz, 797ª1– 34; 802ᵇ5–26). For some time this terminology remained in a state of flux, even inside the mathematical tradition (cf. Proclus, *Comm in Eucl* 75. 10–77. 2; 178. 12–182. 14; see e.g. Heath (1), i. 117–24; (2), 53–7). See esp. VON FRITZ (1955).

(A) *Axioms and Posits*: The distinction between axioms and posits is identical with that drawn at *A* 10, 76ª37–ᵇ2, between 'common' and 'proper' principles; at least, Aristotle uses the terms "the common elements" (*ta koina*) and "the common axioms" (*ta koina axiōmata*) indiscriminately (Bonitz, 400ª2–5), and he does not distinguish between "axioms" and "common axioms" (cf. Euclid's "common notions", *koinai ennoiai*). Though Aristotle held that in a sense the common axioms were familiar to everyone (*Top I* 11, 172ª27–30; *Met B* 1, 995ᵇ8; 2, 996ᵇ27–9; *Γ* 3, 1005ª24), by calling them *common* he indicates not this fact but the fact that they are shared by more than one science. A standard example of an axiom is "Equals taken from equals leave equals" (*A* 10, 76ª41, ᵇ20; 11, 77ª31; Euclid, i common notion 3); this appears to be a specifically mathematical principle, so that the axioms need not be common to *all* sciences. In that case "axiom" is best taken as a relative term—propositions are axioms *for a science*—and Aristotle's definition runs as follows:

(8) *P* is an axiom for *S* = df if anyone knows any proposition in *S*, then he knows that *P*.

The commentators imply an 'absolute' definition:

(9) *P* is an axiom = df if anyone knows anything, he knows that *P*

(cf. *Met Γ* 3, 1005ᵇ15). In that case, the 'equals' principle is not, strictly speaking, an axiom at all.

"Theophrastus defines axioms thus: 'An axiom is a sort of opinion, either applying to items of the same kind (e.g. equals from equals) or else *simpliciter* applying to everything (e.g. either the affirmation or the negation)'" (Themistius, *in APst* 7. 3–4 = frag. 33 Graeser). Thus he in effect accepts both (8) and (9) as accounts of the two different sorts of axiom. As for Aristotle, we cannot take him to mean (8) as his definition; for in that case axioms would no longer be the same as the *common* principles. Yet it remains true that his examples do not fit (9). At *An B* 6, 418^{a}10–11, 16–20, he explains that 'common sensibles' are items which can be perceived by *all* the senses; but his examples indicate—and *Sens* 4, 442^{b}4–10, shows that he knew—that an item is 'common' if it can be perceived by *more than one* sense. Perhaps, then, he means—or should have said—that an axiom is a principle found in *more than one* science. Thus:

(8*) *P* is an axiom = $_{df}$ for at least two distinct sciences, *S* and *S**, if anyone knows any proposition in *S* or in *S**, then he knows that *P*.

Are there axioms, as Aristotle asserts? If (9) is adopted, the only contenders for axiomhood are logical laws; and although it is false that learners must have explicit knowledge of some logical laws, it may be that in some weak sense of "know" all learners must 'know' some logical laws (e.g. they must order their beliefs in accordance with them). If (8) is preferred, we must imagine that, e.g., the 'equals' principle is used in all mathematical proofs; it seems to me improbable that this, or any analogous proposition, is true. (And the suspicion that there are in fact *no* axioms in this sense seems to be tacitly accepted by Aristotle himself: see note to 72^{a}28.)

(B) *Suppositions and Definitions*: 72^{a}19 appears to allow that any type of proposition may function as a supposition (cf. *EE B* 10, 1227^{a}10; ^{b}28–32); and "that something is" is most readily glossed as "that something is the case". (The translation "that it is something", which is also possible, gives essentially the same sense.) Then a definition is a posit "which does not", i.e. which does not suppose that anything is the case. In Book *B* Aristotle maintains that definitions entail existential propositions (cf. *B* 7, 92^{b}4–11); but presumably they do not 'suppose', or directly assert, that anything is the case. Thus definitions are not propositions at all, so that here "definition (*horismos*)" means—as it certainly sometimes does mean—"*definiens*". (Hence we should translate 72^{a}22–3 as: "arithmeticians posit as a unit that which is quantitatively indivisible".) But there is a powerful objection to this interpretation: definitions are posits, posits are principles, and principles (72^{a}7) are propositions. And yet in that case definitions will be 'one part of a contradictory pair', and hence will be a kind of supposition.

Hence we might better follow the majority of the commentators in construing "that something is" as "that there are *F*s", thus taking suppositions to be exclusively existential propositions. In favour of this is the fact that Aristotle's examples are existential (72^{a}24; *A* 10, 76^{a}35); and the argument of *A* 10, 76^{b}3–22, may offer support. (We shall then be obliged to maintain that the word "supposition" is being used in a broader sense at such places as *Phys Θ* 3, 253^{b}5 (cf. *A* 2, 185^{a}12), where it is a supposition of natural science that nature is a source of change.)

But it is hard to believe that by "either of the parts of a contradictory pair" Aristotle could have meant "either the proposition that something exists or the proposition that something does not exist"; nor shall we think that *negative* existential propositions are among the principles of any science.

The account of 'posits' remains baffling (see further MIGNUCCI (1975), 35–9; LANDOR (1981)). It is, however, reasonably clear what Aristotle *ought* to have said, namely: 'Posits are of two kinds—those which say *that* something is (I call these suppositions), and those which say *what* something is (I call these definitions)'. Thus—as Aristotle's example itself indicates—the distinction intended here is the same as the distinction made earlier at *A* 1, 71ᵃ11–17.

Aristotle is clear that principles function as premisses of demonstrations (72ᵃ7); but it is not easy to see how they can do so. A typical axiom is the Law of Excluded Middle; and that is not expressible in syllogistic form. If suppositions are existential propositions, then they too are not syllogistic. Definitions might well seem wholly unamenable to syllogistic expression; Aristotle, however, explicitly says that they have subject–predicate form (*B* 3, 90ᵇ3–4; cf. *Top H* 3, 153ᵃ16)—the notion of definition which this presupposes is not elucidated until Book *B*.

72ᵃ25: Aristotle's argument in 72ᵃ25–32 is this:

(10) If **a** has demonstrative knowledge that *P*, then *P* is known to **a** because *Π* is known to **a**.

—where *P* is a conclusion, and *Π* its principles.

(11*a*) If **b** is *F* because **c** is *F*, then **c** is more *F* than **b**;

(11*b*) If **b** is *F* because of **c**, then **c** is more *F* than **b**.

Hence:

(12) If **a** has demonstrative knowledge that *P*, then *Π* is more known to **a** than *P* is.

This argument is valid if it makes sense (cf. *Met A* 2, 982ᵃ30–ᵇ4). The text at 72ᵃ19 is compatible both with (11*a*) and with (11*b*). The ancient commentators, noting that a murderer is not more dead than his victim, preferred (11*a*); and their interpretation is supported by *Met α* 1, 993ᵇ23–6: "A thing is most so-and-so of the other things that are so-and-so if it is in virtue of it that being so-and-so holds of the others (e.g. fire is hottest; for this is the explanation for the other things of their heat)" (cf. *Phys Θ* 5, 257ᵇ8). On the other hand, Aristotle adheres to:

(13) If **b** is *F* because of **c**, then **b** is *F* because **c** is *F*

('generation is from synonyms': *Met Z* 9, 1034ᵃ21–32; *Θ* 8, 1049ᵇ23–7); and the conjunction of (11*a*) and (13) is equivalent to (11*b*). Zabarella points out that (11*a*) can only be defended if "*F*" is restricted to predicates for which "more *F*" makes sense—a father is not more a man than his son. Even with this restriction (11a) seems to be too imprecise for assessment.

Whatever the value of (11), can we accept (12)? Some would rule it out on the grounds that there are no degrees of knowledge—you cannot know that P 'more' than you know that Q. Aristotle was familiar with this line of argument (cf. *Cat* 8, 8^b29-32; 9^a4-8; 10^b32-11^a5), and the text provides, implicitly, his answer to it: part of the notion of *knowing that P* is *being convinced that P*; since I can be more convinced that P than I am that Q, I can be said, in a reasonably intelligible sense, to know that P 'more' than I know that Q. And (12) can then be defended on Lockean grounds: P is infected by any uncertainty that infects Π and also by any uncertainty that infects the inference from Π to P. If we allow the possibility of complete certainty, then (12) needs a slight modification: P cannot be more known that Π is.

72ᵃ28: "either all or some of them": i.e. 'not all the premisses of an inference need be known before its conclusion'; or, better, 'to know P we need only know beforehand those principles of S on which P depends; there may be other principles of S which are not used in the deduction of P' (cf. *Met B* 3, 998^a25-7).

72ᵃ32: Aristotle infers that **a** must already know Π from the premiss that **a** must be more convinced of Π than he is of P. The argument relies on one further premiss:

(14) It is impossible that (**a** is more convinced of X than of Y, and **a** knows that Y, and **a** does not know that X, and **a** is not more happily disposed towards X than by knowing X).

(The only happier disposition than knowledge is 'comprehension': cf. *A* 22, 83^b34; *B* 19, 100^b8). These premisses warrant the inference that if **a** knows that P, then **a** knows that Π. But it does not follow that **a** knows Π *before* he knows P. And in any case (14) is false: many people are more convinced of certain false beliefs than they are of pieces of knowledge (cf. *EN Z* 3, 1146^b29).

72ᵃ37: The crucial sentence in this paragraph ("in addition, there must be . . .") is doubly ambiguous: first, the genitive *tōn antikeimenōn*, which I translate "*among* the opposites" might equally be read as "*than* the opposites"; and secondly, the antecedent of *hōn* ("from which . . .") may be either "the opposites" or "the principles". There are thus four possible paraphrases:

(A) Nothing must be more convincing than the opposites of the true principles, from which opposites may come a deduction of the contrary error;

(B) Nothing must be more convincing than the opposites of those principles from which . . . ;

(C) Nothing must be more convincing among the opposites of those principles from which . . . ;

(D) Nothing must be more convincing among the opposites of the principles, from which opposites . . .

In (C) and (D) "more convincing" may be expanded to "more convincing ⟨than the true principles⟩" or to "more convincing ⟨than what is being proved⟩".
(A) is traditional, but it obliges us to read "more convincing than the opposites" as "more convincing than that the opposites *are false*". (B) takes "the opposites of those principles from which . . ." as a tortuous paraphrase for "the true principles". (C) says the same as (B), but with less convolution. (D) is the least implausible reading. If we take "the opposites ⟨of *Π*⟩" to be explicated by "from which a deduction of the contrary error may proceed" (i.e. 'from which *AeC*, the contrary of the true conclusion *AaC*, may be inferred'), then we have Aristotle saying that there must be no *Π'* such that **a** is more convinced of *Π'* than he is of *Π* and *Π'* entails the contrary of *P*. The type of case this rules out is illustrated at *APr B* 21, 66^b18–67^a5.

72^b3: "given that anyone who understands . . .": 'If **a** knows that *P*, then he cannot be rationally persuaded that not-*P*; hence he must not be more convinced of *Π'*, for attention to that would then persuade him that not-*P*.' The unpersuadability of knowers was an Academic commonplace (*Tim* 29^c; 51^e; [*Def*] 414^c; *Top E* 2, 130^b15–16; 3, 131^a23–6; etc; cf. *APst A* 33, 89^a5, notes); it is hard to think of any satisfactory argument for it.

CHAPTER 3

72^b5: Demonstrative knowledge is a special case of rational knowledge, or knowledge based upon reasons. The notion of rational knowledge appears to lead to an infinite and vicious regress: if I know that *P*, then my knowledge must be based on some premiss *Q*; hence I must know that *Q*—on the basis of some further premiss *R*. If I know that *P*, I know that *Q*; if I know that *Q*, I know that *R*; and so on: if I know anything, I know infinitely many things.
This regress is adverted to in Plato's *Theaetetus* (209^e–210^b; cf. 201^d–202^d: see Morrow); and it was discussed in the Academy (cf. *Met a* 2; Theophrastus, *Met* 9, 9^b21; cf. Sextus, *adv Math* viii. 347). The present chapter considers three reactions to it—or rather, to the special case in which it is applied to demonstrative knowledge. All three reactions agree that it is impossible to know infinitely many things: one group concludes that knowledge is impossible; a second group denies that demonstrative knowledge yields a vicious regress; the third group denies that all knowledge is demonstrative. The first, sceptical, reaction is ascribed by some scholars to Antisthenes (Cherniss, 65; Ross, 513–14). The second reaction, which calls on the possibility of circular proof, has been attributed to followers of Xenocrates (Cherniss, 68; Ross, 514), or to the Academic geometer Menaechmus (see Proclus, *Comm in Eucl*

72. 23–73. 5); but I am inclined to ascribe it to the youthful Aristotle (see *APr B* 5–7; *APst B* 12, 95^{b}38–96^{a}7, notes; BARNES (1976)). The third view is advocated by Aristotle in our chapter.

The matter of *A* 3 was later developed, by the Pyrrhonists, into a general argument for scepticism. (See Sextus, *Pyrrh Hyp* i. 165–77; Diogenes Laertius, ix. 88–9: BARNES (1990), 113–44.) Suppose that you claim that P_1. Then either (i) you ground P_1 on P_2, P_2 on P_3, . . . , P_n on P_{n+1}, . . . , where each P_1 is distinct from each of its predecessors; or (ii) you ground P_1 on P_2, P_2 on P_3, . . . , P_n on P_{n+1}, . . . , where P_{n+1} is identical with one of its predecessors; or (iii) you ground P_1 on P_2, P_2 on P_3, . . . , P_n on P_{n+1}, where P_{n+1} is ungrounded. But none of these possibilities is legitimate: (i) is an infinite regress, and we cannot grasp an infinite sequence of propositions; (ii) is circular, and circular argumentation is always vicious; (iii) ends in bare assertion, and bare assertion establishes nothing. Thus the Pyrrhonists follow Aristotle in rejecting possibilities (i) and (ii); and they add that Aristotle's own option, (iii), is no better than the others. Plainly, to confute the Pyrrhonists an Aristotelian must claim either that 'bare assertion' is in some cases (viz. in the case of primitive propositions) a respectable operation, or else that his assent to the principles is something more substantial than 'bare assertion'. It is in *B* 19 that we eventually find Aristotle's implicit attempt to confute, proleptically, the Pyrrhonists. (On *A* 3 see also IRWIN (1988), 125–33.)

72^{b}7: ". . . or necessary": i.e., presumably, '. . . or supported by a sound argument'.

72^{b}7: The sceptical argument is subtle and complicated. Aristotle's concise account is helped if we take some science *S* as the potential object of demonstration; *S* is the ordered set $\langle P_1, P_2, . . . , P_n, . . . \rangle$ where each P_i is prior, in the relevant sense, to its predecessor.

The sceptics use two premisses; first:

(1) All understanding comes through demonstration

(72^{b}8—where *allōs* gives the right sense—, 12, 16); in terms of *S*:

(1s) ($\forall i$) (if **a** understands P_i, then **a** has demonstrated that P_i).

The second premiss is implicit at 72^{b}9:

(2) To understand any proposition by demonstration, one must understand it on the basis of one's understanding of some prior proposition,

i.e., in terms of *S*:

(2s) ($\forall i$) (if **a** has demonstrated that P_i, then for some *j* greater than *i* **a** understands P_j and **a** has inferred P_i from P_j).

From (1s) and (2s) there follows:

(3s) ($\forall i$) (if **a** understands P_i, then for some *j* greater than *i* **a** understands P_j and **a** has inferred P_i from P_j).

—so that if anyone understands anything, he understands infinitely many propositions. Since that is impossible, we can infer:

(4s) ¬ (∃i) (**a** understands P_i).

Aristotle applauds this argument. The objection that a certain line of argument 'leads to infinity' is very common in his works (Bonitz, 74^{b}41– 57); the nearest passage to ours is *Met* α 2, 994^{b}16–27, which suggests first that Aristotle has in mind the impossibility of thinking an infinite sequence of thoughts (cf. *A* 22, 82^{b}29; 83^{b}6; 84^{a}3), and secondly that he inferred this impossibility from the fact that "a finite body cannot in a finite time traverse an infinite distance" (e.g. *Cael A* 5, 272^{a}3, 29; *Phys Z* 7, 238^{a}33). (3s) implies that knowledge requires an infinite number of inferences, and hence an infinite sequence of thoughts: Aristotle is surely right to accept the inference to (4s).

We might attempt to stop the inference by supposing that there is a last member of *S*. But let this be P_k. Then, by (1s) and (2s), there follows:

(5s) ¬ (**a** understands P_k).

And since if **a** does not understand P_k then **a** does not understand P_{k-1}, we can again conclude, by a mathematical induction, to (4s).

72^{b}15: "but only on the supposition that they are the case": this is ambiguous between "if *Π* is the case, then **a** knows that *P*" and "**a** knows that if *Π* is the case then *P*". The latter is favoured by the context of the argument, and by Aristotle's few words on the 'hypothetical syllogism' (cf. esp. *APr A* 44, 50^{a}16–^{b}4). But probably Aristotle has not seen the distinction.

72^{b}15: The other party holds that "nothing prevents there being demonstrations of everything". The most reasonable of several possible glosses on this seems to be:

(6s) It is possible that (∀i) (**a** has demonstrated that P_i).

The second party agrees that we cannot produce infinitely many demonstrations, and therefore maintains that *S* contains finitely many propositions. Since the party stands by (1s), it must reject (2s); I shall shortly suggest a premiss it might have substituted for (2s).

Since demonstration involves inference from known premisses, and *S* is, by hypothesis, finite, it is easy to see that (6s) requires:

(7s) It is possible that (∃i) (∃j) (i ≠ j and **a** has demonstrated P_i from P_j and **a** has demonstrated P_j from P_i)

—I say that **a** demonstrates *P* from *Q* if *Q* is a premiss of a demonstration of a premiss . . . of a demonstration that *P*. (7s) represents the claim that "it is possible for demonstrations to proceed in a circle or reciprocally".

In *APr* Aristotle offers a formal definition of circular argument in terms of his syllogistic: "To prove in a circle or reciprocally is to take the conclusion and the one proposition (with its predication the other way about), and to conclude to the remaining proposition which was assumed in the other deduction" (*APr* B 5, 57^b18-21; cf. 58^a34-5). More formally, a circular proof is a set of three interrelated inferences of the following form: (i) $Ax_1B, Bx_2C \vdash Ax_3C$; (ii) $Ax_3C, Bx_1A \vdash Bx_2C$; (iii) $Ax_3C, Cx_2B \vdash Ax_1B$. *APr* B 5–7 goes through the fourteen syllogistic moods and shows that perfect circles are possible only in *Barbara*, when we have: (iB) $AaB, BaC \vdash AaC$; (iiB) $AaC, BaA \vdash BaC$; (iiiB) AaC, $CaB \vdash AaB$. Eight other moods allow 'semicircular' proof, comprising (i) and (ii) or (i) and (iii); and for four cases Aristotle draws a pseudo-circle. Later in the present chapter Aristotle refers back to his discussion of circular argument in *APr* B 5–7, and he evidently thinks that his remarks there yield a formal analysis of the sort of reasoning implicit in (7*s*). In fact, however, the correspondence is not exact; for in the syllogistic circles of *APr* it is not true that every proposition in the circle is proved. Here, as elsewhere, syllogistic does not readily provide a formalization of the argument structures considered in *APst*.

72^b18: Aristotle's own reply to the sceptic falls into two parts.

In *Part (A)* he first denies (1*s*); his statement that "in the case of immediate items understanding is indemonstrable" must be taken to entail:

(8) **a** understands some immediate propositions.

When he says that (8) "must be so" he is naturally taken to mean that it follows necessarily from the propositions he is about to state; but these propositions only yield:

(9) If **a** understands any immediates, then something is understood non-demonstratively.

And the sceptic can cheerfully accept (9). Perhaps in calling (8) necessary Aristotle means only that it is necessary for us to embrace it if we are to evade the sceptic's position. This interpretation relieves Aristotle of a bad argument against the sceptic at the cost of leaving him with no argument at all.

In *Part (B)* the key phrase is "principle of understanding" (72^b24); the same phrase reappears at A 33, 88^b36, and at B 19, 100^b15, where the "principle of understanding" is identified as 'comprehension' or *nous* and said to give knowledge of the principles. Some scholars distinguish between 'comprehension' and 'indemonstrable understanding of the immediates', both here and again at A 33, 88^b35. I do not think this view is tenable; and I prefer the simple and traditional course of identifying the two modes of cognition. In that case, Part (B) of the argument here makes the same point as Part (A); and "We argue . . ." means: 'We can put the point in that way, and we can also express it by saying that . . .'.

It has caused some commentators difficulty that what is referred to as understanding at 72^b18 becomes a principle of understanding at 72^b24

(see p. 93). In fact, the difference between 72^{b}18 and 72^{b}24 merely marks two different ways of expressing the one fact urged in 72^{b}18–24; according to which way is preferred, (1s) will be rejected (we have non-demonstrative *understanding* of certain P_i) or (2) will be modified (to understand P_i we must *know*, but we need not *understand*, P_j).

It seems, then, that Aristotle is telling us that he rejects the sceptic's conclusion but is not giving us any justification for his rejection; this justification is reserved for Book B, the major part of which is occupied with the problem of how we can know the principles of a science.

72^{b}22: "and if things come to a stop at some point": the OCT's punctuation gives: "and if the immediates stop at some point, these . . ." Punctuation before *ta amesa* gives the better sense.

72^{b}24: "by which we get to know the definitions": by comprehension we grasp *all* the principles of a science, and not just the definitions. But Aristotle often speaks as though the only principles are the definitions (B 3, 90^{b}27; *Top* Θ 3, 158^{a}33, ^{b}4, 39; *An A* 1, 402^{b}16–26; *Met B* 3, 998^{b}5; Z 9, 1034^{a}30–2; M 4, 1078^{b}23; *EN Z* 9, 1142^{a}26; 1143^{a}26, ^{b}2). There is no need to invent, as the editors do, some special sense for *horos* here.

72^{b}25: The rest of the chapter gives three arguments against circular demonstration, and hence against the second reaction to the regress.

The *first argument* is straightforward. If there is circular demonstration within S, then every P_i is both prior and posterior to every other; put another way, for every i and j both $i > j$ and $j > i$. The argument is valid; but it only shows that the circular reasoners must abandon (2s).

The clause beginning "except . . ." (72^{b}28) introduces and rebuffs a retort to this argument; the clause is very obscure. I offer what seems on the whole the least implausible paraphrase: 'Unless of course P_i is prior to P_j in *one* sense of "prior" and P_j to P_i in *another*. (See A 2, 71^{b}33–72^{a}5: we are familiar with the latter sort of priority—priority relative to us—in arguments, because inductions regularly proceed from what is prior to us.) But in that case we shall have to suppose either that there are two sorts of understanding, so that the definition at A 2, 71^{b}9–16, which caters only for 'natural' priority, will be incomplete; or else that 'demonstration' from what is prior to us is not demonstration in the unqualified sense'.

This answer is, I think, stronger than it seems to be; its strength can best be appreciated if we recast the whole of Aristotle's first argument.

The circular reasoner must abandon (2s). What he will do, I suggest, is replace it by:

(2s') ($\forall i$) (if **a** has demonstrated that P_i, then for some j distinct from i, **a** understands P_j and **a** has inferred P_i from P_j).

This differs from (2s) only by surrendering the notion of priority; that carries with it the surrender of explanatoriness (cf. A 2, 71^{b}31)— but then certain of Aristotle's contemporaries had denied that explanatoriness was a necessary ingredient at least in mathematical demonstrations (see Proclus, *Comm in Eucl* 202. 9–25—for Aristotle's view see *B* 11, 94^a27–34; *GA B* 6, 742^b23–33; *EE B* 6, 1222^b31–4).

But Aristotle has two retorts to this. First, he will point out that $(2s')$ still contains, implicitly, the notion of temporal priority; for if P_i is inferred from P_j then P_j is known before P_i (cf. *A* 2, 71^b31–3). Thus Aristotle's original argument is still applicable—it need only be recast in terms of temporal priority. Secondly, he will point out that although *S* is finite, nevertheless the circular reasoner is committed to the absurd view that anyone who understands any P_i has performed infinitely many inferences—there are finitely many stops on his Circle Line, but he must call at each of them infinitely many times.

Yet these retorts are far too quick. In particular, it is not clear that the notion of *temporal* priority is of any real importance to the argument. Rather, the central notion is the notion of *epistemic* priority (see p. 95); and the central question is this: Is epistemic priority asymmetrical and transitive? That is, if *P* is epistemically prior to *Q*, does it follow that *Q* is not epistemically prior to *P*? and if *P* is prior to *Q* and *Q* to *R*, does it follow that *P* is prior to *R*? It is easy to suppose—as Aristotle implicitly supposes—that epistemic priority is indeed both asymmetrical and transitive; and in that case his argument against the circular reasoners is sound. But the issue turns out to be far less clear-cut than Aristotle, and we, might initially think. See the discussion in BARNES (1990), 77–87.

However that may be, the circular men might abandon (6s) in favour of:

(10s) ($\forall i$) (it is possible that **a** has demonstrated that P_i).

S is amenable to different axiomatizations; what are axioms under one systematization will be theorems under another.

Now Aristotle need only say against this move that it fails to escape the sceptical argument, which merely has to be relativized to axiom-systems. But he would in fact say more than this: he would point out, correctly, that at most one of the axiomatizations of *S* will yield the sort of understanding defined at *A* 2, 71^b33–72^a5. Thus if Aristotle is right in pressing that definition as explicative of scientific knowledge, (10s) is false.

72^b32: The *second argument* asserts that the 'other party' proves only that if *P*, then *P*; and if *that* counts as proof of *P*, then any proposition is easily proved, since ($\forall P$) (if *P* then *P*). (Cf. *APr B* 16, 64^b39–65^a9; Heath (2), 27–9). Although Aristotle talks of positing *terms*, the variables *A*, *B*, *C* are *propositional* (cf. 64^b39).

Aristotle asks us to posit *three* terms; but he then says that it does not matter whether we take "few or two" for the circular process (*anakamptein*: cf. *An A* 3, 407^a23–30). Presumably he means that it is enough to conduct the argument for the case of the minimal circle of *two* terms (*A*, *B*: 73^a1), but that to set out the argument *three* terms are needed (*A*, *B*, *C*: 72^b38).

The argument, which is less tortuous than I once supposed (see MIGNUCCI (1975), 52), begins with the general truth (72^{b}37–9):

(11) If (if A then B, and if B then C), then if A then C.

The simplest case of circular reasoning is then represented (not wholly felicitously) by (72^{b}39–73^{a}1):

(12) If A then B, and if B then A.

Now, Aristotle says, "Let A be C (*keisthō to A eph' hou to C*)" (73^{a}1–2). He means—as numerous parallels show—that "C" in (11) should represent "A" in (12). The next sentences (73^{a}2–3) are loosely formulated, but their purport is plain. "Hence . . . is to say that C is the case": i.e. "if B then A" in (12) may be rewritten as "if B then C". "And to say this is to say . . .": i.e. given "if A then B, and if B then C" (which is what we are now saying), we may say "if A then C". "But C is the same as A" (73^{a}3–4): i.e. "C" in (11) represents "A" in (12). Hence (73^{a}5) we shall infer:

(13) If A then A.

The argument is open to several objections. First, in syllogistic no proposition can function both as the conclusion and as the sole premiss of an argument: how, then, can *any* demonstration amount to a proof of "If A, then A"? There is a satisfactory, if complex, answer to this; but Aristotle does not give it. Secondly, circular demonstration does not consist in the pair of *implications* conjoined in (12); for a demonstration is not an implication at all, but an argument of the form $A \vdash B$, where the premiss A fulfils certain conditions. Aristotle's argument can be reformulated to meet this point; its conclusion will then be, not that the circular men only prove that if P then P, but that all they do is to 'prove' P on the basis of P.

Finally, nothing in Aristotle's argument shows that the circular men "say *nothing more* than that if A is the case A is the case". Aristotle is trying to express the principle that if someone claims to prove A on the assumption that B and at the same time B on the assumption that A, then all he is doing is showing that A holds on the assumption that it does hold. But Aristotle does not succeed in expressing, let alone in supporting, this principle.

73^{a}6: The *third argument* attaches closely to *APr* B 5–7; A, B, C resume their normal role as term-variables. Aristotle argues that circular demonstration requires convertible propositions (cf. *APr* B 5, 57^{b}32–58^{a}15), and that these are rare in demonstrative sciences; hence at most a few circular demonstrations will be possible in any science. Aristotle's argument is again muddy; its soundness is easily seen if we take a typical small circle: starting from (i) AaB, (ii) BaC, (iii) CaA, we first infer (a) AaC from (i) and (ii), (b) BaA from (ii) and (iii), and (c) CaB from (iii) and (i); then we join the circle by inferring (i) from (a) and (c), (ii) from (b) and (a), and (iii) from (c) and (b). Thus each of (a), (b), and (c) is convertible. (A and B 'convert' (*antistrephein*)—in the commonest sense of that term—or are 'counterpredicated' (*antikatēgoreisthai*: 73^a16) if they 'follow one another', i.e. if both *AaB* and *BaA*. On other uses of *antistrephein* see Ross, 293.) See also BARNES (1981), 38–40.

73^a7: ". . . as properties do": in Aristotle's stricter usage, the notion of a property is defined thus:

(14) *A* is a property of *B* = _{df} (i) ($\forall x$) (necessarily: *Ax* if and only if *Bx*) & (ii) *A* is not part of the essence of *B*.

(*Top A* 5, 102^a18–30). In a laxer usage, condition (ii) is dropped.

73^a8: ". . . I have proved . . .": see *APr A* 25, 41^b36–42^a40 (the commentators offer alternative references); the view is in fact built into Aristotle's definition of *sullogismos* (p. 83).

73^a9: ". . . nor if a single posit . . .": i.e. '. . . nor if only one proposition is premissed'.

73^a14: ". . . as I have proved in my account of deduction": i.e. at *APr B* 5–7. The report is slightly misleading (see p. 106).

73^a16: "or else none concerning the assumptions": In the second figure, one of the premisses and the conclusion are always negative. Hence— since a pair of negative propositions never yields a syllogistic conclusion— there can be no syllogism to the other premiss and therefore no syllogistic circles. The same holds for *Felapton* in the third figure. In four of the remaining third figure moods one of the premisses and the conclusion are particular. Hence—since two particular propositions never yield a syllogistic conclusion—there can be no syllogism to the other premiss and therefore no syllogistic circles. *Darapti* remains. Here you cannot get a syllogism "concerning the assumptions", i.e. you cannot infer from the conclusion and one of the premisses to the other premiss. But you *can* get a syllogistic conclusion from any two of the three components of *Darapti*, granted convertibility. (*Darapti* is:

PaR, *SaR*: therefore *PiS*.

Convert *PiS* and *PaR*, and you will get:

SiP, *RaP*: therefore *SiR*

—which is *Disamis*. Convert *SaR*, and you will get:

PiS, *RaS*: therefore *PiR*

—which is again *Disamis*.)

CHAPTER 4

A 4–6 take up the second of the two necessary conditions laid on understanding at *A* 2, 71^b9–16; the argument starts from the inference that "if there is understanding *simpliciter* of something, it is impossible for it to be otherwise" (71^b16).

73^a21: If **a** knows *X*, *X* cannot be otherwise; hence if **a** knows *X* by demonstration, *X* cannot be otherwise; and hence (cf. *Int* 13, 22^b6–7), if

a knows X by demonstration, X is necessary (cf. *EN Z* 3, 1139^{b}19–23). Aristotle next infers that if **a** demonstrates X from Y, then Y is necessary. This seems to commit him to the view that if P is necessary and P is deducible from Q, then Q is necessary; and he knew this view to be false (*A* 6, 75^{a}2–4).

One way of escape is to suppose that Aristotle is tacitly assuming that the premisses of a demonstration must be known; for if they are known they are necessary. Certainly, Aristotle would be justified in arguing in this way; but it is hard to read the argument into the text.

A second approach points out that Aristotle never satisfactorily distinguishes between propositions which express truths which are necessary (e.g. "Every man is an animal") and propositions which express the necessity of certain truths (e.g. "Necessarily: every man is an animal"). We might suppose that, properly speaking, demonstrative conclusions are of the latter form (their medium is the apodeictic syllogism of *APr A* 8). In that case, Aristotle's argument for the necessity of demonstrative premisses will rely on the very plausible rule that if $\square$ P is deducible from Q then Q is of the form $\square$ R. (The box, "$\square$", abbreviates "necessarily".) This rule, however, is a special case of the scholastic adage *peiorem semper conclusio sequitur partem*; and, notoriously, Aristotle did not accept this rule (*APr A* 9, 30^{a}15–25—there is no good evidence that Aristotle changed his mind about the rule). Moreover, we should not in fact suppose that demonstrative conclusions must be of the form $\square$ P (see p. xxi).

Aristotle has not got a decent argument here; *A* 6 returns to the issue.

73^{a}25: The rest of the chapter gives a rigorous expansion of the common Aristotelian slogan that 'knowledge is of the universal' (cf. e.g. *A* 33, 88^{b}31; *An B* 5, 417^{b}22; *Met M* 9, 1086^{b}5; *EN Z* 6, 1140^{b}31).

73^{a}26: "First let us define . . .": It is helpful to bear in mind the grammatical contexts of Aristotle's three phrases, viz.: (i) "A is said *of every* B" (*kata pantos*), (ii) "A is said of B *in itself*" (*kath' hauto*—more fully: "in virtue of itself"), and (iii) "A is said *universally* of B" (*katholou*). In (ii) the reference of "itself" (in Greek as in English) may be either to A or to B; the parallel with (i) and (iii) suggest that B is intended, but later paragraphs perhaps show that Aristotle was prepared to take it in either way. Both (i) and (iii) are standard Aristotelian ways of expressing the universally quantified proposition that every B is A: here in *A* 4, *kata pantos* is used in a slightly non-standard way; *katholou* is defined in a fashion I think is unique (but perhaps see *Met Δ* 9, 1017^{b}35). Another strange use of *katholou* is introduced at *B* 17, 99^{a}34.

73^{a}28: "We say 'is predicated of every' when one cannot take anything of which the other term will not be said; and 'of none' similarly" (*APr A* 1, 24^{b}28–30). In our passage, the first part of the definition is "Not-(some B is A and some B is not A)", and that is equivalent to "Either AaB or AeB". But 73^{a}32–4 show that Aristotle means "of every" to have the sense he gave it in *APr A* 1.

The second, temporal, clause in the definition (cf. *A* 8; *A* 31, 87ᵇ30–3; *B* 12, 96ᵃ9–19) is explained by *APr A* 15, 34ᵇ7–18: the "is" in "Every *B* is *A*" must not be taken elliptically for "is now"—it is a 'timeless' use of the present tense. Aristotle's 'evidence' is designed to show that the timeless reading is the normal one, at least in argumentative syllogistic contexts; but elsewhere (e.g. *Top E* 1) he distinguishes between "*A* holds of every *B*" and "*A* always holds of *B*". (See also *APr B* 26, 69ᵇ5–8.)

73ᵃ34: Aristotle now distinguishes four ways in which *A* can hold of *B* 'in itself'; only the first two are directly relevant to the characterization of demonstrative propositions (cf. 73ᵇ16–18; *A* 6, 74ᵇ7–10; *A* 22, 84ᵃ12–17), but the third has a central role in the argument of *A* 22. *Met Δ* 18, 1022ᵃ24–36, discerns five uses of "in itself"; only one of these has a clear counterpart in our passage (1022ᵃ27–9 = 73ᵃ34–7: but see Kirwan, 168–9).

Aristotle's account of *the first two uses* of "in itself" is not elegant (see Ross, 520); but it fairly plainly yields the following two definitions:

(1) *A* holds of *B* in itself = ₓₑ *A* holds of *B* and *A* inheres in the definition of *B*;

(2) *A* holds of *B* in itself = ₓₑ *A* holds of *B* and *B* inheres in the definition of *A*.

"In the first case, the subject takes the predicate into its definition; in the second, the predicate takes the subject into its definition" (Philoponus). In (1) "itself" certainly refers to *B* (*B*s are *A* *in virtue of their being B*); in (2) "itself" may perhaps refer to *A* (*B*s are *A* *in virtue of A*). The term *ousia* here evidently amounts to "essence" (see further, p. 177; cf. p. 174 on "what it is").

It is useful to have some brief terminology for referring to these uses of "in itself": A proposition is an *I-predication* if (i) it is of the form "Every *B* is *A*", and (ii) it is true in virtue of the fact that *A* holds of *B* in itself. The proposition is an *I1*-predication if "in itself" is to be taken in sense (1), an *I2*-predication if "in itself" is to be taken in sense (2). There are puzzles in connection with both definitions.

At *Met Δ* 18, 1022ᵃ27, (1) is illustrated by "Callias is a man in himself" ("itself" becomes "himself", and the gender makes the reference plain: cf. *Met Z* 4, 1029ᵇ15); "Animal holds of man in itself" will do equally well, and avoids the ticklish question of the place of singular terms in syllogistic. This suggests that an *I1*-predication is true if and only if every *B* is *A* and *Ba* = ₓₑ *P* & *Aa* (where *P* is any proposition). *I1*-predications are thus, in the Kantian sense, analytic; whether they are what Locke called trifling propositions will depend upon what sort of definition Aristotle has in mind here.

The examples in *A* 4 do not fit this mould easily: "line of triangles and point of lines" seems to give the unpromising candidates "All triangles are lines" and "All lines are points". Some think that, in Academic fashion, Aristotle supposes an 'ontological' dependency of lines on points (cf. e.g. *Met Δ* 8, 1017^{b}18–20; *N* 3, 1090^{b}5–7), and infers a definitional dependency (cf. *Top Z* 4, 141^{b}15–22). Others imagine that Aristotle confuses "*A* is mentioned in the definition of *B*" (which does hold of line and triangle) with "*Ba* = $_{df}$ *P* & *Aa*" (which does not). Philoponus reads "shape of triangles" for "line of triangles", and invokes the non-Aristotelian definition of *line* as *flowing point* (cf. *An A* 4, 409^{a}4; Proclus, *Comm in Eucl* 97. 8–13). Zabarella exhorts us to take the examples *sano modo*: "line" is elliptical for "contained by a line", "point" for "bounded by a point" (cf. Bonitz, 578^{a}1–3; Euclid, i def. 3).

In definition (2), the second conjunct of the *definiens* does not cause such difficulties: number, say, is 'in the definition of odd' inasmuch as "*a* is odd" = $_{df}$ "*a* is a number not divisible by 2" (cf. *Top I* 13, 173^{b}8). (Composite numbers are non-primes; equilaterals are squares; oblongs are non-squares: cf. *Theaet* 147^e–148^b; Euclid, viii def. 16–18). Compare *Met Z* 5, 1030^{b}18–26: ". . . and neither concavity nor snubness is an affection of the nose *incidentally*, but they hold of it in itself—not as whiteness holds of Callias or of a man . . . but as maleness of animal and equality of quantity and every thing which is said to hold of something in itself. These are the things in which there inheres either the account or the name of that of which this is the affection and which cannot be made clear separately—as whiteness can be without man, but not femaleness without animal" (cf. *Phys A* 2, 186^{b}18–23).

What examples can we find of I2-predications? The best case is given at *B* 16, 98^{b}22, where *eclipse* is predicated of *the earth's being in the middle*, and the latter term "inheres in the account" of the former: *AaB*, and *B* is in the definition of *A*. (The truth of the example is another, irrelevant, matter.) Aristotle's examples in *A* 4 are more puzzling. He can hardly have meant such trivial falsehoods as "Every number is odd", "Every line is straight". Perhaps we should think rather of disjunctive predications such as "Every number is either odd or even", "Every line is either straight or curved". This suggestion appears to receive support from 73^{b}19–21 (see notes), *A* 12, 78^{a}16–21, and *A* 22, 84^{a}20 (see notes). Nevertheless, such disjunctive examples are not easily read into 73^{a}37–40, still less into 1030^{b}18–26; they do not seem to 'say one thing of one thing' (cf. *A* 2, 72^{a}9); and they are likely to be, at best, rare in the sciences. (The only examples of disjunctive predicates in syllogistic that I have found are at *APr A* 31, 46^{b}3–19, 30–5; 46, 51^{b}39–41; 52^{a}34–7; *B* 22, 68^{a}3–16.) Retaining the simple predicate "odd", we might try taking not number but a kind of number as subject—e.g. "Every product of odd and odd is odd". But there is no smell of this in the text.

The older commentators take I2-predicates to include properties (see *A* 3, 73^{a}7, note), and properties to include 'in itself incidentals' (see also KULLMANN (1974), 182–3). The queerly named 'in itself incidentals' are defined as follows: "Things are called incidental in another way too—i.e. what holds of a thing in itself without being in its essence, e.g. having two right angles of triangle" (*Met Δ* 30, 1025^{a}30–2). Predicates of this sort, holding of a subject in itself yet not inhering in its essence, are the staple of demonstration (see *A* 7, 75ᵇ2; cf. Bonitz, 713ᵇ43–714ᵃ3). Hence the suggestion that I2-predicates are, or at least include, 'in itself incidentals' is an attractive one. But it will not do: "being capable of understanding" is proper to man; but "All men are capable of understanding" is not an I2-predication. Again, being deciduous is an 'in itself incidental' of vines, but not a property of them. The suggestion does, however, point to a major deficiency in Aristotle's discussion in *A* 4: the chapter does not elucidate the crucial notion of an 'in itself incidental'.

It has also been suggested that *differentiae* are I2-predicates of their genera, so that, e.g., *mortal* is an I2-predicate of *animal* (e.g. GRANGER (1981); FEREJOHN (1981), 291–2; (1991), 96–9). Presumably not all I2-predicates are *differentiae* (e.g. *male* is presumably an I2-predicate of *animal*, but it is not a *differentia*). On the other hand, some *differentiae* are certainly I2-predicates (e.g. *odd* and *even*). But Aristotle nowhere says that all *differentiae* are I2-predicates; and the fact that he sometimes takes *differentiae* to entail their *genus* (i.e. if *D* is a *differentia* of *G*, then *D*a entails *G*a) does not in itself show that *differentiae* are I2-predicates.

I have been assuming that all I-predications are *universal*. It has recently been urged that I2-predications are (typically) *particular* propositions: "Some numbers are odd", "Some triangles are isosceles". (See FEREJOHN (1991), 99–108.) This proposal has one evident advantage: it allows us to produce, without difficulty, *true* I2-predications which (unlike the disjunctive examples I mentioned earlier) might well be thought to feature in the sciences. It has a disadvantage: there is no hint in the text that I2-predications are particular; and in any case it is only universal propositions which Aristotle will allow into the sciences.

73ᵇ5: *The third use* of "in itself" distinguishes things that are (exist) in themselves, i.e. in their own right or independently, from things that exist 'incidentally'. It is sometimes said that Aristotle here leaves logic and turns to ontology; but this 'ontological' use of "in itself" is founded on considerations of predication.

It is convenient to discuss here all the passages in *APst* which bear on the matter; they are identifiable by the occurrence of the difficult phrase "things which are so-and-so in virtue of being something different": *A* 4, 73ᵇ5–10; *A* 13, 79ᵃ6; *A* 19, 81ᵇ25–9; *A* 22, 83ᵃ1–23; 83ᵃ30–2; 83ᵇ23 (cf. *Met A* 6, 987ᵇ23; *B* 4, 1001ᵃ6, 10, 28; *N* 1, 1087ᵃ33, 35; 1088ᵃ28; *Phys A* 4, 188ᵃ8). From *A* 19 and 22 it emerges that the phrase helps to mark a distinction between two types of predication, which the ancient commentators conveniently named 'natural' and 'unnatural' predication. If the proposition *X is Y* is 'natural' Aristotle will say that *Y* is predicated of *X* (82ᵃ20; 83ᵃ15), or that *Y* is predicated *simpliciter* of *X* (83ᵃ16), or that *Y* is predicated of *X* in itself (81ᵇ29); of 'unnatural' predications Aristotle will say that *Y* is not predicated of *X* at all (83ᵃ15), or that *Y* is incidental to *X* (82ᵃ20), or that *Y* is predicated of *X* incidentally (81ᵇ24; 83ᵃ8, 15; cf. *APr A* 27, 43ᵃ34).

Aristotle gives as examples of natural predication: "The man is walking" (83^a3), "The log is large" (83^a3), "The log is white" (83^a9); and as examples of unnatural predication: "The walking thing is walking" (73^b6), "The white thing is white" (73^b7), "The white thing is walking" (83^a2), "That large thing is a log" (83^a2), "The white thing is a log" (83^a5), "The musical thing is white" (83^a11). (Cf. "That white thing is Socrates"; "What approaches is Callias": *APr A* 27, 43^a35.)

The distinction is marked by a variety of formulae:

Natural	Unnatural
(A) "*X* is *Y*" does not mean "something different is *Y*, and that thing happens to be *X*" (83^a10).	
(B) *X* is *Y* without being anything different (73^b8; 79^a6; 83^a13, 32, $^b23$; 987^b23; 1001^a6, 10; 188^a8).	*X*, being something different, is *Y* (73^b6; 1087^a35; 1088^a28).
(C)	"*X* is *Y*" means "That which happens to be *X* is *Y*" (83^a6).
(D) *X* is not said of any other underlying subject (73^b5; cf. 1001^a28; 188^a8).	*X* is said of another underlying subject (73^b9; 1087^a35).
(E) *X* is the underlying subject for *Y* (83^a13).	*X* is not an underlying subject for *Y* (83^a6).
(F) Being *X*, it came to be *Y* (83^a13).	It is not the case that being *X* it came to be *Y* (83^a7).
(G) *X* is a substance (987^b23; 1001^a10, 28).	

(A) allows us to infer that if *X is Y* is unnatural it means "something different is *Y* and that thing happens to be *X*". By "something different" Aristotle means "something different *from just what is X or some particular X*" (see 83^a14). Thus we can define unnatural predication as follows:

(3) *X is Y* is unnatural $=_{df}$ "*X* is *Y*" means "For some *Z* distinct from *X*, *Z* is *Y* and it happens that *Z* is *X*.

The force of "it happens that *Z* is *X*" is "it is not essential that *Z* is *X*"; hence the stipulation that *Z* is distinct from *X* is otiose. The predication, *Z is Y*, may be either essential or non-essential; in the analysis of "The white thing is a man" it will presumably be essential—e.g. "Socrates is a man"; in the analysis of "The white thing is walking" it will be non-essential—e.g. "Socrates is walking". If (3) is simplified, and if the relation of meaning is replaced by entailment (which may indeed be all Aristotle intends), then we can say that *X is Y* is unnatural if and only if:

(4) If *X* is *Y* then $(\exists Z) ((Z$ is *Y*) & (it happens that *Z* is *X*)).

I take it that formula (C) and the commonest formula, (B), are merely abbreviated ways of expressing (A).

(D) and (E) express two supposed corollaries of (A): the subjects of unnatural predications turn out to be dependent entities in two ways.

First, (D). It is true that (D) might be taken to express the trivial consequence of (4), that if X *is* Y is an unnatural predication then:

(5) If X is Y then $(\exists Z)$ (Z is X)

—for this amounts to saying that X is predicated of something, or "said of another underlying subject". But Aristotle means to say something more, viz. that the subject of an unnatural predication is ontologically parasitic on other entities. How is this claim connected with what has been said so far?

It is often supposed that Aristotle was taken in by an ambiguity in his examples: *to leukon estin anthrōpos*, which I translate "the white thing is a man", can also mean "whiteness is a man" (in general, *to A* in Greek does duty both for "the *A*" and for "*A*-ness"). Failing to see this ambiguity, Aristotle imagined that the subject of an unnatural predication was always an abstract, and hence a dependent, entity. This reconstruction is made implausible by the fact that the ambiguity is not present in all Aristotle's examples of unnatural predications; moreover, at *Met Z* 6, 1031^{b}25, the existence of such ambiguities is explicitly noticed. Perhaps Aristotle supposed that if X *is* Y is an unnatural predication, then X *is existent* is also an unnatural predication; hence if X *is* Y is an unnatural predication then:

(6) If X is existent then $(\exists Z)$ (Z is X),

and this might be taken as a formulation of ontological parasitism.

(E) is supported by (F). The term "underlying subject" (*to hupokeimenon*) is often said to be systematically ambiguous in Aristotle between a *logical* subject of predication and a *metaphysical* substratum for change. And the ambiguity is exploited in our passages if anywhere; for in (F), and hence in (E), the *hupokeimenon* grounds changes, while in (D) it grounds predication. How far Aristotle is trapped by this ambiguity, and indeed how far it is vicious, are large questions that cannot be entered into here.

There are problems enough with (F). Aristotle can hardly be meaning to remark upon what changes in fact take place; for white things sometimes become statues (say), although "the white thing is a statue" is an unnatural predication. *A fortiori*, Aristotle's remark is not about the logical impossibility of white things' becoming statues, or the linguistic impropriety of our saying that they do. If Aristotle has a point at all, it must, I think, be this: the subjects of unnatural predications cannot be self-standing starting-points of change; if we do say "That white thing became a statue" our remark only makes sense if it is taken as elliptical for something like "That block of marble, which is white, became a statue". (F) might be an inference from (D): if the subjects of unnatural predications cannot exist without the existence of something to 'support' them, then plainly they cannot exist as independent starting-points of change.

Finally, (G) is simply a restatement of (D).

In sum, then, we can say this. If *X is Y* is a natural predication, then (*a*) *X is Y* does not entail that something else is *Y* and happens to be *X*; (*b*) *X* is not ontologically dependent on anything else; and (*c*) *X* is an independently identifiable subject of change. The latter two points are probably supposed to be inferences from (*a*). And in the third use of "in itself", *X* is or exists in itself if *X is Y* is never an unnatural predication.

73^{b}10: We may now turn to *the fourth use* of "in itself". If *X* and *Y* occur at the same time, yet neither occurs because of the other, then we may say something like "they just happened to coincide", and the Greeks, according to Aristotle, would say *sunebē*, "it was incidental" (see further *Met Δ* 30, 1025^{a}4–30; what is 'incidental' is, as 73^{b}15 shows, the *conjunction* of *X* and *Y*—cf. *APr A* 13, 32^{b}12). Since "incidentally" may thus signify the absence of explanatory connection, "in itself" may do the opposite job and mark the presence of such a connection. "In general, that in virtue of which (*to kath' ho*) will hold in as many ways as the explanation" (*Met Δ* 18, 1022^{a}19–20); in other words, the 'fourth use' of "in itself" is properly a use of *kata X* in general, and not of *kath' hauto* in particular. The example at 73^{b}14 ("*in* the sacrifice", i.e. 'in virtue of the sacrifice') implicitly concedes the point.

The fourth use involves a connection between *events*: "E_1 occurs *kata* E_2". Nevertheless, Aristotle introduces it in the language of predication or 'holding'. If he supposed that E_1 and E_2 were always expressible by sentences of the form "**a** is *F*" and "**a** is *G*", and if he plausibly took "**a** is *F* in virtue of being *G*" to entail "Every *G* is *F*", then he may reasonably have passed from "E_1 occurs *kata* E_2" to "*F* holds of *G* in itself".

73^{b}16: 73^{b}16–18 plainly refers to I1- and I2-predications. The phraseology has caused difficulty. The solution (see MIGNUCCI (1975), 75–6) is that Aristotle here uses *tois katēgoroumenois* ("what is predicated") to refer to the *subject* terms of the propositions. The verb *katēgorein* sometimes means "to apply a predicate to" (e.g. *APr A* 32, 47^{b}1; perhaps *APst A* 22, 83^{b}1), so that *ta katēgoroumena* are the items to which predicates are applied.

Aristotle says nothing to justify the claim that in I-predications *A* holds of *B* 'because of itself'. Presumably he is relying on the fact that, if *A* is in the definition of *B*, then a thing's being *A* explains its being *B* (in the sense of giving a 'formal' explanation: see, e.g. *Phys B* 3, 194^{b}26–9).

In I-predications *A* holds necessarily of *B* "either *simpliciter* or as regards the opposites". "*Simpliciter*" presumably refers to I1-predications, where it is taken as evident that necessarily every *B* is *A*. "As regards the opposites" then refers to I2-predications, and must mean that necessarily every *B* is either *A* or *A'* (where *A'* is the opposite of *A*). Aristotle has an argument for this. He needs to show that:

(7) (∀*x*) (if *Bx*, then (*Ax* or *A'x*))

is necessarily true, given that *A* and *A'* include *B* in their definitions.

One of his premisses is some version of the Law of Excluded Middle (73^{b}23); the other premiss is illustrated by the sentence "even is what is not odd among numbers, in so far as it follows". I take this to mean: 'Even follows what is not odd among numbers'; i.e. 'If **a** is a number, then if **a** is not odd, **a** is even' (cf. e.g. *Met I* 4, 1055^{b}23–6). Thus the premiss is:

(8) ($\forall x$) (if Bx then (if not Ax, then $A'x$)).

From this (7) is readily derived, by means (if you like) of the Law of Excluded Middle.

An I2-predication, then, will be necessary inasmuch as some proposition such as

Every number is either odd or even

is necessary. And there are two difficulties here. First, unless all I2-predications actually are disjunctive in this way, then it is hard to see how they can be said to be necessary at all. Secondly, even if I2-predications are disjunctive, it is hard to see what their status as I2-predications has to do with their necessity. There is indeed a definitory link in them between subject and predicate, and they are indeed necessary. But these are two independent facts; and in particular, their necessity plainly does not depend upon the fact that their subject terms (in whole or in part) inhere in the definitions of their predicate terms. (See also SORABJI (1980), 188–9.)

73^{b}21: It seems clear that Aristotle means to argue as follows: 'Odd is contrary to, or a privation of, even. But contraries and privations are contradictories within their kind (i.e. if F and G are contraries within a kind K, then every element of K is either F or G). But of contradictories, necessarily one or the other holds. Hence of contrary pairs F and G, necessarily one or the other holds (within K).' The received text will not yield this argument; and I can no see no other plausible argument in it. Hence I suggest a minor emendation.

73^{b}23: "... if it is necessary to assert ...": i.e. 'if A holds of $\dot{B}$ in itself, then A holds necessarily of B'; but Aristotle expresses this remarkably badly.

73^{b}25: The rest of A 4 elucidates a singular sense of "universally" (*katholou*). The sense has three components: first, "of every case"; secondly, "in itself" (either in use (1) or in use (2): 73^{b}30); and thirdly, "as such". It follows from this definition and the argument at 73^{b}16 that what is 'universal' is necessary (73^{b}28).

The idiom of "as such" or *qua* (*hēi*) is worked hard throughout Aristotle's philosophical writings (Bonitz, 312^{a}36–44; Wieland, 197–202). It was a piece of Academic jargon; Aristotle's mathematical contemporaries may have held that their theorems should be 'as such' predications (cf. Philip, in Proclus, *Comm in Eucl* 305. 25; cf. 254. 2–3).

Most of the Aristotelian passages might reasonably be used to support the suggestion that A holds of B as such if and only if there is no term C

which explains why A holds of B—in short, if and only if AaB is immediate. Clearly, if AaB is an I-predication, then A holds of B as such; and conversely—though not so clearly—if A holds of B as such, then AaB is an I-predication. (If it were not, then B would have a property not derivable from its essence; but the essence of B is precisely that from which all B's properties are derivable.) Hence being an I-predication and holding as such are logically equivalent, or "the same thing" ($73^{b}29$). (The commentators have worried unnecessarily about this.)

In some passages, however, predicates which are not I-predicates are said to hold as such (e.g. *Top* E 4, $132^{b}2$; $133^{a}30$, $^{b}5$). And the example at $73^{b}31$, despite the implication of the context, must be numbered among these; for *having 2 R* is not an I-predicate of *triangle* (cf. p. 120). To grasp what is happening here we must anticipate some of the theses of *A* 7 and *A* 10. Those chapters suggest that the terms of a demonstrative science fall into two classes: one class lists the genus being studied together with its species, sub-species, etc. (e.g. *animal, carnivore, cat, lion* . . .), the other lists the attributes of the first class (e.g. *being four-footed, having a single stomach, being warm-blooded* . . .). The first class can be set out as a Porphyrean tree; linearly arranged, it will look like this:

$$(\varSigma) \quad G, \; S^0_1, \; S^0_2, \; \ldots, \; S^1_1, \; S^1_2, \; \ldots, \; \ldots, \; S^n_1, \; S^n_2, \; \ldots, \; S^n_m.$$

Here G is the genus, the S^0_is the species, and so on down to the *infimae species*, the S^n_is. Now to say that A holds of S^k_i as such is to say that AaS^k_i and there is no p smaller than k such that AaS^p_j.

The triangle example is plainly an 'as such' predication of this sort, if at all; and it is this type of predication which is discussed, under the title of 'primitiveness', at $73^{b}32-74^{a}3$. But in this sense, 'as such' predications need not be immediate and hence are not necessarily I-predications.

$73^{b}32$: This paragraph either gives a new definition of "universally"; or (better) provides, under the alias of "primitiveness", an elucidation of the term "as such"; or (best) explains how we are to set about *proving* that A holds universally of B, in the sense just defined.

The first condition for such a proof, that A be shown to hold of an arbitrary B, reappears in natural deduction systems of predicate logic: if I can prove Fa for some arbitrary individual **a**, then I may infer $(\forall x) \; Fx$. The criteria for arbitrariness are, of course, precisely specified in modern systems, whereas Aristotle leaves the notion on an intuitive level.

The second condition, that A be proved of B primitively, has no counterpart in modern logic, since it derives from the idiosyncratic elements in *A* 4's notion of universality.

A recipe for universal proof will thus read as follows. Construct the tree $(\varSigma)$. First attempt to prove A of any arbitrary G; if this attempt fails, do the same with each S^0_i; then with each S^1_i; and so on. The first term for which the attempted proof does not fail is the term of which A holds universally. (What if A holds of S^k_i and also of S^k_j but not of any S^p_i

where p is smaller than k? Aristotle does not, I think, consider this possibility here; some of the argument in B 17–18 bears on the matter: see below.)

74^{a}1: "and the demonstration applies to it universally in itself": "in itself" must be taken as equivalent to "as such". Thus: 'Suppose A belongs primitively to S_i^p and derivatively to S_i^k and to S_j^k. Then you can demonstrate A universally of S_i^p as such; but when you demonstrate A of S_i^k and of S_j^k you will not be demonstrating A of S_i^k as such, nor of S_j^k as such—e.g. you won't demonstrate 2 R of isosceles *as such*.' (For a completely different paraphrase see Mure.)

The general thrust of A 4 is clear enough. Aristotle starts from the fact that the objects of understanding—and hence of demonstrative understanding—are necessary; and he asks, in effect, what is the ground of their necessity. He answers that the necessity is ultimately grounded in essential or definitional connections. The elaboration of this answer is thick with difficulties of detail. There is also one major problem: is Aristotle talking about the principles of demonstrative understanding, or about demonstrated theorems, or about both? Aristotle's text is ambiguous. On the one hand, the connection between A 4 and the definition of *understanding* in A 2 implies that it is the necessity of the *conclusion* of a demonstration which Aristotle wants to illuminate: the end of A 4 and the whole argument of A 5 satisfy this implication. On the other hand, the programmatic remarks at 73^{a}25 and the argument of A 6 imply that it is a further feature of demonstrative *principles* which is under consideration. Finally, A 6, 75^{a}29–30, says explicitly that *both premisses and conclusions* are I-predications.

Consider the following propositions, all of which we may suppose to be connected with the science of geometry:

(1) Every triangle is a three-sided rectilineal plane figure.
(2) Every isosceles is a triangle with exactly two equal sides.
(3) Every triangle has three sides.
(4) Every triangle has an angle-sum of 180°.
(5) Every isosceles has an angle-sum of 180°.

Let us suppose, plausibly, that (1) and (2) are among the *principles* of geometry. It is certain that (4) is among the *theorems* of geometry. What of (3) and (5)? We might reasonably expect that both these propositions are also *theorems*: (3) is a theorem inasmuch as it is an utterly trifling consequence of (1); (5) is a theorem inasmuch as it is a trifling consequence of (2) and (4).

It is clear, too, that (1) and (2) are I1-predications: their predicates inhere in—indeed, they constitute—the definition of their subjects. It is equally clear that (3) is an I-predication, and also that (5) is not an I-predication. What of (4)? This sentence appears frequently and in many different contexts as the paradigm of a demonstrable truth; and Aristotle calls it an 'in itself incidental'. Yet surely it is not an I1-predication; for the *definition* of what a triangle is will not advert explicitly to its angle-sum. Equally surely, it is not an I2-predication; for the definition of what it is to have an angle-sum of 180° will not contain any reference to triangles (or to any other sort of figure). (On the problems raised by (4) see TILES (1983).)

Hence we might conclude that the particular type of predication ana-lysed in *A* 4 straddles the distinction between principles and theorems. More precisely, certain I-predications are included among the principles of any science, namely, those I-predications which are primitive in the sense that they cannot be derived from higher I-predications. (And perhaps *all* principles are I-predications? But nothing assures us of this; and the status of the common axioms, and of the suppositions, might lead us to doubt it.) Other I-predications—namely, derivable I-predications—are included among the theorems. But the theorems will also include numerous propositions which, while being deducible from I-predications, are not themselves I-predications. Among these further theorems will be the relevant 'in itself incidentals' (all or at any rate some of them), which are by definition not I1-predications and which in fact are not—or at least not always—I2-predications.

This is perhaps a coherent and even a reasonable position. But it cannot be pretended that Aristotle expressly adopts it. Thus we might well wish that he had said something about those demonstrative pro-positions which are *not* I-predications. (The most we get is the hint, at 74ᵃ1–3, that there will be a demonstration of (5) "in another way, not in itself".) More specifically, we shall have to accuse Aristotle of a straightforward error when he says that (4) is 'universal', and therefore an I-predication. (But on any account of *A* 4, this is an error.) Again, the position is not consistent with the thesis that the logic of the sciences must be thoroughly syllogistic. For, within syllogistic, *no* 'as such' predications can be proved. Any predication of this sort will be a universal affirmative of the form *AaB*. Hence it can only be proved syllogistically in *Barbara*. Hence there must be a prior premiss *CaB*. Hence *B* will not belong to *A* as such.

Perhaps we should distinguish between two types of demonstrable proposition (and two types of demonstration)? Thus '*A*-type' demon-strations conclude to propositions like (5), which are not I-predications in any sense; whereas '*B*-type' demonstrations conclude to I-predications. (The distinction is made by LENNOX (1987), 90–7: he illustrates the two different types of demonstration with examples drawn from the biological works; and he suggests that the distinction itself is alluded to at *B* 17, 99ᵃ21–9.) Sometimes Aristotle is happy to regard *A*-type demonstrations as decent scientific proofs (e.g. *B* 14, 98ᵃ8–12); but sometimes—and most clearly in *A* 4—he takes *B*-type demonstrations to be the paradigm of scientific proof.

And yet the difficulty remains: how can the conclusion of *any* demon-stration be an I-predication? Consider a demonstration of the form

$AaB, BaC \vdash AaC.$

If *AaC* is an I1-predication, then *A* holds of *C* in virtue of itself, i.e. in virtue of the fact that *C*s are *C*. Yet in so far as *AaC* is proved from *AaB* and *BaC*, *A* holds of *C* in virtue of *B*. It is true that if we have a *B*-type demonstration that *AaC*, then *A* does not hold of *C* because it holds of some higher kind, *B*, of which *C* is a sort. Perhaps it is then true that *B* is "an aspect of the subject's specific nature, i.e. something proper to it which makes it that sort of thing" (LENNOX (1987), 93). But from this we may not infer that *A* holds of *C* in itself. Admittedly, it is tempting to conclude that, *in a sense*, *A* holds of *C* in itself. But this conclusion will follow only if we introduce a new account of "in itself", along the following lines:

> *A* holds of *C* in itself if and only if (i) *AaC* and (ii) there is no higher kind, *K*, under which *C* falls such that *AaK*.

No doubt Aristotle does sometimes use "in itself" in this sense; but it is not a sense which he introduces in *A* 4.

Thus we may allow that the distinction between *A*-type and *B*-type demonstrations is genuine, and that it is made, implicitly at least, in Aristotle's biological writings. But it does not solve the main problem set by *A* 4.

These questions were discussed by the ancient commentators (see Alexander, *in APst* frag. 12; MORAUX (1979), 21–4); and they may well have been puzzled over by Theophrastus. In any event, he claimed, against Aristotle, that 'as such' and 'in itself' are not 'the same': rather, all 'as such' predications are I-predications, but not all I-predications are 'as such' predications. In particular, Theophrastus urged that (5) is an I-predication. (See Philoponus, 71. 4–13 = Theophrastus, frag. 34 Graeser.) Now plainly (5) is not an I-predication *in Aristotle's sense*, as Theophrastus must surely have seen. Hence we must infer that Theophrastus gave a new sense to I-predications. What this sense was we cannot guess; but it is reasonable to conjecture that it was designed to ensure that *all* scientific propositions, theorems as well as principles, may be classified as I-predications.

CHAPTER 5

A 5, an appendix to *A* 4, explains and illustrates three types of case in which we are prone to think we have shown that *A* holds universally of *B*, when in fact it does not; the three cases form a hierarchy of mounting heinousness.

The *first case* is described at 74^{a}7–8 and illustrated at 74^{a}16–17: if the only triangles we had met with were isosceles, we might come to believe that 2 R held universally of the isosceles (cf. *Met Z* 11, 1036^{b}1); for we would have no concept of *triangle* as such ("there is nothing higher we can take apart from the particular case"). This interpretation construes "particular" (*to kath' hekaston*) at 74^{a}8 as "species" (cf. above p. 83); others read it as "individual", leaving the first error unillustrated.

(At 74^a8 the received text reads: "the particular or the particulars". Zabarella excised "or the particulars"; see Ross, 525.)

The *second case* is stated at 74^a8–9 and illustrated at 74^a17–25 (cf. *B* 14, 98^a13–19). The general theory of proportion (Euclid, v) to which the illustration alludes (cf. *A* 24, 85^a36–^b1) had recently been discovered by Eudoxus (cf. Eudoxus D 30–57 Lasserre; Heath (2), 43–6). For comparable generalizations see Proclus, *Comm in Eucl* 390. 8–392. 19 and 67. 15 (on Theudius).

At *Met E* 1, 1026^a25–7, Aristotle refers to a "universal mathematics"; and this has rightly been taken as an allusion to the Eudoxan generalization (see G.-G. GRANGER (1976), 308–9). It has been thought (see e.g. KULLMANN (1981), 252–4) that the admission of such a 'universal' mathematics contradicts Aristotle's insistence on the distinctions between the specific mathematical sciences and his prohibition on 'kind crossing' (see *A* 7, notes). But there is no inconsistency here; and *Met E* 1 itself shows that Aristotle simultaneously held both that there was a universal mathematics and that there were distinct mathematical subsciences.

74^a18: "that proportion alternates": i.e. that $a:b::c:d$ if and only if $a:c::b:d$ (Euclid, v. 16).

74^a24: ". . . but as *this*": i.e. as quantities, or as magnitudes, which all numbers, lengths etc. are. (Euclid uses "magnitude", the Aristotelians "quantity" (cf. *Cat* 6, 4^b20–5); see Heath (2), 44).

The *third case* is stated at 74^a9–10 and illustrated by Euclid, i. 29 at 74^a13–16.

74^a9: "the proof applies to something which is in fact a partial whole": i.e. '*C*, of which *A* is proved, is actually a species of *B*, of which *A* holds universally'. *C* is a whole in so far as *AaC*, but partial with respect to *B* (i.e. a part of *B*: cf. *EN E* 4, 1130^a14).

74^a14: "because it holds of every perpendicular": i.e. 'Observing that all perpendiculars are parallel, we wrongly infer that *this* is what, in the strict sense, we demonstrate'.

In outline, Aristotle's illustration is clear enough. Take a straight line AB, and suppose that it is cut by a second straight line CD at E and by a third straight line FG at H, thus:

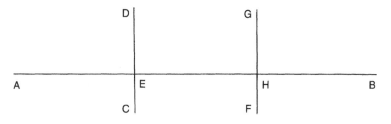

Now if the angles DEB and GHB are each 90°, you might prove that "perpendiculars do not meet", i.e. that CD and FG are parallel. But this is not a genuine demonstration; for the proof depends not on the fact that DEB and GHB are each 90° but, quite generally, on the fact that DEB = GHB.

The details, however, are obscure. (i) It is not clear exactly what theorem or exactly what proof Aristotle has in mind. (ii) The phrase *hai orthai* at 74^{a}13 might be taken as elliptical either for *hai orthai* ⟨*grammai*⟩ ("right lines", i.e. perpendiculars) or for *hai orthai* ⟨*gōniai*⟩ ("right angles"). In the former case—which my translation adopts—there is an inelegance at 74^{a}16, where "they are equal" must mean "the *angles* are equal". In the latter case there is an inelegance at 74^{a}13, where "right angles do not meet" must be taken to mean "⟨a pair of lines cutting another line at⟩ right angles do not meet". See MIGNUCCI (1975), 94–6.

74^{a}25: This section is commonly taken to present a second illustration of the second case of error; but the species of triangle do not lack a common name.

We are to suppose that a man has proved something of each of the three sorts of triangle. With some obvious abbreviations this is expressible as:

(1) **a** knows that: ($\forall x$) ($Ex \to Rx$) & **a** knows that: ($\forall x$) ($Sx \to Rx$) & **a** knows that: ($\forall x$) ($Ix \to Rx$).

Aristotle's point is simply that from (1) we can infer neither (74^{a}27):

(3) **a** knows that: ($\forall x$) ($Tx \to Rx$)

nor (74^{a}29):

(4) **a** knows that: (R holds universally of T).

Indeed, not even with the help of (74^{a}29):

(2) ($\forall x$) ($Tx \to (Ex$ or Sx or Ix))

can we infer either (3) or (4).

The connection of thought indicated by "for this reason" (74^{a}25) is opaque; perhaps it is this: '(4) cannot be inferred from (1); for **a** in (1) is to all intents and purposes in the same position as the pre-Eudoxan students of proportion'. But the analogy is not as close as this implies.

74^{a}31: "except in number...": Aristotle wants to distinguish two different ways in which you might be said to known of every triangle that it has 2 R. The second way must be the one represented by (3); there, **a** has knowledge in respect of the sort, triangle. The other way should be:

(5) ($\forall F$) (if F is a species of T, then **a** knows that: ($\forall x$) ($Fx \to Rx$)).

Unlike (3), (5) does follow from (1) and (2); so in *this*, 'sophistical' (cf. *A* 1, 71^{a}24) sense, someone of whom (1) holds *may* be said to know of every triangle that it has 2 R.

74^{a}32: The final paragraph of *A* 5 offers further elucidation of the issue discussed at *A* 4, 73^b32–74^a3. The argument assumes that *R* holds of *T* as such, and that **a** knows that *RaE*. Then **a** will have knowledge *simpliciter*, i.e. will know that *R* holds universally of *E* only if being *E* and being *T* are the same, i.e. only if "*E*" and "*T*" are synonymous. The qualification "(either for each or for all)" is puzzling. Since it would be absurd to think that "*T*" *always* meant "*E*", the sentence "if it were the same thing to be a triangle and to be equilateral" must be taken as a brachylogy; the qualification then offers two alternative expansions of the brachylogy, viz.: "*T*" means "*E*" and "*T*" means "*I*" and "*T*" means "*S*" ("for each": i.e. "*T*" is ambiguous); or: "*T*" means "*E* or *I* or *S*" ("for all"). (So Pacius; there are different suggestions in Mure and Ross.)

At 74^a37 Aristotle offers a recipe for discovering of what subject a given predicate holds universally and primitively. The text is unusually telegraphic. Aristotle supposes a sequence of terms of increasing generality, thus:

(Σ*) bronze isosceles, isosceles, triangle, figure, limit, . . .

He takes the predicate "has 2R" and asks of which member of the sequence it holds universally. His answer is this: 'Remove the members of (Σ*) one by one, beginning with the least general term. After a certain number of removals the predicate "has 2R" will no longer hold of all the items falling under the remaining terms. Take the *first* term after the removal of which "has 2R" no longer holds: "has 2R" holds universally of this term.'

The illustrative example at 74^a38–^b4 shows that this is Aristotle's meaning. But it is hard—perhaps impossible—to extract it from the received text of 74^a37–8. The text reads: the predicate holds universally "when, after the removal of items, it holds *prōtōi*". If we take "*prōtos*" here to mean "first", then Aristotle says the opposite of what he should say. If we take it to mean "primitive", then Aristotle's recipe is tautologous ('It holds primitively of the term of which it holds primitively')— and, in addition, the sense of "*prōtos*" changes from 74^a38 to 74^b2. Hence I prefer to take "*prōtos*" in the sense of "first", and to insert a negative particle before the verb.

74^b1: The last few sentences may then be paraphrased as follows: 'But *R* does not hold of any member of the series if *figure* and *limit* are abstracted.—But *figure* and *limit* are not the first terms after whose abstraction *R* fails to hold.—Then what *is* the first term after whose abstraction *R* fails to hold?—*Triangle*; and so *R* holds primitively of triangle.'

CHAPTER 6

A 6 first argues that demonstrative principles are I-predications; then offers four arguments to show that they are necessary propositions; and finally appends a number of loosely connected remarks.

74^{b}5: The argument that demonstrative principles are I-predications has four premisses:

(1) If P is demonstrated from Π, then Π is necessary.
(2) If Π is an I-predication, then Π is necessary.
(3) All propositions are either I-predications or incidental predications.
(4) No incidental predications are necessary.

This argument is valid, but unhappy. First, the conclusion follows from (1), (3), and (4) alone; and the text gives the impression of offering an *in*valid argument from (1) and (2) and hastily supplementing this by (3) and (4). Secondly, Aristotle cannot have both (3) and (4): (3) is true if "incidental" is defined as "non-I" (*A* 4, 73^{b}4); but then (4) is false, since predications of properties and 'in itself incidentals' are necessary but not I-predications. (4) is true if "incidental" is defined as "non-necessary" (*Top A* 5, 102^{b}6–7); but then (3) is false. Thirdly, (1) is supported by the assertion that "what you understand cannot be otherwise", which probably encapsulates the bad argument at *A* 4, 73^{a}21–4. (For "it holds in what it is", 74^{b}8, see *A* 22, 82^{b}37, note.)

74^{b}13: The paragraph begins as though it were about to present a further argument for the thesis that the principles are I-predications; but in fact it offers *the first argument* for (1). (1) is to be inferred from the posit that "demonstration is necessary", i.e. from:

(5) If P is demonstrated, P is necessary.

The inference is supported by:

(6) If P is inferred from Π, and Π is necessary, then P is demonstrated.

But (5) and (6) do not yield (1); and (6) is false.

74^{b}18: The *second argument* for (1) is similar in type to that at *A* 4, 73^{a}32. 'If someone claims to demonstrate that P by deducing it from Π, then we may object to the claim by urging that Π is not necessary— either that it is not in fact necessary or else that nothing has been done to show that it is necessary. Hence we suppose that the principles of a demonstration must be necessary.' Note that here, as often, Aristotle is content to argue from the actual practice of the sciences, and in particular from the way in which scientific argument is actually conducted.

74^{b}21: This paragraph constitutes a curious aside; we would expect the argument to run: 'It is silly to be satisfied with premisses which are merely reputable and true—for demonstrative principles must be necessary.' But in fact Aristotle appeals not to necessity but to primitiveness and appropriateness.

"Reputable", and not "probable" or "plausible", is the correct translation of *endoxos*; criteria for repute among propositions are laid down at *Top A* 1, 100^{b}21–3.

The sophists' assumption can be found in argumentative context at *Euthyd* 277^b; *Theaet* 197^a.

74^{b}26: The *third argument* for (1). Suppose I 'demonstrate' the necessary proposition *AaC* from non-necessary premisses: then I do not know why *AaC*; hence (cf. *A* 2, 71^{b}10–11) I do not understand *AaC*; hence (71^{b}18) I have not given a *demonstration* that *AaC*. Aristotle explains that if the premisses are contingent then *AaC* cannot hold because of them; thus he is committed to the general law that if *P* holds because *Q* holds, then if □ *P* then □ *Q*. Perhaps he is treating explanations as expressions of necessary as well as sufficient conditions: if *Q* is a necessary condition for *P*, then *P* implies *Q* and so if □ *P* then □ *Q*. Or perhaps it just seemed absurd to suppose that a contingent fact could be sufficient to account for a necessity.

74^{b}28: "If, in a case where there is a demonstration . . .": i.e. 'when *AaC* is in fact demonstrable'; or perhaps 'when a man has 'demonstrated'—i.e. thinks, wrongly, that he has demonstrated—that *AaC* (at 74^{b}30 "demonstrate" means "'demonstrate'").

74^{b}29: Does the supposition that "*B* . . . does not hold from necessity" mean that both *AaB* and *BaC* are contingent, or that just *BaC* is contingent? It is clear that Aristotle requires both premisses in a demonstration to be necessary; and that perhaps supports the view that his supposition is the contradictory of this, viz. that one premiss is not necessary. In that case the would-be demonstrator may be imagined to be offering a syllogism in *Barbara* of the form: □ *AaB*, *BaC* ⊦ □ *AaC*. Notoriously, Aristotle held this mood to be valid (*APr A* 9, 30^{a}15–23). This is a piquant thought, but perhaps too subtle; and 75^{a}4 favours the other reading of the supposition.

74^{b}32: The *fourth argument* for (1) relies on the complex premiss:

(7) If, where t_1 is earlier than t_2, (i) **a** does not know at t_2 that *P*, and (ii) both at t_1 and at t_2 **a** has a reason *R* for holding that *P*, and (iii) **a** was alive at t_1 and is alive at t_2, and (iv) *P* is true at t_1 and true at t_2, and (v) **a** has not forgotten that *P* between t_1 and t_2—then **a** did not know at t_1 that *P*.

Here (ii) dilutes "possesses *the* account" to "has *a* reason"; without this dilution the argument makes no sense. (iv) offers a sober version of the quaint phrase "the object is preserved" (*sōzomenos*: see *An B* 3, 428^{b}6; cf. the use of "remain", *diamenein*, at *Top* Θ 2, 157^{b}15, and of "perish", *phtheiresthai*, at 74^{b}34; *APr A* 33, 47^{b}31; *Top E* 9, 139^{a}12; *Met* Θ 3, 1047^{a}2). "The object" refers to the subject of the proposition *P*, and its 'preservation' consists in its retaining the predicate ascribed to it by *P* (cf. *Met* Θ 8, 1050^{b}14).

(7) appears to be true; indeed, (i) and (v) seem by themselves to imply the consequent of (7). (iii) seems peculiarly otiose (but cf. *Met* Γ 8, 1012^{b}25); it may be present purely for the sake of symmetry: knowledge is maintained from t_1 to t_2 provided that the *knower* is preserved; the object *known* is preserved; and the relation *between* knower and object is preserved.

Now let P be the conclusion AaC; and R the premises AaB & BaC, which are supposed contingent. Thus R may 'perish', i.e. cease to be true; but if R is false at t_2, then (i)–(v) are satisfied and it follows that **a** did not know at t_1 that AaC.

This brings out clearly the presupposition already implicit in (iv), that a proposition may change its truth-value. This presupposition underlies the whole of Aristotle's logic (cf. e.g. *Cat* 5, 4^a34–^b13; *APst A* 33, 88^b31–4; *Top Δ* 2, 123^a15–17; *I* 22, 178^b25–9; *Met Θ* 10, 1051^b13–15); but it works ill for Aristotle here. For we can now construct a counter-example to (7): let t_1 be 1950, t_2 1960, P "No one has run a three-minute mile", and R "No one has run a four-minute mile"; and suppose that I regularly assented to P from 1949 to 1961, and regularly gave R as my reason for holding P. Then (i)–(v) are satisfied; yet surely I may, in 1950, have known that P—an ancient interest in athletics ensured that my belief that R was well-founded in 1950; the interest waned, and the belief, now turned false, remained. To avoid such counter-examples it is necessary to add a further condition to (7), viz. (vi) R has the same truth-value at t_2 and at t_1—but with this addition Aristotle's application of (7) no longer works.

74^b37: "And if, although the middle term has not perished...": Aristotle has supposed that R *is* false at t_2; but what if, though it is *possible* for R to be false at t_2, nevertheless R is in fact true then? Aristotle's answer relies on:

(8) $(\neg R \rightarrow X) \rightarrow (\Diamond \neg R \rightarrow \Diamond X)$

—where "X" is "the result" (*to sumbainon*, 74^b37), and the diamond, $\Diamond$, represents possibility. (8) is a case of a general principle enunciated at *APr A* 15, 34^a5–12, and *Met Θ* 3, 1047^b14–17. What is "the result"? If we assume:

(9) **a** knows at t_1 that AaC,

then (7), (9), and $\neg R$ lead (Aristotle would argue) to:

(10) (**a** knows at t_1 that AaC) & (**a** does not know at t_1 that AaC).

Hence, (by (8)) the assumption that $\Diamond\neg R$, together with (7) and (9), will entail that (10) is possible; but it is not. This argument can, I think, be made to work, though it needs a slightly stronger principle than (8).

74^b38: "but it is impossible to have knowledge under such conditions": i.e. 'it is impossible for (10) to be true'; or, perhaps better, 'You cannot know that AaC if you rely on contingent premisses' (Zabarella).

75^a1: This section is a further aside; it propounds three theses, which generalize to:

(11) It is *not* the case that if P follows from $Q_1, Q_2, \ldots, Q_n$, and if $\Box P$, then for some i $\Box Q_i$.
(12) If P follows from $Q_1, Q_2, \ldots, Q_n$ and for every i $\Box Q_i$, then $\Box P$.

(13) If P follows from $Q_1, Q_2, \ldots, Q_n$, and if $\neg \, \square \, P$, then for some i $\neg \, \square \, Q_i$.

(11) is supported by analogy with:

(14) It is *not* the case that if P follows from $Q_1, Q_2, \ldots, Q_n$ and P is true, then for some i Q_i is true.

Aristotle argues for (14) at *APr B* 2–4 (see Patzig, appendix). (12) entails (13); both are illustrated by *Barbara*. In the case of (13) "the middle term is not necessary" means "it is not the case that $\square \, AaB$ & $\square \, BaC$"; hence I have read the same interpretation into (12).

75^{a}12: If **a** infers AaC from AaB and BaC, when $\square \, AaC$, $\neg \, \square \, AaB$ and $\neg \, \square \, BaC$, then first **a** will not know *why* AaC holds (see 74^{b}26–32), and secondly **a** will not know that $\square \, AaC$ (presumably because he cannot validly infer it from his premises). These two implications answer to the two parts of the definition of understanding at *A* 2, 71^{b}10–12. (But the Greek at 75^{a}14 may rather mean: "you will understand neither why ⟨it is *necessary* for it to be the case⟩ nor . . ." (see BURNYEAT (1981), 111 n. 27).)

75^{a}15: "either you will wrongly think . . .": i.e. 'either **a**, supposing wrongly that $\square \, AaB$ and $\square \, BaC$, does indeed *think*—but does not *know*—that $\square \, AaC$; or else he will not even think that $\square \, AaC$, alike if he simply infers AaC from AaB & BaC or if he knows "the reason why through immediates"'. The last clause is baffling (cf. Ross, 529–30). Conceivably Aristotle is imagining a completely different argument, in which **a** infers DaF from DaE & EaF, where the premises are immediate and necessary truths but **a** does not realize that they are. Then he does, in a sense, "know the reason why"—for he knows the propositions which in fact give the reason why; but he does not think that $\square \, DaF$.

75^{a}18: The thesis that there is no understanding of 'incidentals' is readily inferred from the matter of *A* 2 and *A* 6 (see also *A* 30); but Aristotle's argument here equivocates on "incidental" (see p. 126), and the longer argument at *Met E* 2, 1026^{b}2–24 and 1027^{a}19–28, is laborious and obscure.

75^{a}18: "Of incidentals which do not hold of things in themselves . . .": this seems to mean 'incidentals which are not "in itself" incidentals' (cf. p. 113); but "in itself" is immediately glossed by reference to *A* 4, 73^{a}34–^{b}5, and 'in itself' incidentals are not I-predicates.

75^{a}22: The puzzle is this: 'If incidental predications are non-necessary, then what is the point of arguing for them in the way we do, i.e. of looking for *relevant* premises from which to infer them (why do we bother to ask *these* particular questions about them)? For if Q is not necessary, *any* argument of the form "P, so necessarily Q" will be equally good—since *no* argument of that form will be any good.' The puzzle is solved by distinguishing between *necessitas consequentiae* and *necessitas consequentis*: if $P \vdash Q$ is a valid argument then it follows that $\Box\ (P \to Q)$; but it does not follow that $\Box\ Q$. Aristotle is evidently trying to formulate this distinction; but he does not succeed. He contrasts with $\Box\ Q$ first:

(15) $\Box$ (If **a** says that P, then **a** says that Q),

and then:

(16) $\Box$ (if P is true, then if **a** says that Q then **a** says truly that Q).

Of these, (15) neither entails nor is entailed by $\Box\ (P \to Q)$, and (16), though entailed by it, does not entail it. (See further Patzig, ch. 2.)

75^a28: The final paragraph of the chapter returns to the thesis, and repeats the argument, of the first.

75^a30: ". . . demonstrations are concerned with what holds of things in themselves and . . . proceed from such items"; i.e. 'in a demonstration both conclusion and premisses are I-predications'.

75^a33: "(e.g. deductions through evidence)": see *APr B* 27.

75^a34: "For you will not understand in itself . . .": i.e. 'you will not understand that A holds of C in itself'.

CHAPTER 7

A 7 turns to 'appropriateness' (cf. *A* 2, 71^b23; see e.g. G.-G. GRANGER (1976), 68–72). Note that the modern division of *APst* into chapters is particularly misleading here. As the word "thus (*ara*)" shows, the main thesis of *A* 7 follows directly from the conclusion of *A* 6: see 75^b10–12, which rehearse 75^a35–7. (See DE GANDT (1975–6), 73.) A principle *Π* may be inappropriate to a conclusion *P* either because it is 'too general' (e.g. *Π* concerns animals in general, *P* only mules: cf. *GA B* 8, 747^b30–748^a11), or because it is specific to a kind different from the kind *P* is concerned with (e.g. *Π* concerns lions, *P* mules). It is the second sort of inappropriateness that Aristotle discusses here.

75^a38: This tripartition of the "things involved in demonstrations" recurs more than once (see p. 143). The *first* element seems straightforward: it is "the conclusion". But the parenthetical gloss ("this is what holds . . .") indicates that the first element is *not* the conclusion as a whole, *AaC*, but rather the predicate of the conclusion. And *A* 10, 76^b15, confirms this indication by talking simply of "the affections" (*ta pathē*). The *second* element both seems and is straightforward. Just as "the conclusion" is really the predicate of the conclusion, so the *third* element—"the underlying kind"—is in fact the *subject* of the conclusion. This is made clear in the explanatory clause at 75^b1, and is corroborated by Aristotle's use of "underlying" (*hupokeimenon*), his standard term for 'subject'.

I shall postpone the difficult question of the relationship between this tripartition and the other ways in which Aristotle classifies the elements

of a demonstrative science (see p. 143); the immediate problem is
to determine how the tripartition bears on the requirement of 'appropriateness' or the prohibition on kind crossing.

A kind, or *genos*, is a sequence of terms of the type (Σ) of p. 119.
Suppose two such kinds (Σ_a) and (Σ_b), and let T_a stand for an arbitrary
term in (Σ_a) and T_b for an arbitrary term in (Σ_b). Then a demonstrative
chain D will 'cross' from (Σ_a) to (Σ_b) if and only if D concludes to AaT_b
from premisses including AaT_a.

The burden of Aristotle's argument is contained in 75^{b}7–12: he
assumes that the kind-crossing argument must contain the proposition
T_aaT_b. This, like all demonstrative premisses, must be an I-predication
(75^{b}11); hence T_a and T_b must come from the same kind (75^{b}10)—
presumably because if one 'inheres in the account' of the other it will
necessarily fall under the same general kind. Thus if D crosses, T_a and
T_b belong to the same kind. But, trivially, if D crosses, (Σ_a) and (Σ_b) are
distinct; hence D does not cross.

This argument tacitly assumes that a term belongs to at most one kind.
If we suppose that we can distinguish terms which make up the 'kind'
from attributes or affections of the kind, and if we adopt as constitutive
of kind construction the principle that if AaB is an I-predication then A
and B belong to the same kind, then it becomes possible to show that
kind crossing is a logical impossibility; and this is what Aristotle in effect
does. But plainly he hopes to do rather more than this: "kind" is
occasionally used for "branch of knowledge" (e.g. *Top Γ* 1, 116^{a}16);
and *APst* regularly supposes it proved that D cannot cross from e.g.
arithmetic to geometry. Aristotle has not proved this; to do so he needs
to prove that the existent 'kinds' or branches of knowledge are 'kinds' in
the technical sense required by the argument of *A* 7. He cannot prove
this; and the example he discusses at *A* 13, 79^{a}13–16, refutes it (see
p. 160). (It has been argued that in *MA* Aristotle implicitly relaxes his
prohibition on kind crossing, allowing in particular that cosmology and
biology are not wholly separate sciences (see NUSSBAUM (1985), 107–42);
but see KUNG (1982).)

75^{b}2: "Now the items from which . . .": i.e. the axioms used in demonstrations from different kinds may be the same; for a more precise
account see *A* 10, 76^{a}37, notes.

75^{b}5: "unless magnitudes are numbers": the hypothesis is jocular (cf.
A 10, 76^{b}38, note). Magnitudes (*megethē*), in Aristotle's terminology,
are the subject-matter of geometry (e.g. *Cael A* 1, 268^{a}7—contrast
Euclid's usage, above, p. 123).

75^{b}6: "how . . . this is possible . . .": cf. 75^{b}9 ("either *simpliciter* or in
some respect"); 75^{b}14–17; *A* 9, 76^{a}9–15, 23–5; *A* 12, 77^{b}1–2; and esp.
A 13, 78^{b}34–79^{a}16 (see notes there).

75^{b}13: That there is 'a single science of contraries' is an Aristotelian
commonplace (see Bonitz, 247^{a}13–21), with a wide range of application.

Thus a doctor, say, cannot know about therapeutic drugs unless he knows about poisons; and he cannot know how to cure a patient unless he knows how to kill him.

75^{b}13: "two cubes make a cube": i.e. if $m = x^3$ and $n = y^3$, then for some z $m \cdot n = z^3$ (Euclid, ix. 4); cf. Heath (2), 46.

75^{b}17: "Nor indeed anything . . .": this is not an illustration of kind crossing; Aristotle's point is this: if AaT_a is an I-predication, then you cannot prove AaT_b by the principles of (Σ_b) alone—you are bound to use at least one principle from (Σ_a), viz. AaT_a. By the earlier argument, this would in fact make (Σ_a) and (Σ_b) identical: Aristotle in effect allows this, but he singles out (Σ_b), a sub-class of (Σ_a), as a 'subordinate' science. His only motive for this can be the fact that in current scientific practice (Σ_b) (e.g. geometry) was a science in its own right.

75^{b}18: "Whether straight lines are the most beautiful of lines": Aristotle preferred the circle (*Cael A* 2, 269^{a}19–30); for the place of beauty in mathematics see *Met B* 2, 996^{a}29–^{b}1; *M* 3, 1078^{a}31–^{b}6.

75^{b}19: "Whether they are contrarily related to curved lines": cf. *Cael A* 4.

75^{b}20: ". . . in virtue of something common": sc. to lines and other genera. Contrariety is a relation holding between things *qua* beings (cf. *Met Γ* 2, 1003^{b}33–1004^{a}2; and esp. 1005^{a}11–13); *qua* what are things beautiful?

CHAPTER 8

This chapter breaks rudely into the train of thought uniting *A* 7 and *A* 9; Zabarella proposed to place it after *A* 10. It expands on matter already hinted at in *A* 4, 73^{a}28–34, and *A* 6, 74^{b}32–9. In an interesting passage at *GA B* 6, 742^{b}17–34, Aristotle argues against the contrary view, which he ascribes to Democritus, that there cannot be demonstration of *eternal* objects.

The argument at 75^{b}21–6 goes as follows: Suppose that *P* is demonstrable. Then *P* is of the form *AaC*. Hence (by *A* 4, 73^{a}28) for all *t*, *AaC* holds at *t* (*P* is "eternal"). Hence *C*s are not 'perishable', and there is no knowledge, in the full sense, of "perishable things". (Cf. *EN Z* 3, 1139^{b}22–4.)

The commentators suppose Aristotle to be arguing that there is no demonstration of *individuals*; and they might have compared the argument at *Met Z* 15, 1039^{b}27–1040^{a}7. But in our passage Aristotle speaks explicitly of *perishables*; and he did not think that all individuals were perishable.

It is true that the individual Socrates has perished, and that hence we can have no demonstrative understanding about him—no demonstrative deduction will conclude to a proposition of the form "*A* (Socrates)". It is also true that every human is perishable; but we shall not ascribe to

Aristotle the view that no demonstration may conclude to a proposition of the form "Every human is A". (The text might seem to suggest this view—but it cannot be Aristotle's meaning.) Rather, although every human is perishable, there is a sense in which—on Aristotle's view of nature—humans are imperishable: there will always be humans, humans will not die out. A demonstrative deduction may conclude to a proposition of the form "Every C is A" only if Cs are imperishable in *this* sense, i.e. only if there will always be some Cs about.

Two dubious moves have been discerned in Aristotle's argument. First, the inference from "P is eternal" to "P is about eternal objects" seems to confuse the eternal holding of facts with the eternal existence of objects (cf. e.g. *Phys Δ* 12, 222^a3–9; *Θ* 1, 252^b2–4; *Cael B* 11, 281^a4–7; *GA B* 6, 742^b25–8; *EN Γ* 3, 1112^a21–3; S. Mansion, 86–8; 115–18). Aristotle could be defended here if we took "Cs are imperishable" to mean "Cs cannot cease to be A" (where A is the attribute demonstrable of C)—cf. *Met Θ* 8, 1050^b14. But Aristotle thought that if Cs are perishable in the absolute sense (if they can cease to be), then they are perishable relative to every attribute (they can cease to be A); in terms of syllogistic, AaC is not true if there are no Cs. Secondly, the move from "P is about eternal objects" to "P is about imperishable objects" seems to confuse what *does* perish with the perish*able*. There is considerable evidence that Aristotle consciously adhered to this 'confusion' (cf. Hintikka (1)). It is possible, however, that he has in mind here an argument of the type he deployed at *A* 6, 74^b32–9.

75^b26: 'If P is non-eternal, and **a** 'demonstrates' that P from Q and R, then "one of the propositions must be non-universal and perishable".' There is no reason to construe "one of the propositions" as "the minor premiss"; rather, it means "at least one of the premisses". "Non-universal" does not mean "singular", as the reference to "its subjects" (75^b29) shows. It might mean "particular" (i.e. 'of the form AiC'); but then Aristotle could infer not merely that P is not omnitemporal but, more strongly, that P is only a particular judgement of the form AiC. Rather, he has in mind a proposition AaB which only holds for a given time. The text at 75^b28 and 75^b29 is uncertain. At 75^b29 I translate the conjecture *hote men estai hote d'ouk estai ta eph' hōn*. This gives Aristotle a good argument: AaB is non-universal because sometimes the Bs will be (i.e. will exist; or perhaps, will be A) and sometimes they will not be. The MS readings give: 'Some of the Bs will be (A) and others will not be (A)'; if this is correct, then particular judgements are intruded, misguidedly, into the argument of the chapter. At 75^b28 Aristotle means: 'Either AaB or BaC is perishable; for ($\forall t$) (AaB_t & $BaC_t \rightarrow AaC_t$): hence if ($\forall t$) AaB_t and ($\forall t$) BaC_t then ($\forall t$) AaC_t. But by hypothesis AaC is perishable, i.e. ($\exists t$) ¬ AaC_t' (see Ross, 534).

The long and the short of this is very simple: if **a** 'demonstrates' AaC from AaB and BaC, when AaC does not hold omnitemporally, then either AaB or BaC only holds for part of the time.

75^{b}30: "The same goes for definitions . . .": i.e. 'if Cs are perishable, then C cannot be defined' (cf. *Met Z* 15, 1040^{a}2). The argument relies on the classification of definitions at *B* 10, 94^{a}11–14, and is scarcely intelligible apart from the argument of *B* 10.

75^{b}33: Given that we can only have knowledge of what is eternal, how can we know—as we surely do know—about, e.g., eclipses of the moon? For these do not, fortunately, *always* occur. (These cases are sometimes assimilated to what happens 'for the most part' (cf. esp. *A* 30); but the moon is not eclipsed for the most part.)

Aristotle's answer to this question is obscure—and the text is uncertain at a crucial point. If, with the OCT, we read *hēi men toioude*, Aristotle asserts that 'demonstrations of what happens often hold always (are universal) in so far as they hold of such-and-such a sort of thing'. The point is then simple and true: even though eclipses do not *happen* always, we may still produce universal demonstrations to the effect that *every* eclipse is thus and so. (Whether Aristotle is entitled to this answer is another matter; for—as this very chapter shows—he wishes to construe universal propositions as requiring the eternal existence of their subjects.) But then the next clause in the text must mean that 'demonstrations of what happens often are particular in so far as they do not hold always'; and it is difficult to make any sense of this. Hence I prefer the suggestion in VERDENIUS (1981), 347: read *hēi men toiaide* and suppose that the subject to be understood is *hai ekleipseis*: demonstrations are universal in so far as the eclipses are such-and-such (i.e. in so far as the demonstrations involve propositions of the form "Every eclipse is . . ."), and they are particular in so far as eclipses do not always occur. But it must be admitted that this construe is difficult.

CHAPTER 9

75^{b}37: Aristotle now turns to the first of the two sorts of inappropriateness (p. 130), where the principles of a proof are too general.

The argument is hampered by the reference to Bryson, a Megarian contemporary of Aristotle's (cf. Bonitz, 144^{a}17–20; DÖRING (1972), 62–7). The problem of Bryson's attempt to construct a square equal in area to a given circle (see *Top I* 11, 171^{b}12–18; 172^{a}2–7; cf. *Cat* 7, 7^{b}30–3) "is one of the most baffling in the history of Greek geometry" (Heath (2), 48; see MORAUX (1979), 25–32; MUELLER (1982)). *A* 5, 74^{a}15–25, suggest a simpler example of the error Aristotle has in mind: an argument of the sort Aristotle is objecting to might run:

(1) All proportional numbers are B;
(2) Everything B alternates.

Therefore:

(3) All proportional numbers alternate.

We are to suppose that (1) and (2) are immediate truths (75^{b}40). Even so, Aristotle says, the argument is unsatisfactory because it applies "to other items which are not of a kind with them" (76^{a}1; *Top I* 11, 172^{a}4–6). Thus "numbers" can be replaced in (1) by, say, "lengths"; so that the argument proves "in virtue of a common feature"—viz. *B*, which is common to numbers and lengths.

No doubt this is true; but what does it matter? Aristotle says that on the basis of (1)–(3) "you do not understand the item as such"; this presumably means (cf. *A* 6, 75^{a}34) that you will not know that *A* belongs to *C* as such. That is true; but it is true because *A* does not belong to *C* as such—in general, if *AaC* is concluded from *AaB* and *BaC* then *A* will belong to *C* not *as such* but *as B*. If Aristotle's words are to be pressed here, he will have to abandon the possibility of demonstrative knowledge.

There is a further difficulty, which my supplementary example exposes in stark form. How can the premisses in such a case be "indemonstrable and immediate"? It is plain that (1) is *not* immediate; and it is plain, more generally, that if *AaB* and *BaC* are both immediate, then they must be 'appropriate' to the conclusion.

76^{a}4: The argument runs thus: 'We understand *A*—or rather that *AaC*—if we have derived it through a term *B* which does in fact explain why *AaC*, and if our derivation rests on principles which are I-predications of *B*. . . . Hence if *BaC* must also be an I-predication, then if we are to know *AaC* our middle term must be from the same kind as *C*.'

This suggests a different criticism of (1)–(3): *B* is not the term in virtue of which *A* belongs to *C* (cf. *Top I* 11, 171^{b}17); *B* cannot explain why *numbers* that are proportional alternate, because it explains in general why proportional *quantities* alternate. This is perhaps an intelligible complaint; and it links with some of the things Aristotle says in *B* 18. But it must be said first, that if the complaint is justified then (1) and (2) cannot after all both be immediate propositions; and secondly, that it indicates at most that (1)–(3) is not in itself enough to demonstrate (3)—a longer chain of demonstrations is needed for that.

76^{a}9: The paragraph is obscure. "Otherwise, it will be like . . .": i.e. if the middle term is not in the same kind, then we shall have a proof of the sort which we find, e.g., in harmonics. "Things of this sort . . .": i.e. proofs in harmonics are indeed *like* standard proofs—but there is also a crucial difference. Take a demonstration

AaB, BaC ⊢ AaC

—where *AaC* is a theorem of harmonics. Then *AaB* may be a principle of arithmetic, while *BaC* is a principle of harmonics. Thus the principles of the two sciences have something in common, namely, the term *B*. (And *BaC* is a 'bridge' principle, which links harmonics to arithmetic.) This may seem reasonably clear in itself. Yet it is quite unclear why the same may not be said, *mutatis mutandis*, of the Brysonian proof, which also works "in virtue of a common feature"—especially if (as Aristotle is apparently prepared to allow) the premisses of the Brysonian proof may be indemonstrable and immediate. (For the matter in 76ᵃ9–16 see notes to *A* 13, 78ᵇ34–79ᵃ16.)

76ᵃ16: Suppose that Π_g is a proper principle of geometry, and it is demonstrated. This demonstration must depend on some principles, say Π; and Π must also apply to some science other than geometry ("there will be principles of everything", 76ᵃ17). (If Π applies *only* to geometry, then it is a proper principle of geometry; and Π_g is, after all, a theorem and not a principle.) But this is not possible, since "a demonstration does not attach to another kind" (76ᵃ22).

This interpretation gives Aristotle a valid argument; but it is obliged to gloss "there will be the principles of everything" as "there will be principles of more than one science". (But compare the use of "everything", *pas*, at *An B* 6, 418ᵃ11: see above, p. 100.) And it breaks the natural connection between this argument and those at *A* 32, 88ᵇ23–9 and *Met B* 4, 997ᵃ2–11, which unequivocally attack the notion of a single science which is sovereign over all others in the manner of Platonic dialectic (cf. Cherniss, 73 n. 55).

Suppose that *AaB* is a principle of arithmetic, i.e. that it cannot be proved within arithmetic and contains terms specific to arithmetic. Any putative proof of this principle must—within syllogistic—use the premisses *AaC* and *CaB*. But both *A* and *B* are *arithmetical* terms. Hence *AaB* can after all be proved within arithmetic. Hence if there are any principles proper to a science, they cannot be proved at all.

There is a subtle discussion of the passage in MIGNUCCI (1975), 178–84. According to Mignucci, when Aristotle refers to "the proper principles" he has in mind only those principles which are not *common* to a subordinate and a superordinate science: the principles of a subordinate science *can* be proved—from the principles of the superordinate science. Moreover, Aristotle intends only to show that the proper principles of one science cannot be proved *from the principles of a co-ordinate science*. Against the first of these points there is the following to be said. The argument which I have just offered will apply as well to the principles of harmonics as to the principles of arithmetic, and I do not think that Aristotle anywhere suggests that the principles of subordinate sciences can be proved. What is peculiar to the subordinate sciences is not that their *principles* can be proved but rather that in the proofs of their *theorems* you will (sometimes) invoke principles of the superordinate science as well as principles of the science itself. (Indeed, if all the principles of a subordinate science could be proved from the principles of a superordinate science, then the 'subordinate science' would be simply a fragment of the superordinate science and not a distinct science at all.) As for Mignucci's second contention, it seems to me to have no support in the text, which claims quite generally (and quite rightly) that the proper principles of a science cannot be proved.

The function of 76ᵃ18–22 is to show why understanding the putative principles of everything will be 'sovereign'. Such understanding will be the best possible sort of understanding, since it will be based on the highest possible explanations, namely, on explanations which admit no further explanation.

The paragraph proves that Aristotle did not think that the proper principles of a science were demonstrable. Many commentators, both ancient and modern, have claimed that, in Aristotle's view, *metaphysics* can prove the proper principles of the sciences (see e.g. Simplicius, *in Phys* 15. 29–16. 2); and they have accordingly supposed that *A* 9 affirms only that the sciences cannot demonstrate *their own* proper principles. But the supposition is untenable; and the claim is ill-founded. (It has rested principally on *A* 12, 77ᵃ29–31, and on *Met E* 1, 1025ᵇ10–18; but for the latter text see GOMEZ-LOBO (1978).)

A 10 elaborates the classifications of principles already introduced in *A* 1 and *A* 2.

76ᵃ31:   With this paragraph cf. *A* 1, 71ᵃ11–16, and notes.

Just as the propositions of a demonstrative science divide into primitive axioms and derived theorems, so the terms of such a science can be divided into primitive terms and defined terms. In several passages Aristotle appears to grasp both the distinction between primitive and defined terms, and the parallel between this distinction and the distinction between axioms and theorems: see *A* 23, 84ᵇ15; 28, 87ᵃ38; *B* 9; *Top Z* 4, 141ᵃ27–31; *Met A* 9, 982ᵇ32; *B* 3, 998ᵇ5. Scholz, who has an excellent discussion of all this, argues that in our passage "the primitives" and "the principles" mean "the primitive terms", and "the items proceeding from them" means "the defined terms"; for Aristotle's examples are all of terms and not of propositions.

Had Aristotle developed the line of thought present in these several passages he would doubtless have grasped the distinction Scholz ascribes to him. He was, of course, well aware that some of the terms in a science would be defined by means of others—the whole notion of an I-predication depends on this. But he did not, I think, reach any great degree of sophistication. First, the parallelism between propositions and terms is not explicitly noticed in *APst*; the definition of "principle" at *A* 2, 72ᵃ7, leaves no room for term-principles; and the several places in which termlike objects are referred to as principles reflect a general muddiness rather than a clear perception of the parallelism between terms and propositions. Secondly, the distinction between types of item at 76ᵃ31–6 is not one between defined and undefined terms; for Aristotle explicitly says that we assume the meanings *both* of the dependent items *and* of the primitives—i.e. in both cases we assume their definitions. (Scholz later recanted: see the passage quoted by DE GANDT (1975–6), 56 n. 153.)

There is a further difficulty. If we must assume the meanings both of the primitive and of the dependent terms, then how are the two sorts of term to be distinguished? And what exactly do we do when we assume what a term means? It is natural to suppose that such an assumption will be expressed by a proposition of the form:

T means so-and-so,

or perhaps simply:

Ts are so-and-sos

—where this proposition is taken to show what T means. Let Σ_t be the set of terms $\{T_1, T_2, \ldots, T_n\}$ for a science S. If there is a defining proposition for *every* member of Σ_t, then T_i will be a *dependent* term just in case its defining proposition uses some other T_j in Σ_t. (For example, in geometry, the defining proposition for "triangle" will include the term "line", which is itself a geometrical term.) What of the defining propositions for primitive terms? There seem to be two possibilities here. First, they might be 'homophonic', so that the defining proposition for, say, "point" might be simply:

"Point" means a point.

Secondly, they might be 'analytical', e.g.:

"Point" means a unit with position.

Presumably it is the second possibility which Aristotle embraces. But in that case we must surely ask why the terms used in the 'analytical' account of e.g. "point" are not *themselves* geometrical terms.

76ᵃ37:   The distinction between common and proper "items used in the demonstrative sciences"—i.e. common and proper principles—has already been adumbrated in *A* 7 and *A* 9 (see also *Rhet A* 2, 1358ᵃ1–35). What exactly is the role of the common principles? Aristotle is clearly glossing his unqualified statement at *A* 7, 75ᵇ2; but the precise qualification he is making is unclear. Let us take the common axiom:

   (1) Equals taken from equals leave equals

and the application of the axiom to geometry:

   (2) Equal magnitudes taken from equal magnitudes leave equal magnitudes.

(For (1) see Euclid, common notion 3. Note that (1) is restricted to *quantities*: thus a principle must count as 'common' if it applies to *more than one* kind of thing—although 77ᵃ26 might suggest that "common" is elliptical for "common *to all*" (see above, p. 100).) Then take any geometrical proof (e.g. that of Euclid, i. 2) which relies on the axiom. Does Aristotle mean that the proof *need* contain only (2)? (He seems to state as much at 76ᵃ42.) Or that it *must* contain (2)? (This may be his meaning at 76ᵃ39: the axiom is only useful, i.e. only yields results, if applied in form (2).) Or that it must *not* contain (1)? (This may be the burden of his claim that the common axioms appear "by analogy"; and it is perhaps supported by the argument of *A* 9.) The evidence from outside our passage is unsure: at *Met Γ* 3, 1005ª23–6 (cf. *K* 4, 1016ᵇ20–4) Aristotle in effect asserts that geometers only need (2) and as a matter of fact only use (2). At *APr A* 24, 41ᵇ13–22, he appears to argue that (1) is necessary if the proof is not to 'beg the question'.

76ᵇ3: "Proper too . . .": the proper principles illustrated at 76ª40 were all definitions; Aristotle now adds existential propositions (or, more precisely, the subject-*terms* of such propositions).

76ᵇ6: "They assume that there are such items, and that they are *such-and-such*": i.e. 'geometry (e.g.) assumes that there are lines and that a line is by definition such and such'.

76ᵇ9: "Irrational or inflection or verging": a line *A* is *irrational* in relation to *B* if there are no integers *n, m* such that *A* = *nB/m*; a line *AC* *inflects* at *B* if the angle *ABC* ≠ 180°; and *AB verges* to a point *C* if the angle *ABC* = 180°.

76ᵇ10: "through the common items and from what has been demonstrated": Ross (56, 531) stresses the difference between the prepositions in this phrase ("through", *dia*, and "from", *ek*) and asserts that to prove *from X* is to use *X* as a premiss, while to prove *through X* is to use *X* as a rule of inference. But elsewhere Aristotle uses "from" of the common axioms (e.g. 75ª42; 76ᵇ14; 77ª27) and "through" of premisses (e.g. 78ª30; *Top A* 1, 100ª26); and the account of the common principles which he has just given scarcely suggests that they are to be read as rules of inference.

On the alleged distinction between *dia* and *ek* see the full discussion in MIGNUCCI (1975), 141–3. As far as I know, the two prepositions are used promiscuously in later Greek logical texts too; and I have found no clear recognition among the ancient logicians of the distinction between rules of inference and premisses (see BARNES (1990), 111–18). On pp. 198–9 Mignucci rightly underscores a further oddity in these lines: Aristotle makes no reference at all to the *proper* principles of a science, writing as though the demonstrations he has in mind here could rely simply on common axioms and previously proved theorems. There is a more general problem: how, in Aristotle's view, will an arithmetician prove that 'odd is', i.e. that there are some odd numbers? In theory, Aristotle imagines that there will be a syllogism the conclusion of which states (or at least directly entails) that some numbers are odd and the premisses of which are either common axioms (in their arithmetical specification) or else theorems of arithmetic. I have no idea how Aristotle might hope to give concrete sense to this theoretical schema.

76ᵇ11: See *A* 7, 75ª39–ᵇ2. The assertion that a science may "ignore" some of these three elements is a bow to the enthymematic nature of actual scientific reasoning; for 'by nature' (i.e. when presented in their full, unabbreviated form) demonstrative arguments will show all three elements. Cf. e.g. *APr A* 44, 50ª36; *MA* 7, 701ª25–33. (See also *A* 1, 71ª11, note.)

76^{b}23: The distinction between postulates and the type of supposition defined here is new. These things fit ill into the structure of demonstrative sciences: being provable, they are not principles; and being unproved, they are not theorems. Presumably Aristotle is thinking of the teacher who wants to start, as it were, from Book II of the *Elements*; he may use the theorems proved in Book I, but since he has not proved them himself or to this pupil he will be 'postulating' or 'supposing' them.

The clause at 76^{b}23–4 is perhaps most naturally translated as follows: "What must be the case because of itself and must be thought to be the case". (The word-order suggests that *di' hauto* should be construed only with the first of the two conjuncts.) In that case, it would be reasonable to take "what must be the case because of itself" to refer in general to the principles of the science in question; and they form a proper contrast to the provable postulates and suppositions. But two things tell against this.

First, there is Aristotle's argument for the thesis he is propounding. The picturesque phraseology, no doubt suggested by Plato's description of thought as "the argument which the soul has with itself about whatever it inquires into" (*Theaet* 189^e), is unique in Aristotle; but the contrast it makes is familiar enough: it is simply that between saying that *P* and believing that *P* (a contrast usually made by *logos* and *dianoia*: e.g. *Met Γ* 5, 1009^{a}17; cf. Bonitz, 433^{a}22–33). Thus: 'Demonstration starts from principles which must be admitted. It is no use objecting that a man can admit and refuse to admit whatever he likes. He may of course *say* what he likes, but there are some things which, once set before him, he cannot help believing; and demonstration, being concerned with teaching and truth, is directed to what a learner actually believes and not to what he merely says' (cf. *Top Θ* 5, 159^{a}28–30; the same type of point at *Met Γ* 3, 1005^{b}23–6; *EN H* 3, 1147^{a}18–24). (It is odd of Aristotle to say that deduction in general is not aimed at 'external argument' (76^{b}25); it can be, and by the sophists regularly was.)

Secondly, there is the phrase ". . . and must be thought to be": the phrase itself, and the argument just analysed, intimate a class of propositions which everyone is bound to believe—or rather, a class *K* such that if *P* is in *K* then if anyone entertains *P* he believes *P*. *Met Γ* 3, 1005^{b}11–34, argues that it is impossible to believe that the Law of Contradiction is false. This is as close as Aristotle gets to arguing of any axiom that it belongs to *K*: he nowhere argues that *every* axiom belongs to *K*—indeed *Met Γ* 3 implies that its argument only applies to the Law of Contradiction. (It is, I suppose, tempting to construe "must" in "must be thought" as hypothetical, offering the gloss: 'anyone who is to learn the theorems of the science must assent to these propositions' (cf. *A* 2, 72^{a}16). But so construed, the thesis is given no support by the following lines.)

Thus it is not the principles in general but specifically the common axioms which are being contrasted with postulates and suppositions at

76ᵇ23. But in that case, why did not Aristotle simply say that, since postulates and suppositions are by definition demonstrable, they are distinct from principles of whatever sort? A different interpretation of the text is perhaps possible. We might construe *di' hauto* ("because of itself") with *dokein* as well as with *einai*, and suppose that Aristotle is referring in general to the principles of a science and not specifically to the common axioms (let alone to a special class of those axioms). What must be the case 'because of itself' is what cannot be proved on the basis of anything else: you do not—or perhaps should not—suppose or postulate such items precisely because they are to be believed 'because of themselves'. My revised translation opts for this second construe: it yields a better sense—but it is, I think, less natural than the first construe.

76ᵇ27: For the term "supposition" see *A* 2, 72ᵃ18–20, notes. "Postulate" (*aitēma; aitein*) is regularly used in a more relaxed way than the one suggested here (see Bonitz, 22ᵃ56–ᵇ8; cf. [*Rhet ad Alex*] 20, 1433ᵇ17–28); later, the term was used quite differently by Euclid, and in yet another sense by Archimedes (cf. Proclus, *Comm in Eucl* 180. 23–184. 10; Heath (2), 53–7).
If (A) *P* is provable, and
(B) **a** assumes that *P* when demonstrating something to **b**,
then if
(i) **b** believes that *P*
then
a *supposes* that *P* and *P* is a *supposition* in relation to **b**;
and if
(ii) **b** either does not believe that *P*
or believes that *Q* where *Q* entails not-*P*,
then
a *postulates* that *P* and *P* is a *postulate* in relation to **b**.
Thus "postulate" and "supposition" are relative terms; recognition of this is explicit in 76ᵇ30 and implicit in the phrase "if you make *the same* assumption" (76ᵇ31—i.e. in assuming that *P* **a** may suppose relative to **b** and postulate relative to **c**).
The final sentence of the section is perplexing. The MS text gives: "a postulate is what is *hupenantios* to the opinion of the learner or [*ē*] what, though demonstrable, is assumed and used without being proved". This is insane. The excision of *ē* improves the text, but still leaves a difficulty; for then the account of what a postulate is appears to ignore the first disjunct in clause (ii). (See MIGNUCCI (1975), 210–11.) This difficulty would be solved were we to distinguish between *enantios* at 76ᵇ31 and *hupenantios* at 76ᵇ32, taking the latter term to mean not "contrary to" but rather something like "not in accordance with". Then both the

disjuncts of (ii) are covered. I have translated the word in this way; but I confess that I have found no good parallel.

76ᵇ35: "Terms" translates *horoi*, which may equally mean "definitions". The commentators think that Aristotle is talking of definitions here: first, a contrast between definitions and suppositions properly follows a paragraph which has distinguished axioms from suppositions; secondly, confusion between terms and suppositions seems too crass to warn against (unless Aristotle thought Plato guilty of it at *Rep* 510ᶜ); thirdly, the language of 76ᵇ35–6 has appeared to parallel that of *A* 2, 72ᵃ18–24, which unequivocally talks of definitions. On the other side, definitions at *A* 2, 72ᵃ20–4 are a species of thesis, and hence are propositions; but *horoi* are here distinguished from suppositions by the fact that suppositions are propositions. This point seems to me to outweigh the opposing reasons.

The text at 76ᵇ35–6 is controversial; but if *horoi* are terms, the received reading, which I have translated, may stand: "⟨terms⟩ are not said to be or not be anything" means 'in uttering a term, e.g. *man*, one is not yet saying that men are or are not anything.' (See *Int* 3, 16ᵇ19–22: "Said by themselves verbs are names and signify something ... but they do not yet signify whether anything is or not"; cf. 1, 16ᵃ9–18.)

76ᵇ38: "unless you are going to say ...": i.e. unless the grasping of a term is itself reckoned as a supposition. The suggestion is deliberately absurd (cf. *A* 7, 75ᵇ5; *A* 31, 88ᵃ10; *Top B* 1, 109ᵃ32; *Met Γ* 4, 1006ᵇ20; *M* 4, 1079ᵃ2).

76ᵇ39: The connection between this paragraph and its predecessor becomes clearer if the first clause is paraphrased as follows: 'Nor do the falsehoods which (according to some) geometers utter function as suppositions in their demonstrations.' This paraphrase is confirmed by the parallel discussions at *APr A* 41, 49ᵇ33–50ᵃ4; *Met M* 3, 1078ᵃ19–21; *N* 2, 1089ᵃ22–5 (cf. *Mem* 1, 450ᵃ1; *Rep* 510ᶜ).

The geometer says, e.g., "Let *AB* be the given finite straight line" (Euclid, i. 1), and he draws a line in the sand. But "perceptible lines are not such as the geometer says them to be (for no perceptible thing is either straight or curved in this way; for a circle does not touch the tangent at a point, as Protagoras said in refutation of the geometers) ..." (*Met B* 2, 997ᵇ35–998ᵃ4; see also Aristoxenus, *Elementa Harmonica, B* 33: "a geometer ⟨who says, e.g., 'Let this be a straight line'⟩ does not make use of his faculty of perception; for he does not train his sight to judge badly or well what is straight or curved or anything of this sort"; cf. Heath (2), 204–5).

Plato and Aristotle agree that when the geometer says "Let *AB* be a foot long" he does not refer to the line he is drawing in the sand; but they disagree about the nature of "what these lines show". Both Plato and Aristotle apparently want the geometer to be saying *truly* of some line that it is straight; a modern geometer would be interested in the consequences of the supposition and not in its truth—he might even agree with Protagoras that all his suppositions were (strictly speaking) false, while maintaining that this impugned neither the validity nor the utility of geometry.

76^{b}42: "a line . . . is a foot long": i.e. 'is one unit long' (*Met I* 1, 1052^{b}33); but in what proof would a geometer use such a premiss?

77^{a}3: A second argument for the thesis of 76^{b}35 that terms are not suppositions.

77^{a}4: "either universal or particular": Aristotle holds that definitions are universal propositions (*A* 14, 79^{a}24–9; *B* 3, 90^{b}3–7); this gives further proof that *horos* means "term" and not "definition" here.

The various classifications of the elements of demonstrative science have now all been introduced. Aristotle himself makes no attempt to co-ordinate them; and so it may be of some use to assemble them here and to state their interconnections, where these are discoverable.

(A) (i) of some things we must know beforehand that they are; (ii) of others what they mean; (iii) of others both that they are and what they mean (*A* 1, 71^{a}11–17).

(B) Principles divide into (i) axioms; and (ii) posits; and posits into (*a*) suppositions, and (*b*) definitions (*A* 2, 72^{a}14–22).

(C) The elements of demonstrations are (i) axioms; (ii) affections-in-themselves; (iii) the underlying kind (*A* 7, 75^{a}39–^{b}2; 10, 76^{b}11–22).

(D) There are (i) principles or primitive things; (ii) what depends on them (*A* 10, 76^{a}33).

(E) (i) of some things we assume both that they are and what they mean; (ii) of others, what they mean (*A* 10, 76^{a}32–6).

(F) Of the things used in demonstrations (i) some are common; and (ii) others are proper (*A* 10, 76^{a}37–^{b}2; *A* 32, 88^{b}28).

(G) The sciences prove (i) through certain things; (ii) from certain things (*A* 10, 76^{b}10).

(H) In demonstrations there are by nature (i) that about which; (ii) that of which; and (iii) that from which the proof is (*A* 10, 76^{b}22; *A* 11, 77^{a}27–8; *A* 32, 88^{b}27; *Met B* 2, 997^{a}8, 19–21; *HA A* 6, 419^{a}13–17).

(J) There are (i) axioms (?); (ii) suppositions; (iii) postulates; (iv) terms (*A* 10, 76^{b}24–77^{a}4).

Of these nine classifications, (A) is preparatory and gives way to (E); (G) is specious; and (J) is not properly a classification of demonstrative elements at all. The remaining six classifications are related as follows: (Bi) = (Ci), and perhaps (Bii*a*) = (Fii); (Ci) = (Hiii), (Cii) = (Hii), and (Ciii) = (Hi); (Di) = (Ei), and perhaps (Dii) = (Eii); (Eii) = (Cii); (Fi) = (Hiii), and perhaps (Fii) = (Hi) + (Hii).

The distinctions which Aristotle should have made, and therefore can be supposed to be groping towards, are those between (A') rules of inference and demonstrative propositions; (B') propositions and terms;

(C') primitive and derived elements; (D') common and proper elements. There is in Aristotle no trace of (A'), unless in (G) (see p. 139); (B') is never made explicit in *APst* (see p. 137); (C') is present, in a muddy form, in (D) and (E); and (D') is identical with (F).

CHAPTER 11

The first section of *A* 11 dispenses with subsistent universals; the rest of the chapter takes up various questions about the role of the common axioms. Some commentators have felt the first section to be out of place; but it felicitously follows the Platonic issues canvassed at the end of *A* 10, and its thesis is put to use later in the chapter at 77^{a}20.

77^{a}5: Demonstration requires that, in a sense, 'there are universals': it does not require, as the Platonists argued (e.g. *Met A* 9, 990^{b}12), that there are self-subsistent universals 'apart from' (*para*: see Bonitz, 562^{a}38–44; cf. *B* 19, 100^{a}7) the particulars; but it does require (cf. e.g. *Met B* 4, 999^{b}26) that there are universal predicates true of (*kata* or *epi*: Bonitz, 368^{a}34–55; 268^{a}13–31) more than one thing.

Aristotle means that demonstrative science requires true pairs of propositions of the form *AaB* & *AaC*, where *B* ≠ *C*; but that it does not require subsistent universals. (Note that, *pace* IRWIN (1988), 118–19, this does not commit Aristotle to a 'nominalist' account of universals.) He does not put the matter cleanly. First, his proposition that "one thing holds of many" is naturally read as "(∃*x*) (∃*y*) (*x* ≠ *y* & *Ax* & *Ay*)"; but it must be taken as "(∃*B*) (∃*C*) (*B* ≠ *C* & *AaB* & *AaC*)". Secondly, he normally says that 'the universal' is "what *by nature* is predicated of more than one thing", i.e. 'what *can* be predicated of more than one thing' (e.g. *Int* 7, 17^{a}39; *Met Z* 13, 1038^{b}11; cf. *APr A* 1, 24^{a}18 + 24^{b}28–30). That there are universals in this sense does not imply that "one thing holds of many". Thirdly, there is the requirement that the universal be 'non-homonymous'. This is, I think, unlikely to be a rejection of ambiguous terms as such (Aristotle elsewhere seems prepared to argue that *all* terms are ambiguous: *Top I* 1, 165^{a}6–17). Perhaps the meaning is this: it will not do to have a 'universal' *A* which holds of many things, $B_1, B_2, \ldots, B_n$, if "*A*" means something different in each *AaB_i*.

The word I translate "forms" (*eidē*) is regularly translated "Ideas"; and it is certain that Aristotle's chief, if not his sole, target is Plato's theory of Ideas (cf. *A* 22, 83^{a}32–5; 24, 85^{a}32–^{b}2; 85^{b}15–22). But from a logical point of view Aristotle's argument is not limited to *Platonic* universals; and *eidos* does not *mean* "Idea".

This section deals with a special case of what has become a standing crux in Aristotelian exegesis, the Problem of the Universality of Knowledge: the objects of knowledge are universal; everything real is particular: how, then, can we have knowledge of the real? (Cf. *Met B* 4, 999^{a}24–^{b}24; *M* 10.) The answer Aristotle should have given is perfectly

144

clear: knowledge is of universal *propositions*; only particular *objects* are real: universal propositions do not require universal objects as their subject-matter. Aristotle is groping for this answer in our passage; but he does not grasp it properly, and his more explicit treatments of the Problem are no better. Nevertheless, it is clearly a mistake to offer this Problem as a genuine difficulty for Aristotelian epistemology.

77^{a}10: This section is exceedingly difficult (see esp. Husik). The difficulties are caused partly by the extremely crabbed nature of Aristotle's style, and partly by the fact that Aristotle's main theme is obscured by a subsidiary subject.

The *main* theme is this: demonstrations do not assume as a premiss the Law of Contradiction unless their conclusion too is to be (an instantiation of) LC. (Although LC is rarely a premiss, nevertheless all demonstrations in some sense depend on it: cf. *Met Γ* 3, 1005^{b}32.) The body of the section discusses the case of those demonstrations which *do* premiss LC; of course, even in these cases, LC is only assumed "in so far as is sufficient" (cf. 77^{a}23–4; and esp. *A* 10, 76^{a}37–^{b}2, notes). The *subsidiary* point is this: in those atypical demonstrations, LC need be assumed in only *one* of the premisses. Aristotle's argument falls into three parts, which I shall discuss in order.

Part (A): 77^{a}12–15 give the general form of LC-demonstrations. Their conclusions will, I suppose, look like:

(3) not-(*AaC* & not-*AaC*).

The LC premiss, as Aristotle offers it (77^{a}12), is:

(1) (true: *AaB*) & (not-true: not-*AaB*).

This simplifies (cf. e.g. *Int* 9, 18^{a}34–^{b}5) to:

(1a) *AaB* & not-(not-*AaB*).

To reach (3) we need a second premiss; plainly:

(2) *BaC*.

It is hard to see how (3) is meant to follow from (1) and (2); certainly there is no simple syllogism present. Rather than elucidate this, Aristotle proceeds to state his subsidiary point: "It makes no difference if you assume that the middle term is and is not." This appears to mean that one does *not* have to assume as the second premiss:

(2a) *BaC* & not-(not-*BaC*).

Finally, Aristotle adds the puzzling sentence: "and the same holds for the third term". Since there is no question of a third *premiss*, we are obliged, if this sentence is to be understood, to suppose that Aristotle is thinking of *term*-negations, i.e. is construing "not-*XaY*" as "(not-*X*)*aY*". With this construe, we can expand the puzzling sentence as follows: 'Such demonstrations require the negative term not-*A*, but they require neither not-*B* nor not-*C*.' Even so it remains obscure how we should state the further unnecessary assumption: the older commentators identify it as "not-*Ba*(not-*C*)"; Ross prefers "not-*Ca*(not-*C*)".

However that may be, (2a) must now be restated with term-negations, thus:

(2b) *BaC* & not-[(not-*B*)*aC*].

By parity of reasoning, instead of (1a) we should have:

(1b) *AaB* & not-[(not-*A*)*aB*].

How, then, does (3) come from (1b) and (2)? Aristotle gives no clear indication, and I am unable to construct a valid line of syllogistic reasoning for him. I suggest, hesitantly, the following: from (1b) infer:

(1c) *AaB* & (not-*A*)*eB*.

Then from (1c) and (2), by *Barbara* and *Celarent*, infer:

(3c) *AaC* & (not-*A*)*eC*,

whence:

(3d) *AaC* & not-(not-*A*)*aC*,

from which (3) follows immediately. This reconstruction involves the false equivalence, "*XeY* ↔ not-(*XaY*)". Later in *APst* there are clear examples of this equivalence (see pp. 158, 163, 188), and that is why I presume to ascribe it to Aristotle here. (See also SMITH (1982a), 118–32, for an attempt to explain how Aristotle came to accept the equivalence.)

Although (3) does indeed follow from (3d), so that it is possible to find some sort of argument behind the text, I find it very hard not to suspect that—despite the sentence at 77ª10—(3) does not really have any place in Aristotle's thought. Rather, I suspect that he means to say this: 'In a demonstration you need only *affirm* e.g. *AaB*—you do not also need to *deny* not-*AaB*. Unless, of course, you want your conclusion to include a denial as well as an affirmation. And even in these unorthodox cases you do not need to deny not-*BaC* as well as affirming *BaC*.' In these unorthodox demonstrations, then, you are not really assuming that 'it is not possible to affirm and deny'; rather, you are assuming an affirmation and the negation of its denial.

Part (B): 77ª15–18 illustrate the argument-schema (1)–(3): "animal" is *A*, "man" *B*, and "Callias" *C*. (Here, as often, singular terms creep into Aristotelian syllogisms. Aristotle tacitly treats them as general terms, and I shall do the same here and elsewhere.) The text is probably corrupt (I follow the readings of the OCT); and it is certainly compressed. I paraphrase thus: 'Suppose that (2) *BaC*. ["You are given something of which it is true to say that it is a man".] It does not matter whether (not-*B*)*aC* is also true. If in addition you assume that *AaB* and not-(not-*A*)*aB*, then you may infer that *AaC* and not-(not-*A*)*aC*.'

This leaves the phrase "even if not Callias". The least implausible interpretation of the words is this: 'even if the same is true of not-Callias; i.e. even if not-Callias is *also* a man and not a not-man'. And the phrase must connect with the puzzling reference to the "third term" at 77ª15. If this means that we need not also assume that not-*Ba*(not-*C*), then Aristotle's remarks have some sort of sense: 'The argument will go

through without the assumption that not-*Ba*(not-*C*). True, if we also
have *Ba*(not-*C*), then we shall be able to conclude that *Aa*(not-*C*) and
not-(*Aa*(not-*C*)). But this conclusion will not bar the way to the desired
conclusion, namely (3*d*).'

There is a further question: Why does Aristotle go through this
rigmarole? It is indeed *true* that demonstrations do not need to assume
LC (or any specification of it). But why should Aristotle bother to *say*
so? Had someone denied it, or said something which appeared to deny
it? Again, it is perhaps true that a demonstration *could* assume LC (or
rather, could assume something of the form (1*a*)). But why should
Aristotle want to *say* so? Surely no scientific demonstrations ever *do*
assume premisses of this form? The commentators offer various unsatisfactory answers to these questions. Perhaps Aristotle was simply interested in the logical intricacies which the section follows out.

Part (*C*): 77ª18–21 offer an 'explanation'. What is explained appears
from 77ª21 to be the subsidiary point that (2*a*) is superfluous. The
explanation is desperately obscure. The sentence "even if the middle
term both is it and is not it" should refer to the fact that it does not
matter if we assume "not-*BaC*" as well as (2); such an assumption is an
innocent, if indolent, addition to the argument. Aristotle's sentence thus
paraphrases as: 'even if both *B* and not-*B* appear as the middle term, i.e.
even if both *BaC* and (not-*B*)*aC* are assumed'.

The explanation of the innocence of "(not-*B*)*aC*" is supported by:

(4) AaB & $(\exists X)$ $(X \neq B$ & $AaX)$

—which is inferred from the principle enunciated in 77ª5–9. But it is
hard to see how (4) bears on the issue at all. Waitz replaces (4) by

(5) AaB & Aa(not-*B*).

Then the presence of "(not-*B*)*aC*" does not matter because together
with (5) it will yield *AaC*. If this is right, then Aristotle is arguing that we
may assume "(not-*B*)*aC*" *instead of*, rather than *in addition to* (2). But
the text will hardly bear this; and Aristotle is in any case not entitled to
(5). (For a different interpretation see SMITH (1982*a*), 120.)

However that may be, Aristotle has certainly not grasped the correct
explanation of the innocence of "(not-*B*)*aC*": in general, if *P* & *Q*
together entail *R*, then *P* & *Q* & *S* (for any *S*, including not-*Q*) entail *R*.

77ª22: Aristotle now turns to the Law of Excluded Middle. He does
not explain how LEM is assumed in *reductio ad impossibile*. *Reductio* is
a special case of 'hypothetical' reasoning, the general form of which
consists of a conditional proposition *if P then Q* and a syllogism concluding to *P*; thus *Q* is proved 'on the supposition (*hupothesis*)' that *P*
(cf. e.g. *APr A* 23, 41ª37–ᵇ1). Aristotle says that in *reductio* the conditional is so obvious that there is no need to state or agree upon it (*APr
A* 44, 50ª35–7; *B* 11, 61ª25; 61ᵇ14; 12, 62ª26). Patzig (156) infers that the
conditional has the form *if not-not-P then P*; and we might suppose that
Aristotle takes this to represent LEM, to which it is equivalent. But

Aristotle's illustrations of 'obvious' conditionals do not support Patzig's inference.

Aristotle's thought is surely a simple one. In a *reductio* proof you set out to infer a conclusion, Q, from a set of premisses, Π, by first assuming that not-Q. From Π and not-Q you reach something impossible; hence you must reject not-Q. Thus—since either not-Q or Q—you infer that Q. LEM is thus employed, in a specific form (i.e. in the form "Q or not-Q"), in the last stage of the *reductio*. Aristotle says that in a *reductio* you *assume* LEM. If we take this literally, we must suppose that (some specification of) LEM actually figures as a premiss in a *reductio*. There is, of course, no difficulty in formulating the *reductio* in this fashion—but neither Aristotle nor any other ancient logician does so in practice.

77ᵃ25: "as I said earlier": at *A* 10, 76ᵃ37–ᵇ2.

77ᵃ26: Dialectic is "a method by which we shall be able to argue about any problem which is presented to us" (*Top A* 1, 100ᵃ18–20; cf. *I* 34, 183ᵃ37–9; *Met Γ* 4, 1004ᵇ19–20); thus it deals with what is 'common', and so, in a sense, with everything (e.g. *Top I* 11, 172ᵃ12; *Rhet A* 1, 1345ᵃ1–3; 1355ᵇ8–9; 2, 1356ᵃ30–3). And so it "is not concerned with any determined set of things" (77ᵃ32).

Dialectic also "covers the same kind as philosophy" (*Met Γ* 3, 1004ᵇ22— a 'kind' only by courtesy, of course). "We must say whether it is the task of one or more sciences to investigate what the mathematicians call the axioms, and substance. It is clear that the investigation of these belongs to one science, that of the philosopher" (1005ᵃ19–22). The easy inference from these two passages is that logic too investigates the axioms; but Aristotle does not draw this inference in the *Organon* (see IRWIN (1988), 537 n. 20).

Thus dialectic might be thought to 'associate with all the sciences' in either of two ways: first, since it argues on every topic from general principles, it will presumably use any common element that any science uses. In this way, dialectic 'associates' with the sciences in the same sort of fashion in which they all associate with one another; for they do so in so far as each uses its own instantiations of the common elements (cf. *A* 10, 76ᵃ38). Secondly, in its role as investigator of the principles, dialectic will actually discuss the common axioms which the sciences use. 77ᵃ30 seems to show that Aristotle has the latter association uppermost in his mind.

The phrase "any science which attempted to give . . . proofs" is regularly taken to refer to metaphysics or first philosophy (see p. 137). But, first, metaphysics, though it investigates the first principles, does not and cannot *prove* them (cf. *Met Γ* 4, 1006ᵃ5–11). And secondly, the heavily hypothetical syntax of our sentence makes it plain that Aristotle has no actual science in mind.

Dialectic is not concerned with any single kind or *genos* of things; if it were, it would be demonstrative, and if it were demonstrative it would not 'ask questions' (but cf. *A* 12, 77ᵃ36, and notes). ". . . none of the arts that prove some nature [i.e. that are about some determinate kind] asks questions; for it cannot grant either one of the parts ⟨of a contradiction: cf. *A* 2, 72ª9⟩; for a deduction does not come about from both. But dialectic does ask questions; and if it did prove, even if it asked about *some* things, it would not ask about the primitives and the appropriate principles. For if they were not granted, it would no longer have anything from which to argue against the objection" (*Top I* 11, 172ª15–21).

77ª33: In demonstrative argument you cannot ask questions "because the same thing cannot be proved from opposite assumptions"; i.e.:

(6) It is impossible to prove that *Q* both from *P* and from not-*P*.

This is true, since proofs must have true premisses and both *P* and not-*P* cannot be true. Aristotle probably refers not to *APr B* 4, 57ª36–ᵇ17, which enunciates a false principle (cf. Patzig, appendix), but rather to *APr B* 15, which argues that "whereas from falsehoods it is possible to deduce a truth, as was said earlier, it is not possible to deduce a truth from opposites" (64ᵇ7–9); this, viz.:

(7) If *P* and *P'* are opposites and *Q* is true, then *Q* does not follow both from *P* and from *P'*

is sufficiently close to (6) to warrant Aristotle's reference.

CHAPTER 12

77ª36: Since Aristotle has just denied that the demonstrator asks questions (*A* 11, 77ª32–5), it is strange to find him talking here of "scientific questions". As a 'question' is said to be "a proposition stating one part of a contradictory pair" (cf. *A* 2, 72ª8) we might excuse Aristotle by supplying an etiolated sense for the word "question" here. But this kindness is not tolerable: first, propositions themselves are, at least in the *Topics*, unequivocally interrogative (see *A* 4, 101ᵇ29–32; *Θ* 2, 158ª14–24; cf. *Int* 11, 20ᵇ22–30—contrast *APr A* 1, 24ª16–ᵇ3). And secondly, the example at 77ᵇ33 contains a pair of naked and unabashed questions. Perhaps these questions, though interrogative in form, are not so in intent (they are, as we should say, rhetorical); perhaps they are 'scientific' questions only in the sense that they have to do with the subject-matter of the sciences and not in the sense that they form part of scientific argument itself; or perhaps *A* 12 is part of an early stratum of *APst*, written before Aristotle had become clear about the relation between demonstrative argument and questioning.

77ª40: "It is plain, then . . .": i.e. 'Given a demonstration *P* ⊢ *Q*, *P* is a geometrical proposition if and only if *Q* is a theorem either of geometry or else of one of the sciences subordinate to geometry' (cf. *A* 13, 78ᵇ32–79ª16, notes). Aristotle's syntax is contorted.

77ᵇ3: "For these items . . .": i.e. the theorems of the sciences subordinate to geometry.

77ᵇ5: Why should a geometer not "supply arguments" about the principles of geometry? The major part of the paragraph implies that Aristotle is giving a bit of practical advice to the geometer (see esp. *Phys A* 2, 185ᵃ14–17; cf. *Θ* 3, 253ᵇ2–6; *Met Γ* 3, 1005ᵇ29–33). The advice is based on a simple logical point: to argue about *P qua* geometer is to try to infer *P* from the propositions of geometry; since the principles of geometry cannot be inferred from the propositions of geometry, any attempt to argue about them *qua* geometer is certain to fail—and therefore better left alone (*Top A* 2, 101ᵃ37–ᵇ1).

77ᵇ9: "If you argue in this way . . .": either 'if you argue from geometrical principles . . .' (in which case we have another condemnation of Bryson (cf. *A* 9, 75ᵇ37–76ᵃ3): just as Bryson at best attained 'incidental' knowledge of geometrical theorems, so at best he refutes the geometers incidentally); or else 'provided you do not argue about the principles of geometry' (in which case the point is new but trivial; for the geometer is genuinely refuted though not 'as geometer', i.e. not on a point of geometry).

77ᵇ16: Three questions are asked in this paragraph: (*a*) Are there non-geometrical questions? (*b*) Are there ignorant questions in geometry which are nevertheless in a sense geometrical? (*c*) What is a deduction of ignorance in geometry? The questions are answered only elliptically; and these answers depend on a distinction of meaning which applies alike to "non-geometrical" and to "ignorant". (On ignorance see further *A* 5, *A* 16–18.)

77ᵇ18: "And are ignorant deductions . . . ?": the commentators find three ignorant deductions in the text: (i) 'deduction from the opposites', i.e. a deduction taking as its premisses the contradictories of certain geometrical truths; (ii) a geometrical paralogism, i.e. an invalid argument from true geometrical premisses; and (iii) deduction 'from another art', i.e. an argument from premisses which have nothing to do with geometry.

Aristotle defines "paralogism" as follows: "Besides all the above-mentioned deductions there are the paralogisms that come about from things appropriate to certain sciences, as happens to be the case in geometry and the sciences cognate to it . . . ⟨The pseudographer⟩ constructs his deduction from assumptions that are appropriate to the science but not true; for he constructs his paralogism either by inscribing circles as he should not or by drawing lines as they should not be drawn" (*Top A* 1, 101ᵃ5–17; cf. *I* 11, 171ᵇ34–8; Euclid's *Pseudaria* was a compilation of such paralogisms (see Heath (1), i. 7)). Thus a paralogism is a valid argument from false but geometrical premisses. This sense appears to fit the present paragraph better than the sense "invalid argument". In that case, (ii) collapses into (i), and the text requires the punctuation I have given it. The 'musical question' illustrates (iii); thinking that parallels meet (cf. *APr B* 17, 66ᵃ13) illustrates (i).

77^{b}24: "There is an ambiguity here": the two ways of being non-geometrical answer to (iii) and (i) respectively. Aristotle holds that words of the form "un-F" or "non-F" (in Greek, words prefixed by an alpha privative) are ambiguous: *Met Δ* 22, 1022^{b}31–6 (cf. *An B* 10, 422^{a}26–31; *EE Γ* 2, 1230^{a}38–^{b}5; *Phys E* 2, 222^{b}10–17). (Elsewhere he says that a thing cannot be non-F (as opposed to not being F) unless it is capable of being F (*Met I* 4, 1055^{b}4–11; cf. *APr A* 46, 51^{b}25–8); presumably that ruling is dropped here—for a musical question is hardly 'capable' of being geometrical.)

77^{b}26: "It is the latter type of ignorance": *agnoia* ("ignorance") is an alpha-privative compound. (The old noun "unknowing" is an exact translation.) Hence it too has a pair of senses; to be ignorant about P (where P is some true proposition) is either not to know that P or to 'know badly' that P—i.e. to think that not-P. These two senses are distinguished at *A* 16, 79^{b}23, as 'ignorance in virtue of negation' and 'ignorance in virtue of a disposition'. (Cf. *Top Z* 9, 148^{a}3–9, criticizing *Rep* 585^b; see Cherniss, 26.)

The implicit answers to the three questions are, then: (*a'*) There are non-geometrical questions, and that in two senses. (*b'*) Questions that are ignorant in the sense of exhibiting 'bad' knowledge are in a sense geometrical. (*c'*) Deduction from false geometrical propositions is deduction of ignorance in geometry.

77^{b}27: 'Paralogism depends on ambiguity in the middle term; ambiguities are easily detected in mathematics: hence paralogism tends not to occur in mathematics.' Here paralogism includes or comprises fallacy of equivocation (cf. *Top I* 4, 165^{b}30–166^{a}6); thus the term suffers an abrupt and unannounced shift of sense between the last paragraph and this. (If such a shift of sense is deemed intolerable, then we must suppose, with most scholars, that *paralogismos* at 77^{b}20 means "invalid argument (from true premisses)". In that case (i) and (ii) will offer two distinct ways in which a deduction may be 'non-geometrical' in the sense of exhibiting poor geometrical skill: either (i) the deduction starts from premisses which have a geometrical content but are false; or else (ii) it has true geometrical premisses but proceeds invalidly to its conclusion (see MIGNUCCI (1975), 262–3.) If this is correct, then Aristotle's example of a paralogism at 77^{b}31–3 is ill chosen; for its second premiss ("The epic is a circle") is hardly a *geometrical* proposition.)

Aristotle's argument for his first premiss is that the middle term is the only one which occurs twice in the premisses (*ditton*—"ambiguous" or "twofold"—is a pun): any term may be equivocal, but only an equivocal middle term can give rise to fallacy.

The argument for the second premiss is hard. The things that we "as it were see in thought" are presumably mathematical objects (cf. p. 86) (though the subject of "they escape notice" ought to be something like "equivocations"). Yet Aristotle's illustration refers to the *actual* drawing of a diagram. The train of thought is perhaps this: 'The first premiss of the paralogism, that every circle is a shape, is accompanied by a drawn circle which, as it were, guides our inward gaze toward geometrical circles; if we are then offered as a second premiss that epic poems are circles we at once see that *such* circles are quite different from the things we are contemplating. Thus we are not taken in by the attempted fallacy.' (Cf. *Top I* 1, 165^{a}6–16: fallacies of equivocation occur because we cannot always carry about with us examples of whatever we may talk about.)

An alternative interpretation is possible if *mathēmasi* is not taken in its narrow and normal sense of "mathematics", but in its larger and original sense of "learnings"; if we understand "learnings" as 'didactic or demonstrative arguments' (cf. e.g. *Top I* 20, 177^{b}16), we may paraphrase the argument thus: 'In didactic contexts you know that paralogism can only arise from an ambiguous middle term; and you can detect ambiguities by, as it were, mentally gazing at the things talked about: hence paralogism is rare.' (See 78^{a}10, note.)

77^{b}30: "you do not say "all" of what is predicated": i.e. 'One does not quantify the predicate in a syllogistic proposition' (cf. *Int* 7, 17^{b}13; *APr A* 27, 43^{b}17–22). Or perhaps, more pertinently: 'The predicate (of the middle term) is not said to be all (something else)'—i.e. *CaD* is not premissed; and so *C* does not occur twice.

77^{b}31: "In arguments . . . they escape notice": i.e. 'in dialectical (as opposed to mathematical, or to demonstrative) arguments'; or better: 'if they are just stated (and not seen in thought)'. See 78^{a}12, note.

77^{b}32: "Is every circle a shape? . . .": cf. *Top I* 10, 171^{a}10; the sense in which epic is describable as a 'circle' is uncertain.

77^{b}33: This puzzling paragraph may be designed to reveal yet another form of error. But there is something to be said for the suggestion that the antecedent of *auto* ("it" in "objection against it") is the question "Is the epic a circle?"

Aristotle's argument seems to be this:

(1) Deductive propositions must hold of more than one thing.
(2) Any objection can serve as a deductive proposition.

Hence:

(3) Objections must hold of more than one thing.

For the interpretation of (1) see *A* 11, 77^{a}9, notes. An 'objection' (*enstasis*) is, in a wide sense, any means of blocking an argument (cf. *Top Θ* 10, 161^{a}1–15; *Rhet B* 25, 1401^{a}29–1403^{a}15), and in a narrower sense "a proposition opposite to a proposition" (*APr B* 26, 69^{a}37). "But it differs from a proposition in that an objection may be particular but a proposition may not—either never or at least not in universal deductions" (69^{a}38–^{b}1). This contradicts (3); nor can we say that (3) is restricted to demonstrative objections, since 77^{b}39 explicitly denies this.

The phrase "inductive proposition" (77^{b}34) might mean either "proposition got by induction" or "proposition used in induction"; the latter sense is more likely. If the inductive proposition is the objection, then Aristotle may mean that you should not object to, e.g., "Epics are circles" by means of the singular proposition "The *Iliad* is not a circle", since that proposition only holds of one thing, contrary to (3). This is, to say the least, a silly argument. If the inductive proposition is what the objection is aimed against, then Aristotle may mean that you should not object to, e.g., "The *Iliad* is a circle" by means of the singular proposition "The *Iliad* is not a circle", since again that proposition offends against (3). But this is equally silly.

On this desperate paragraph see MIGNUCCI (1975), 269–79. Mignucci's tentative suggestion amounts to this: 'If your opponent produces an argument which contains a singular proposition (an "inductive proposition"), then you should not proceed by objecting to *this* proposition, i.e. by affirming its negation. For in that case your objection (i.e. the negation of his singular proposition) will not be able to function as a premiss in an argument to the contradictory of his conclusion.' This suggestion makes more sense of the paragraph than do most; but it can hardly be said to make everything plain.

77^{b}40: To argue 'non-deductively' is to argue invalidly; the fallacy of inferring *BaC* from *AaC* & *AaB* (cf. *APr* A 28, 44^{a}20–4) has little enough connection with the matter of the chapter. Caineus was a Lapith; Aristotle is probably referring to a play, perhaps to Antiphanes' comedy *Caineus* which he cites at *Poet* 21, 1457^{b}21. "Multiple proportion" probably means "geometrical proportion"; it is generated quickly in the sense that the terms in a geometrical progression soon become large.

78^{a}5: "Sometimes . . .": the commentators take Aristotle to mean that sometimes you *can* infer *BaC* from *AaC* and *AaB*, e.g. if *AaB* converts to *BaA*. But in no case does *BaC* follow from *AaC* & *AaB*; and it is preferable to take the sentence in isolation from its predecessors, as a true if unexciting jotting.

78^{a}6: Suppose "it were impossible to prove truth from falsehood", i.e.:

(4) If *P* entails *Q*, then necessarily if *Q* is true *P* is true.

(I take it that "prove" is being used in the weak sense of "validly infer", and that Aristotle is adverting to the thesis which he refutes at length in *APr* B 2–4). Then "the propositions would convert", i.e.:

(5) If *P* entails *Q* then *Q* entails *P*.

(For this use of "convert" (*antistrephein*), cf. e.g. *Top* I 15, 167^{b}1–3.) Hence in order to prove *A* we need only find some syllogistic conjunction *B* such that *A* entails *B* and *B* is true.

78^{a}7: "to make analyses": i.e. 'to discover premisses from which to prove the conclusion'. "In analysis we assume that which is sought as if it were already done, and we inquire what it is from which this results" (Pappus, *Collectio* ii. 634; cf. *EN Γ* 3, 1112^{b}20–4; *Top* I 16, 175^{a}17. The ancient texts also describe a quite different procedure as analysis; and the whole matter is controversial.)

78ᵃ10: "In mathematics conversion is more common . . .": Definitions 'convert' in the sense that if *AaB* is a definition then *BaA* (e.g. *Top Z* 1, 139ᵃ31). Thus if we have one definitional premiss, *AaB*, and a putative conclusion, *AaC*, we can infer the second premiss *BaC*. But why does this bear on mathematics in particular? After all, definitions rather than incidental predications form the principles of *all* the sciences and not just of mathematics. (Does *mathēmasi* mean "learnings" rather than "mathematics" (cf. 77ᵇ27, note)?) Again, how is this compatible with Aristotle's assertion that conversion is rare in the sciences (*A* 3, 73ᵃ17)? Aristotle has observed that mathematical theorems often do 'convert'; but he has not got to grips with his observation.

78ᵃ12: ". . . in this too they differ": "too" seems to refer back to 77ᵇ31; in that case it forces us to read *en tois logois* there as "in dialectical arguments" (perhaps cf. *Top Θ* 3, 159ᵃ1–2).

78ᵃ14: This paragraph has no connection with the body of *A* 12; Aristotle, though he does not say so, is talking of the way in which a *science* 'increases', i.e. gains more theorems (cf. *APr A* 25). Suppose that a science starts with the minimum number of principles, viz. two: *AaB* & *BaC*. It does not increase "through the middle terms", i.e. by adding new principles of the form *AaG*, *GaB*, *BaH*, *HaC*; for if *AaB* and *BaC* are principles they are immediate. It may increase "by additional assumptions" in two ways. The first way is exemplified by "e.g. *A* of *B* . . ."; i.e. we take new *principles CaD, DaE* . . . The second, 'lateral', way is exemplified by "e.g. *A* both of *C* and of *E*". Here *AaC* and *AaE* turn out to be the conclusions which the laterally increased science can obtain. The new principles must be *AaD* and *DaE*. The difference between the two methods of increase can be illustrated diagrammatically:

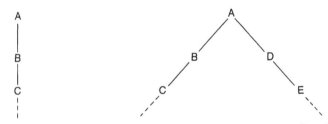

The concrete illustration of the second mode of increase is puzzling. The adjective "definite" (*posos*) is nowhere else applied to numbers by Aristotle (or, so far as I know, by anyone else). It has been taken to mean either "finite" or "particular" (so that *B* is, e.g., 7—a particular odd number). The latter interpretation is wrong, since 7 cannot be predicated of *C*, "odd number". The former interpretation, however, is very strange. "Odd number" (*C*) and "even number" (*E*) may stand for particular numbers, e.g. 7 and 8. *A* should then be simply "number"; some interpreters achieve this by reading the phrase "definite (or even indefinite) number" as "number (whether definite or indefinite)".

CHAPTER 13

The first part of *A* 13 discusses some of the issues raised by Aristotle's requirement that understanders 'know the explanation' of what they understand (*A* 2, 71ᵇ9–16). In general see PATZIG (1981).

We might well think we could distinguish between understanding a fact and understanding an explanation in less subtle ways than those Aristotle devises; but in fact Aristotle, despite his language, is not concerned with this distinction at all: rather, he wants to distinguish between understanding a fact 'through' its explanation (i.e. knowing that *P* on the basis of *Q*, where *Q* explains why *P* is the case), and understanding a fact not through its explanation (i.e. knowing that *P* on the basis of *Q* where *Q* does not explain why *P* is the case). Cases of the second type, which Aristotle divides into two groups, are not, strictly speaking, cases of understanding at all; perhaps with ordinary usage in mind, Aristotle is here countenancing a weaker sense of "understand" than his official one.

78ᵃ22: *Group (A)*—"first in the same science"—lasts until 78ᵇ34; Aristotle announces two subdivisions within this group, but the commentators have discerned more than two. The passage may be divided, uncontroversially, into five sections. (i) 78ᵃ23–6 describes the first of the two cases which 78ᵃ23 announces, and (ii) 78ᵃ26–ᵇ11 describes the second case. (iii) occupies 78ᵇ11–13, (iv) is 78ᵇ13–27, and (v) is 78ᵇ28–34. Whereas (ii) discusses cases in which there are *converting* terms, (iii)–(v) deal with non-converting terms. Hence (iii)–(v) do not offer further instances of the second case announced at 78ᵃ23. Hence either (iii)–(v) offer illustrations of the first case announced at 78ᵃ23, or else they add further cases to the two which were initially announced. If we prefer the former option, then we must suppose that (i) and (iii)–(v) all consider syllogisms which do not proceed through immediates and in which the middle terms, while mentioning explanatorily relevant factors, do not pick out the *primitive* explanation. This supposition is perhaps consistent with the text; but it is not enormously plausible.

78ᵃ23: *Section (i)*: Aristotle has not said that in order to understand something we must know its *primitive* explanation, though his remarks at *A* 9, 76ᵃ18–22, come close to implying it; the statement is made explicitly at *Phys A* 1, 184ᵃ12–14; *B* 3, 194ᵇ17–20. The phrase "primitive explanation" (*prōton aition*) can be taken in two ways: in a sequence $P_1, P_2, \ldots, P_n$, where each P_i explains its predecessor, either P_n (the 'ultimate' explanation) or P_2 (the 'proximate' explanation) may be called the "primitive explanation" of P_1 (cf. esp. *Met Δ* 4, 1015ᵃ7–10, on prime, or 'primitive', matter). Aristotle does not say which sort of primitiveness he has in mind here: suppose that we have as immediate propositions *AaD, DaB, BaC*, and we want to demonstrate *AaC*. We might do so either from *AaD* & *DaC* or from *AaB* & *BaC*; several passages (*A* 9, 76ᵇ18–22; 24, 85ᵇ23–86ᵃ3; *Met α* 2, 994ᵃ11–16) suggest that *AaD* & *DaC*, the ultimate explanation, is the required premiss-pair; but *B* 18 plumps rather for *AaB* & *BaC*, the proximate explanation, and the examples at 78ᵇ13–32 seem to support this view (cf. also *Top Z* 5, 143ᵃ17–32). Aristotle certainly thinks that he has to decide which explanation 'really' explains *AaC*; but in a fully explicit demonstrative science, all the relevant immediate propositions will be used in the demonstrative chain leading to *AaC*, and it is fatuous to attempt to single out any subset of these as constituting the 'real' explanation of the fact.

78ᵃ26: *Section (ii)*: We argue: *AaB, BaC* ⊢ *AaC*. But *B* is not the explanatory term: it is in fact *A* that explains why *B* belongs to *C* and not *B* that explains why *A* belongs to *C*. We are misled by the fact that *A* and *B* are convertible (i.e. that *AaB* & *BaA*), and that *B* is "more familiar" (sc. in relation to us: *A* 2, 71ᵇ21), i.e. that we are more ready to assent to *BaC* than to *AaC*.

Aristotle says that in this case our demonstration is "through immediates"; but though *AaB* may be immediate, *BaC* is not.

78ᵃ30: 78ᵃ30–ᵇ11 illustrates section (ii) (for the examples see *Cael B* 8, 290ᵃ13–24; *B* 11); there is a further illustration in *B* 16. Just as "understanding" was used in a weak sense at 78ᵃ22, so "demonstrate" is used in an analogously weak sense at 78ᵃ36.

It should be noted that *both* of Aristotle's planetary syllogisms would count as explanatory on the orthodox modern account of scientific explanation; both infer a fact from a set of observationally significant general laws and boundary conditions. Thus if Aristotle is correct to distinguish between the two syllogisms, and to hold the one explanatory and the other not, then the orthodox account of scientific explanation is wrong. Moreover, the Humean notion of causation, which is a presupposition of that account, goes too: as far as Hume is concerned, the major premisses of both syllogisms are equally causal. (See further Brody; VAN FRAASSEN (1980), 28–35.) If Aristotle's view is to be upheld, then he must tell us how we can judge that non-scintillation is explained by, and does not explain, proximity; any such account is obliged to wait upon the discussion of essence in Book *B*: it is finally offered at *B* 16, 98ᵇ21–4.

78ᵇ11: *Section (iii)*: At first sight we might take this as a case in which we infer *AaC* from *AaB* & *BaC*, where *AaB* does not convert and in point of fact *A* rather than *B* is explanatory. But if *A* is explanatory of *BaC*, then *BaC* is deducible from *BaA* & *AaC*; so that *AaB* does convert.

Perhaps, then, the following argument illustrates Aristotle's point: "The wallaby has a pouch; all pouched animals are mammals: therefore the wallaby is a mammal." The second premiss does not convert; and the fact that wallabies are marsupial is more familiar than the fact that they are viviparous (which is, let us suppose, the actual explanation of their being mammals). If this illustration is apposite, then here as at 78^{b}15 "the explanation is not stated".

78^{b}13: *Section (iv)*: Aristotle now turns to cases in which "the middle term has outside position". This phrase has divided the commentators (see e.g. Alexander, *in APst* frag. 19; MIGNUCCI (1975), 304–12). Some take it to mean "in the second figure". This is supported by the parallel phrase at *APr A* 5, 26^{b}39 (see Patzig, 10–14); and also by the fact that the illustration is a second figure syllogism and is expressly marked as such (78^{b}24). We should then suppose that section (iii) deals implicitly with first figure syllogisms. But there are difficulties. First, 78^{b}14 will then imply that no second figure syllogism can present a genuine demonstration. But *A* 14 implies that demonstrations may be made in the second figure; and consider, e.g., the argument:

> Having lungs holds of all breathing things
> Having lungs holds of no walls
> _____
> Breathing holds of no walls.

This is a syllogism in *Camestres*; and its terms satisfy (let us allow) the conditions which Aristotle lays down for explanations. Moreover, the connection between sections (iv) and (v) is then hard to fathom.

Other scholars therefore hold that the phrase "the middle term has outside position" refers not to the structure of a syllogism but rather to the remoteness of the explanation which it offers: it is then an accident that the case is illustrated by a second figure syllogism. This interpretation has the advantage of making sense of the sequence (iii), (iv), (v): section (iii) deals with cases where the middle term is non-immediate but 'near', section (iv) with remote middles, and section (v) with very remote middles.

However that may be, the argument in section (iv) is illustrated by a syllogism in *Camestres* (*AaB, AeC ⊢ BeC*). The argument rests on a general principle about explanation (78^{b}17–18) which requires a rather complicated formulation:

(1) If (∀x) (if not-Fx, then not-Fx because not-Gx) then (∀x) (if Fx, then Fx because Gx).

(For the illustration of (1) cf. e.g. *Top Z* 2, 139^{b}21; *Phys H* 3, 246^{b}4. The corollary of (1)—78^{b}20–1—is simply its contrapositive. Cf. *Phys A* 7, 191^{a}7; *B* 3, 195^{a}12 = *Met Δ* 2, 1013^{b}12.) This principle is false: if my matches won't strike because they are not dry, it does not follow that when matches do strike they strike because they are dry; non-striking may be adequately explained by the absence of just one of a set of conditions all of which must be employed in an explanation of successful striking.

It turns out, however, that (1) is an unnecessarily strong principle for Aristotle's purposes; all he needs is:

(2) If not-*P* is among the conditions explanatory of not-*Q*, then *P* is among the conditions explanatory of *Q*.

And this principle seems to be true.

(2) has now to be applied to the wall. If *AeC* is among the conditions for *BeC*—i.e. if the *Camestres* syllogism is genuinely explanatory—then if *BaC* were the case, *AaC* would be among its explanatory conditions. (The contradictory of *BeC* is *BiC*, not *BaC*; Aristotle seems to be assuming that only universal propositions figure in demonstrations—see p. 146.) But then the *other* condition for *BaC* would have to be *BaA*; and *BaA* is not true ("not every animal breathes"—e.g. fish and insects don't: *PA Δ* 13, 697^{a}21; 5, 678^{b}1). (By "a deduction giving an explanation" at 77^{b}23 Aristotle means a *putatively* explanatory deduction.)

78^{b}28: *Section* (*v*): On Anacharsis see e.g. Herodotus, iv. 76–7; Diogenes Laertius, i. 101–5.

78^{b}34: *Group* (*B*): Aristotle turns now to a topic he has already touched upon more than once (cf. *A* 7, 75^{b}6, note). The *fons et origo* of Aristotle's discussion, as of so much in his classifications of the sciences, is Plato's *Philebus* (55^c–59^b).

Group (B) is quite distinct from group (A). If we suppose that *AaB*, *BaC* ⊢ *AaC* is a full-blooded explanatory demonstration, then (A) indicates how a man might miss it and be tempted instead by some related but non-explanatory argument; (B), on the other hand, indicates how the different propositions in the demonstration may fall under the province of different sciences (so that, e.g., even though *AaC* is a theorem of medicine, the doctor *qua* doctor cannot explain why it holds: *AaB* is a theorem of another art).

In the five passages bearing on the topic Aristotle offers the following illustrations:

　(i) harmonics, arithmetic (75^{b}16; 76^{a}10, 24; 78^{b}38; 87^{a}34);
　(ii) optics, geometry (75^{b}16; 76^{a}24; 78^{b}37);
　(iii) mechanics, stereometry (geometry) (76^{a}24; 78^{b}37);
　(iv) star-gazing, astronomy (78^{b}39);
　(v) nautical astronomy, mathematical astronomy (79^{a}1);
　(vi) acoustical harmonics, mathematical harmonics (79^{a}2);
　(vii) study of the rainbow, optics (79^{a}10);
(viii*) medicine, geometry (79^{a}14).

With the exception of (viii*), he implies or states that all these pairs are on a par. The following relations are said to hold between the members of each pair:

　(*a*) *x* falls under *y* (75^{b}15; 78^{b}36; 79^{a}4; cf. 13);
　(*b*) *x* is proved through *y* (76^{a}10);
　(*c*) the demonstrations of *y* apply to *x* (76^{a}22; cf. 75^{b}4);
　(*d*) *x* is proved from the same things as *y* (77^{b}2);
　(*e*) the kind of *x* is different from the kind of *y* (76^{a}12; cf. 75^{b}2, 9; 76^{a}23);

(f) the 'in itself' attributes of x are the same as those of y (76^a13);
(g) the fact belongs to x, the reason why to y (76^a11; 78^b34; 79^a11, 15);
(h) x is like particular, y like universal knowledge (79^a5);
(j) x is studied by empirical, y by mathematical scientists (79^a3);
(k) x uses and y is about forms (79^a7);
(m) x is less exact than y (87^a31-3).

These items raise a number of acute problems, only some of which can be indicated here.

The first members of (i), (ii), and (iii)—harmonics, optics, and mechanics—are classed by Aristotle as "the more mathematical of the natural sciences" (cf. *Phys B* 2, 194^a10; *Met B* 2, 997^b15-21; *M* 3, 1078^a14-18). Aristotle is said to have written works on all three subjects, but the surviving *Mechanica* (cf. Heath (2), 227–54) and *Musical Problems* are spurious. Pseudo-Euclid's *Optics* contains an axiomatized mathematical treatment of the subject and no doubt is a sophisticated version of the sort of thing Aristotle had in mind. Mechanics was given a mathematical treatment by Archytas; but Plato spurned it, and it did not recover until Archimedes (cf. Solmsen, 130–5). Some commentators have been worried by the fact that Aristotle at 76^a24 places mechanics under geometry rather than under stereometry; but the term "geometry", in Greek as in English, may include stereometry (cf. e.g. *Met M* 3, 1078^a25).

Astronomy, too, is one of the more mathematical of the sciences (*Phys B* 2, 194^a10; *Met B* 2, 997^b15-21; A 8, 989^b33; A 8, 1073^b3-8— Aristotle wrote a treatise on this, too); and so we should expect (iv) to parallel its predecessors and pair astronomy with dynamics. The terminology of (iv) disappoints this expectation: "astronomy" there seems parallel to the *first* members of (i)–(iii), and its subordinate, "star-gazing" (literally "the appearances", *ta phainomena*), looks observational rather than mathematical (see esp. *APr A* 30, 46^a19-21; cf. *PA A* 1, 639^b7; note, however, that Euclid gave his axiomatic treatment of astronomy the title *Phainomena*.)

The pair (vii) shares a member with (ii), and thus together they yield a triad:

(a) study of the rainbow, optics, geometry.

The study of the rainbow (cf. *Metr Γ* 2–5) presumably stands as an *example* of what the science subordinate to optics studies. Study of the rainbow was later included in 'catoptrics' (cf. pseudo-Euclid's *Catoptrica*). Aristotle did not have a term for catoptrics; when he talks of "optics *simpliciter* or mathematical optics" (79^a12) he means that we should call the second member of (vii) mathematical optics since "optics" without qualification might include both members of (vii).

(v) and (vi) appear comparable to (vii), the more so if the second member of (vii) is properly "mathematical optics". Thus we might expect two more triads:

(β) acoustical harmonics, mathematical harmonics, arithmetic;
(γ) nautical astronomy, mathematical astronomy (or star-gazing), astronomy (or dynamics).

(The pairs (v) and (vi) are distinguished at *Rep* 529^c–530^d (cf. [*Epin*] 990^a) and 530^d–531^c; the distinction in (vi) was rejected by Aristoxenus, *Elementa Harmonica*, *B* 32–3.) The natural and orthodox account of (iv), however, obliges us to identify (iv) and (v), and hence to abandon (γ).

The commentators suppose that when Aristotle says that "some of these sciences bear almost the same name as one another (*sunōnumos*)" (78^{b}39) he is using *sunōnumos* in the technical sense of *Cat* 1, 1^{a}6–7 (roughly, *x* is *sunōnumos* with *y* if *x* and *y* are both *F* in the same sense of "*F*"); but the non-technical sense, "having the same name as", seems more probable here (cf. *Phil* 57^b). However that may be, the point is that there are two different sorts of astronomy and harmonics.

Finally, (viii*) is not on a par with the other pairs, as Aristotle makes clear. Yet it is more scandalous than Aristotle allows. The doctor learns by observation that curved wounds heal slowly (cf. Cassius, *Problems* 1); the geometer explains this by the fact (say) that among plane figures circles have the highest area/periphery ratio. (The demonstration needs the further premiss that speed of healing is dependent on the area/periphery ratio of a wound.) Thus, the geometer explains, or helps to explain, the doctor's theorem: on any account of kind crossing, this violates the thesis of *A* 7.

It is clear that the constitutive relation for the pairs (i)–(vii) is (*a*), subordination (cf. esp. 76^{a}10–13; 79^{a}13). Relations (*b*)–(*f*) are in one way or another explicative of (*a*). (*b*) and (*c*) are too vague to be helpful. (*d*), too, is not very precise; it appears to imply that the principles of *x* are included in those of *y*. But it is implied by (*e*) that *y* has proper principles of its own; and it is not clear whether or why Aristotle thought that *x* uses the same instantiations of the common principles as *y*. Presumably (*d*) only means that *some* of the principles of *x* are also principles of *y*.

(*e*) and (*f*) are thus crucial. 75^{b}9 indicates that the kind of *x* is not wholly distinct from the kind of *y*; the obvious inference to make is that the elements in the kind of *x* are *species* of those of *y*: thus whereas *line* is one of the items in the kind of geometry, *line from the eye to the object of vision* or *ray* (*opsis*) is an item in the kind of optics (cf. [Euclid], *Optics*, definitions). And this gives a sense to the assertion that *x* falls *under* (*hupo*) *y*: the predicate terms of *x*, according to (*f*), are the same as those of *y*; we might then imagine that if *AaC* is a theorem of *y*, there is a term *B* in *x* such that *C* falls under *B* and *AaB* is a theorem of *x*. This gives a neat sense to Aristotle's general account of the relation between *x* and *y*; but it seems to trivialize the notion of a subordinate science.

Relation (*g*) is inferred from (*e*) and (*f*). If *AaC* is a theorem of *y*, and its demonstration proceeds from *AaB* & *BaC*, then by (*e*) *C* is a term of

y and by (f) A and B are terms of x. Hence the explanation for AaC is not demonstrable within x but requires the principles of y.

Relation (j) cannot be intended to apply to all the pairs (if it is applied both to (i) and to (vi) it leads to a contradiction) but only to (v), (vi), and (vii). Aristotle's point at 78^{b}40–79^{a}4 is this: the facts of e.g. astronomy are discovered by empirical scientists, the theories supplied by the mathematicians. More striking is his claim that the mathematicians, who know the explanations, may be in ignorance of the facts. Plainly, they cannot know that P explains Q unless they know (the fact that) Q: Aristotle must mean that they may know P without knowing Q, although as a matter of fact P explains Q. The presence of (j) has been taken to show that Aristotle is muddling up two quite different things: in (α)–(γ) the *first* two items are related as empirical to mathematical, whereas the *second* two are related as applied to pure. But the fact that the pairs do not share *all* their relations does not show that they do not share *some*; and in particular, it does not show that the relation of subordination does not hold for (v)–(vii) as it does for (i)–(iii). The observational sciences bring forward propositions based on perception and induction (e.g. "The rainbow contains seven hues"). Suppose AaC is a theorem of catoptrics, and the explanation of this is by AaB & BaC: then C will belong to catoptrics, and A and B to optics; hence AaC is explained through optics and not through catoptrics. (It should perhaps be added that the surviving treatises on catoptrics are no more observational than the Euclidean *Optics*; and Aristotle's treatment of the rainbow is one of the most mathematically sophisticated parts of his corpus (Heath (2), 180–90).)

Relation (h) is readily intelligible; for the relation of AaB to AaC is precisely that between universal and particular. (On the thesis of 79^{a}2–6 cf. *A* I, 71^{a}24–^{b}8, and notes; see also *Met A* I, 981^{a}12–^{b}6—the connection made there between the subordinate sciences and practice is perhaps carried here in the name *nautical* astronomy.)

Relation (k) is stated at 79^{a}6–9. The lines are difficult to understand. In the opening clause, "The items in question are things which . . .", "the items" has been referred both to acoustical harmonics and to mathematical harmonics. The former seems to give a slightly better argument, viz.: 'Acoustical harmonics and the like, though they are essentially different from mathematical harmonics and the like, still make use of forms; for mathematics, on which they rest, is about forms.' Aristotle's argument that "mathematics is concerned with forms" appears to paraphrase as follows: 'Mathematical objects are forms, because they are self-subsistent. Geometrical objects, perhaps, are not self-subsistent, but even so geometry studies them as though they were.' This *seems* to credit Aristotle with a Platonist view of the objects of mathematics—in which case we must suppose that the paragraph represents an early (or a temporary) phase of his thought. But a better interpretation is possible. The key sentence is "for even if . . .": Aristotle presumably means that the mathematical sciences are 'about forms' only in the sense that they treat their objects *as though* they were self-subsistent forms. The geometers produce theorems of the type "Every triangle is . . .": they use the term "triangle" as though it picked out a substance (just as a botanist's theorems of the form "Every deciduous tree is . . ." pick out a substance). But in point of fact, triangles are not substances—and the reality behind the geometers' theorems is the ordinary world of physical objects. (On Aristotle's view of the objects of mathematics see BARNES (1985); MIGNUCCI (1987).)

Finally, relation (*m*) is expounded in *A* 27 (notes).

CHAPTER 14

79^a17: This paragraph seems to conflate two arguments. (A) 'As a matter of fact the paradigmatic sciences use first figure syllogisms.' This assertion is false; indeed, syllogistic reasoning as a whole is unsurprisingly absent from Greek mathematics. Presumably Aristotle had observed that most mathematical arguments made use of affirmative universal propositions; and he inferred from this that they were, potentially at least, in *Barbara*. (B) 'Demonstrations that reveal the explanation are usually in the first figure.' Presumably because *a*-propositions, the paradigm *explananda*, are only deducible in *Barbara*.

79^a24: The next argument presupposes that knowledge of essences (of "what a thing is") is important for science; the nature and extent of this importance emerges in Book *B*. The connection between demonstration and knowledge of what a thing is is discussed at length in *B* 2–10. The main conclusion there is that there cannot be a demonstration whose conclusion expresses an essence: if the 'hunt for essence' is carried on syllogistically it will at best find its quarry caught in the concatenation of premisses and conclusion. It is true that the argument in our passage seems to envisage essences as being expressed in conclusions; but when the argument is restated at *B* 3, 90^b3–7, that appearance vanishes.

79^a29: "it is not in a certain respect . . .": i.e. 'it is not as *such and such* that men are two footed, so that only *some* men, viz. those who are such and such, are two-footed'.

79^a29: It is not figures but propositions which are 'thickened' or 'increased'. Thus the second figure, say, needs the first figure inasmuch as any thickening of the premisses of a second figure syllogism must be done by way of a first figure syllogism. To 'thicken' or 'increase' a proposition *AxB* is to find a term *C* such that *AyC*, *CzB* ⊢ *AxB* (cf. *A* 23, 84^b35; 25, 86^b13; Einarson, 158); evidently, thickening may continue until the premisses it produces are immediate.

Aristotle's text implies the following proposition: if *P, Q* ⊢ *R* is a syllogism whose premisses must be thickened, then, whatever figure it is in, at least one of the two thickening syllogisms will be in the first figure. This is false: *Ferio* (I), *Festino* (II), and *Ferison* (III) may each be thickened by (say) *Cesare* (II) and *Darapti* (III). Aristotle might reply either that he is only interested in syllogisms with universal conclusions; or that after the *first* thickening process, his argument holds even for these three syllogisms. Thus no demonstrative chain of any length can be entirely independent of the first figure, whereas chains of any length may contain nothing but first figure arguments.

CHAPTER 15

The term "atomically" (*atomōs*) is needlessly introduced as a synonym for *amesōs*, "immediately" (I can find no distinction between the two terms; but see Hintikka (2), 60–1). *Atomos* has several other senses in the *Organon* (Bonitz, 120ᵃ32–ᵇ6). My translation of *A* 15 prefers the barbarous "to not hold" to the ambiguous "not to hold".

79ᵃ36: The initial statement of the first two conditions under which AeB is not immediate or atomic suggests that they are:

(1) $(\exists X)$ $(XaA$ & not-$XaB)$;
(2) $(\exists X)$ $(XaB$ & not-$XaA)$

(For the sense of "in as in a whole" see *APr A* 1, 24ᵇ26–8). But Aristotle's arguments show that instead of (1) and (2) he means:

(1′) $(\exists X)$ $(XaA$ & $XeB)$;
(2′) $(\exists X)$ $(XaB$ & $XeA)$.

Given (1′), there is a syllogism in *Camestres* yielding AeB, so that AeB cannot be atomic (79ᵃ38–ᵇ1). Case (2′) naturally yields *Cesare*, but the text presents *Celarent* (79ᵇ1–4).

The third case is simply the conjunction of (1) and (2). But it must be observed that Aristotle's statement at 79ᵃ36–8 does not propound (1) and (2) at all. What he actually *says* amounts to this: 'If either $(\exists X)$ (XaA) or $(\exists X)$ (XaB) or $(\exists X)$ $(XaA$ & $XaB)$, then it is not possible for AeB to hold atomically.' This is straightforwardly false. Hence I previously took Aristotle to *mean* that AeB cannot be atomic under conditions (1) and (2); and MIGNUCCI (1975), 337–40, argued that the *ouk* at 79ᵃ37 modifies *prōtōs* rather than *endechetai*, so that Aristotle actually says "If either . . . , then it is possible for AeB to hold non-primitively." But 79ᵇ37–8, 80ᵃ1, and 81ᵃ7–9 show that Aristotle meant just what he said—and hence that he erred.

79ᵇ5: A series of terms $A, A_1, \ldots, A_n$ is a chain (*sustoichia*: cf. Bonitz, 736ᵇ33–737ᵃ19; Waitz, 338–40) if each holds universally of its predecessor. A chain α $(A, A_1, \ldots, A_n)$ and a chain β $(B, B_1, \ldots, B_m)$ overlap (cf. Bonitz, 264ᵇ51–265ᵃ6) if some member of α stands in the *i*-relation to some member of β. Suppose, then, that α and β do not overlap. Then, by definition, A_1aA; and also A_1eB (for if not-A_1eB, then A_1iB and there is an overlap). Thus $(\exists X)$ $(XaA$ & $XeB)$.

79ᵇ12: If AeB, and $\neg$ $(\exists X)$ (XaA) & $\neg$ $(\exists X)$ (XaB), then AeB is atomic. The proof is straightforward.

79ᵇ18: In the second figure there will be a proof of *AeB* either in *Cesare* (in which case the proposition with *B* as subject will be affirmative) or else in *Camestres* (in which case the proposition with *A* as subject will be affirmative). This is plainly what Aristotle intends to say. What the received text (which I have translated) makes him say appears a flat contradiction—or else encourages the reader to look vainly for a distinction between negative and privative propositions. Perhaps we should boldly change *amphoterois* ("both") to *hekateron* ("one or the other")?

CHAPTER 16

A 16–18, on ignorance, attach to *A* 5 and *A* 12; for the two sorts of ignorance see *A* 12, 77ᵇ26, note. In general, see LEAR (1980), 90–7.

79ᵇ23: The classification Aristotle is after is this:

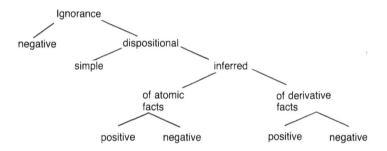

This 'division' is accurately mirrored in the structure of *A* 16–18, but negligently stated at 79ᵇ23–7 (unless the text is corrupt).

79ᵇ26: "when you believe *simpliciter*": i.e. 'when you have come to believe that *P* not on the basis of inference'. "simple" (*haplous*) may also mean "single"; and Aristotle puns when he says that for simple belief (i.e. uninferred belief) the error is simple (i.e. there is only one way of being wrong).

79ᵇ26: "that something holds or does not hold": throughout *A* 16–17 only *universal* propositions are under consideration; "*X* holds of *Y*" is always *XaY*; and "*X* does not hold of *Y*" is always *XeY* (cf. *A* 15, 79ᵃ36, notes).

79ᵇ29: (A) *Inferred dispositional ignorance of negative atomic facts.* I infer *AaB* from *AaC* & *CaB*, when in fact *AeB* is an atomic truth.

Case (i), 79ᵇ33–40, in which both premisses are false, will hold if and only if *AeC*, *CeB*, and atomic *AeB* are compossible (cf. *APr A* 4, 26ᵃ9–16). Aristotle's argument must be paraphrased thus: 'Atomic *AeB* is compatible with *AeC*, for some chosen *C*; but atomic *AeB* and *AeC* yield *CeB* (for if not-*CeB*, then *CaB*, and hence *AeB* is derivable).' Case (ii), 79^{b}40–80^{a}2, would require the compossibility of *AeC*, *CaB*, and atomic *AeB* (cf. *APr A* 4, 25^{b}40–26^{a}2: *Celarent*). Case (iii) requires the compossibility of *AaC*, *CeB*, and atomic *AeB* (cf. *APr A* 4, 26^{a}2–9): 'Atomic *AeB* is compatible with atomic *AaC*; and together they entail *CeB*.' As 80^{a}5 points out, the stipulation that *AaC* is atomic is unnecessary. (Note that "holds" and "is predicated" at 80^{a}3 must cover both affirmative and negative holding and predication; cf. e.g. *A* 19, 82^{a}14.)

80^{a}6: (B) *Inferred dispositional ignorance of positive atomic facts.*

80^{a}9: (*a*) *in Celarent*: I infer *AeB* from *AeC* and *CaB* when in fact *AaB* is an atomic truth.

There is no argument for case (i), 80^{a}11–14, the compossibility of *AaC*, *CeB*, and atomic *AaB* (cf. *APr A* 4, 26^{a}2–9).

Case (ii), 80^{a}14–20, requires the compossibility of *AeC*, *CeB*, and atomic *AaB* (cf. *APr A* 4, 26^{a}9–16): 'Atomic *AaB* is compatible with *AeC*; and they yield *CeB*—for *CaB* & *AaB* would yield *AiC* and hence not-*AeC*; and *CaB* & *AeC* would yield *AeB* and hence not-*AaB*.'

Case (iii), 80^{a}21–4, requires the compossibility of *AaC*, *CaB*, and atomic *AaB*. The argument mirrors the previous one.

80^{a}26: "the deduction may be false": i.e. 'the *conclusion* will be false' (cf. e.g. *APr B* 18, 66^{a}21).

80^{a}27: (*β*) *In the second figure*: Aristotle first asks whether both premisses can be false; his answer would have been best put by saying that it *is* possible for both premisses to be false, although it is *not* possible for their contraries both to be true. Instead of saying this, he distinguishes between total and partial falsity: "I mean by false as a whole the contrary proposition, i.e. if what holds of none is assumed to hold of all, or what holds of all of none" (*APr B* 2, 54^{a}4–6). Thus *AaB* is false as a whole if *AeB*, and *AeB* is false as a whole if *AaB*; and to say that the premisses cannot both be wholly false is just to say that their contraries cannot both be true. Partial falsity is not defined; but Aristotle plainly means that *AaB* is partially false if *AoB* & not-*AeB*; and *AeB* is partially false if *AiB* & not-*AaB*. Thus to say that both the premisses may be partially false is in fact to say something stronger than that both may be false. (Aristotle adopts this curious procedure because his attention in *A* 16–17 is concentrated on universal propositions. The jargon of partial truth is a refinement of common usage; cf. e.g. *Top Z* 12, 149^{b}8; *Θ* 2, 157^{b}28; 7, 160^{a}26.)

AeB must be deduced either from *CaA* & *CeB* (*Camestres*), or from *CeA* & *CaB* (*Cesare*). If both premisses are wholly false "they will be the other way about when assumed in the contrary way", i.e. 'their contraries will have the opposite truth-values', i.e. 'it will be the case that *CeA* & *CaB*, or that *CaA* & *CeB*'. But from *AaB* it follows that ¬ (∃*X*) (*XeA* & *XaB*) & ¬ (∃*X*) (*XaA* & *XeB*).

If both premisses are partially false, then *CiA*, *CoA*, *CiB*, *CoB*, and atomic *AaB* are compossible (cf. *APr A* 5, 27^{b}36–9).

80ᵃ34: "i.e. *C* might hold both of some *A* and of some *B*": Ross
paraphrases: 'i.e. if *CoA* & *CiB*', taking "hold" to cover both positive
and negative holding. But if partial falsity is defined as I suggested,
Aristotle needs the stronger condition: 'i.e. if *CiA* & *CoA* & *CiB* &
CoB'. If this is right, "hold" is taken in its normal positive sense, and
"of some *X*" means "of some but not all *X*".

80ᵃ38: "And if the privative is posited the other way about": i.e. in
Cesare. Aristotle does not ask whether one premiss might be wholly false
and the other partially false.

80ᵃ39: "For what holds of every *A*...": i.e. 'Assuming *AaB*, (∀*X*)
(*XaA* → *XaB*). So if you infer *AeB* from *CaA* & *CeB*, and *CaA* is true,
then *CeB* is false'. This shows that *AaB*, *CaA* and *CeB* are not compatible; but it does not show that *CaA*, *CaB*, and atomic *AaB* are
compossible, which is what Aristotle needs to show. The same goes for
the other three arguments in this paragraph.

80ᵇ17: (C) *Inferred dispositional ignorance of positive derivative facts*:
(α) *in Celarent*: In case (i), 80ᵇ17–26, *AeB* is inferred from *AeC* & *CaB*,
when in fact *AaB* holds, and *C* is the 'appropriate' middle term—i.e.
AaC, *CaB* ⊢ *AaB* is the proper demonstration of *AaB*. This is the
"deduction of the contradictory ⟨of *AeB*⟩". ("Contradictory" is used
loosely: cf. e.g. *Top I* 25, 180ᵃ23–31.)

Thus in the erroneous deduction *CaB* must be true and *AeC* false.
(*AeC* is the proposition "on the major extreme", i.e. 'containing the
major term' (cf. Bonitz, 641ᵃ39–50).)

80ᵇ25: "for it does not convert": i.e. 'if it is replaced by its contrary, no
valid inference is possible'; yet another sense for the Protean *antistrephein*.

80ᵇ26: Case (ii), 80ᵇ26–32, is, logically speaking, exactly like case (i);
for illustration see *A* 29.

80ᵇ32: In case (iii), 80ᵇ32–9, *AaD* & *DeB* hold; in case (iv), 80ᵇ40–
81ᵃ4, *AeD* & *DeB* hold. In (iii) and (iv) *D* is 'inappropriate' because it
cannot figure in a sound argument for *AaB*; in (ii) *D* is 'inappropriate'
because the argument for *AaB* which it yields is, though sound, not
demonstrative.

81ᵃ5: (β) *In the second figure*: 81ᵃ8 refers back to *A* 16, 80ᵃ27–33; from
a logical point of view the arguments here only repeat what was said at
80ᵃ27–ᵇ14.

81ᵃ15: (D) *Inferred dispositional ignorance of negative derivative facts*.
We infer *AaB* from *AaC* & *CaB*, when in fact *AeB*; Aristotle assumes
that *AeB* is demonstrable by *Celarent*. Case (i), 81ᵃ15–20, parallels
80ᵇ18–26; case (ii), 81ᵃ20–4, parallels 80ᵇ26–32.

Case (iii), 81ᵃ24–7, occurs when in fact *AaD* & *DeB* hold; case (iv),

81^a27-31, occurs when AeD & DaB hold; and case (v), 81^a31-2, occurs when AeD & DeB hold. Thus (iv) is identical with (ii).

81^a33: "Thus it is clear...": The received text ascribes an unintelligible error to Aristotle. Ross excises the whole sentence; and he may be right. I have preferred to emend the text (on the model of 79^b40-1). For a similar proposal see MIGNUCCI (1975), 382.

CHAPTER 18

81^a38: (E) *Negative Ignorance*. Aristotle is clearly arguing for some sort of empiricist thesis; and his argument is clear enough in outline: 'no knowledge without induction, no induction without perception; so no knowledge without perception'. But what exactly the thesis is, and how exactly the argument runs, are matters far less clear. Compare, in general, *A* 31 and *B* 19.

The first sentence of the chapter could be read as:

   (1) $(\exists y)$ (**a** has not perceived y) $\rightarrow$ $(\exists P)$ (P & **a** does not know that P).

But Aristotle's argument will not yield (1). The argument does yield:

   (2) (**a** has perceived nothing) $\rightarrow$ (**a** knows nothing).

This is stated at *An* Γ 8, 432^a7-8; but it is hard to read it into 81^a38. It is better to read the thesis as saying:

   (3) (**a** lacks some sense-faculty) $\rightarrow$ $(\exists P)$ (P & **a** does not know that P).

Since the senses each have their proper objects (*An B* 6, 418^a11-16), (3) is entailed by:

   (4) $(\exists A)$ (**a** has not perceived As) $\rightarrow$ $(\exists P)$ (P & **a** does not understand that P).

Aristotle can then be construed as arguing for (4) from the following premisses, not all of which are explicit in the text:

   (5) **a** understands that AaB $\rightarrow$ **a** has learned that AaB;

   (6) **a** has learned that AaB $\rightarrow$ (**a** has demonstrated that AaB) or (**a** has induced that AaB);

   (7) **a** has demonstrated that AaB $\rightarrow$ $(\exists C)$ (**a** has inferred that AaB from AaC & CaB);

   (8) **a** has inferred P from Q $\rightarrow$ **a** has considered Q;

   (9) **a** has considered AaC $\rightarrow$ $(\exists D)$ (**a** has induced that AaD);

   (10) **a** has induced that AaD $\rightarrow$ **a** has inferred AaD from n perceived instances of the type Ab & Db;

   (11) **a** has inferred P from a perceived case C $\rightarrow$ **a** has perceived C.

From these premisses there follows:

(12) **a** understands that $AaB \to$ **a** has perceived As.

Premiss (5) is implicit at 81ᵃ39–40. For (6)—expressed at 81ᵃ40—cf. e.g. *APr A* 23, 68ᵇ13; *Phys* Θ 1, 252ᵃ22; *Met A* 9, 992ᵇ30–2; *EN Z* 3, 1139ᵇ27 (cf. above, p. 81). (7) is trifling, and (8)–(9) are found at 81ᵇ2. For (10)—81ᵇ5–6—see esp. *Top A* 12, 105ᵃ13–16 (see above, p. 83). (11), again, is trifling. Since the argument is concerned with understanding, it is reasonable to limit its scope to universal propositions (but no doubt *AeB* should be allowed, as well as *AaB*).

The conclusion does not quite yield (4); and some of the premisses leave something to be desired. But it is, I think, an easy, if tedious, matter to tidy up the argument in such a way that its only disputable feature is the proposition that, if *A* is any proper sensible, then **a** knows that *Ab* only if **a** has perceived some *As*. This proposition seems defensible to me; but to discuss it would involve a wholesale treatment of the foundations of empiricism.

81ᵃ38: "if some perception is wanting . . .": *ekleloipen*, "is wanting", could also be translated "has been lost"; but this deprives the argument of plausibility.

81ᵇ1: "induction on particulars": particulars here are *individuals*, the objects of sense-perception (cf. p. 83).

81ᵇ3: "even the items . . .": i.e. 'even if *C* is an abstraction, it is possible to show by induction that, say, *A* holds of *C* as such (even though *Cs* are not separable, i.e. self-subsistent)'. The parenthesis is obscure, and the commentators offer several different glosses. It is clear enough, however, that Aristotle is offering an *a fortiori* defence of (9). Even if the defence succeeds, its conclusion is not strong enough; for it argues only that induction *can* make abstractions familiar, when Aristotle needs to argue that abstractions *can only* be made familiar by induction. *An Γ* 8, 432ᵃ3–6, offers a different and stronger argument for the view that "objects of comprehension, both what are called abstractions and the affections and qualities of sensible things, are in the sensible forms" and hence cannot be considered apart from perception.

By "the items we speak about on the basis of abstraction" Aristotle means the quasi-objects which we consider when we mentally abstract from ordinary objects some of their actually inseparable properties; among such quasi-objects are the objects of mathematics (cf. e.g. *Cael Γ* 1, 299ᵃ16; *An A* 1, 403ᵇ14–15; *Γ* 4, 429ᵇ18–20; 7, 431ᵇ12–17). Thus what Aristotle says commits him to the Millian view that some (not all) the propositions of mathematics are learned by induction. Aristotle's philosophy of mathematics leads him toward the conception of mathematics as an applied science, or at least to the view that mathematical theorems state truths about the ordinary furniture of the world. Such a view sits well with the Millian thesis: *applied* mathematics is an empirical science.

81ᵇ6: The last lines of the chapter are extremely puzzling (see MIGNUCCI

(1975), 384–6). With much hesitation, I place a light stop after *adunaton* and a heavy stop after *aisthēsis* at 81ᵇ6 (the OCT punctuates the other way about). And I take *ou gar* ... *aisthēseōs* at 81ᵇ6–9—despite the *gar*—to offer a brief summary of the argument of the whole chapter. For an alternative suggestion see VERDENIUS (1981), 351.

CHAPTER 19

A 19–23 form a continuous argument for the thesis that there cannot be predicational chains of infinite length; it follows from this thesis that there cannot be demonstrative chains of infinite length. There is a more general, but far briefer, argument against infinite explanatory chains in *Met* α 2. The thesis connects, and is connected (82ᵃ7), with the argument of *A* 3. On the whole argument see LEAR (1980), 15–33.

A 19 states the thesis and analyses the question of its truth into three subquestions; these questions are answered in the succeeding three chapters.

81ᵇ10: "One type ... the other ...": only syllogisms with universal conclusions are in question.

81ᵇ14: "Thus it is clear that the principles ... are items of these types": i.e. '... are propositions of the form *AaB* or *AeB*'. This is evident from the fact that the principles form the ultimate premisses from which demonstrations are derived.

81ᵇ18: The predications in the syllogistic chains must be *true* and they must be *natural*.

Truth: cf. in general *APr A* 30, 46ᵃ3–10; on opinion/truth cf. *APr B* 16, 65ᵃ35–7; on "reputable" see *A* 6, 74ᵇ21, note. The words translated "opinion", "reputable", and "is thought" all come from the root *dok-*; and Aristotle plays on the fact: the dialectician starts from reputable premisses (*enDOXa*), so he is content if there is thought (*DOKei*) to be a middle term, since he is only arguing with regard to opinion (*kata DOXan*—i.e. it is enough if his conclusions are believed).

Natural Predication: see pp. 114–17; the significance of this stipulation emerges in *A* 22.

81ᵇ30: This section analyses the main question of the chapter into its three subquestions; Aristotle first considers chains of affirmative propositions. The three subquestions are these: first, can the sequence of immediate propositions *AaB, CaA, DaC,* ... continue indefinitely, or must it stop? Secondly, can the sequence of immediate propositions *AaB, BaC, CaD,* ... continue indefinitely, or must it stop? Thirdly, can the non-immediate proposition *AaB* be indefinitely thickened by the interposition of propositions *AaC, CaD,* ..., *ZaB*, or must the thickening stop?

It is worth stating these questions a little more precisely. Take the sequence of terms:

(S) $\ldots A_n, \ldots, A_m, \ldots, A_k, \ldots$

such that $(\forall i)\,(\forall j)\,(i > j \rightarrow A_i a A_j)$. (Aristotle thinks of a *vertical* line ascending from A_n to A_k.) Then the three questions are:

  (i) Given that (S) has a first term—i.e. a term A_0 such that $\neg\,(\exists i)\,(A_0 a A_i)$—can there be infinitely many terms to the right of (or 'above') A_0?

  (ii) Given that (S) has a last term—i.e. a term A_1 such that $\neg\,(\exists i)\,(A_i a A_1)$—can there be infinitely many terms to the left of (or 'below') A_1?

  (iii) Can there be two terms A_i, A_j in (S) such that there are infinitely many terms between A_i and A_j? (Equivalently, can there by any term in (S) which has no immediate neighbour? i.e. can there be an A_i such that for all j neither $A_i a A_j$ nor $A_j a A_i$ is immediate?)

Aristotle does not explicitly consider the possibility that every term in (S) has infinitely many terms to its right and infinitely many to its left.

82^a6: "This is the same as to inquire . . .": "This" refers to question (iii): demonstration, in Aristotle's view, requires the existence of immediate propositions; it does not require that there is only a finite number of them. The question whether there is demonstration of everything involves the issue of 'circular' proof (A 3, 72^b25–73^a20), and that is not taken up in these chapters; rather, Aristotle is backing up his stand at A 3, 72^b18–25, against the view that there is *no* understanding. His remarks must be taken loosely: if there are no immediate propositions there will be premisses available for the proof of any given proposition—but of course no proof at all would be possible in such a situation.

82^a9: Negative propositions are now brought into the picture, and yield a fourth question. Aristotle says "I say the same . . ."; and so we might reasonably expect him to have in mind a sequence of terms, like (S), for which $A_i e A_j$. But the expectation is disappointed. (In effect such a sequence is considered implicitly in the next paragraph, at 82^a15; for all the terms in such a sequence will convert with respect to the *e*-relation.) Rather, Aristotle is interested in "privative *deductions* and propositions"; and the sequence he has in mind is this:

  (S*) $\ldots, AeB_n,\ AeB_{n+1},\ AeB_{n+2}, \ldots$

where $B_i a B_j$. This sequence of privative propositions yields a sequence of privative deductions, all of them in *Celarent*. (AeB_{n+1}, $B_{n+1}aB_n \vdash AeB_n$; etc.) And Aristotle's question is this:

  (iv) Can the sequence (S*) contain infinitely many members?

When, in A 21, he turns to answer the question we shall find that it is broadened in scope: the limitation to syllogisms in *Celarent* is removed.

82^a14: "The prior terms of which A holds": "hold" is here used in the neutral sense (see p. 165).

82^{a}15: Aristotle now turns, parenthetically, to a sequence (S^c), in which all the terms are counterpredicable, i.e. such that every term in it is universally predicable of every other. He does not say whether (S) may contain counterpredicable terms, but his later argument indicates that it does not; if that is so, then he does not consider series of terms only some of which are counterpredicable.

What does Aristotle mean to say about (S^c)? "It is not the same" for it inasmuch as questions (i) and (ii) cannot be posed for it; and if it has infinitely many members, then both (i) and (ii) are answered affirmatively for (S). (This translates *ei t'* ... *ep'* ...; most MSS give *eit'* ... *eit'* ... : "whether its predicates ... or the items we are puzzling over ..." This seems to make little sense.)

82^{a}16: "... there is none of which any is predicated primitively or ultimately": i.e. '(S^c) has no first subject of predication (i.e. no term which is not predicated of anything) and no ultimate subject of predication (i.e. no term of whose predicate nothing is predicated).'

82^{a}19: "unless it is possible ...": i.e. 'unless each counterpredicated pair contains one natural and one unnatural predication'.

CHAPTER 20

A 20 argues correctly that if the answers to (i) and (ii) are negative, then the answer to (iii) is also negative. (He might have been content (*pace* LEAR (1980), 19–21) with the weaker thesis that if either the answer to (i) or the answer to (ii) is negative, then the answer to (iii) is negative: see SCANLAN (1982), 2–4.)

82^{a}30: An objector says that in the infinite series *A*, *B*, *F* (where *B* represents infinitely many terms: 82^{a}25), it might be the case (*a*) that some of the predications are immediate, and (*b*) that the terms not appearing in immediate predications cannot be grasped.

Aristotle does not bother to answer (*b*): he would agree that not all the terms of *A*–*F* can be grasped (cf. e.g. *Met A* 2, 994^{b}20–7) but hold that *A*–*F* may still contain infinitely many terms (cf. e.g. *Phys Γ* 6, 206^{a}21–5). He does answer (*a*): what he should say is that *A*–*F* may have infinitely many members even if some subset, say B_j–B_k, is finite; his actual answer is less clear.

82^{a}32: "whichever of the *B*s I take ...": if this sentence is not to be the merest tautology it must be understood as follows: 'Even if some subset of *A*–*F* is finite, it remains the case that for any B_i either *A*–B_i or B_i–*F* is infinite.'

82^{a}34: "It makes no difference ...": Aristotle seems to have the following argument in mind: 'Suppose that B_j–B_k are immediately connected to one another: that makes no difference. For the series up to *F* is infinite whether it starts being infinite immediately after *A* or only after

B_k'. But of course, if B_k-F is infinite, then so too is $A-F$; a set does not 'start' being infinite at any point. (But see LEAR (1980), 24–5.)

CHAPTER 21

The aim of A 21 is to show that there cannot be an infinite sequence of negative demonstrations if there are no infinite sequences of positive demonstrations. In effect, then, Aristotle will try to prove that if the answers to questions (i) and (ii) are negative, then a negative answer must also be given to question (iv). Or rather, to a revised version of question (iv). For question (iv), and its sequence (S*), was limited to syllogisms in *Celarent*; whereas in A 21 Aristotle wants to exclude *any* infinite sequence of negative syllogisms.

There are nine syllogistic moods which yield a negative conclusion, so that there are—we might infer—nine different types of sequence for Aristotle to investigate. In fact, he limits himself to three ways. According to the received text, these three ways are *Celarent*, *Camestres*, and *Bocardo*. The commentators generally assume that the argument of A 21 is incomplete: in order to complete it, we must consider the remaining six negative moods. But I shall argue that the three ways which Aristotle has in mind are *Celarent*, *Camestres*, and *Cesare*, that he is limiting his attention (as he usually does in *APst*) to universal propositions, and that his argument is therefore complete as it stands.

82^b5: Suppose that we have a connected sequence of arguments in *Celarent* (AeB, BaC ⊢ AeC): can this sequence be infinite? Aristotle first remarks, truly but impertinently, that we cannot have an infinite sequence of propositions leading to the second premiss, BaC: here "we must arrive at immediates", since—by hypothesis—the sequence (S) has an uppermost or right-most member. (At 82^b7 "interval" (*diastēma*) means "proposition": see Bonitz, 189^b11–17.) Secondly, Aristotle remarks—truly and pertinently—that if the sequence of proofs associated with AeB were infinitely long, then the sequence (S) would have no right-most or uppermost member. To see that this is correct it is enough to look at sequence (S*): associated with every AeB_i there is a B_iaB_j. Hence if there are infinitely many of the former, there are infinitely many of the latter, so that (S) will go on *ad infinitum* to the right.

82^b13: *Camestres*: the case is parallel to that of *Celarent*. Instead of (S*) we need to consider:

(S**) $\ldots, A_neB, A_{n+1}eB, A_{n+2}eB, \ldots$

where A_iaA_j. (*Cesare* requires a different—and a more complicated—sequence.)

82^b14: "If you must next prove this": i.e. *BeC*.

82^b16: "the second will now be proved": presumably "proved" means something like "exhibited" (the root meaning of *deiknunai* is "show").

82^{b}17: "If you prove in this way . . .": for the text of this very difficult sentence I now follow MIGNUCCI (1975), 427–31.

82^{b}21: As the text stands, Aristotle here turns to *Bocardo*. But the text presents several peculiarities. First, in the lettering of *Bocardo C* stands unusually for the major and *A* for the minor term. Secondly, 82^{b}24 says that "this [i.e. *CoB*] will be proved . . . in the ways described above"; but neither *Celarent* nor *Camestres* yields an *o*-conclusion. Thirdly, if it is the three figures with which Aristotle is concerned, we must suppose that *Celarent*, *Camestres*, and *Bocardo* are representatives of their respective 'ways' and not (as the text leads us to believe) those 'ways' themselves. Fourthly, it is hard to see why Aristotle should have made provision for *particular* conclusions to demonstrations; and it is harder to see why he should tacitly allow the scientific respectability of particular negatives without giving some analogous hint about particular affirmatives.

Finally, the clinching argument: at 82^{b}15 "the third way" cannot refer to the third *figure*—for Aristotle is referring to the proof of *DeC*, and universal negatives cannot be proved in the third figure. Here, then, we are obliged to take Aristotle to be referring to the three *moods* which yield a universal negative conclusion. Hence throughout *A* 21 the three ways are these three moods. And *Bocardo* has no place in the chapter. (Compare *A* 23, 85^{a}1–12, where the three *tropoi* are clearly the three *moods* with universal negative conclusions. Here too the MSS falsely shove *Baroco* into the text. See MIGNUCCI (1975), 512–14.)

I conclude that 82^{b}21–8 is a glossator's addition. Aristotle meant to refer only to *Celarent*, *Camestres*, and *Cesare*, the three *tropoi* which yield *e*-conclusions; he sketched the argument for the first two moods and perhaps simply added "the third is proved likewise". A later improver filled this note out, and filled it out wrongly.

82^{b}29: "It is clear that . . .": Aristotle's conclusion is true, but his argument for it is unsound; see LEAR (1980), 27–30, who provides a sound argument.

82^{b}31: A consequential emendation is necessary at 82^{b}30–1, where there is an explicit occurrence of the word "figure" (*schēma*). We might excise *schēmatos* or else replace it by *tropou*; but I suspect that the whole clause, from *hote men* to *tritou*, should be expunged.

82^{b}34: The term "general", *logikos*, is often used by Aristotle to designate an argument not employing notions or principles proper to any given science (thus it is more or less synonymous with *dialektikos*): "But perhaps a general demonstration would seem more persuasive than what has been said—I call it general for this reason, that the more universal it is, the further it is from the appropriate principles" (*GA B* 8, 747^{b}27–30). Again: "A problem is general (*logikon*) if a quantity of fine arguments (*logoi*) might be raised against it" (*Top E* 1, 129^{a}29–31)—the more general a proposition is, the more ways of testing it, and so possibly of refuting it, there are. (See further *APst A* 22, 84^{a}7~8; 32, 88^{a}19~30; Bonitz, 432^{b}5–11; cf. e.g. G.-G. GRANGER (1976), 98–9.

CHAPTER 22

This chapter contains three arguments for the thesis that the set (S) is finite—i.e. for negative answers to questions (i) and (ii). The first two arguments are 'general', and occupy 82^{b}37–83^{b}31 and 83^{b}32–84^{a}6; the third argument, at 84^{a}7–28, is 'analytical'.

82^{b}37: *Argument (A).* The strategy of the first argument is this: Aristotle first contends that there cannot be an infinite series of essential predicates (82^{b}37–83^{a}1); then he establishes, in a rambling and digressive passage, the parasitic nature of non-essential predication (83^{a}1–39); and finally he infers that non-essential predicates cannot generate infinite sequences either (83^{a}39–^{b}31).

As 83^{b}1 shows, 82^{b}37–83^{a}1 offers a self-contained argument against an infinite series of essential predicates. It is worth trying to set the argument out fairly explicitly; and I shall begin with a few terminological points.

I use "what a thing/something/it is" for *to ti esti.* This phrase reads literally "the what is it?"; hence "the answer to the question "What is it?"", and so, for short, "what it is". (There is no pronoun in the Greek answering to "it"; since "it" in English is regularly anaphoric, it is often necessary to use "a thing" or "something" in its place.) To answer the question "What is *X*?", as it is here used, one must state the 'essence' or give a definition of *X*. Sometimes, however, Aristotle uses the phrase in such a way that a proper answer to "What is *X*?" will state only the kind or genus under which *X* falls. To indicate that a complete definition, and not merely a specification of the genus, is in question Aristotle will sometimes use a different phrase, *to ti ēn einai,* which I render as "what it is to be a thing/something/it". The literal translation of this bizarre expression is "the what was to be?"; hence "the answer to the question 'What was to be?'", and so, for short, "what was to be". The past tense here is a Greek idiom that does not go over into English; thus we get to "what is to be". Several passages indicate that this is elliptical for "what, for so-and-so, it is to be such and such" or "what it is for **a** to be *X*". Since the question, "What is it for **a** to be *X*?" is to be understood as a request for a definition of "*X*" as it occurs in "**a** is *X*", stating what it is for **a** to be *X* amounts to giving a definition or account of *X*.

The "items predicated in what something is" are presumably the same as the items which "inhere in the account which says what something is" (*A* 4, 73^{a}35; cf. *Top A* 5, 102^{a}32–5). Thus when Aristotle says that such items are finite, we might take him to mean merely that if a term is defined by the conjunction of a set of predicates $\{A_1, A_2, \ldots, A_n\}$, then n must be finite. And this is surely true. It has, however, little to do with sequences of terms such as (S); for the A_is will not by themselves generate such a sequence.

Aristotle must be thinking of definition by genus and differentia: in order to define a term G_0 I must give the genus G_1 and the specific difference D_1 of members of G_0; and similarly, to define G_1 I must give

G_2 and D_2. Now each G_i is "predicated in what G_0 is"—genera are essential to their species. Moreover, genera are predicable of their species (e.g. *Cat* 3, 1^{b}13), so that the G_is will form a sequence.

(Sg) ..., G_0, G_1, G_2, ..., G_n, ...

which has the same feature as (S): it is ordered by the *a*-relation; ($\forall i$) ($\forall j$) ($i > j \rightarrow G_i a G_j$).

We can now construct an argument as follows: Suppose that **a** knows what it is for a thing to be a G_n. Then, since being a G_n is being a G_{n+1} that is D_{n+1}, **a** knows what it is to be G_{n+1}. Hence if every term in (Sg) has a successor, **a** knows infinitely many truths of the form "being a G_i is being a G_{i+1} that is D_{i+1}". Now infinite knowledge of this sort is impossible (cf. *A* 3, 72^{b}10, notes); and evidently some people do have knowledge of some essences: hence (Sg) cannot be infinite in length.

At 83^{b}2 Aristotle asserts that this argument disposes of infinite chains both in the upward and in the downward direction. But at most it deals with the upward direction: for all that Aristotle has said, every G_i in (Sg) may be preceded by a G_{i-1}.

It is far from clear that Aristotle's argument works even for the upward direction. In a weak sense of the phrase, many men do know what, say, a horse is; for they can pick horses out from other animals, they can name some of the salient features of horses, and perhaps they can offer an account of what the term "horse" means. But in this sense it does not seem to be the case that in order to know what G_n is you must know what G_{n+1} is—a child may, in this sense, know what a horse is without knowing what an animal is. If Aristotle replies that he is using a stronger notion of knowing what so and so is, then we may legitimately wonder why he is confident that anyone has any knowledge of this sort; certainly, if we suppose that to know what X is is to grasp the real essence of X, then there is room for scepticism, in a Lockean vein, about our knowledge of what things are.

83^{a}1: Aristotle now turns to the second leg of argument (A), which attempts to establish the finitude of non-essential predicates. 83^{a}1–24 performs three preliminary tasks: (i), it distinguishes between 'natural' and 'unnatural' predication; (ii), it asserts that demonstration is concerned only with natural predication; and (iii), it connects this with the doctrine of the categories of being.

For *task (i)* see the notes to *A* 4, 73^{b}5–10. Three points of detail arise. First, Ross finds two varieties of unnatural predication, typified by "The white thing is a log" and "The musical thing is white". But Aristotle only recognizes two sorts of predication (83^{a}4, 14); and he offers the same type of analysis for the two sentences just quoted (83^{a}10–11).

Secondly, at 83^{a}13 I translate *hoper kai egeneto* by "which came to be white"; logs become white but white things do not become logs (cf. 83^{a}6–8). Ross translates "which is what we made it in our assertion" (cf. Bonitz, 533^{b}25–8); even if the Greek can mean this, it seems to make little sense in the context.

Thirdly, "just what is some particular white" translates *hoper leukon ti*. Aristotle regularly uses "*Y* is *hoper X*" to mean "*X* is the genus of *Y*" (cf. esp. *Top* Γ 1, 116ᵃ23–8; *APr* A 39, 49ᵇ6–8; see Bonitz, 533ᵇ36–534ᵃ18). But sometimes it is used less strictly so that *Y* is *hoper X* if *X* is in the essence of *Y* (cf. e.g. *Top* Δ 1, 120ᵇ21–6; *Met* Γ 4, 1007ᵃ33). The customary translation, "just what *X* is", suggests precisely the wrong sense. (At 83ᵃ7 the text should probably be emended to read "just what is white or some particular white" (*hoper leukon on outh' hoper leukon ti* for *leukon on outh' hoper leukon ti*). Philoponus seems to have read this.)

Task (ii): By "this is the way in which demonstrations demonstrate" (83ᵃ20) Aristotle must mean 'these are the sorts of predication occurring in demonstrations'. The two types of predication were illustrated exclusively by *singular* propositions; and these do not properly appear in demonstrations. Thus we must first apply the distinction to universal propositions; presumably such an application will yield the result that *YaX* is an unnatural predication if and only if:

(1) *YaX* → (∃*Z*) (*YaZ* & it happens that *XaZ*).

If this is right, then demonstrations *do* deal with unnatural predications; indeed, in Aristotle's view, any proposition of the form *YaG*—where *G* is any geometrical term, e.g. "triangle"—will be unnatural. For triangles are not independent entities; it is (*pace* Ross) no answer to say that geometry proceeds 'as if' triangles and the like were independent entities.

Why should Aristotle have thought that unnatural predications are not found in demonstrations? His thesis amounts to the claim that the subject-term of any scientific proposition will denote a substance: the items which metaphysics determines as the primary realities are the very items with which science is concerned. The constraints which this thesis imposes on the sciences—and not just on the mathematical sciences—are severe; and yet the attraction of the thesis is evident. Perhaps Aristotle had something like the following thought in mind. If a sentence expresses a *true* non-natural predication, then there will always be an associated sentence which expresses the natural truth which underlies the unnatural predication. (Thus "The sculptor, who is musical, made the statue" can be associated with "The musical man made the statue".) When a science appears to deal in unnatural predications, it may always be construed as dealing in the associated natural predications.

Task (iii): Aristotle does not say elsewhere that the division of predicates into the 'categories' only applies to natural predications. Presumably his thought is that if *X is Y* is unnatural then *Y* is not, properly speaking, a predicate of *X* but rather of whatever it is that happens to be *X*; *a fortiori Y* will not express a quality or quantity or relation etc. of *X*.

The first category, that of substance, is here designated by the phrase "what the item is". This can only refer to essential predication; and the next paragraph expressly equates essential and substantial predication. Thus it seems that Aristotle confuses substantial with essential predicates—for even if all substantial predicates are essential (see *Cat* 5, 2^{b}8–10, 29–37), the converse does not hold (see the example of *white* at 83^{a}7, 29; cf. e.g. *Top A* 9, 103^{b}27–37; *Met Z* 4, 1030^{a}18–27). Aristotle might, I think, retort that if only natural predicates fall under the categories, and if the subjects of natural predicates are substances, and if all essential predicates of substances are substantial, then all essential predicates are substantial. (See further Ackrill, 78–80.)

83^{a}21: Only eight of the ten categories are listed: cf. *Cat* 4, 1^{b}25–2^{a}4; Bonitz, 378^{a}45–^{b}15.

83^{a}22: "when one thing is predicated of one": cf. *A* 2, 72^{a}9, notes.

83^{a}24: This paragraph makes four further preliminary points.

First, substantial predications are essential predications: if *AaB* and *A* is in the category of substance, then *A* is in the essence of *B*.

Secondly, non-substantial predications are non-essential and so (in one of the many senses of the term) incidental. It is an obvious objection to this that *differentiae*, such as *being two-footed*, are essential and yet non-substantial (a *differentia* states a quality: *Top Z* 6, 144^{a}15–22; *Met Δ* 14, 1020^{a}33–^{b}1). 83^{b}1 shows that *A* 22 counts *differentiae* as substances.

Thirdly, non-substantial predicates do not signify *ousiai*. There are two main uses of the word *ousia*: in the form "*x* is an *ousia*" it amounts to "*x* is a substance"; in the form "*x* is the *ousia* of *y*" it amounts to "*x* is the essence of *y*". Thus a crude account of *ousia* might say, without being unduly misleading, that *ousia* is ambiguous between "essence" and "substance". Ross takes *ousia* to mean "essence" at 83^{a}30, thus making the third point the converse of the first. But *ousia* can hardly bear this meaning at 83^{a}30 if it means "substance" at 83^{a}24.

Fourthly, Aristotle again rejects independent Platonic forms (see *A* 11, 77^{a}5–9 and notes); the Idea of White, for example, would be something which was white 'without being anything different'. The argument here is precisely parallel to that at *EN A* 6, 1096^{a}34–^{b}5 + ^{b}32–1097^{a}14: 'There are no Ideas, and even if there were they would have no bearing on our problems.' Nonny-noes, *teretismata*, are the sounds produced by people who sing without uttering sentences (cf. [*Probl*] *IΘ* 10, 918^{a}30).

83^{a}36: Most commentators suppose that 83^{a}36–^{b}17 is a unit and deals with counterpredication. But in that case we must conclude that Aristotle's line of thought is infernally turbid, the reprise of 82^{b}37–83^{a}1 at 83^{b}1–7 being wholly out of place. I now incline to suppose (after MIGNUCCI (1975), 463–9) that the issue of counterpredication occupies only 83^{a}36–9, and that at 83^{a}39 Aristotle returns, after various preliminary observations, to the main argument. This supposition certainly does not make everything plain; but it is perhaps preferable to the orthodox view.

83^{a}36: "Again . . . to counterpredicate truly": text and interpretation are uncertain here; Aristotle's premiss is either: 'If *X* is a quality of *Y*, then Y is not a quality of X'; or else 'If X is a quality of Y, then Z is not a quality of X'. From either of these premisses Aristotle can correctly infer that X and Y are not counterpredicable; for even if we can "truly say" Y of X (cf. 83ᵃ2) we cannot naturally predicate Y of X. It follows that (S^c)—the set of counterpredicable terms—cannot contain any non-substantial terms; *a fortiori*, (S^c) cannot contain infinitely many non-substantial terms. (Note that "quality" in this argument stands for any of the non-substantial categories of predicate.)

83ᵃ39: "Either a term . . .": we now return to the main argument. Consider the sequence of predications:

$$(\Sigma) \quad \ldots, A_{n+2}aB, A_{n+1}aB, A_naB, \ldots$$

Aristotle urges (*a*) that (Σ) cannot be infinite if the predications in it are essential (83ᵃ39–ᵇ10), and (*b*) that (Σ) cannot be infinite if the predications in it are incidental ("Nor is anything . . .": 83ᵇ10–12). Argument (*a*) is an elaboration of the argument at 82ᵇ37–83ᵃ1. Aristotle claims, mistakenly, that the argument excludes a downward as well as an upward infinity of predicates.

83ᵇ1: ". . . of what is predicated": i.e. of the subject. For this use of "predicate" see *A* 4, 73ᵇ17, and note.

83ᵇ9: "Terms will not be counterpredicated . . .": i.e. in terms of (Sg), it cannot be the case that G_jaG_i if $j < i$ (a species cannot be predicated of its genus). This is perhaps true—but what is its function in the economy of Aristotle's argument? I cannot discover any role for it, and I lamely enclose it within parentheses.

83ᵇ10: "Nor is anything . . .": the text is elliptical (there is no verb explicit in the Greek), and it is also ambiguous. I construe it as expressing what I have called argument (*b*), thus '⟨Or else, (*b*), the predicates in (Σ) are accidental. But in that case the sequence cannot be infinite;⟩ for nothing at all is predicated—i.e. predicated *simpliciter*—of accidents.'

83ᵇ13: "They will not be . . .": 'Every A_i is either an incidental or an essential predicate; every sequence of essential predications is finite, and there is only a finite number of kinds of incidental predicate: therefore, (Σ) is finite in the upward direction.' This appears to be the argument; but there are two puzzling features about it. First, the fact that the number of *kinds* of predicate (of 'categories') is finite is irrelevant: even if there were infinitely many categories (and hence infinitely many incidental predicates), it would not follow that any *sequence* of predications could be infinite. Secondly, it is unclear how the paragraph attaches to its predecessor. In so far as Aristotle says that the sequence will not be infinite in the upward direction, we might be inclined to infer that he has just shown that it will not be infinite in the *downward* direction. (And we shall be more strongly so inclined if we translate *oud'* by ". . . in the upward direction *either*". But *oude* need not bear this sense: see e.g. 84ᵃ22.) But nothing in the previous paragraph relates to the downward rather than to the upward direction—indeed, as I have said, it is precisely the *downward* direction for which Aristotle has not argued. (No doubt there cannot be a downward sequence of incidental predications, since every natural predication has a substance in subject position. But the downward sequence of essential predications has not been closed off.)

83^{b}17: The paragraph repeats some salient points of its predecessors, and prepares the way for the final statement of the argument.

83^{b}18: "items . . . are not predicated of themselves": i.e. a sentence such as "The white thing is white" does not express a natural predication. White is not predicated 'of itself': rather, "The white thing is white" is true in so far as 'something different' (some substance) is white. Cf. *Top A* 9, 105^{b}35–9.

83^{b}19: "though some hold of things in themselves": for 'in itself incidentals' see p. 113.

83^{b}22: "We posit nothing . . .": i.e. 'For in the case of every incidental predicate *I*, there are *I*s only in so far as for some substance-term *S*, *S* is *I*—i.e. only in so far as *I* is predicated of something other than an *I*-term.' (At 83^{b}24 the MSS reading is untenable, but the sense is clear.)

83^{b}24: This concludes argument (A). Strangely enough, in the enunciation of the conclusion Aristotle omits the crucial word "infinitely".

83^{b}26: "the incidentals . . .": this closes off the downward path: if *X is Y* is an incidental predication, then *X* is a substance-term; thus the downward series from *X is Y* (*Z is X, A is Z*, . . .) consists solely of substantial predications, and hence of essential predications. And essential predications are finite.

83^{b}27: "and in the upward direction . . .": this picks up the argument of 83^{b}12–17.

83^{b}28: Aristotle's statement of the general conclusion to the argument is irritatingly obscure. With some hesitation, I take him to mean this. 'Hence (*a*) "there must be some term . . .", i.e. there must be *immediate* predications, . . . *DaE, EaF*, . . . [for, as *A* 20 has argued, if sequences are limited in the upward and in the downward directions, then there cannot be infinitely many terms in between]; and (*b*) "this must come to a stop", i.e. the sequence of immediate predications cannot extend *ad infinitum* in either direction; or in other words (*bi*) "there must be items . . .", i.e. each sequence will have a last item, *YaZ*, such that *Z* is not predicated of anything, and (*bii*) there must be items "of which nothing else . . .", i.e. each sequence will have a first item, *AaB*, such that nothing is predicated of *A*.' But it is not easy to read (*bii*) into the Greek. An alternative gloss on the last clause: '. . . or in other words (*b**) there must be a term *A*, predicated of *B*, such that (i) *A* is not predicated of anything prior to *B* [*AaB* is primitive] and (ii) nothing is predicated of *A*'. This second interpretation is closer to the Greek; but it omits any mention of a *last* item in the sequence.

83^b32: *Argument* (*B*). The gist of the argument, which has connections with *A* 3, is this. Suppose an infinite sequence of propositions:

$$P_1, P_2, \ldots, P_n, \ldots$$

—where each P_i is prior to its predecessor. Then each P_i is demonstrable ("there will be demonstrations of all of them": 84^a2). Hence you know that P_i only if you have demonstrated that P_i on the basis of P_{i+1}. Hence you must know that P_{i+1}. Hence you must have demonstrated that P_{i+1}. Hence you know that P_i only if you have demonstrated each of the infinite sequence of P_is. But this is impossible. Hence if there is any demonstrative knowledge, then not every (S) is infinite. (See *A* 3, 72^b5-18.) Aristotle cannot, of course, conclude that no (S) is infinite; nor even that if there is demonstration no (S) is infinite.

83^b38: "*simpliciter* and not on the basis of something else": cf. *A* 3, 72^b15, notes.

84^a1: "the predicates in between": I paraphrased Aristotle's argument in terms of the priority of propositions; it is more complicated if expressed properly in terms of the priority of predicates. *AaC* is demonstrable only if $(\exists X)$ (*AaX* & *XaC*); and the supposition of the argument, strictly expressed, is that there are infinitely many terms between *A* and *C*.

84^a7: *Argument* (*C*). Finally, the 'analytic' argument (cf. *A* 21, 82^b35, notes). In fact (C) is not an independent argument, for it uses the conclusion of (A) at 84^a26; and it is non-'general' only in so far as it refers to the fact that demonstrative propositions are I-predications. 84^a19-25 argues that there cannot be infinite sequences of I2-predicates, and 84^a25-6 argues that there cannot be infinite sequences of I1-predicates. The argument for I1-predicates consists merely in a reference to argument (A), 82^b37-83^a1.

The argument for I2-predicates is more complex. It seems to run like this: Take a sequence of I2-predicates:

$$(Si) \quad I_1, I_2, \ldots, I_n, \ldots$$

Each I_i inheres in the definition of I_{i+1}; *inhering in* is clearly transitive, so that $(\forall i)\ (\forall j)\ (j < i \rightarrow I_j$ inheres in the definition of I_i). But then if (Si) is infinitely long, there will be infinitely many things inhering in the definition ·of one thing; but this is not possible (presumably, again, for the reasons given at 82^b37-83^a1).

This argument is invalid: every I_i will have *finitely* many predecessors. Philoponus saw this and suggested that Aristotle meant only that it is not possible for I_1 to have infinitely many predicates, which it would have were (Si) infinite (at 84^a22 Philoponus read "hold *of* a single item" for "hold *in* a single item"); but this replaces an invalid argument with no argument at all. Aristotle could have presented a valid argument against the *downward* infinity of (Si): since each I_i contains all its predecessors, it can only have finitely many predecessors (again by 82^b37-83^a1). It is therefore tempting to change the text at 84^{a}22 to read "they will not be infinite in the downward direction" (*katō* for *anō*); but this is ruled out by 84^{a}26–8.

84^{a}20: "and if this is prime, number . . .": I_1 is *number*, I_2 *odd* (i.e. *odd or even*, since the I_is convert), and I_3 *prime* (i.e. *prime or composite*: cf. *A* 4, 73^{a}40); then I_1 inheres in everything which holds of I_3. This, I take it, is Aristotle's rather cumbersome way of indicating that *inhering in* is transitive. (This interpretation punctuates after *prōton* (Philoponus). Most scholars punctuate before *prōton*; "and if this is so, then, first, number . . .".)

84^{a}23: "Moreover, they must . . .": by construction $I_i a I_{i-1}$; but I_{i-1} is in the definition of I_i, so that $I_{i-1} a I_i$; hence every $I_i a I_j$ converts. (On 'exceeding', *huperteinein*, see Bonitz, 793^{b}17–19.) But if the content of this sentence is clear, its function in the argument is opaque (see MIGNUCCI (1975), 492–3).

84^{a}25: Aristotle's argument assumes that *all* the I1-predicates of a term inhere in its definition.

84^{a}28: "Hence they will come to a stop in the downward direction too": this does not follow (see notes to 82^{b}37).

84^{a}29: "And if so . . .": by the argument of *A* 20.

84^{a}32: "as we asserted at the beginning": *A* 3, 72^{b}6–7.

84^{a}32: "For if there are principles . . .": if we take the text *au pied de la lettre* Aristotle argues that if the terms are finite then there must be principles on the grounds that if there are principles then the terms are finite.

84^{a}36: "by interpolating . . .": cf. *A* 12, 78^{a}14, notes.

None of the arguments in *A* 22 is successful; and they cannot be reformulated in such a way as to furnish a proof of Aristotle's contention. The fundamental insight from which Aristotle starts is the thesis that proofs can have only finitely many steps. But in *A* 22 he makes or implies far bolder claims than this; for he supposes first that there are only finitely many things capable of proof, and secondly that there are only finitely many truths. Consideration of the infinite sequence of true and provable propositions in even elementary arithmetic is enough to dispose of these two bolder suppositions.

CHAPTER 23

84^{b}3: From the conclusion of *A* 22 Aristotle correctly infers:

(1) It is not the case that: ((*AaC* & *AaD* & not-*CaD* & not-*DaC*) → ($\exists X$) (*AaX* & *XaC* & *XaD*)).

The conjuncts not-*CaD* and not-*DaC* are needed, for otherwise *C* or *D* would itself be the common feature in virtue of which *AaC* & *AaD* (e.g.

2 R would belong both to triangle and to isosceles in virtue of triangle).

84^b15: "The terms must . . .'': 'But C and D must belong to the same kind as one another, i.e. must be defined in terms of the same primitives (cf. A 10, 76^a33, note), if there is a common item—a middle term B—such that BaC and BaD are I-predications' (cf. A 7).

84^b19: Aristotle next infers that all mediated propositions are demonstrable and all immediate propositions principles. His argument supports neither of these views; and A 13 shows that the first is false.

84^b22: "either all of them or the universal ones": there are in fact twice as many immediate premisses as middle terms, hence the strained parenthesis. The 'universal' premiss, in this sense, is the premiss containing the most universal of the three terms, i.e. AaB; at A 25, 86^b30, Aristotle repeats that this premiss (by itself) is the 'principle' of the demonstration. (If this is right, then "either X or Y" here must mean "X—or rather, Y"; see note on 84^b25.)

84^b23: "this is the path to the principles": the phrase is Platonic (cf. EN A 5, 1095^a32); Aristotle means only that if AaB is immediate, it is a principle (cf. 84^b26).

84^b25: "if there is either a middle or a prior term". There is "a prior term (sc. than B) of which A does not hold" only in the case of *Celarent*. Thus it is probable, as Ross says, that Aristotle is thinking only of *Celarent*; and that here again "either X or Y" means "X, or rather Y".

84^b26: "there are as many elements as terms": i.e. as *middle* terms.

84^b31: 84^b31–85^a1 expand upon 84^b19–24; 85^a1–10 expand upon 84^b24–31.

84^b33: "No proposition and no term holding outside A": the sense of "outside" here is obscure. What Aristotle says can be made true on the assumption that the following equivalence holds:

(2) If AaB or AeB, then (i) C is outside A if and only if CaA, and (ii) C is outside B if and only if BaC.

Ross in effect takes (2) to define "outside"; it is more probable that Aristotle has some diagrammatic representation in mind, and that "outside" refers literally to spatial position in the diagram.

84^b35: "they become indivisible and single": AaB is single *simpliciter* just in case it cannot be 'divided' into two propositions AaX & XaB. The locution is not very felicitous in itself, and it encourages the fatuous comparisons with weight and pitch: just as the ounce, the 'principle' of weight, is not itself divisible into ounces, so the immediate proposition, the 'principle' (in a perfectly different sense) of deduction, is not 'divisible' into propositions. There is nothing in this comparison. (Aristotle's point about measurement, however, is sound and simple: all measurement and counting requires a unit; this will differ materially from one set of measurables or countables to another, but it will have the same formal properties in all cases. Cf. *Met Δ* 6, 1016^{b}17–24; *I* 1, 1052^{b}24–1053^{a}14; *N* 1, 1087^{b}33–1088^{a}14.)

85^{a}1: First (85^{a}1–7), *Celarent*: Aristotle says truly that the middle term may not fall outside *A*; he should have added that it may not fall outside *B* either; secondly (85^{a}7–10), *Camestres*: at 85^{a}10, as at 85^{a}3, "hold" is used neutrally; and thirdly (85^{a}10–12), *Cesare* (see Ross).

85^{a}9: "and of no *E*": the MSS add "or not of every ⟨*E*⟩", which Ross rightly excises.

85^{a}11: "the middle term will never pass outside . . .": i.e. 'The middle term will never be outside either *B*, the term of which we are to deny *A* ("of which we must make a privative predication"), or *A*, the term which is to be denied of *B* ("which we must predicate privatively").'

CHAPTER 24

The three comparisons Aristotle sets himself to discuss at the beginning of this chapter occupy *A* 24, *A* 25, and *A* 26. What Aristotle has in mind when he says that one demonstration is 'better' than another can only be gleaned from the arguments used to support his evaluations.

85^{a}13: Two terminological points need to be made. First, the terms "universal" and "particular" are used to make three distinctions: (*a*) that between syllogistic propositions of different 'quantity'—i.e. between *a*- and *e*-propositions on the one hand and *i*- and *o*-propositions on the other; (*b*) that between general and singular propositions; and (*c*) that between more general and more specific *a*- and *e*-propositions. Since Aristotle treats singular propositions as the limiting case of *a*- and *e*-propositions, he tends to conflate distinctions (*b*) and (*c*); and this conflation is evident in the present chapter. D_1 is a more universal demonstration than D_2 if either the conclusion of D_1 is more universal than that of D_2 (e.g. 85^{a}37–^{b}1, ^{b}10–13) or the premisses of D_1 are more universal than those of D_2 (e.g. 85^{b}23–7; 85^{b}27–86^{a}3). Aristotle switches without warning from one to the other of these notions.

Secondly, *e*- and *o*-propositions, and demonstrations concluding to such propositions, are called indifferently negative (*apophatikē*) and privative (*sterētikē*); *a*- and *i*-propositions, and demonstrations concluding to them, are affirmative (*kataphatikē*) or positive (*katēgorikē*). But demonstrations leading to *a*- and *i*-propositions are also called from time to time probative (*deiktikē*); this is peculiarly unfortunate since the term *deiktikē* is also used for 'direct' proofs as opposed to *reductio* arguments. Thus at 85^{a}19 Aristotle says that, having treated the universal/ particular dispute, he will turn to "demonstrations which are said to prove (*deiknunai*)": this is naturally taken to mean 'direct' proofs; yet it is possible, and preferable, to refer the phrase to affirmative proofs—for then all three subjects for study are listed in their proper order.

A 24 first cites two arguments for the superiority of particular over universal proof; then rejects these arguments; and finally marshalls seven arguments for the superiority of universal proof.

85ᵃ20:   *Argument* (*A′*). The illustrative example of Coriscus compares the following two situations: (i¹) a^1 knows that Coriscus is musical; (ii¹) b^1 knows that a man (who is, at it happens, Coriscus) is musical. In this case a^1 knows Coriscus' musical ability better than b^1. The application of this to the example of the triangles should yield the following two situations: (i²) a^2 knows that isosceles triangles have 2 R; (ii²) b^2 knows that triangles (which in fact include isosceles triangles) have 2 R. In this case a^2 knows the properties of isosceles triangles better than b^2. And the generalization is straightforward: if (i⁰) a^0 knows that *AaC*, and (ii⁰) b^0 knows that *AaB* (where in fact *BaC*) then a^0, who has the more particular knowledge, knows better—for he has better knowledge of the properties of *C*s.

85ᵃ31:   *Argument* (*B′*) puts its conclusion differently from (*A′*): (*A′*) argued that it is better to have particular knowledge that *P* than to have universal knowledge that *P*; (*B′*) argues that it is better to know that *P* than to know that *Q*, where *Q* is on a higher plane of abstraction than *P*.

85ᵃ33:   "a sort of natural object . . .": literally: "a sort of nature (*phusis*) . . . e.g. ⟨a nature⟩ of triangle . . .". "Metaphorically and generally, every substance is called a nature, because nature is a sort of substance" (*Met Δ* 4, 1015ᵃ11–13).

85ᵃ38:   "as . . . in the case of proportion": cf. *A* 5, 74ᵃ17–25, notes. Students of proportion theory are allegedly inclined to suppose that the magnitudes they talk about are somehow entities over and above numbers, lines, planes, etc. (cf. *Met M* 2, 1077ᵃ9–12, ᵇ17). The more general one's proofs, the more numerous and the more abstract are the entities one feels tempted to postulate.

85ᵇ4:   *Argument* (*A*) tries to turn the tables on (*A′*): (*A′*) asserts that a^2 knows about *I* in its own right and not in virtue of something else, viz. *T*; Aristotle retorts that b^2 knows about *R* in its own right, in so far as it belongs to *T* as such.

The generalization of the argument uses the odd phrase "know something as it holds" (*ho eidōs hekaston hēi hekaston huparchei*). I take it that "**a** knows *A* as *A* holds" means "**a** knows that *AaZ*, where *A* holds of *Z* as such"; but Aristotle does not express this with any great clarity. If this is right, Aristotle's general point is this: a^0's knowledge cannot be of something that holds of its subject as such, but b^0's knowledge may be; thus by the principle that knowledge of something in itself is better than knowledge in virtue of something else, b^0 has the better knowledge.

If I am right, Aristotle does not in fact succeed in turning the tables; for his argument does nothing to show that b^0 has better knowledge *that AaC*. Rather, he produces a point in favour of universal demonstration that roughly balances the first point in favour of particular demonstration.

$85^{b}10$: "Thus if triangle extends further . . .": cf. A 4, $73^{b}32-74^{a}3$. The conditions Aristotle states are not sufficient for R's holding of T as such; he should conclude that "the isosceles, if anything, has such an angle-sum as triangle".

$85^{b}15$: *Argument* (B) makes two points against (B'). The first point at first sight reads like an avowal of Platonism. But the reference to what is 'imperishable' (cf. A 6, $74^{b}32-9$; A 8) indicates the following gloss: genuinely universal propositions cannot change their truth-value and thus are more real than those particular propositions (i.e. *singular* propositions) that can.

The second point is simpler: it is mistaken to infer from " 'F' signifies some single feature in the objects to which it applies" to "There exists some real object, F-ness". And this inference is just as mistaken in the case of the terms used by the demonstrator as "in the case of those other items"—items such as colours and sizes. The presupposition of this argument is that the only thing about abstract demonstrations that might lead us to postulate universals is the fact that they talk about abstract things; and the argument is that this inducement is insufficient. On both counts Aristotle is right.

$85^{b}23$: *Argument* (C) claims that a deduction which uses AaB *as a premiss* is better than one which uses AaC *as a premiss*.

The parenthetical argument for the explanatoriness of universal premisses is this: 'A universal premiss is primitive, i.e. immediate; but if AaB is immediate, then the only answer to the question: Why are Bs A? is: Because they are B. (B, of which A holds, is itself explanatory of its own being A: cf. A 31, $88^{a}7$.) Thus if you want to know why Cs are A the answer which is most explanatory, because it gives the ultimate explanation, is that AaB.' Here "universal" does not have the meaning "general": if Aristotle is to attach the parenthesis to the main argument he needs two further premisses, first that primitive propositions are the most general propositions; and secondly, that if the most general pro-positions are the most explanatory, then if P is more general than Q, P is more explanatory than Q.

$85^{b}27$: *Argument* (D) is presented as a new argument, though it is evidently closely tied to (C). It states quite clearly that knowing that P requires knowing the *ultimate* explanation of P (cf. A 13, $78^{a}22$, notes).

As B 11 shows, Aristotle believes that the market-place example (for which cf. *Phys B* 5, $196^{b}33-197^{a}5$) can be formulated within syllogistic, and that it is precisely parallel to the angle-sum example except in so far as it makes use of a different type of explanation.

The theorem that the sum of the external angles of a polygon is 4 R (see B 17, $99^{a}19$) is not in Euclid, though it is standardly derived as a corollary of Pythagoras' theorem (Euclid, i. 32: cf. Proclus, *Comm in Eucl* 382. 22–383. 16); Menaechmus proved it (Proclus, *Comm in Eucl* 73. 1–4).

86ᵃ3: *Argument* (*E*). The 'infinite' items to which particular demonstration tends are individuals (cf. e.g. *Top B* 2, 109ᵇ14); individuals are infinite in kind (cf. *Phys A* 4, 187ᵇ7–9), i.e. they are indeterminate in character: "For if there is nothing apart from the particulars, and the particulars are infinite, how can one get understanding of the infinites? For we recognize everything in so far as it is one and the same and in so far as something universal holds of it" (*Met B* 4, 999ᵃ26–9; cf. α 2, 994ᵇ20–7; Γ 5, 1010ᵃ25; Z 10, 1036ᵃ8). Aristotle thinks of individuals as in themselves bare particulars, devoid of all distinguishing properties; as individuals and infinite, things cannot be grasped; for to grasp something is to put it under a concept, to see it as an *F*.

This correct point is the foundation of Aristotle's argument; but the superstructure is built on its false shadow; for particular demonstrations do not tend to bare particulars—as a description becomes ever more specific it does not approach the nature of the bare particular. Nor does it follow from the fact that bare particulars cannot be known as such that the more abstract an argument is the better it is.

It is worth noting that the sense in which 'the infinite is unknowable' in this passage is quite different from that of *A* 22, 82ᵇ37 (see notes); and a third way in which 'the individual is unknowable' is mentioned at *Rhet A* 2, 1356ᵇ30–3.

86ᵃ5: "universal demonstrations tend to the simple" because principles are simple (*A* 23, 84ᵇ37); principles are 'limits' because there are no propositions 'beyond' them (there is a pun on *peras*, "limit", and *apeira*, "infinites").

86ᵃ9: "for correlative items . . .": R^* is a relative property if R^* **a** ↔ ($\exists x$) (*Rax*); R^{*1} and R^{*2} are correlative if (R^{*1}**a** ↔ ($\exists x$) (R^1**a**x)) & (R^{*2}**a** ↔ ($\exists x$) (R^2**a**x)) & R^1 is the converse of R^2). Aristotle means that if R^{*1} and R^{*2} are correlative, then **a** is more R^1 to **b** if and only if **b** is more R^2 to **a** (**a** loves **b** more if and only if **b** is more loved by **a**.) The thesis only applies to those relations which "admit the more and the less" (cf. *Cat* 7, 6ᵇ19–27): *demonstrate* and *be demonstrated by* admit the more and the less in so far as *know* and *be known through* do (see p. 102).

86ᵃ10: *Argument* (*F*): See *A* 1, 71ᵃ24, notes; and below 86ᵃ22–9.

86ᵃ13: *Argument* (*G*) can be turned on its head. Suppose that *AaB*, *BaC*, *CaD* are all immediate; then Aristotle claims that *AaB* & *BaD* ⊢ *AaD* is "more exact" (*akribes*: see *A* 27) because it "proceeds from a principle". But *AaC* & *CaD* ⊢ *AaD* equally "proceeds from a principle": in both demonstrations one premiss is an immediate principle and the other is at one remove from principlehood. Aristotle assumes without argument that it is better to have an immediate major premiss than an immediate minor.

86ᵃ22: *Argument* (*H*) repeats and corrects (F); (D) and (F) are 'general' in the sense of *A* 21, 82ᵇ35.

86ª29: *Argument* (*J*) is a jotting; presumably the thought is this: 'Demonstrations containing comprehensible propositions (i.e. propositions known by comprehension or *nous*) are better than those containing propositions whose truth is apprehended by sense-perception. But the more universal a demonstration, the further from perception and the nearer to *nous* its propositions come.'

CHAPTER 25

A 25 contains four arguments for the superiority of affirmative over negative demonstration.

86ª33: *Argument* (*A*), as it stands in the text, is embarrassingly bad: having shown that if D_1 has fewer premisses than D_2 then D_1 is preferable to D_2, the text observes that affirmative and negative demonstrations have equally many premisses, and infers that affirmative demonstration is the better. Only surgery can save Aristotle's reputation: a bold sawbones will excise the "universal argument" at $86^a36-{}^b7$, together with the false disjunction "postulates or suppositions or propositions" at 86ª34. That leaves the following argument: D_1 is preferable to D_2 if it "depends on fewer items", i.e. if it makes fewer conceptual demands than D_2. And probative deductions make fewer demands than privative ones; for the latter, as Aristotle points out, require the concept of negation.

86ª34: "postulates or suppositions or propositions": cf. *A* 10, 76^b23-34. If the disjunction is Aristotelian, it probably only means "fewer propositions of whatever sort".

86ᵇ2: "Thus that *A* holds of *D* . . .": *AaD* and *AaE* are "on a level" in that each depends on three premisses.

86ᵇ5: "that through which . . . is more convincing": cf. *A* 2, 72^a29-32, notes.

86ᵇ10: *Argument* (*B*): see *A* 21; and, for the terminology of 'increasing', *A* 14, 79^a29.

86ᵇ10: "we have proved": cf. *APr A* 7, 29^a19-29; 24, 41^b6-31.

86ᵇ15: "it is impossible . . .": Aristotle states a trivial consequence of his syllogistic; but he undoubtedly has a more complicated consequence in mind. Suppose that a deduction in *Celarent* is to be increased. The first stage of the increase will consist of two syllogisms, one in *Barbara* and one (e.g.) again in *Celarent*. The next stage of increase will consist of four syllogisms, three in *Barbara* and one in (e.g.) *Celarent*. And in general, the *n*-th stage will contain 2^n syllogisms and thus 2×2^n or 2^{n+1} premisses; of these premisses $(2^{n+1} - 1)$ will be affirmative and only one negative.

86ᵇ23: "the same holds for the other deductions": i.e. for *Camestres* and *Cesare* (but see Ross).

86ᵇ28: "privative demonstrations . . .": the Greek is elliptical, no noun being expressed. Grammar allows "propositions" to be supplied after "privative", and logic encourages this supplement. But the consequent of the conditional shows that "demonstrations" is the correct supplement; thus we must take "prove" loosely—D_1 is 'proved through' D_2 if D_2's conclusion is a premiss of D_1.

86ᵇ30: *Argument* (*C*) is virtually identical with (A), if my interpretation of 86ᵇ36–ᵇ9 is right. If "universal immediate propositions" refers to the major premiss, then the argument applies to *Celarent* and *Cesare* but not to *Camestres*. Probably Aristotle is thinking only of first figure syllogisms.

Affirmation is prior to negation (cf. *Int* 5, 17ᵃ8; *Cael B* 3, 286ᵃ25) in that we cannot understand a negation unless we understand the corresponding affirmation; for we cannot understand not-*P* unless we understand *P* ("just as being the case is prior to not being the case").

86ᵇ37: *Argument* (*D*) is a jotting; it is hard to see how it could swell into a different argument from its predecessors.

CHAPTER 26

A single argument shows the preferability of negative over reductive argument; contrast *Top Θ* 2, 157ᵇ34–6.

87ᵃ3: The *reductio* which is compared to a direct proof in *Celarent* seems to be invalid. We are to prove that *AeB* (87ᵃ7), and so "we should assume that it does hold" (87ᵃ8)—i.e. *AaB*. *AaB* & *BaC* yield *AaC*, but the impossibility of *AaC* then licenses only *AoB* and not *AeB*; if, on the other hand, we assume *AiB*, *AaC* is not deducible. Aristotle himself makes both these points explicitly at *APr B* 11, 61ᵇ23–30, in the course of a long discussion on the relation of indirect to direct proof (*B* 11–14). His error here is explained, though not excused, by the fact that *APst* often limits its interest to universal propositions, and hence treats *AaB* and *AeB* as exhaustive alternatives (see p. 146).

Let us suppose, then, that the two arguments to be compared are:

(1) *AeB*, *BaC* ⊢ *AeC*;
(2) *AeC*, *BaC*. Not-*AeB* ⊢ *AaB*. ⊢ *AaC*. ⊢ *AeB*

—where (2) uses *reductio*. In (1) and (2) the arrangement of the terms into propositions is the same (87ᵃ12); thus preference between (1) and (2) must be based on the arrangement of the propositions in them. Since (1) is a demonstrative syllogism its premisses are prior to its conclusion (*A* 2, 71ᵇ30); thus (2) uses as a premiss a proposition—*AeC*—which is posterior to its conclusion. Hence (2) is inferior to (1).

Aristotle's argument does not turn on the nature of *reductio* as such: it shows that *any* argument proving one of the premisses of a demonstration by way of its conclusion is inferior to the demonstration itself; it does not show that every *reductio* must bear this relation to some

demonstration. (For that, Aristotle might have appealed to *APr*
B 11–14.)

87^{a}15: "the conclusion (that it is not the case) is more familiar": i.e.
'*AeC* (the genuine conclusion: 87^{a}20–2) is more familiar to us than *AeB*
("the proposition in the deduction")'. Or possibly we should translate:
"that the conclusion is not the case is more familiar", i.e. 'that *AaC*, the
'conclusion' of the *reductio* syllogism, is false is more familiar to us . . .'
(cf. *APr B* 14, 62^{b}35–7).

87^{a}21: "For if it follows . . .": You might object: 'Both (1) and (2) are
sound arguments (let us grant), and the premisses of an argument are
prior to its conclusion; hence in both cases the ordering of the propositions is perfectly proper.' Aristotle should answer by stating that
only in *some* valid arguments do premisses and conclusion stand in the
relevant priority relation (cf. *A* 13); instead he tries to argue that (2)
does not really contain premisses and conclusion at all. For the apparent
premisses of (2) are not "related as whole to part or part to whole".
Aristotle sometimes uses this phrase in such a way that the premisses of
all valid inferences must stand as part to whole or whole to part (see esp.
APr A 41, 49^{b}37–50^{a}2; cf. 25, 42^{a}8–12; 32, 47^{a}10–14). Does Aristotle
then mean to imply that all *reductio* arguments are invalid? The answer
to this question should emerge from 87^{a}24–5, where Aristotle specifies
which items in the *reductio* fail to satisfy the part–whole condition. The
MSS give: "The propositions *AC* and *AB*"; but these two propositions
do not appear as (apparent) premisses in argument (2). I once suggested
reading "The propositions *BC* and *AB*": Aristotle is then alluding to the
derivation of *AaC* from *AaB* and *BaC*, and he means that *AaB* and *BaC*
do not stand in the part–whole relation inasmuch as *AaB* is *false*. The
OCT reads "The propositions AC and BC"; for *AeC* and *BaC* are
indeed the (apparent) premisses on which *AeB* depends in argument (2).
I now follow this reading—but without confidence, for *AeC* and *BaC* are
the premisses of *Felapton* so that their presence can hardly mark an
argument as invalid. See further STRIKER (1977), 317–18.

CHAPTER 27

"exact" translates *akribēs*. The adjective is a favourite of Aristotle's
(Bonitz, 27^{b}43–28^{a}47), and he applies it to the senses (e.g. *An B* 9,
421^{a}12), the intellect (e.g. *Top Z* 4, 141^{b}13), units of measurement (e.g.
Met I 1, 1053^{a}1), definitions (e.g. *Cael A* 9, 279^{a}29), and arguments (e.g.
Rhet B 22, 1396^{a}33–^{b}3). Aristotle himself glosses the word by "clear"
(*saphēs*: *Top B* 4, 111^{a}9); and in general being *akribēs* seems to amount
(vaguely enough) to being of good epistemic quality. In some contexts,
the relevant quality is certainty; in others, rigour; in others, exactness or
precision. In the first edition I translated *akribēs* in a heterodox fashion
by "certain"; but this, I now think, is misleading (see BURNYEAT (1981),

115 n. 35), and I prefer the more orthodox "exact". (Yet, in truth, I doubt if the notion of *akribeia* is itself very exact.)

The view that the sciences differ in exactitude runs throughout Aristotle's thought (see esp. *EN A* 3, 1094^{b}11–27); its source is to be found at the end of Plato's *Philebus* (56^{c}seqq). See KULLMANN (1974), 122–32; G.-G. GRANGER (1976), 312–15.

A 27 offers three criteria for comparative exactness: (i) on the distinction between sciences 'of the fact' and sciences both 'of the fact' and 'of the reason why' see *A* 13, 78^{b}39–79^{a}13, and notes. (ii) On sciences whose objects are not "said of an underlying subject" see p. 161. Cf. *Met α* 3, 995^{a}15–16: "Mathematical exactitude of argument (*akribologian*) is not to be sought in all things, but in those which do not have matter" (cf. *Cael Γ* 7, 306^{a}27). (iii) "Additional posit", *prosthesis*, is the opposite of "abstraction", *aphairesis*: see Bonitz, 646^{a}13–19; for the connection with exactness cf. *Met A* 2, 982^{a}25–8; *M* 3, 1078^{a}9–14 (where exactness is associated with simplicity).

Elsewhere Aristotle mentions at least two further criteria: (iv) a science is less exact if its theorems hold only 'for the most part': *EN A* 3, 1094^{b}11–27; *Γ* 5, 1112^{b}1–9. (v) At *A* 24, 86^{a}16–17, one demonstration is said to be more exact than another if its premisses are closer to the principles of the science (cf. *EN Z* 7, 1141^{a}16–18).

Criterion (iv) derives from (ii) (cf. e.g. *GA Δ* 10, 778^{a}4–9); criterion (v) perhaps grounds (i). The criteria are held together, in a loose way, by the notion of priority (cf. 87^{a}31): one science, S_1, is prior to another, S_2, if S_2 in some way depends upon S_1; and each of (i)–(v) expresses a mode of dependence. And if S_2 depends on S_1, then there is a sense in which S_1 might be thought to be of better epistemic quality than S_2: any good qualities which S_2 has will derive from S_1, and the good qualities will tend to dissipate in the course of the derivation. (This is a miserably flabby thought; but I can find nothing less flabby in the text.)

87ᵃ36: "a point a substance having position": for the definition see Bonitz, 701^{b}25–9; according to Proclus it is Pythagorean (*Comm in Eucl* 95. 21; cf. Heath (1), i. 155–8).

CHAPTER 28

With *A* 28 cf. *A* 7.

87ᵃ38: "whatever items come from the primitives": i.e. derived *terms* (cf. *A* 10, 76^{a}32, notes; for the verb *sugkeitai* see *B* 13, 96^{b}21; *Met Δ* 25, 1023^{b}19–23).

87ᵃ39: "parts or attributes of them in themselves": "them" may refer either to the primitive or to the derived terms. For the sense of "parts" see *Met Δ* 25, 1023^{b}23: "Again, the items in the account which makes a thing clear are also parts of the whole". Thus the "or" is epexegetic— "parts" means "attributes in themselves". The "whatever . . ." clause is presumably explanatory of the notion of a kind; here, then, a kind is determined by its subject-terms and by its predicate-terms. This is singular: cf. e.g. *A* 7, 75^{a}42; *Met B* 2, 997^{a}21; *Γ* 2, 1003^{b}20; *I* 4, 1055^{a}31.

87^{a}40: "One science is different from another": the text is usually read as asserting that $S_1 \neq S_2$ if and only if $\neg \, (\exists Q) \, (Q \to \Pi_1 \, \& \, Q \to \Pi_2)$ —where Π_i is the set of principles of S_i. But then difference between sciences is explained by reference to axioms, while identity is explained by reference to terms. Perhaps the relation of *depending on* is to be taken not as *deducible from* but as *constructed from*—i.e. as a relation between propositions and the terms they contain. Thus $S_1 \neq S_2$ if and only if the terms in Π_1 differ from those in Π_2. Since theorems cannot introduce new terms this condition amounts to saying that $S_1 \neq S_2$ if and only if the terms of S_1 differ from those of S_2; and this is the contradictory of the identity criterion.

87^{b}1: "There is evidence for this . . .": It is hard to get a clear argument from the text; perhaps Aristotle means this: 'Suppose there are two putatively distinct sciences S_1 and S_2, with principles Π_1 and Π_2 and theorems T_1 and T_2. Then if all the items in T_1 are in the same kind as one another, T_1 is in the same kind as Π_1. Similarly for T_2. And if Π_1 and Π_2 are different in kind, then S_1 and S_2 are distinct sciences.'

CHAPTER 29

Aristotle shows only that there can be several valid arguments for the same conclusion, not that there can be several demonstrations of the same fact; the latter thesis entails that there may be several explanations for the same fact: how far this can be the case is discussed in *B* 16–18.

87^{b}6: "non-continuous middle terms from the same chain": *X* is "non-continuous" (*mē . . . suneches*) in relation to *AaB* if *AaX* and *XaB* are not both immediate. On chains cf. *A* 15, 79^{b}7, note.

87^{b}7: "but also . . . from different chains": the two chains are *A*, *D*, *B* and *A*, *G*, *B*, where not-*DaG* and not-*GaD*. As 87^{b}14 notes, the chains must overlap (cf. *A* 15, 79^{b}11, note) since $(\exists X) \, (DaX \, \& \, GaX)$— whence, by *Darapti, DiG*.

87^{b}8: "E.g. let *A* be altering . . .": the Platonic analysis of pleasure (*EN H* 11, 1152^{b}13: cf. e.g. *Tim* 64^{cd}; *Phil* 42^d) is rejected in *EN* (cf. *H* 12, 1152^{b}25–1153^{a}17; *K* 3, 1173^{a}29–^{b}20); it is used illustratively again at e.g. *Rhet A* 11, 1369^{b}33. "Alter" (*metaballein*) and "change" (*kineisthai*) are normally used interchangeably (but cf. *Phys E* 5, 229^{a}30–2, ^{b}11–14). It is not clear why coming to rest is not a species of change on this account.

87^{b}16: "Inquire in how many ways . . .": for similar memoranda see *APr A* 21, 67^{b}26; 26, 69^{b}38; *Top I* 6, 169^{a}5; etc.

CHAPTER 30

On chance see *Phys B* 4–6; *EE Θ* 2 = *H* 14; *Rhet A* 5, 1362^{a}1–12. Demonstrations of what holds for the most part are discussed at *B* 12,

96^{a}8–19 (see notes; cf. *APr* A 27, 43^{b}32–6; *Rhet* A 2, 1356^{b}16–18; 1357^{a}22–32).

For Aristotle's argument, see A 6, 75^{a}4–7. There is a more general argument at *Met* E 3, 1026^{b}27–1027^{a}28, which purports to establish that there cannot be any sort of understanding of what is incidental or by chance.

87^{b}24: "if they hold for the most part, so too does the conclusion": the notion of 'what holds for the most part' is of some importance in the Aristotelian scheme of things—in the world of sublunary nature, and also in the world of human practice, many things hold not always and invariably but only for the most part. Yet the notion raises difficulties. First, Aristotle categorically states that the objects of scientific knowledge are all *necessary*: if **a** understands that P, then it is necessary that P. But the objects of scientific knowledge include many items which happen 'for the most part', and what happens (only) for the most part does not happen by necessity. Aristotle must either relax his requirement that the objects of understanding be necessary, or else revise his view that many items in nature hold only for the most part. (KULLMANN (1974), 273–7, urges that what holds for the most part is necessary in so far as it is natural; but it is hard to reconcile this view with the Aristotelian texts.)

Secondly, it is far from clear how we are to construe the notion of something's holding 'for the most part'. (1) "For the most part" is sometimes contrasted with "every", so that it is tempting to take it as a plural quantifier: "For the most part, As are B" will be true if and only if most As are B. See e.g. *HA* E 14, 545^{a}14–18; *PA* Γ 2, 663^{b}28. (2) "For the most part" is often contrasted with "always", so that it is tempting to construe it in temporal terms: "For the most part, P" will be true if and only if "P" is true for most of the time. See e.g. *APst* B 12, 96^{a}18–22; *Top* E 1, 129^{a}6–16; *Phys* B 5, 196^{b}10. (3) "For the most part" is frequently contrasted with "necessarily" (e.g. *Int* 9, 19^{a}18–22; *APr* A 13, 32^{b}5–10; *Top* B 6, 112^{b}1–9) and assimilated to "possibly" (e.g. *APr* A 3, 25^{b}14–15; A 13, 32^{b}4–11), so that it is tempting to read it as a sort of modal operator; and since it is often associated with "naturally" (e.g. *APr* A 3, 25^{b}14; A 13, 32^{b}4–13; *Top* E 5, 134^{a}7–11; *GA* A 19, 727^{b}29; Δ 8, 777^{a}19–21) it might seem that "For the most part, P" will be true if and only if (say) it is a natural but not a necessary fact that P. These three interpretations are mutually incompatible; each fits some of the Aristotelian texts well; none fits all the Aristotelian texts. Aristotle's immediate successors were apparently unhappy with what he said about 'for the most part' propositions; and no later commentator has been able to produce a coherent interpretation. (See e.g. MIGNUCCI (1981); also Barnes, 133–6; MIGNUCCI (1975), 585–91; BARNES (1982). The best attempt to find a coherent doctrine in Aristotle is in JUDSON (1991): he argues that interpretation (1) is correct, denying that any passages unequivocally support (2) (84 n. 26) and urging that the equivalence on which (3) is based is substantive and not definitional (82 n. 23; 95–8).)

At 87^{b}24 Aristotle claims that 'for the most part' premisses entail a 'for the most part' conclusion. The claim is false on interpretation (1): "Most Cs are B" and "Most Bs are A" do not together entail "Most Cs are A"—they do not even entail "Some Cs are A". (Most centenarians are women, and most women are under 70.) The claim is also false on interpretation (2). If, say, "AaB" and "BaC" are each true for most of the time, it follows that "AaC" is true for some of the time, but it does not follow that it is true for most of the time. (If "AaB" is true on Mondays to Fridays, and "BaC" is true on Wednesdays to Sundays, then "AaC" will be true on Wednesdays to Fridays.) Finally, if Aristotle's claim is interpreted in style (3), it may well seem to have some plausibility. But in the absence of a clear analysis of what it is for something to hold 'by nature', we can say no more than that.

CHAPTER 31

With A 31 compare A 18 and B 19. The general line of argument is clear, despite the suspicion that "universal" vacillates between "universally quantified proposition" and "universal property": perception cannot constitute knowledge since if P truly reports a perception it must contain singular terms (references to particular individuals, times and places) and hence cannot be universal in the fashion required for understanding.

87^{b}29: "even if perception is of what is such and such": "And similarly perception is affected by what has colour or flavour or sound—but not as each of them is called but as *such* and such" (An B 12, 424^{a}21–4; cf. 6, 418^{a}20–5; APst B 19, 100^{a}15). When, e.g., I see the son of Diares, the proper object of my perception is a coloured thing of such and such a shape. We see individuals incidentally; i.e. to see **a** is to see an F (where F is some sensible quality) which in fact is **a**. Thus perception is, in a sense, 'of the universal'; and so (one might infer) reports of perception may encapsulate knowledge. Aristotle rejects the final inference, but his rejection relies on a tenuous distinction between having perception of X and perceiving X. His answer should be something like this: 'Although a strictly correct reply to the question "What are you perceiving?" must be of the form "an F" or perhaps "That F" and cannot be of the form "**a**" (where "**a**" is a proper name), nevertheless any proposition reporting the contents of your perception must contain or imply some reference to individual objects, times, or places; and this must be so because the act of perception is necessarily tied to some individual time and place.'

87^{b}35: "even if we could perceive . . .": Aristotle's point is not that one cannot perceive mathematical objects at all (see p. 86), but that such perception, no less than perception of physical objects, can only be reported by sentences containing singular terms.

87^{b}37: "as some people say": Zabarella refers to Heracliteans, Ross to Protagoras; but there is no good evidence for any identification.

87^{b}39: Since perception cannot yield universal propositions it cannot yield explanations (cf. *Met A* 1, 981^{b}10–13); for to explain (Aristotle implies) is to subsume under some universal law. For the example see *B* 2, 90^{a}26.

88^{a}2: "Nevertheless, if we observed . . .": the ascent to explanation appears to have three stages: first, we simply observe several eclipses of the moon; then we hunt for what is common to all these cases, and thus adopt a universal proposition; and finally we formulate a demonstration using this universal proposition. At 88^{a}11 Aristotle says that the hunting is not always necessary, and *B* 2 says that it is not so in the eclipse case.

88^{a}7: "which have an explanation . . .": i.e. cases in which *X* is *Y* because it is *Z* (where *Z* ≠ *X*); cf. *A* 24, 85^{b}25, note.

88^{a}10: "unless you say that . . .": cf. *Met B* 5, 999^{b}3; *APst A* 10, 76^{b}38, note.

88^{a}11: "Nevertheless, certain features . . .": although perception is not a sufficient condition for knowledge, it is (as *A* 18 argued) a necessary condition—and gaps in our knowledge may be explicable by deficiencies in perception. It is, of course, impossible to provide genuine illustrations of such cases; and Aristotle's example must be taken hypothetically: 'If we could see the internal structure of glass—which might, perhaps, turn out to be porous—then we would know why light passes through it.' (For the example see *B* 11, 94^{b}28–31; cf. Empedocles frag. 84; [*Probl*] *IA* 58, 905^{b}2–9; *KE* 9, 939^{a}10–15. The OCT has Aristotle refer to the properties of a burning-glass.)

88^{a}16: "even if we see . . .": i.e. 'If we could see the internal structure we should be able to grasp the explanation—even though we see each particular case separately and yet must grasp them all together in comprehending a universal fact.' (The commentators take *hama*, "at a single time", to mean "at the same time ⟨sc. as the seeing⟩". But sense, syntax, and the contrast with "separately", *chōris*, favour my interpretation.)

CHAPTER 32

The issue in *A* 32 goes back to Plato's *Republic* (511^b), which describes the vision of a unified science all of whose theorems are derived from a single principle (cf. *A* 9, 76^{a}16–25; *Met A* 9, 992^{b}24; *Λ* 4, 1070^{b}5). Conceivably some Platonizing mathematicians had tried to realize this vision in the context of their own science (Solmsen, 111–12; but see Cherniss, 73 n. 55).

The thesis that "all deductions have the same principles" is open to more than one interpretation: the arguments "in general terms" (cf. *A* 21, 82^{b}34) seem to be aimed against:

(1) There is a consistent set of principles *Π*₁ such that every proposition whatever is deducible from *Π*₁.

This is certainly false, and certainly not a fair formulation of Plato's vision. When Aristotle leaves the 'general' arguments and turns to argue "on the basis of what we have laid down ⟨sc. in the earlier part of *APst*⟩" (88ᵃ30), it is hard to know what he is attacking. Perhaps he has in mind something like:

(2) There is a coherent set of principles Π_2 such that all scientific truths are deducible from Π_2.

A 32 first offers seven arguments against (1) and (2); and then deals with three reinterpretations of the Platonic thesis.

88ᵃ19: *Argument (A)*: By "true (false) deduction" Aristotle means "deduction with a true (false) conclusion" (cf. *Top I* 18, 176ᵇ31–3). Thus Aristotle wants to infer the falsity of (1) from the fact that some deducible propositions are true and others false. He relies on the principle that "every false conclusion proceeds from falsehoods, whereas true conclusions proceed from truths". But the second part of this principle is false, as *APr B* 2–4 shows—and 88ᵃ20 acknowledges its falsity. Nor is it true, as 88ᵃ20–6 argues, that any chain of syllogisms whose last member has false premisses and a true conclusion can contain at most one true proposition. Aristotle's argument relies on the principle that if the conclusion of a syllogism is false, then so are both its premisses. The principle is false, as *APr B* 2–4 knows.

88ᵃ27: *Argument (B)* correctly observes that there are pairs of propositions whose members are incompatible with one another and both false. This disproves (1); it is surprising that under (A) Aristotle did not note that a truth and a falsity might be incompatible.

88ᵃ30: *Argument (C)* in effect urges that Π_2 in (2) cannot be the axioms of any given science (cf. *A* 7). "Principles" here seems to denote primitive terms. Take the subject terms of any two sciences, say arithmetic and geometry, hierarchically arranged (see p. 119):

(Σa) $A, A_1^0, A_2^0, \ldots, A_1^1, A_2^1, \ldots, A_1^n, A_2^n, \ldots, A_k^n$.
(Σg) $G, G_1^0, G_2^0, \ldots, G_1^1, G_2^1, \ldots, G_1^m, G_2^m, \ldots, G_p^m$.

Suppose that we have to prove some geometrical theorem, of the form XaG_j^i, from arithmetical principles. Then G_j^i must attach to (Σa): it may do so in one of three ways (I simplify slightly): (i) ..., A_q^k, G_j^i, $A_{q+1}^k, \ldots$ ("as a middle term"); (ii) ..., A_k^n, G_j^i ("from below"); (iii) G_j^i, $A, \ldots$ ("from above"). (The fourth possibility, "or else some of the terms ...", is the conjunction of (i) and (iii); Aristotle is thinking of the general case in which *all* geometrical theorems are proved from the principles of arithmetic, so that *every* G_j^i must attach to (Σa). For the terminology see *A* 19, 81ᵇ40; 23, 84ᵇ33, notes.) Now if every G_j^i attaches to (Σa) in this way, then for every T_a in (Σa) and every T_g in (Σg) either T_aaT_g or T_gaT_a. (By "X attaches to Y" (*epharmottein*: cf. *A* 7, 75ᵇ4) Aristotle must mean "*XaY* or *YaX*".) But "unit" is in (Σa), and "point" in (Σg), yet these terms are not tied together by the *a*-relation.

If some T_a does not attach to (Σg), then some arithmetical truth cannot be derived from geometrical principles; and if some T_a does not attach to any science other than (Σa), then there is some arithmetical truth which cannot be derived within any science other than arithmetic. Hence not all truths can be derived from the same set of principles. The weakness of Aristotle's argument is the general weakness of his individuation of the sciences: it is not at all plain what the criteria for a scientific genus or kind are. Take the axioms of geometry and those of botany, and form their conjunction. From this conjunctive axiom-set, all the theorems of geometry and of botany can be derived. Why does this not constitute a new science? Plainly, because the conjoined set of axioms is not unified or coherent—it does not stick to a single kind. But then Aristotle owes us an account of unification or coherence. (Take a set of principles, Π, and the set of theorems, T, which are derivable from them. Suppose that both Π and T can be divided into two exhaustive and exclusive subsets, Π_1 and Π_2, T_1 and T_2, such that all the items in T_1 derive from Π_1 and all the items in T_2 derive from Π_2: could we say that Π lacks coherence under these conditions and only under these conditions?)

88ᵃ36: *Argument* (*D*) claims that Π_2 cannot consist solely of common principles. Aristotle is usually taken to say that in addition to common principles every proof needs some 'proper' principles (cf. *A* 10, 76ᵃ37–ᵇ2); alternatively he may mean to recall his view that the common principles have to be tailored to fit the genus to which they are being applied (cf. *A* 10, 76ᵃ37–ᵇ2). But neither of these interpretations fits the text well. Rather, Aristotle argues that *some* of the principles in any science will be restricted to items in the relevant 'category' (the 'kinds of existent things' are the categories): the common principles alone will not suffice—in addition we need *at least* principles specific to a given category. Hence Π_2 cannot form a coherent set. (But why cannot the principles of a science include reference to items from more than one category?)

88ᵇ3: *Argument* (*E*): to find premisses for AxC you must get a third term B (either 'interpolating' it or assuming it in addition: *A* 22, 84ᵃ36–7). Hence there will be twice as many premisses as conclusions. ("The principles are not much fewer . . ." means "It is not the case that the principles are much fewer . . ." and not "The principles are only a little fewer . . .") This argument makes the unwarranted assumption that if one set of principles sufficed for all deductions, there would be many fewer principles than conclusions. And it falsely asserts that "the propositions are principles". (Ross offers a completely different interpretation, which attaches to *APr A* 25; but he does not give Aristotle a decent argument.)

88ᵇ6: *Argument* (*F*): (i) If the terms are finite, the premisses are finite, and hence the conclusions too are finite; (ii) if the principles are finite they will be infinitely fewer than the conclusions, contrary to the previous argument. Perhaps, then, we should interpret Argument (F) a little less strictly: 'The Platonists must be prepared to specify some pretty small, finite, set of principles; but their claim is that all true propositions are generable from this set: yet we have no idea how many such propositions there may be.' In other words, the opponents, taking a finite set of n principles, thereby fix the number of true propositions at $\frac{1}{2}(n(n-1))$; but the number of truths is 'infinite', i.e. it is, for all we know, much greater than $\frac{1}{2}(n(n-1))$ for any n the Platonists may care to fasten upon.

88^{b}7: *Argument (G)*: There are contingent principles because there are contingent conclusions (i.e. 'for the most part' propositions: see *A* 30 and notes) and every contingent conclusion depends upon at least one contingent premiss (*APr A* 24, 41^{b}27–31). Aristotle does not explain why a single set of principles may not contain both necessary and contingent propositions.

88^{b}9: The *First Reinterpretation* yields:

(3) For any scientific truth P there is a set of principles Π_3 such that P is deducible from Π_3.

Here "the principles of the sciences are the same" is read as 'the principles of the sciences are self-identical'. ("*X* is the same" can mean—at least in Platonic Greek: e.g. *Soph* 256^{ab}—"*X* is self-identical".) The use of "calculation" (*logismos*) to denote arithmetic is Platonic (e.g. *Rep* 510^c; *Phil* 56^e).

88^{b}15: *Second Reinterpretation*: 'the principles of the sciences are the same' in that "anything must be proved from everything"—i.e. (88^{b}22):

(4) There is a set of principles Π_4 such that every scientific truth is deducible from Π_4 and from no subset of Π_4.

According to the MSS, Aristotle sets himself to show that (4) is not "the same as seeking the same principles for everything", i.e. is not a reasonable interpretation of the Platonic view. But in fact he proceeds to argue that (4), whatever its relation to the Platonic view, is a naïve falsity. (We should perhaps emend the text at 88^{b}16 to eliminate this inconcinnity.)

The falsity of (4) is both obvious to any mathematical tiro (for different proofs use different principles), and analytically demonstrable. 'Suppose a proof *AaB*, *BaC* ⊢ *AaC*; to get a new conclusion *AaD* we need to add a premiss, *CaD*. Since *CaD* is *added*, it did not form one of the set of principles on which *AaC* depended; hence *AaC* does not depend on *all* the principles.'

88^{b}20: "And if someone were to say . . .": i.e. 'It is really only the *first* immediate proposition which is a principle, so that both *AaC* and *AaD* depend on the same principle, viz. *AaB*.' Aristotle retorts that even so, *each kind* will have one such principle so that not all conclusions will depend on the same first immediate principles. (For different readings see Mure and Ross.)

88^{b}21: The *Third Reinterpretation* gives:

(5) There are sets of principles Π_5^a, Π_5^b, . . . , Π_5^m, such that all the Π_5^xs

are of the same kind and every truth of science S^x is deducible from the set Π^x_S.

This has been ascribed to Speusippus (Cherniss, 73 n. 55; KULLMANN (1974), 149 n. 43; TARÁN (1981), 420–2).

CHAPTER 33

A 33–4 turn from the theory of demonstration to more general epistemo-logical matters.

88^{b}30:   88^{b}30–89^{a}10 seems to be arguing for:

(1) It is not the case that: (**a** understands that *P* if and only if **a** opines that *P*).

The conclusion rests on two premisses, the first of which is:

(2) If **a** understands that *P* then necessarily-*P*,

which was argued for in *A* 6. For his second premiss Aristotle needs:

(3) It is not the case that: (if **a** opines that *P* then necessarily-*P*).

The argument down to 89^{a}4 supports this premiss by arguing that objects of opinion include contingencies, on the grounds that contingencies cannot be the objects of any other cognitive attitude. And that (3) is indeed in Aristotle's mind is confirmed by 89^{a}11–16 (see notes).

89^{a}4–10, however, suggests a different premiss. Here Aristotle appeals to two sets of 'appearances' (*phainomena*) or commonly accepted beliefs. First, that opinion and non-necessities are alike "unstable" (*abebaios*: cf. *Phil* 59^b). This appears to support not (3) but rather:

(4) If **a** opines that *P* then not necessarily-*P*.

By saying that opinion is unstable Aristotle does not mean that opiners are always hesitant, or lack 'subjective certainty' (see *EN H* 3, 1146^{b}26–30; cf. *Gorg* 454^e; but see perhaps *EN Θ* 8, 1159^{a}22). Rather, stability is a matter of objective fixity (cf. *Phaedo* 90^c; *Rep* 503^c). Thus Aristotle may mean that opiners are inherently liable to change their minds (cf. *A* 2, 72^{b}3, and notes); or he may be referring to his view that opinions are inherently liable to change their truth-value. (Cf. p. 128. See *Met Γ* 4, 1008^{a}16, where an opinion is stable if not both *P* and not-*P* are true; and further *EN Z* 3, 1139^{b}21–2; *APr B* 21, 67^{b}1; *Top E* 3, 131^{b}21–2; *Met Z* 10, 1036^{a}6; 15, 1040^{a}2—all connected with opinions founded on perception.)

The second 'appearance' or common belief perhaps represents an ordinary use of language (see *A* 2, 71^{b}9–16, and notes). To support (3) Aristotle needs something like:

(5) We sometimes think we opine that *P* (say "I opine that *P*") even though we think that not necessarily-*P*.

But what he in fact says implies:

(6) Whenever we think that necessarily-*P* we think we know and do

not opine that P (say "I know that P" and not "I opine that P").
This seems directed at (4) rather than at (3). (Its falsity is illustrated
every time a mathematician speaks tentatively.)

(4) is stronger than (3); it entails it but is not entailed by it. (2) and (4)
yield something stronger than (1), viz.:

(7) ¬ (∃P) (**a** understands that P & **a** opines that P).

If we take Aristotle's official argument to be the one from (2) and (3)
to (1), then he might consistently accept:

(8) If **a** understands that P, then **a** opines that P.

If we prefer the argument from (2) and (4) to (5), then Aristotle cannot
entertain (8).

88^{b}36: "by comprehension I mean . . .": cf. *A* 2, 72^{a}24, notes; the point
of the parenthesis is to indicate that Aristotle is not thinking of the
quasi-perceptual *noēsis* of mathematical objects.

88^{b}36: "nor indemonstrable understanding": indemonstrable understanding and comprehension are identical; "nor" (*oude*) means "i.e.
not".

89^{a}1: "and what is called after them": presumably: 'what is comprehensible, understandable, or opinable'.

89^{a}3: "Opinion is belief in a proposition which is immediate and not
necessary": Aristotle has no reason to limit opinion to *immediate* propositions; and the sentence at once raises the unanswerable question of
what attitude of mind governs *mediated* non-necessities. It should be
excised.

89^{a}11: 'How, then, can opinion and understanding be differentiated
when they are directed towards the same object?' Aristotle's question
appears to ask how (8) is possible, and hence to presuppose that (8) *is*
possible. And that might be thought to clinch the view that Aristotle's
argument is from (2) and (3) to (1). It turns out, however, that Aristotle
does not after all countenance the possibility of (8).

The discussion of (8) occupies 89^{a}11–38.

89^{a}13: "A knower and an opiner will follow the same path": Ross
happily paraphrases 'will keep pace with one another'.

89^{a}16: Aristotle's suggestion amounts to this: If AaB is an I-predication
and **a** believes that AaB, then **a** knows that AaB if and only if **a** believes
that AaB is an I-predication; and **a** opines that AaB if and only if **a** does
not believe that AaB is an I-predication. This is not very persuasive.
First, on pain of a regress Aristotle will have to allow that opining that
AaB is an I-predication and understanding that AaB is an I-predication
are indistinguishable. Secondly, it is hard to see how opinion that AaB is
an I-predication can amount to knowledge that AaB (or, in general, how
belief that P can amount to knowledge that P'), given that any opinion
may be adopted at random and irrationally. Aristotle's suggestion omits

the essential trait of knowledge, that it must be reasonable (however that is ultimately to be explained).

89ᵃ17: "if you believe something which cannot be otherwise . . .": 89ᵃ20 shows that "what cannot be otherwise" is being used to denote predicates which are necessary to some given subject; similarly, "definitions" must refer to *definientia*. Thus: 'If **a** believes of some necessary predicate *A* that it holds of *B* in itself—just as he will believe of a *definiens D* that it holds of *B* in itself—then he understands and does not merely opine that *AaB*.' (The stressed "*these* items" (*tauta ge*) contrasts *A* with *D*.)

89ᵃ20: ". . . in virtue of its essence and in virtue of its form": i.e. 'in itself'—the essence or form of *X* is, in one sense, its 'account'; and *A* holds of *B* 'in virtue of its account' if *AaB* is an I-predication.

89ᵃ23: I discuss the difficulties of the next paragraph under five heads.

(i) The argument turns on the fact that "things are called the same in several senses". Aristotle catalogues the senses more than once (e.g. *Top A* 7, 103ᵃ6–39; *Met Δ* 9, 1017ᵇ27–1018ᵃ11; *I* 3, 1054ᵃ32–ᵇ3); but these passages throw no light on the present argument. What Aristotle means is that there is more than one criterion of identity for objects of cognitive attitudes, and that there cannot be both knowledge and opinion that *P* under all identity criteria.

(ii) The paragraph distinguishes two ways in which one might be thought to have knowledge and opinion of the same thing; and it elucidates this distinction by an allegedly parallel distinction between two ways in which it might be thought that there could be true and false opinions of the same thing. The latter distinction is merely hinted at in the text. The first way probably occurs if:

(9) (∃*t*) (at *t* **a** opines truly that *P* & at *t* **b** opines falsely that *P*).

The criterion of identity for objects of opinion is here identity of the propositional objects of those attitudes. As Aristotle says, (9) is absurd: there cannot be true and false opinion of the same thing in this way. (Temporal quantification is explicitly introduced at 89ᵃ38; it is needed in (9) if Aristotle is to allow for the possibility that *P* may change its truth-value.) It is not clear whether "some people say" (89ᵃ26) that (9) is true, or only that (9) is a proper interpretation of "there is true and false opinion of the same thing".

Aristotle says that (9) leads to many absurdities, in particular to the conclusion that "you do not opine what you falsely opine". It is not clear just how the inference should go. Perhaps thus: 'Suppose that **a** truly opines that *P* and that **b** falsely opines that *P*; then what **b** opines cannot be *P*—for *P*, as **a**'s case shows, is true, and what **b** opines is false. Thus a false opiner does not opine what he falsely opines.' The argument will go equally well for the case of the true opiner; and we should perhaps omit "falsely" (*pseudōs*) at 89ᵃ28.

(iii) The second way of there being true and false opinion of the same thing is contained in the sentence "because the diagonal with which the opinions are concerned is the same" (89ᵃ31). Thus:

(10) ($\exists t$) (at t **a** opines truly that X is Y & at t **b** opines falsely that X is Z).

(It emerges later that Z must be read as not-Y.)

In (10) "they are of the same thing—although what it is to be each of them in respect of its account is not the same" (89ᵃ32): i.e. 'the essence of the two opinions is different'—the opinion that X is Y and the opinion that X is Z are about the same thing, but what it is to opine that X is Y and what it is to opine that X is Z are not the same.

(iv) The application of (9) and (10) to the case of knowledge and opinion should yield:

(11) ($\exists t$) (at t **a** understands that P & at t **b** opines that P);

(12) ($\exists t$) (at t **a** understands that X is Y & at t **b** opines that X is Z).

where (11) is inadmissible but (12) permitted. Aristotle's illustration of (12) appears to be:

(12a) ($\exists t$) (at t **a** understands that a man is just what is an animal & at t **b** opines that a man is an animal).

Moreover, the argument at 89ᵇ1–5 requires that the object of **b**'s opinion is "a man is an animal, but not just what is an animal".

This position is even stricter than the one implicit in 89ᵃ11–23: let *"P'"* abbreviate "men are animals" and *"P"* "men are just what are animals". Then 89ᵃ11–23, although it rules out anything answering to (8), still allows the possibility of:

(13) ($\exists t$) (at t **a** understands that P & at t **b** opines that P).

But now (11) denies the possibility of (13): we are allowed only:

(14) ($\exists t$) (at t **a** understands that P' & at t **b** opines that P).

(v) Finally, two small points. First, the use of "understanding (opinion) is of X" in 89ᵃ34–6 differs from its use earlier in *A* 33; for at 89ᵃ34–6 X denotes the *predicate* of the proposition understood or opined. Secondly, by "they are the same" (89ᵃ36) Aristotle means "the objects of understanding and opinion are the same"; perhaps we should read *tou autou* for *to auto*.

89ᵃ38:   Aristotle asserts that (14) is possible only if **a** ≠ **b**. His argument rests on the general principle:

(15) ((**a** understands that P) or (**a** opines that P) → **a** believes that P).

The word for "believe" is *hupolambanein*: although Aristotle sometimes uses this as a synonym for "opine" (*doxazein*), its official use is to mark out the genus of cognitive attitudes of which understanding and opinion are two species (cf. *An Γ* 3, 427ᵇ25). Thus the concern of *A* 33 is not (as we might unwarily suppose) the distinction between knowledge and belief: that distinction it takes for granted, and investigates the distinction between the two species of belief, knowledge and (let us say) mere opinion. It seems an obvious suggestion that mere opinion might be *defined* as belief which is not knowledge, i.e.:

(16) **a** opines that $P =_{\mathrm{df}}$ **a** believes that $P \,\&\, \neg$ (**a** knows that P).

Had Aristotle got this clear the puzzles of the chapter could have been resolved more simply; for many of the contortions Aristotle goes through are due to his tendency to treat (mere) opinion and belief as identical. In particular, the argument that (14) requires that **a** ≠ **b** might go, more cleanly, thus: 'Given (16), (11) cannot hold if **a** = **b**. Now in (14), P' immediately entails P. If R immediately entails Q, then if **a** knows that R **a** knows that Q. Hence (14) cannot hold if **a** = **b**.' This argument is more respectable than the one Aristotle offers; whether or not it is sound depends on the question whether a decent sense can be given to the notion of immediate entailment.

89ᵇ7: I take it that "the remaining items" are the other objects of cognitive attitudes rather than the other "operations of thought", as Ross somewhat vaguely has it. These questions are discussed at *EN* Z 3–7 (moral study) and *An Γ* 4–7 (the study of nature).

CHAPTER 34

For acumen, *agchinoia*, see *EN* Z 10, 1142ᵇ5–6; [*Epin*] 976ᵇᶜ; [*Def*] 412ᵉ.

The sharp man quickly seizes upon what is in fact the correct explanation; but presumably he does not *know* the correct explanation until he has observed the relevant correlations in a number of cases (cf. *A* 31, 88ª2–5, notes).

89ᵇ14: "he gets to know all the explanatory middle terms": i.e. 'in all cases he apprehends the explanatory middle term' (Pacius).

CHAPTER I

Aristotle's four question-types, which he names *to hoti, to dioti, ei estin,* and *ti estin,* appear to come to this: we may ask:

(1) whether it is the case that *P*;
(2) why it is the case that *P*;
(3) if *X* is;
(4) what *X* is.

(For the use of "is" in (3) see p. 84.)

Aristotle has two attempts at expressing the distinction between (1) and (3). First, he employs different subordinating conjunctions: in the case of (1) we ask *whether* and we know *that*; in the case of (3) we ask *if* and we know *if*. But this is unsatisfactory; for in the case of (3) we can with equal propriety ask *whether,* and strictly speaking we know *that* and not *if* ("a knows if there are *X*s" does not mean the same as "a knows that there are *X*s", and it is the latter which is the required analogue to "a knows that *P*"). The second attempt renders the subordinate clause in (3) as "*X* is *simpliciter (haplōs)*", and contrasts this with "*X* is something *(ti)*" or "*X* is partially *(epi merous)*". ("*X* is *Y*" says that *X* is 'partially' because "*X* is" is a part of "*X* is *Y*": cf. *Top I* 5, 166ᵇ37–167ᵃ4; for "*X* is something" cf. *Top I* 25, 180ᵃ32–8.) Thus (1) and (3) are to be distinguished by the content and not the form of their interrogations; and we may therefore replace "*P*" in (1) by "*X* is *Y*". *B* 2, 90ᵃ9–14, confirms that (1) asks after the possession of a predicate; and in addition it states unequivocally that (3) is restricted to subject-terms. Thus it lies near to interpret the four question-types as follows: Of any subject term *S* we may ask:

(1*a*) if *S* is *P*;
(2*a*) why *S* is *P*;
(3*a*) if there is such a thing as (an) *S*;
(4*a*) what *S* is.

There are objections to this reconstruction. First, we might well wonder if (1*a*)–(4*a*) represent *all* the questions we may ask. A possible reply is that (1*a*)–(4*a*) do indeed cover all the questions which a demonstrator might ask in connection with any given syllogistic proposition. (And *B* 2 makes it clear that only syllogistic propositions are in question.) Secondly, however, even a demonstrator might be inclined to ask:

(5*a*) if there is such a thing as (*a*) *P*;
(6*a*) what *P* is.

A possible answer is that (5*a*) and (6*a*) analyse as cases of (1*a*) and (2*a*): see *Met H* 2, 1042ᵇ25–1043ᵃ12. Thirdly, the illustration of (3) at *B* 2,

90^a5, substitutes "night" for "X": if we read (3) as $(3a)$, we must interpret "night" as a subject-term. But I suppose that this can be done.

In sum, I incline to accept $(1a)-(4a)$ as the proper interpretation of Aristotle's four questions; at all events, I shall use this interpretation in what follows. (For a different account see GOMEZ-LOBO (1980).)

89^b26: "whether the sun is eclipsed": either 'whether the sun is now in eclipse' (cf. B 2, 90^a30) or 'whether the sun suffers eclipses'.

89^b27: "Evidence for this . . .": ' "Surely in addition to $(1)-(4)$ we can ask whether *or not P*?" No: this merely reformulates (1). For suppose we are seeking whether or not P: if we find out that (*hoti*) P, we think our search is successfully terminated. Thus seeking whether or not P is seeking the fact (*to hoti*).'

89^b29: "When we know the fact we seek the reason why" (cf. e.g. B 8, 93^a17; B 10, 93^b32; *APr A* 30; *HA A* 6, 491^a7; *PA A* 1, 639^b5; *IA* 1, 704^b8: see KULLMANN (1974), 204–20). If P because Q, then P; and if **a** knows that (P because Q), then **a** knows that P. Hence if you ask "Why P?" you presuppose *that P*; and it is—not impossible but—futile to ask why P unless you actually take it to be the case that P. But if you *understand* that P, then you know that (P because Q). Hence when **a** asks why P, he knows, or truly supposes, that P, but he does not understand that P. (See ACKRILL (1981), 364–8).

89^b34: ". . . having come to know . . . that it is, we seek what it is": see e.g. B 2, 89^b38, 90^a22; 7, 92^b4-8; *Phys Γ* 4, 202^b35. If **a** knows that X is, then **a** knows what X is; and in asking "What is X?", **a** presupposes that X is. But in some cases (A 2, 72^a23; 10, 76^a34; B 2, 90^b30; 9, 93^b24), we start from knowledge of what X is and then prove that X is. There appears to be an inconsistency here: the appearance is (implicitly) shown to be illusory in B 7–8.

89^b34: "Then what is a god?": "Aristotle keeps the example of God but not that of centaur; for since there are no centaurs, we cannot seek or know what a centaur is, but only what its name signifies—as will be explained in more detail in chapter 8" (Pacius).

CHAPTER 2

89^b39: Questions $(1a)$ and $(3a)$ of B 1 are reduced to:

    (7) Is there a middle term?

and $(2a)$ and $(4a)$ are reduced to:

    (8) What is the middle term?

In the case of $(1a)$, (7) has the form:

    (71) Is there a Z such that X is Z and Z is Y?

Or rather, we must think of something like:

    (71*) Is there a Z such that X is Z, Z is $Y \vdash X$ is Y is a demonstrative syllogism?

For the search for a 'middle term', as 90^a6 makes clear, is the search for an *explanatory* middle term, i.e. the search for a middle term which may figure in a demonstrative proof. (This confirms the suggestion that Aristotle is not displaying a wholly general interest in any questions which anyone might think to ask: he is concerned exclusively with those questions which, in his view, are appropriate to scientific research.) However that may be, a negative answer to (71*) is compatible with an affirmative answer to (1*a*) if *X is Y* is immediate. Conceivably the use of "understand" at 89^b23 is meant to indicate that *B* 1–2 are restricted to mediable propositions.

The application of (7) to (3*a*) is less simple. Probably Aristotle has in mind:

(73*) Is there a *Z* such that *X is Z* is an I-predication and there are Zs?

Met Z 17 perhaps suggests that (3*a*) is analysable as "*M is F*" where *M* is the matter and *F* the form of *X*; but it is not clear that such propositions are mediable. A negative answer to (73*) is compatible with an affirmative answer to (3*a*) if *S* is unanalysable.

Consequently, for (8) we need something like:

(82*) What is the *Z* such that *X is Z, Z is Y ⊢ X is Z* is a demonstrative syllogism?

The thesis that (82*) is equivalent to (2*a*) is discussed in more detail in *B* 11.

Similarly, for (4*a*) we need something like:

(84*) What is the *Z* such that *X is Z* is an I-predication, and there are Zs?

89^b39: "either partially or *simpliciter*": i.e. '⟨i.e.⟩ either ⟨the fact that it is⟩ partially or ⟨the fact that it is⟩ *simpliciter*'. The two ways of distinguishing (1) from (3) are here put side by side (see p. 203).

90^a6: The proposition that "the middle term is the explanation" (90^a7) must be read as: 'For any facts p^1 and p^2, if p^1 explains p^2 then there is a demonstrative syllogism *AaB, BaC ⊢ AaC* such that *AaC* expresses p^2 and the middle term expresses p^1.' Thus since we are always asking for explanations, we are always after middle terms, and (1*a*)–(4*a*) reduce to (7) and (8).

This may well seem to be simply false—and also to be known by Aristotle to be false. For the supposition seems to imply that everything can be explained. (If "Is it the case that *P*?" amounts to "Is there an explanation of why *P*?", then if there is no explanation it follows that it is not the case that *P*.) Moreover, the supposition seems to imply that the very form of the question "Is it the case that *P*?" carries the notion of a possible explanation. But we can sensibly suppose that some events have no explanation; and Aristotle recognizes as much in his discussions of chance events. Here, again, it must be assumed that Aristotle is thinking only of *scientific* questions. Science does not deal with chance events; and when we ask, in scientific vein, whether it is the case that P, we presuppose that chance events have been excluded. (And if it turns out that it is a scientific *principle* that P? Then there is an explanation inasmuch as P is 'self-explanatory'.)

Ross thinks that questions (3) and (4) "which in ch. 1 referred to substances, have in ch. 2 come to refer so much more to attributes and events that the former reference has almost receded from Aristotle's mind". On the contrary, the present section provides the main evidence for the interpretation of (3) and (4) by (3a) and (4a).

90^a14: The purport of this paragraph is uncertain. If "all these cases" (90^a14) are the predicates that Aristotle has just listed, then he may be making the point that to ask "What is P?" is the same as asking "Why is S P?" (see p. 203). But 90^a31–4 state unambiguously that the reduction of 'what' to 'why' questions goes through for subject-terms as well as for predicates: *Any* answer to the question: What is F? will answer the question: Why is **a** F? To say what a man is (e.g. that he is a featherless biped) is to explain—in one sense of explanation—why Socrates is a man (because he is a featherless biped). On this interpretation, the word "these" (90^a14) has no referring function: Aristotle might better have said "in all cases".

90^a21: "Can the high and the low harmonize? . . .": this last example seems to introduce two new questions: "*Can X be Y?*"; and "What sort of Z is X?" Aristotle probably does not mean to distinguish the first question from (1a) (cf. *B* 7, 92^b19, note). His train of thought may be this: 'Assuming we know what Y is (say that Y is Z), then our question: Is X Y? becomes: Is X Z? Suppose that X is Z. Then if our interest is in some special case of X, say X^* (some particular pair of high and low notes), we know that X^* is Z, but we will want to ask what particular case of Z X^* is. And in fact this question amounts to asking what is the middle term Z^* for X^* *is Z*.'

90^a24: 'If, observing that X is Y, we actually perceive the middle term Z, we do not cast around for an answer to the question "Why is X Y?" Hence in *this* case having Z is knowing the explanation; and so in general the middle term is the explanation.' But a single glance cannot give us the explanation (A 31, 87^b39–40). And although from perception (i.e. from a series of perceptions) "the universal would come about", this does not distinguish the lunar from the mundane cases; for *all* universal knowledge comes about from perception (A 18), and thus *all* middle terms, if they can be known at all, are in this weak sense 'perceptible'. What Aristotle should say is that in some cases we do not have to *cast around* for a middle term: for moon-dwellers, observation of the eclipse involves observation of the interposition of the earth; and having observed several eclipses, they will at the same time have come by knowledge of the middle term. (The example is more ingenious than apposite; for moon-dwellers would hardly observe an eclipse of the moon.)

CHAPTER 3

B 3 begins the main burden of the book: to what extent, if at all, can definitions be demonstrated? The introductory chapters, as Aristotle stresses, are aporematic.

90^b1: "to the neighbouring arguments": the thread connecting *B* 3 to *B* 1–2 is this: 'To answer the four types of question one has to find a middle term; and this will express what something is; how, then, can we show that we have found a genuine middle term which does express what something is?' Thus it is reasonable to take "neighbouring" to mean "immediately preceding" rather than "following", even though the word *echomenos* normally has the latter reference.

90^b1: Aristotle sets himself at 90^b2 to consider whether anything can both be a definition and be demonstrated; let us abbreviate this to:

(1) ($\exists P$) (Dem:P & Def:P).

90^b1–17 presents four arguments against:

(2) ($\forall P$) (Dem:$P \rightarrow$ Def:P),

and 90^b18–27 offers two arguments against its converse:

(3) ($\forall P$) (Def:$P \rightarrow$ Dem:P).

Only at 90^b28–91^a6 does (1) officially enter the argument; Aristotle there gives three reasons for denying it.

The three theses are not clearly stated inasmuch as Aristotle's remarks about definition are neither uniform nor precise; it seems, however, that his meaning is adequately represented if we take "Def:P" to be true if and only if P is of the form AaB and $Ba =_{\text{df}} Aa$.

90^b4: *Argument (A) against (2)*: cf. *A* 10, 77^a4, note.

90^b7: *Argument (B) against (2)* has two premisses:

(4) Dem:$P \rightarrow \Box:(K_a:P \rightarrow \text{Dem}_a:P)$;
(5) Dem:P & Def:$P \rightarrow \Diamond (\exists x) (K\text{def}_x:P$ & not-Dem$_x$:P).

("$K\text{def}_a$:P" means "**a** knows that P by reason of knowing definitions only"; $K\text{def}_a$:P thus entails $K_a:P$—"**a** knows that P".) The argument is valid. Premiss (4) is used at *A* 22, 83^b35 (see notes); and (5) seems to be true. Aristotle, I infer, accepts this argument *in propria persona*, even though it appears among the puzzles. As it is presented, Argument (B) claims to show only that not every conclusion of an argument in *Barbara* is knowable by definition; but in fact it establishes, if sound, the falsity of (1).

90^b13: *Argument (C) against (2)*.

90^b16: In *Argument (D) against (2)*, *ousia* (see p. 177) is usually construed as "substance" (cf. *Met Z* 4, 1030^b4–7; 5, 1031^a1–5). But it is better to take it as "essence": the point is that such predicates as *having*

2 R, which *Barbara* may demonstrate, do not form part of the essence of their subjects.

90^{b}19: *Argument (A) against* (3) is the same as (B) against (2); premiss (4) is generalized, but the generalization is vague, since Aristotle does not explain his criteria for identifying 'modes of understanding'.

90^{b}24: *Argument (B) against* (3): "it has been proved earlier": cf. A 3, 72^{b}18–33; A 22, 84^{a}29–^{b}1.

90^{b}28: *Argument (A) against* (1) is an expansion of 90^{b}16–17; that demonstrations assume 'what a thing is' has in effect been stated at A 10, 76^{a}32–3; cf. A 1, 71^{a}11–17.

90^{b}33: *Argument (B) against* (1) takes "definition" in the sense of "*definiens*" (see p. 200); though "two-footed" and "animal" are not related as subject and predicate in "man is a two-footed animal" (*Met Z* 12, 1037^{b}19–24; but cf. *H* 3, 1043^{b}31), it is by no means so clear that "two-footed animal" is not here predicated of "man"—indeed, 90^{b}4 implies that it is. (The Greeks do not seem to have had a term for "plane figure"; perhaps, then, the definition Aristotle has in mind is that of triangle as "plane figure bounded by three straight lines". He says "*nor indeed* figure of plane" because the unwary might forget the existence of non-plane figures.)

90^{b}38: *Argument (C) against* (1).

91^{a}3: "unless one . . . as a part to the whole": if D_1 concludes to AaB and D_2 to AaC, and in fact BaC, then D_2 is a 'part' of the whole D_1, and AaC is a 'part' of AaB. See A 1, 71^{a}24 and notes.

CHAPTER 4

91^{a}12: Despite Aristotle's remark, the puzzles (*aporiai*) continue until the end of B 7, and their topic is the same as before.

91^{a}14: "as the argument just now supposed": i.e. 'as B 3 argued' (cf. *GA E* 8, 788^{b}20, for this use of "suppose").

91^{a}15: 'Suppose that AaC gives a definition of C or expresses what C is. (Suppose, as I shall put it, that $Aa_{df}C$.) Now if we are to prove that AaC, we must take as premisses AaB and BaC. There are four possibilities: (1) $Aa_{df}B$ & $Ba_{df}C$, (2) $Aa_{df}B$ & not-($Ba_{df}C$), (3) not-($Aa_{df}B$) & $Ba_{df}C$, (4) not-($Aa_{df}B$) & not-($Ba_{df}C$). Now it is clear that we can only prove that $Aa_{df}C$ in case (1). But in case (1) we already have $Ba_{df}C$—i.e. we already have a definition of C—, and hence we are assuming what we were hoping to prove. If we do not make the assumptions "in this double fashion", i.e. by making double use of the subscript "df", then we shall not be able to reach $Aa_{df}C$.'

That this is the general structure of the argument seems clear. But there are several difficulties of detail. First, Aristotle explicitly considers case (2); but he does not explicitly mention cases (3) and (4). Presumably case (3) falls to the same objection as case (1), in that it already assumes the definition of C. And if case (2) can be ruled out, then perhaps case (4) is ruled out *a fortiori*.

Secondly, it is not clear precisely how case (2) is meant to be ruled out; and thirdly, it is not clear why Aristotle begins the argument by remarking that properties and definitions *convert*. These two difficulties may best be considered together. At 91ª21–3 Aristotle considers case (2); and at 91ª24 he remarks that "both will contain what it is". We *might* take "both" to refer to AaB and AaC, both of which—in case (2)—do indeed carry the subscript "df". And then we might take the following sentence ("therefore B too will hold . . .") to encapsulate the following argument. 'Suppose $Aa_{df}B$ and $Aa_{df}C$. By conversion, $Aa_{df}C$ yields $Ca_{df}A$; and by transitivity of a_{df} (91ª17–21), $Ca_{df}A$ and $Aa_{df}B$ yield $Ca_{df}B$, which in turn, by conversion, gives $Ba_{df}C$. But we were assuming that not-($Ba_{df}C$). Hence case (2) leads to a contradiction.' This is clever enough—but it demands a very generous reading of the text. Moreover, when the phrase "both contain what it is" is repeated at 91ª25, the word "both" clearly refers to AaB and BaC; hence we should probably construe the reference in the same way at 91ª24. In that case, the sentence (and its successor) merely restate case (1). But this, too, is an unsatisfactory conclusion; for if it is correct, then there is no argument in the text to rule out case (2) (and in addition, the reference to conversion becomes entirely pointless).

Fourthly, it is in any case false that definitions convert in the sense that $Aa_{df}B$ implies $Ba_{df}A$ (rather, $Aa_{df}B$ implies not-($Ba_{df}A$)). Of course, if $Aa_{df}B$, then AaB converts and BaA follows—but it is hard to see how this fact might bear upon Aristotle's argument.

Finally, it is far from clear that cases (2) and (4) can be excluded on purely logical grounds. For case (2) consider "two-footed animal" for A, "human" for B, "man" for C; for case (4) take "two-footed animal", "creature capable of laughter", and "man".

Thus Aristotle's argument is less than satisfactory. But in so far as B 4 is still part of the preliminary puzzling, we need not be too distressed.

91ª35: The theory that the soul is a 'self-moving number' was put forward by Xenocrates (frags. 60–5 Heinze ≃ 165–212 Isnardi Parente; see Cherniss, 33–4). Xenocrates' argument must be this: 'The soul is what is explanatory of life; what is explanatory of life is a self-moving number: therefore the soul is a self-moving number.' (This argument is, formally speaking, on a par with Aristotle's own implied argument at *An* B 2, 413ª11–20.) Why does Aristotle say that Xenocrates here "proves through conversion"? And why does he think that Xenocrates *postulates* that "soul is just what is a number . . ."?

The commentators suppose that Xenocrates attempted to prove the first premiss of his argument from the conclusion and the conversion of the second premiss. If this is right, then Aristotle's strictures achieve an *ad hominem* success; but they do not show why a definition cannot be demonstrated in the Xenocratean way as long as the demonstrated definition is not subsequently used to prove a premiss of its own demonstration.

Aristotle's criticism ceases to be *ad hominem* if we give up the supposition that Xenocrates tried to prove the first premiss of his argument. We may then imagine that the argument is "through conversion" in the weak sense of using a convertible premiss (cf. 91ᵃ15–18); and that when Aristotle says "it is necessary to postulate that X is Y in the sense of being the same thing" he means "it is necessary to postulate that X is Z, where $Z = Y$"—i.e. Xenocrates must postulate that the soul is a number inasmuch as he postulates that the soul is explanatory of its own life and being explanatory of one's own life is (on his account) one and the same thing as being a self-moving number.

91ᵇ1: 91ᵇ1–7 reasserts the conclusion of the previous section: you cannot infer $Aa_{df}C$ from AaB & BaC—not even if $Aa_{df}B$. There are some difficulties of detail:

91ᵇ3: "Rather, it is true to say only that A will hold of C": i.e. 'but you can conclude only AaC, not $Aa_{df}C$'. (The MS text is defensible.)

91ᵇ3: "even if A is just what is some B": i.e. 'even if $Aa_{df}B$'. But this is a hard gloss; and the MSS may well be corrupt.

91ᵇ4: "For what it is to be an animal...": i.e. 'Suppose that *being F* is what it is to be an animal, and that *being G* is what it is to be a man. Then, just as animal belongs to every man, so *FaG* (this is the sense of the parenthesis). But of course *being F* is not the same as *being G*. Now substitute "F" for A, "animal" for B and "man" for C in our syllogism: then $Aa_{df}B$ & BaC will alike be true; but $Aa_{df}C$ will be false—for in fact $Ga_{df}(man)$ and $F \neq G$.'

91ᵇ10: Aristotle accuses Xenocrates of 'assuming what was set at the beginning' (*lambanein to en archēi*—traditionally, "to beg the question"). Xenocrates does not literally assume his set thesis; but he assumes something which is 'the same' as it. Aristotle wrongly thinks that such assumptions are inevitably bad; and he misidentifies Xenocrates' error by trying to bring it under this dialectical foul.

CHAPTER 5

Xenocrates' straight road to the demonstration of definitions is impassable. What, then, of Plato's method of 'division'?—cannot that demonstrate definitions? Aristotle argues that it cannot: "Division is a sort of weak deduction; for it postulates what it has to prove ... But at first this escaped the notice of all those who made use of it, and they attempted to persuade us on the assumption that it was possible for there to be demonstrations about essences and what something is" (*APr A* 31, 46ᵃ32–7). The present chapter repeats the arguments of *APr A* 31, to which it refers at 91^{b}13; *B* 13 explains in what ways division is a useful tool in definition. (See also *PA A* 2–3, which criticizes dichotomous division as a tool of definition and develops Aristotle's mature view of the proper role and function of division: in general see Balme, 101–6; LLOYD (1961); KULLMANN (1974), 54–72, 342–6; PELLEGRIN (1981); BALME (1987).)

91^{b}12: Aristotle first points out that in a division the 'conclusion' is not deduced from the 'premisses', but is merely 'asked', i.e. taken as an assumption. (On 'asking the conclusion' see *Top Θ* 2, 158^{a}7–13).

91^{b}18: The divider wants to define man: he assumes that everything is A_1 or A_2, and then assumes that man is A_1; next, he assumes that every A_1 is B_1 or B_2, and assumes that man is B_1. Having carried on like this for as long as he pleases (the length makes no odds to the logic), he concludes that man is, by definition, $A_1 B_1 \ldots$

Aristotle appears to make four criticisms of this procedure. (i) Every step in the divider's 'proof' is an assumption and not an inference. (ii) Even when he *could* deduce the divider does not. (iii) Even if the divider's conclusion, that man is $A_1 B_1 \ldots$, is true, he has no warrant for supposing that it gives the *definition* of *man*. (iv) The division gives no grounds for thinking that $A_1 B_1 \ldots$ contain all and only the elements of the definition of *man*.

On (ii) see *APr A* 31, 46^{a}37, and 46^{b}9: from his premisses the divider could, but does not, validly infer that man is A_1 *or* A_2, etc.

Point (iii) is stated at 91^{b}25. (Ross finds it at 91^{b}20; but this says only that the final step (to "man is $A_1 B_1 \ldots$") is an assumption, like its predecessors.)

Point (iv) seems to be a restatement of (iii); for what could be wrong with the conclusion that man is by definition $A_1 B_1 \ldots$ if not that $A_1 B_1 \ldots$ contains a non-definitory element ("positing some additional item...") or omits some definitory element ("removing something or passing over something")? (On 'passing over' see *Top Z* 5, 143^{a}15–28.)

91^{b}28: The way of solving the difficulties—i.e. objections (iii) and (iv)—is developed at length in *B* 13. The word translated "ignored" (*parietai*) normally means "left aside" (Bonitz, 569^{a}42–50); most of the commentators translate "these errors are committed".

91^{b}29: "make the division consecutive": literally, "make consecutivity (*to ephexēs*) for the division"; two things are 'consecutive' if there is no third thing of the same sort in between them (cf. *Phys E* 3, 226^{b}34–5).

91^{b}31: "This is necessary...": this notorious crux has been variously emended. The text is intelligible as it stands in the MS tradition, but only by reference to *B* 13, 97^{a}35–^{b}6 (see notes); I suppose that some intelligent reader, acquainted with *B* 13, jotted it in his margin whence it crept into the text.

91^{b}37: "conclusions without middle terms": i.e. 'conclusions drawn enthymematically'. (On 'asking why' see *Top I* 6, 168^{a}28–33.)

92^{a}2: "He will say...": 'If you ask the divider why man is mortal, he will answer "Because all animals are either mortal or immortal" (and he thinks wrongly that this proposition is proved by his division). But the most that this will give him is the proposition that man is either mortal or immortal, and an account of this sort does not qualify as a definition. So even if the divider did succeed in proving something, what he proved would not be a definition.'

CHAPTER 6

Can definitions be demonstrated, if not absolutely, at least hypothetically? With *B* 6 compare *Top H* 3.

92ᵃ6: *The first hypothetical argument* is this:

(1) A defines B if and only if A is proper to B, and A is a complex each of whose components is in B's essence;

(2) $X_1, X_2, \ldots, X_n$ are the only things in Y's essence;

(3) X_c—the complex of the X_is—is proper to Y.

Hence:

(4) X_c defines Y.

For (1) see *B* 4, 91ᵃ15–16; this is presumably the supposition or hypothesis, though Aristotle does not say so explicitly.

"Next, note that a certain account of what a definition is and how one should define is the task of a different treatise, and that here we shall only say as much as suffices for our present need; hence we shall say just this—that it is possible for there to be a deduction of a definition and of what it is to be something" (*Top H* 3, 153ᵃ11–15). The next few lines offer an argument that is in all interesting respects the same as the present argument; and Aristotle sums up: "Now, that it is possible for there to be a deduction of a definition is evident" (153ᵃ23–4). The relationship between *APst B* 6 and *Top H* 3 has aroused a considerable dispute (see esp. A. Mansion, 64–7): either, as I believe, the texts are incompatible, in which case it is reasonable to infer that *APst B* 6 was written to correct *Top H* 3; or else we must suppose that *Top* is prepared to admit as a '*dialectical*' syllogism something which *APst* denies to be a *demonstrative* syllogism. See further BARNES (1981), 44–6.

92ᵃ9: The first objection to argument (1)–(4) has been glossed in two ways: 'Argument (1)–(4) needs to import a middle term if it is to work, and that term would have to be a definition of *Y*'; and: 'Argument (1)–(4) uses as a middle term the definition of *Y*'. The second gloss is preferable; Aristotle means that (2) in effect expresses the definition of *Y* in as much as it lists all and only the elements in *Y*'s essence.

92ᵃ11: The second objection runs: 'In a deduction one does not premiss an account of what deduction is; hence in a deduction one does not premiss an account of what definition is.' The inference is dismal and is only slightly improved by emendation to: 'In a deduction one does not state what deduction is; so in a definition—however it may be established—one does not state what definition is' (Philoponus). The premiss is peculiar: Aristotle must mean that it is *illegitimate* to use the definition of deduction as a deductive premiss; and he argues for this on the grounds that such a definition could not be 'whole or part', i.e. of the form *AaB* or *AiB*. But elsewhere Aristotle says that definitions are of the form *AaB* (see p. 143); and even if they were not, that would not matter. ((1)–(4) is in any case non-syllogistic.) Ross thinks that Aristotle is here drawing "the very important distinction between premisses from which we reason and principles according to which we reason". But he does not seem to be doing this; rather he is stating, falsely, that certain propositions cannot figure as premisses from which we reason.

92ᵃ13: "so too what it is to be something must not be in the deduction": i.e. 'an account of what we mean by "what it is to be something" must not figure as a premiss'; the same laxity of expression recurs at 92ᵃ18.

92ᵃ15: "Then if anyone disputes . . .": this and the next sentence seem intended to provide a second reason for keeping the definition of definition out of the premisses. When, in ordinary deductions, we are challenged to show that we have made a valid deduction, we want to say, pointing to the form of our argument, that that is what deduction is. If this answer is to have any force, it must not simply repeat something we have already said in the original premisses; hence our deductions must not assume 'what deduction is'. Similarly, Aristotle suggests, anyone who wanted to demonstrate a definition would have to hold back the definition of definition, in order to produce it later if challenged. The point is feeble.

92ᵃ20: *The second hypothetical argument* draws on an Academic method and example (see Ross; Cherniss, 36–8; TARÁN (1981), 443–4: 92ᵃ20–7 = Speusippus, frag. 82 Tarán). The method is discussed at some length at *Top Z* 9, 147ᵃ29–ᵇ25 (cf. *H* 3, 153ᵃ26–ᵇ24), where Aristotle seems to hold that it can be used within certain limits. Here he rejects it entirely, at least as a method for *demonstrating* definitions. The example of *good* and *bad* appears at *Top Z* 9, 147ᵇ4–25, where Aristotle argues that it is wrong to define *good* in terms of *bad*, but implies that a definition of *bad* in terms of *good* would be acceptable. Here, confusingly, the same example is employed to illustrate the illegitimacy of the Academic method as a whole.

The text of this paragraph is in parts very uncertain; one reason for this is that Aristotle is trying to state highly technical propositions in an untechnical language.

Let *D(X, Y)* abbreviate "*X* is the definition of *Y*", and *C(X, Y)* "*X* and *Y* are contraries". Then the conclusion of the illustrative argument is:

(9) *D*(indivisible, good),

and three of its premisses are:

(6) *D*(divisible, bad);

(7) C(good, bad);
(8) C(indivisible, divisible).

The fourth premiss, given at 92^{a}21, states the general principle that warrants the inference of (9) from (6)–(8). The text at 92^{a}21 is uncertain, and Aristotle's expression is in any case opaque; but it is plain what principle Aristotle's argument needs. I paraphrase thus: 'If X has a contrary, Y, then being X is a matter of being the contrary of what being Y is.' One way of making this reasonably precise is this:

(5) If $C(X, Y)$, then $D(W, X)$ if and only if $(C(W, Z)$ and $D(Z, Y))$.

This principle, together with (6)–(8), yields (9).

Aristotle objects that (5)–(9), like its precursors, assumes what it sets out to prove. The obvious retort is that the illustration certainly assumes a definition—but a *different* definition from the one which it attempts to prove. Aristotle's answer to this is telegraphic. One interpretation takes it thus: 'Certainly, it is different in a sense. After all, if in an ordinary demonstration you want to prove AaC, you assume BaC where B is different from A. In ordinary cases, however, B is different from A ("not the *same* item": 92^{a}27) in the strong sense—i.e. A and B do not have the same account (92^{a}27), and do not convert. But in (5)–(9) the terms, though verbally different, are not different in this strong sense.' A and B must be different in the strong sense in ordinary demonstrations; for if B and A have the same account then AaB & BaC cannot be prior to and explanatory of AaC. Applied to (5)–(9), Aristotle's point looks like this: 'In (7) *being contrary of bad* is said of *good*; but by (6) *being contrary of bad* is identical, in the strong sense, with *being contrary of divisible*; and by (8) this is the same as *being indivisible*. But *being indivisible* is just what is said of *good* in (9). Hence in the strong sense we do assume, in (7), just what we try to prove in (9).'

92^{a}27:   None of the attempts to deduce definitions can account for the unity of the *definiens*; see further *B* 10, 93^{b}35–7, and esp. *Met Z* 12 and *H* 6, which professedly carry on where *APst* leaves off.

It is easy to see how the divider must face the problem of the unity of definition, but less easy to land the hypothetical reasoner with it. Perhaps we should think specifically of the *first* hypothetical argument: in premiss (2), the deducer lists the defining characteristics of his chosen term separately, and simply assumes, in (3), that they 'form a unity'.

CHAPTER 7

B 3–6 have discussed the question whether definitions can be *demonstrated*; in *B* 7 Aristotle first puzzles over the more general question of whether the definer can offer *any* sort of proof (92^{a}34–^{b}3); then he produces three more arguments against the view that definers can prove what they express (92^{b}4–25); and finally he rejects the thesis that definitions merely say what certain terms mean (92^{b}26–34).

92^{a}34:   Demonstration has already been ruled out; induction is dismissed with an argument resembling that of *B* 3, 90^{b}38–91^{a}6; and 'ostensive' definition is passed over with a pun. (*deiknunai*, "prove", means originally "point out". Aristotle does not mean that ostension cannot convey the sense of a term (cf. *Met E* 1, 1025^{b}12) but only that it cannot provide a proof.)

92^{b}4:   *The first argument* runs like this. We know that

(1) If **a** knows what *X* is, then **a** knows that there are *X*s.

Hence:

(2) If **a** proves what *X* is, **a** thereby proves that there are *X*s.

But:

(3) One proof proves one item,

and:

(4) What *X* is and that there are *X*s are distinct items.

Hence:

(5) What *X* is cannot be proved.

Premiss (1) is supported by:

(6) If there are no *X*s then **a** cannot know what *X*s are.

And this in turn is defended by the distinction between knowing what *X* is and knowing what "*X*" means (on the goat-stag see Bonitz, 767^{b}5–7). The argument is presented here as a 'puzzle'; Aristotle makes serious use of its different elements in *B* 8.

92^{b}12:   *The second argument* runs: 'We demonstrate that there are triangles, and we assume what "triangle" means; hence all that a definer could prove would be what triangles are. But if he could do this, then he would be able to know what triangles are without knowing whether or not there are any triangles.'

92^{b}13:   "existence is not the essence of anything . . .": '*X is Y* must be demonstrated for all non-essential values of *Y*; but "exists" is never an essential predicate: hence *there are X*s is always demonstrated and not shown by definition.' (This paraphrase rests on Ross's reading *ho ti* for *hoti* at 92^{b}13; see also S. Mansion, 179 n. 88.)

The second premiss is supported by the consideration that "the things that exist do not constitute a kind" ('being is not a genus'). Aristotle offers a short, bad, argument for this at *Met B* 3, 998^{b}22–7. The premiss requires the further claim that 'existence is not a difference'; and elsewhere Aristotle urges that *being* is predicated of everything and thus cannot differentiate one set of things from another (cf. e.g. *Top Δ* 1, 121^{a}18, ^{b}6; *Met Z* 16, 1040^{b}16–24; *H* 6, 1045^{b}1–7). It is not clear how Aristotle would reconcile these views with his remark that goat-stags do not exist.

92^{b}15: "And this is what the sciences as a matter of fact do . . .": see *A* 1, 71^{a}15, notes.

92^{b}19: *The third argument* aims at a different conclusion: it purports to show, not that definers do not prove what something is, but that they do not prove that anything is. (But Aristotle does not signal the change of interest, unless we may see a signal in the word "too" (*kai*) at 92^{b}19; and it is possible that the text is awry.) Geometers define a circle as a plane figure all of whose extreme points are equidistant from its centre (cf. *Rhet Γ* 6, 1407^{b}27; Euclid, i def. 15). Aristotle offers two criticisms of the view that this might amount to a proof.

First, the geometers do not show that there are any circles. Having the definition, we may still ask *why* what satisfies the *definiens* exists: no doubt there *is* a plane figure of the sort defined—but *why*? And if the geometers have not told us *why*, they have not *proved* anything. (This interpretation is strained; but it is required—unless we emend the text.) 92^{b}23 says that the geometers do not show that the circle is possible (cf. *B* 2, 90^{a}21). This anticipates the point later stressed by Leibniz that in a satisfactory definition the *definiens* must be consistent. Aristotle is commonly taken to imply that consistency is *sufficient* for mathematical existence; but this does not square with his general views on mathematical objects, and 92^{b}23 only shows that consistency is a *necessary* condition for existence.

Secondly, why should we suppose that the geometer has defined the *circle* and not something completely different? (Mountain-copper is yellow copper ore; cf. *Critias* 114^a). ". . . for the defining account should not only make the fact clear, as the majority of definitions do, but the explanation too should inhere in it and appear through it. But as it is, the accounts of the terms are like conclusions: e.g. what is squaring?—there being an equilateral rectangle equal to an oblong. Such a definition is an account of the conclusion; but one which says that squaring is the discovery of a mean proportional states the explanation of the object" (*An B* 2, 413^{a}10–20). Thus Aristotle's contemporaries offered as definitions propositions which are not immediate;. but proper definitions, being principles, must be immediate.

92^{b}26: Aristotle seems to argue that because definitions cannot *prove* what *A* is, they can only *state* that "*A*" means "*B*". In fact he need not be taken to argue thus. I paraphrase: 'If definitions are proved, then they express either what something is or what a word means. We have shown that definers cannot prove what something is, and hence that definitions do not express what something is. Hence definers must prove, and definitions must express, what a word means.' The argument depends on the hypothesis that definitions are *proved*, a hypothesis which Aristotle is of course arguing against.

92^{b}28: *Argument* (*A*): For the view that non-substances cannot be defined see esp. *Met Z* 5, 1031^{a}1–11; 13, 1039^{a}19–20.

92^{b}30: *Argument (B)* is repeated at *Met* Z 4, 1030^{a}7–9, with the same example. "For it is not necessary if we set this down that there be a definition of this—whatever means the same as an account—but only of what means the same as a certain sort of account; and this will be the case if it is of some unity—not a unity by being continuous, like the *Iliad* or whatever is one by connection . . ." (1030^{b}7–13; cf. *H* 6, 1045^{a}12–14; *Poet* 20, 1457^{a}28–30; *APst* B 10, 93^{b}36; *Int* 5, 17^{a}15–16). We might regard Humpty-Dumpty's use of "glory" as an anti-social but logically innocent foible. Aristotle would not have done so, for the *definiens* of "glory" is not a unity. The argument is thus the same as that of *B* 6, 92^{a}27–33.

92^{b}32: *Argument (C)* is obscure. I take it that by "no demonstration *would* demonstrate . . ." Aristotle means "no demonstration *does* demonstrate . . .". Thus: 'No demonstration gives a conclusion of the form *"A" means "B"*; hence, if definitions are proved, definitions cannot express the idea that *"A" means "B"*.'

CHAPTER 8

B 8 begins Aristotle's positive treatment of the issues introduced in *B* 3–7; it is excessively difficult and it has amassed a considerable body of literature (besides the commentators see e.g. S. Mansion, 183–96; G.-G. GRANGER (1976), 235–9; BOLTON (1976); ACKRILL (1981); SORABJI (1981); GOMEZ-LOBO (1981); LANDOR (1985); GUARIGLIA (1985); DEMOSS and DEVEREUX (1988)).

93^{a}3: *B* 2 argued that knowing what *X* is and knowing why there are *X*s is 'the same' (cf. 90^{a}31–4).

93^{a}3: The clause at 93^{a}5 ("the account of the fact that something is is the explanation") is usually translated thus: "the reason for this is that the explanation is something". I can make no sense of this; and I have altered the standard punctuation of the text to permit a different (and admittedly banal) translation.

93^{a}5–6: 'self-explanatory' cases (see above, p. 185) will be discussed in *B* 9. The commentators suppose that *substances* are self-explanatory and non-substances non-self-explanatory. There is no evidence for this in Aristotle's text, and it does not fit the general context of his thought. Rather, it is the denotata of the primitive terms of any science which are self-explanatory: thus that there are men, say, will be 'explained' by the fact that there are featherless bipeds—even though men are substances; and conversely, that there are units is self-explanatory—even though units are non-substantial.

Which explanations will be 'indemonstrable'? Does Aristotle mean to say that some explanations *cannot* be revealed through a scientific demonstration, or is he perhaps merely noting a logical possibility? The latter is suggested by 93^{b}18. (For a different interpretation of 93^{a}3–9 see LANDOR (1985).)

93ᵃ6: What does Aristotle mean when he says that the explanation is "either demonstrable or indemonstrable"? Since the explanation has to be a middle term (93ᵃ8), we must take "demonstrable" in a weak sense: 'In some cases the explanation of P is demonstrable in that we can construct an explanatory demonstration concluding to P.' P must then be of the form AaC (cf. 93ᵃ9); and yet P is supposed to say "that X is" (cf. 93ᵃ4). Here at least we are obliged to suppose that in Aristotle's view "X is" can be analysed as a syllogistic proposition (see p. 205).

93ᵃ9: The way "just examined" is that of B 4, 91ᵃ14–ᵇ11; this is now dismissed as not a demonstration but only a "general deduction" (*logikos sullogismos*). The standard sense of *logikos* in *APst* (cf. A 21, 82ᵇ34, note) does not fit here with any particular appropriateness; and Aristotle's two other uses of *logikos sullogismos* (*Top* Θ 12, 162ᵇ27; *Rhet A* 1, 1355ᵃ13) do not help. Perhaps Aristotle wants to say only that the argument, though not demonstrative, is none the less sound. (See further Le Blond (1), 157–66. Much of the discussion has been vitiated by the ancient error of identifying the 'general deduction' with the argument at 93ᵃ16–35.)

93ᵃ15: The rest of the chapter tries to show in what way it *is* possible to demonstrate what a thing is; Aristotle's conclusion is that, in some cases at least, what something is can be revealed in but not proved by a demonstration.

Aristotle first recalls the thesis of B 7, 92ᵇ4–5, that knowing what X is entails knowing that X is. But here he distinguishes two cases of knowing that there are Xs. (The issue is put quite generally; "X" is not restricted, as Ross states, to 'properties and events'—cf. 93ᵃ24.) The first case is marked down as 'incidental' knowledge; the second occurs when we "grasp something of the object itself" (93ᵃ22). What is this 'something'? It is often supposed that it is the 'nominal definition' of the object: we know that there is an eclipse, knowing what the word "eclipse" means (see e.g. BOLTON (1976); SORABJI (1980), 196). An 'incidental' knower will then be a man who does not know what "eclipse" means: he has seen what we have seen, but he cannot report his observation by saying, intelligibly, "There's an eclipse". In a sense, he "does not even know that it exists" (93ᵃ26). Aristotle's examples, however, (93ᵃ22–4) can scarcely be interpreted as 'nominal definitions'; and B 10, 93ᵇ32–5, seems to set possessors of nominal definitions in the opposite camp, among 'incidental' knowers. A second suggestion is that to know 'something of the object' is to know some of its non-essential properties. This suggestion receives some support from the example at 93ᵃ36–ᵇ2, and it agrees with the general remarks at *An A* 1, 402ᵇ21–5; but again, this interpretation hardly fits with the examples at 93ᵃ22–4. It seems, then, that the 'something' which we grasp must be a part of the essence of the object. *Met Z* 17, 1041ᵇ2–9, and *H* 4, 1044ᵇ9–20, suggest that the 'something' is the matter of the object, and that we are still in search of its form; alternatively, we might take the 'something' for the kind or genus of the object, and think that we are still in search of its difference.

But neither suggestion fits all the examples at 93ᵃ22–4; and a less specific interpretation is better: if the set of predicates $E_1, E_2, \ldots, E_n$ expresses what X is, then we "grasp something" of X if we know that X is E_i for at least one i. (See further ACKRILL (1981), 370–6.)

If this is right, what is it to have 'incidental' knowledge that there are Xs? The moon-gazer who does not know what "eclipse" means may still serve; but there will be more interesting cases than his if the nominal definition of "X" contains no reference to any of the features of the essence of X—for then someone might intelligently and truly say "There are Xs", and yet not have any grasp at all of what it is to be X. (Ross thinks that we have incidental knowledge of something if we "have inferred it to exist because we know something else to exist of which we believe it to be a concomitant"; but the notion of inference is absent from the text.)

Incidental knowledge that there are Xs does not help us; but a knowledge which grasps 'something of the object' does. This might lead to the following interpretation of Aristotle's general claim that definitions may be revealed through, but not proved by, demonstrations. Take a standard demonstration in *Barbara* (cf. 93ᵃ8): AaB, $BaC \vdash AaC$. The conclusion represents our knowledge of 'something of the object', and thus gives a *partial* definition of C (e.g. a lunar eclipse is a deprivation of light). The middle term, B, explains why A holds of C (e.g. B may be "screening by the earth"). And from the whole demonstration we may read off a *complete* definition of C.

(1) Deprivation of light holds of screening by the earth.
(2) Screening of the earth holds of eclipse.

Therefore:

(3) Deprivation of light holds of eclipse.

Thence we can see that a lunar eclipse is the deprivation of light by the screening of the earth. This interpretation, which gives a clear purpose to the grasp of 'something of the object', makes reasonably good sense in itself; and it receives strong support from *B* 10, 94ᵃ1–9 (see notes).

93ᵃ29: Aristotle's illustrative example is developed in a moderately clear fashion. First, we ask whether or not the moon is eclipsed; i.e. we ask if there is a middle term. (Strictly speaking we do not "seek whether B is or not" (93ᵃ31–2): rather, we seek whether or not there is a middle term at all.) When we have found a middle term, then, in favourable cases, we thereby grasp the explanation. (Aristotle describes the favourable cases as those in which "we proceed through middle terms", i.e. through 'genuine' middle terms which give the appropriate account. The OCT prints *di' amesōn* ("through immediates"), the reading of one MS, for *dia mesōn*. But, as *A* 13 shows, not all cases of proceeding 'through immediates' are favourable. See HADGOPOULOS (1977).) In unfavourable cases (93ᵃ36–ᵇ2) we have further seeking still to do. When we are successful, we may present a demonstration such as the following:

(4) Eclipse holds of screening by the earth.
(5) Screening by the earth holds of the moon.

Therefore:

(6) Eclipse holds of the moon.

But this syllogism is crucially different from syllogism (1)–(3). There, we read a definition of C out of the syllogism as a whole: here, the first premiss is a definition of A. (Aristotle is perfectly explicit on the point: 93^b6–7.) There, our antecedent grasp of 'something of the object' played an evident role in the argument: here, it seems to play no role at all. (Aristotle says nothing explicit on this point. Perhaps we should assume that our grasp of 'something of the object' is presupposed by the argument: we are in a position to construct syllogism (4)–(6) in so far as (6) is plain (93^b4); and in order for (6) to be plain, we must have some grasp on what an eclipse is.)

93^b7: In the thunder example we are again explicitly said to be presented with a definition of A in the first premiss of the syllogism. (For Aristotle's own account of thunder, quite different from the one used here, see *Metr B* 9.) And the example contains a further "oddity. The term A is said first to be "thunder" and then to be "noise". If the thunder syllogism is to run precisely parallel to the eclipse syllogism, then A ought to be "thunder". If A is "noise", then we shall get the following syllogism:

(7) Noise holds of extinction of fire.
(8) Extinction of fire holds of the clouds.

Therefore:

(9) Noise holds of the clouds.

None of the terms in this syllogism is defined in it, whether explicitly or implicitly. But we can read off from the syllogism the definition of a *fourth* term. Given our antecedent knowledge that thunder is a sort of noise in the clouds, we may draw a complete definition from (7)–(9): thunder is the noise of the extinction of fire in the clouds.

In itself, (7)–(9) is as respectable as (4)–(6). Moreover, Aristotle claims to show that definitions are "made plain through deductions and through demonstrations" (93^b17–18); and this claim seems more appropriate to (7)–(9)—and to (1)–(3)—than to (4)–(6). None the less, it is hard to avoid the suspicion that (7)–(9) is a phantom and that the identification of A as "noise" at 93^b11 is a mere carelessness on Aristotle's part. (It might also be objected that (7)–(9) can scarcely be reconstructed as a genuine demonstration in *Barbara*, inasmuch as its conclusion cannot be represented as having the form AaC. This is true. But it applies equally to (4)–(6). Although Aristotle speaks expressly of first figure syllogisms at 93^a8, it is difficult if not impossible to cast his illustrative arguments into orthodox syllogistic form.)

93^b12: "If there is another middle term . . .": i.e. 'If, after all, AaB is not an immediate proposition, and B does not give the definition of A, then we must look at the other putative accounts of A which we have at our disposal.' If this is what Aristotle means, then he is adverting to the possibility of unfavourable searches, which he had illustrated at 93^{a}36–^{b}2. But the sentence is very obscure.

93^{b}15: Aristotle's concluding remarks make three claims. (i) "There are no deductions and no demonstrations of what something is": i.e. if AaB, $BaC \vdash AaC$ is a demonstration, then AaC is not a definition. (In claim (i) "and" must have the force of "i.e.": Aristotle allows that there can be 'general' deductions of definitions: 93^{a}15.) B 8 has said nothing to support this claim, which relies on the various arguments of B 3–7. (ii) "What something is is made plain . . . through demonstrations." As we have seen, Aristotle has illustrated this claim in at least two, and perhaps three, different ways. It is tempting to disregard (7)–(9) as a minor aberration; and perhaps we should also dismiss (1)–(3), inasmuch as it receives no explicit illustration in the text of B 8. (But see below, B 10, 94^{a}1, note.) Anyone who thus maintains that (4)–(6) represents Aristotle's considered view must admit that it illustrates and supports claim (ii) only if that claim is interpreted in a peculiar way. (iii) "Without a demonstration you cannot get to know what something is." Strongly construed, this claim is entirely unsupported: B 8 has done nothing to show that we can *only* come to grasp a definition by first constructing an appropriate demonstration. But perhaps Aristotle has a weaker thesis in mind: whenever you have grasped a definition, you can always construct an appropriate demonstration without more ado.

CHAPTER 9

The results of B 8 are explicitly limited to things which are not self-explanatory (93^{a}7, ^{b}19); Aristotle now argues that in the case of what is self-explanatory not even that weak connection between definition and demonstration holds. His argument is muddled.

First, he argues from the fact that some propositions are self-explanatory or immediate to the conclusion that some essences are immediate and hence principles. To say that the essence of A is immediate should mean that the proposition stating the essence of A is immediate; but in this sense (B 8, 93^{a}36) all essences are immediate.

Secondly, *all* definitions are 'supposed' (or rather, posited: A 2, 72^{a}18–24; but see e.g. *Met E* 1, 1025^{b}11); 'supposition' is not a way of 'making clear' but is compatible with various ways of making clear, including the ways described in B 8 and also the method of ostension (cf. *Met* l.c.; *EN A* 7, 1098^{b}3–4).

Through this muddle we might hope to discern a significant point: B 9 hints at the distinction between primitive and derived terms (cf. A 10, 76^{a}32, note). Primitive terms are 'immediate' in the sense that they are unanalysable; and as they are unanalysable, they have no parts which can be exhibited in the terms of a demonstration and they must be made familiar in some way other than that described in *B* 8. (For a different interpretation see DESLAURIERS (1990).)

CHAPTER 10

93^{b}29–94^{a}10 appear to distinguish *four* sorts of definition; but the summary at 94^{a}11–14 enumerates just *three* sorts, apparently omitting the sort described at 93^{b}29–37 (cf. *A* 7, 75^{b}31–2). The older commentators explain that the sort of definition distinguished at 93^{b}29–37 is *nominal* definition, and that Aristotle deliberately omitted this scientifically uninteresting notion from the enumeration at 94^{a}11–14. (These lines do not, *pace* Ross, give a "definite statement that there are just three kinds" of definition; they list three kinds but do not say that the list is exhaustive.) Ross offers a different explanation. He argues that *B* 10 only ever countenances three sorts of definition; he thinks that 93^{b}29–37 does not have anything to do with nominal definition, and that 94^{a}7–9 does not introduce a new sort of definition into the discussion.

93^{b}30–1 are traditionally translated thus: "one type will be an account of what its name means, or some other name-like account"; "name-like account" (*logos onomatōdēs*) is then glossed as "nominal definition" (indeed it is the origin of this term) and "or" is read epexegetically. Thus: 'One sort is an account of what a name means, i.e. is a nominal definition.' Ross rightly objects that the gloss does not do justice to the word "other", and that *onomatōdēs* can scarcely mean "nominal". His own version of the sentence is given in my translation, thus: 'One sort is a statement of what a word or longer nominal phrase means.' (For 'accounts of accounts' see, e.g. *Top A* 5, 102^{a}1; 7, 107^{a}37; *Z* 11, 148^{b}23–5.) But though Ross is correct on this point, he does not show that 93^{b}29–37 has nothing to do with nominal definition; and in fact the lines are explicitly about "what a name . . . means". Thus the first type of definition is 'nominal' definition—though Aristotle does not call it that.

If, as Ross has it, 94^{a}7–9 merely reminds us of 93^{b}29–37, then it too must deal with nominal definition. But in fact it deals with the partial definitions of *B* 8, which express 'something of the object itself'. And these are unlikely to be nominal definitions (see p. 218).

Other scholars have essayed other ways of reducing the number of types of definition to three. Thus BOLTON (1976), 522 n. 14, agrees with Ross that 94^{a}7–9 should be associated with 93^{b}29–37; but he takes both passages to be concerned with nominal definitions. In support of this view he cites *Phys A* 1, 184^{a}16, and *An B* 2, 413^{a}11–20; but neither of these texts seems to confirm his interpretation. Again, CHARLES (1990), 146 n. 1, urges that 93^{b}29–37 describes not a genuine type of definition but only "*a sort of* definition", where "a sort of" (*tis*) should be construed as an 'alienating' particle. (Thus Aristotle will describe self-control as *a sort of* virtue, although it is not a genuine virtue.) But this suggestion will not strike everyone as linguistically plausible.

Thus we are, after all, stuck with four sorts of definition; and the traditional explanation of them seems the best. It should, however, be added that only two of the four are genuine cases of definition: a 'definition' of the third sort is merely a part of a definition of the second sort; and the fourth sort (see notes to *B* 9) is the product of an Aristotelian confusion.

Finally, a word about 'nominal' definitions. The phrase "nominal definition" is often bandied about as though its sense were clear and univocal. In fact, it seems to have been used to express several different notions, among them these:

A nominal definition is:

(*a*) Any truth of the form "*W* means *X*";
(*b*) Any truth of the form "*Y* is *X*", where in fact "*Y*" means *X*;
(*c*) Any truth of the form "*W* means *X*" which also says what *X* is;
(*d*) Any truth of the form "*Y* is *X*", where "*Y*" means *X*, which also says what *X* is.

If we opt for either (*c*) or (*d*)—with e.g. BOLTON (1976), 523–6—then there will not even be nominal definitions of such terms as "goat-stag", since there is no such thing as what a goat-stag is; and all definitions, including nominal definitions, will have 'existential import'. There are severe difficulties with this view, and most scholars implicitly opt for (*a*) or (*b*).

93^{b}32: "When we grasp that this . . .": i.e. 'When we know that there are triangles we ask why there are; but if we have only a nominal definition it is hard to attain the explanation, since we do not yet know if there are any triangles.' "in this way" (*houtōs*) means "having only a nominal definition"; the 'difficulty' has been explained already at *B* 8, 93^{a}20 (where it was an impossibility). If this interpretation is correct, then we have 'incidental' knowledge that there are *X*s when we know (only) the nominal definition of *X* (see p. 219). (For different interpretations see e.g. SORABJI (1981), 217 n. 30; GUARIGLIA (1985), 92–7.)

93^{b}35: "An account is one in two ways . . .": see *B* 7, 92^{b}30, note. The unexpressed moral of this parenthesis is that every definition must be 'one account'; but that nominal definitions may be one in the first, Homeric, way, whereas real definitions must be one in the second way.

93^{b}36: "by showing one thing of one thing non-incidentally": i.e. 'by predicating one thing of one' (cf. *A* 2, 72^{a}9, note); but the parallels (cf. *B* 7, 92^{b}30) make it probable that Aristotle means 'reveals a unity', and "of one thing" (*kath' henos*) should perhaps be excised.

93^{b}38: A definition states what something is; what something is is the same as the reason why it is (see *B* 2, 90^{a}14–23, notes): hence every definition "shows why something exists". How, then, can Aristotle use this phrase to characterize one species of definition? The commentators generally take Aristotle to be singling out a special sort of definition which applies only to a special sort of object or event. Objects or events which are essentially caused or brought about in one specifiable way must be given a *causal* definition: X is Y caused by Z ("Thunder is noise in the clouds caused by the extinction of fire"). But there is no hint of this in the text, where Aristotle's illustrative definitions do not contain any *explicit* references to causation. Rather, we should admit that this second 'species' of definition is in fact the *only* genuine sort of definition which Aristotle's sciences will admit. Since the other three 'species' of definition enumerated in *B* 10 are not definitions at all, Aristotle can correctly characterize the second 'species' by a description which applies to every definition.

93^b39: "Hence the former . . .": i.e. 'Nominal definition states that X means Y but does not show that X is Y (or even that there are Xs).'

94^a1: "like a demonstration . . .": The demonstration which Aristotle has in mind is this:

(1) Noise in the clouds holds of extinction of fire.
(2) Extinction of fire holds of thunder.

Therefore:

(3) Noise in the clouds holds of thunder.

Here (3), the conclusion of the demonstration, is a partial or quasi definition of thunder, of the sort countenanced at 94^a7–9. And from (1)–(3) as a whole we can read off a complete definition of thunder: Thunder is the noise of the extinction of fire in the clouds. Note that this syllogism is precisely parallel to syllogism (1)–(3) of *B* 8. *B* 10 contains nothing to parallel syllogism (4)–(6) of *B* 8. This suggests that, despite the attention given to (4)–(6) in *B* 8, the proper illustration of Aristotle's thesis in that chapter is given by (1)–(3). (But see ACKRILL (1981), 360–3, who urges that the differences between the two syllogisms, while genuine enough, are unimportant in their context: "against an appropriate background either syllogism can be used in illustration of Aristotle's theory about the relation of definition to demonstration".)

94^a2: "differing in arrangement (*thesis*) . . .": the same fact is expressed at 94^a12 by the expression "differing in aspect" (*ptōsis*). For the terms see Bonitz, 372^b8–12; 658^b58–659^a31. There is no very clear parallel to their use here. Some interpreters take *thesis* in the sense of "supposition", and think that different things are 'supposed' in the demonstration and the definition (see esp. Robin, 190–2); but this reasoning makes dubious sense and cannot be applied to *ptōsis*. A standard meaning of *ptōsis* is "grammatical form" (*ptōsis* = Latin *casus*, whence the English grammatical term "case")—cf. *APr A* 36, 48^b37–49^a5. Aristotle, then, may mean here that the demonstration and the definition use the same terms but in different grammatical forms; when he says that they differ in 'arrangement' (*thesis*) he may mean that they contain the same terms but arrange them in a different way. But it is probably wrong to see anything very significant in Aristotle's terminology: he wants to point out that, though closely connected, the demonstration and the definition are not identical.

94ª7: "a continuous demonstration" (*suneches*): i.e., probably, 'a demonstration that has immediate premisses'.

94ª14: The summary refers to: (i) *B* 8, 93ª15–ᵇ14 ("in what sense there are demonstrations . . ."); (ii) *B* 9 ("in what cases there are . . ."); (iii) *B* 10 ("and, further, in how many senses . . ."); (iv) *B* 8, 93ª15–ᵇ14 ("in what sense they prove . . ."); (v) *B* 9 ("in what cases they do . . ."); (vi) *B* 3–8 ("and, further, how they are related . . .").

Up to this point Aristotle has been speaking of the definition or 'formal' explanation as something revealed in, though not proved by, a demonstration; in this chapter he argues that each of the four types of explanation is "proved through the middle term". He means that the only scientific way of exhibiting an explanation of whatever sort is through a demonstrative syllogism.

The structure of the chapter is admirably clear: Aristotle first lists the types of explanation and states that each can appear in a demonstrative deduction; then he attempts to prove his statement *seriatim* for each type of explanation; and finally he considers the possibility of there being more than one explanation for a thing. In detail, there is less clarity; in particular, Aristotle's examples are often hard to understand and often seem, when understood, curiously inapposite. It is not without reason that Ross judged *B* 11 one of the most difficult chapters in Aristotle.

Some scholars have passed a still less favourable judgement: the whole aim of the chapter, they say, is hopelessly misguided. Roughly, their argument is this: 'Only 'formal' explanations can appear in demonstrations, for otherwise the premisses will not be I-predications. Aristotle's attempt to accommodate other types of explanation to demonstrative exhibition succeeds only in so far as he tacitly treats all explanations as though they were formal.' (This view is forcefully advanced by Robin; see also Le Blond (1), 94–6.) It is true that if a demonstrative premiss *AaB* is an I-predication, then *A* and *B* are essentially, or 'formally', connected; but it does not follow that no demonstration can reveal any non-formal explanation. A formal explanation may incorporate non-formally explanatory elements; at any rate, Aristotle thinks that this can, and often does, occur: thus the definition of natural objects will typically include reference to their matter (e.g. *Phys B* 2); the definition of artefacts will typically include reference to their aim or function (e.g. *Met Z* 17, 1041ª27–30; *H* 2, 1043ª9); and the definition of events will typically include a reference to 'what initiates change' (cf. *B* 8). Thus *B* 11 can introduce non-formal explanations into demonstration without thereby extruding formal explanation: demonstration reveals the formal explanation, and this in turn will reveal one or more of the three other types of explanation. (*B* 11 implies that all four explanations are logically on a par here; but that is only a minor slip.)

94ᵃ20: Of the four canonical types of explanation or *aitia* (cf. *Phys B* 3; *Met A* 3; *Δ* 2), three are unmistakably present here. Where we expect a name for the fourth member of the tetrad, 'matter', we find the phrase "if something holds it is necessary for this to hold". That is, we explain a fact *p* by producing another fact that necessitates it. (That this is Aristotle's meaning emerges clearly enough from 94ᵇ27–95ᵃ9.) The form in which Aristotle first states this is strongly reminiscent of his standard account of what a deduction is (*APr A* 1, 24ᵇ19); and indeed he identifies a necessitating cause of *p* with a premiss-set that entails *P* (the proposition expressing the fact *p*). Thus, loosely speaking, we can say that an explanation of the sort in question is a set of premisses that entail a statement of the *explanandum*. Now Aristotle twice says that the premisses of a deduction are the 'matter' or material explanation of its conclusion (*Phys B* 3, 195ᵃ15–18 = *Met Δ* 2, 1013ᵇ17; *Met Δ* 1, 1013ᵃ15); and the commentators infer that the phrase "if something . . ." (94ᵃ21) means "deductive premisses" and denotes the material explanation. Thus we have the canonical tetrad under a non-canonical description.

Ross assembles a battery of arguments against this conclusion; his most impressive gun is this: Aristotle expressly remarks at *Phys B* 9, 200ᵃ15–30, that premisses are unlike material explanations in that the former necessitate their conclusions whereas the latter do not necessitate their *explananda*—the fact that there are bricks and mortar does not necessitate the construction of a house. If this is so, it is hard to think that Aristotle should designate the material explanation by a phrase which means "necessitating condition". Ross himself identifies the necessitating explanation with the 'ground' or *causa cognoscendi*.

I do not think that Ross's solution will do—Aristotle is not concerned with epistemological 'causes' in *B* 11. Moreover, there is reason to believe that Aristotle had material factors in mind as necessitating causes; for at *PA Δ* 2, 677ᵃ18, he uses the phrase "if something . . ." precisely to express material necessitation. It seems, then, that the non-canonical type of explanation is a special case of material explanation—viz. the case in which the fact that the matter of *X* is such and such does necessitate *p*.

It is clear that such material explanations can be accommodated within demonstrative deductions. Moreover, it seems to be the case that if the matter of *X* is genuinely explanatory, then it can always be syllogistically accommodated in this way: if *M* is some material predicate, and *X* is necessarily *M* (as it might be, men are necessarily of flesh and bones), and if *M* really explains why *X* is *Y* (e.g. why men are mortal), then there will be a demonstration *X is M, M is Y ⊢ X is Y*.

Thus the non-canonical type of explanation is, after all, 'matter'. Its unusual designation reflects the fact that citing the matter of *X* is not always genuinely explanatory. *B* 11 represents a sophisticated and not a naïve version of the notion of material explanation; for it distinguishes between ascertaining in general the matter of *X* and ascertaining a material explanation of *X*'s being *Y*. (See further SORABJI (1980), 51 n. 24.)

94^{a}24:   First, then, the material, or quasi-material explanation. Aristotle offers an abstract argument for the thesis that this type of explanation can appear in a demonstration. It seems to be this: 'If *p* necessitates *q*, then *P* must be a conjunction of at least two elements and these must have a middle term in common; hence there will be a middle term which explains *Q*.' The conclusion is a *non sequitur*; and the premiss relies first on the thesis that deductions require more than one premiss (cf. *A* 3, 73^{a}9) and secondly on the implicit claim that if *p* necessitates *q*, then *P* entails *Q*.

The abstract argument is followed by a geometrical illustration. (On explanation in geometry see p. 107—a 'material' explanation might seem peculiarly inapposite in mathematics, but the example is satisfactory enough.) The theorem is Euclid, iii. 31, and the proof which Aristotle presupposes is probably Euclid's (see NOVAK (1978)). The bit of it that concerns us can be set out syllogistically:

(1) *R* belongs to every angle that is half of two rights;
(2) Being half of two rights belongs to every angle in the semicircle.

Therefore:

(3) *R* belongs to every angle in the semicircle.

(Aristotle himself gives hints of a non-syllogistic formulation by means of equations: that, of course, is how the geometers would have set the argument down.)

The middle term in (1)–(3) expresses, in a sense, the 'matter' of the minor (the reference is to 'intelligible' matter, or extension: *Met Z* 10, 1036^{a}9–12; 11, 1037^{a}2–5; *H* 6, 1045^{a}33–6); for, as the proof itself indicates, the angle in the semicircle is constructible out of the halves of two right angles, which are thus its 'matter' (cf. *Met Z* 10, 1035^{a}12). Evidently, too, being half of two rights necessitates being right. And anyone who wanted an explanation of (3) might properly, if elliptically, be told: 'Because it's half of two right angles'.

94^{a}34:   "And this is the same as . . .": the commentators paraphrase: '*B* is the essence of *A*; for the account of *A* states *B*.' This ascribes to Aristotle the absurd view that *being half of two right angles* is the essence of *being a right angle*. (Reference to Euclid, i, def. 10 is no help.) The alternative is to paraphrase: 'For *B* is the essence of *C*; for the account of *C* signifies *B*.' *Being half of two right angles* is (part of) the essence of *being an angle in the semicircle* for the same reason that finding a mean proportional is the essence of squaring (*An B* 2, 413^{a}17–20): the properties of the latter in each case are dependent upon the former. (See the proof at Euclid, iii. 31.)

94ᵃ35:   The text, sense, and import of this sentence are all obscure. As to the text, I have followed the majority of the MSS; as to the sense, I follow Zabarella in taking *to meson* as the subject of *dedeiktai* (the genitive, "of what it is...", is 'constitutive'—i.e. 'explanatory in the sense of saying what it is...'). The sentence can be read in at least two ways. It may be taken in isolation, as Aristotle's sole indication that the 'formal' explanation can appear as a middle term; the point is here briefly expressed since it has already been laboriously argued for in *B* 8. Alternatively, the sentence may be tacked on to its predecessor, making the following argument: 'This is the same as the essence, and we have already shown that the middle term is an essence.' The word "also" (*kai*) favours the first interpretation.

Of what does the middle term state the essence? 94ᵃ27–34 suggests that it is the essence of the *minor* term, *C*, which is at stake; but 94ᵇ19–21 and *B* 8, 93ᵇ6–7 (see notes) pick out the essence of the *major* term. Perhaps Aristotle thinks that the middle term may state the essence now of one and now of the other extreme; he does not observe, however, that this is only possible if the major premiss converts, and even then only in deductions of the sort illustrated in *B* 8.

94ᵃ36:   If the illustration of efficient explanation is put into syllogistic form, its terms are best read as follows: *A*, "warred upon"; *B*, "aggressor"; *C*, "the state of Athens" (for the facts see Herodotus, v. 97–102). The syllogism so formed may in a sense exhibit the 'efficient' explanation of the war; but it is not a demonstration: its minor premiss is contingently true, its major contingently false. Ross remarks (647) that "it is only by exercising a measure of good-will that we can consider as syllogisms some of the 'syllogisms' put forward by Aristotle in this chapter"; he notes that Aristotle does not use the term *sullogismos* in *B* 11, and that elsewhere (*EN Z* 12, 1144ᵃ31–3) he employs a concept of 'quasi-syllogism'. The moral (which Ross does not explicitly draw) is that the arguments of *B* 11 are not meant to be interpreted as full-blooded demonstrations, but as some weaker variety of explanatory deduction. I doubt this: first, the notion of a quasi-syllogism is unaristotelian, for the 'practical' syllogisms of *EN Z* 12 are, logically speaking, on all fours with 'theoretical' syllogisms (cf. *MA* 7—but the issue is notoriously complicated); and secondly, *B* 11 stands in the middle of a discussion of scientific demonstration—for Aristotle to shift, without warning, to a laxer mode of explanation (which he nowhere describes or even mentions) would be intolerably gauche.

Aristotle's illustrative example is ill chosen; and it is not easy to find a good illustration. Perhaps something like this may serve:

(4) All ducks have webbed feet.
(5) All things with webbed feet are good swimmers and waders.

Therefore:

(6) All ducks are good swimmers and waders.

The middle term, having webbed feet, explains why ducks are good swimmers; and the webbing is (part of) the *efficient* explanation of their swimming prowess. But there is a difficulty with the example: the premisses of an explanatory demonstration are all supposed to be *necessary*; yet it is not clear that (4) expresses a necessary fact about ducks. More generally, efficient explanations—unless they are trifling—will be attached only contingently to their *explananda*. (Perhaps Aristotle recognizes this at *Met Λ* 4, 1070^b22, where he distinguishes between "the explanations which inhere in (*enhuparchein*)" their *explananda* and efficient explanations, which lie "outside" them.)

94^b8: The section on 'final' explanation is miserably obscure. The first sketch of the valetudinarian example at 94^b9 (cf. *Top I* 11, 172^a8; *Phys B* 3, 194^b34 = *Met Δ* 2, 1013^a34) suggests the following argument:

(A) Socrates is healthy.
Healthy men take constitutionals.

Socrates takes constitutionals.

For here the middle term explains the conclusion, and does so by stating Socrates' purpose, health (though it does not state that health is Socrates' purpose). Some scholars have changed the terms of (A): first, 94^b11–12—"Why should you walk . . ."—indicates that the major term is "*should* take constitutionals"; secondly, the middle term is more appropriately taken as "desirous of health". The modified argument is a 'practical' syllogism, stating the reason why Socrates should go for walks; to that extent it is less congenial to the chapter than (A) itself.

However that may be, Aristotle's fuller exposition of the example (94^b12–21) is nothing like (A); rather it is something like this:

(B) Good digesters are healthy.
Perambulators are good digesters.

Perambulators are healthy.

(In this argument I take "hold of" in its normal logical sense: "making the foodstuffs not remain on the surface holds of walking about" means "Everyone who walks about digests well". Ross thinks that "holds of" means "is caused by", and he accuses Aristotle of equivocation.)

Unfortunately, (B) will not serve Aristotle's purposes: the middle term does not answer the question "*For what purpose* are perambulators healthy?"—if indeed that question makes any sense at all. Pacius supposed that Aristotle must have been aware of this and can have had no intention of presenting (B) as an example of final reasoning; rather, the illustration of final explanation is contained in 94^b8–10, and 94^b11 initiates a discussion of the interrelations between final and efficient explanation. There is no hint of this in the text; and I am inclined to think that (B) was indeed meant as an illustration of final explanation. But perhaps Aristotle became aware of its infelicity, and expressed his awareness in the Delphic injunction to "*metalambanein* the accounts" in order that everything may become "clearer" (94^b21)?

94^{b}8

POSTERIOR ANALYTICS

The word *metalambanein* is common enough in the *Organon* (Bonitz, 460^{a}35–49). Sometimes *metalambanein* X means "take X in a different way" (e.g. *APr* A 17, 37^{b}15; B 4, 56^{b}8), where the vague "way" is explicated by the context. Most commentators apply this usage to our passage and suppose that "taking the accounts in a different way" means "changing the order of the terms in (B)". The change which they prefer yields:

(C) Healthy men are good digesters.
Perambulators are healthy.
_____
Perambulators are good digesters.

They choose (C), which has the conclusion *BaC*, for the following reason. At 94^{b}20 the sentence which I translate as "Why is B explanatory for C" is elliptically expressed: the Greek text has no word answering to "explanatory". Then "Why is B for C?" might rather be expanded to "Why does B hold of C?"; and we may then take this question to be answered by the 'changed' argument, which must then be argument (C).

Against this there are three objections. First, it is not clear that (C) is any improvement on (B): health is, perhaps, the purpose of perambulators; but it hardly answers the hardly sensible question "With what purpose are perambulators good digesters?" Ross appeals to "the very strong teleological element in Aristotle's biology"; but (C) is not a piece of biology. Secondly, in (C) the middle term is not an account, nor even "as it were an account" (94^{b}19—i.e. a partial account) of either of the extremes. Ross suggests that the phrase "*metalambanein* the accounts" caters for this objection by inviting us to change the *definitions* of the terms. If we define "good digestion" as, e.g., "movement of food designed to secure health" the middle term in (C) is after all a partial account of the major. But at 94^{b}21 Aristotle says that *having a good digestion* gives the essence of *health*, thus precisely inverting the relationship Ross finds. Finally, the introduction of a revised argument at 94^{b}20 is intolerably abrupt.

I thus suppose that the question "Why is B explanatory for C?", together with its answer, merely repeats 94^{b}18–20. Thus argument (C) is not expressed in the text at all.

We might then feel free to construct a different improvement on (B): instead of (C) let us offer:

(D) Healthy men are perambulators.
Good digesters are healthy.
_____
Good digesters perambulate.

This is better than (C), but not good enough: *healthy* will not serve as an 'account' of either extreme term.

Metalambanein X is also used as elliptical for *metalambanein* X *anti* Y, or "take X instead of Y". A common substituend for X in this phrase is *tous logous*, "the accounts" (e.g. *Top* E 2, 130^{a}39; Z 4, 142^{b}3; 9, 147^{b}14); and *metalambanein* amounts to replacing a term by its definition. It is

230

plausible to take *metalambanein* thus in our passage. Aristotle is then remarking, parenthetically, that if you replace "healthy" in (B) by its definition you will see more clearly that *having a good digestion* is a constituent in that definition. If that is so, the Delphic remark at 94^b20 does not pretend to *modify* example (B), but only to make it more persuasive: the attempt fails, and we are left with (B) and its faults. (For a somewhat different suggestion see Fortenbaugh.)

These problems are, however, peculiar to the valetudinarian example. The text at 94^b10 sketches another example which is precisely adapted to Aristotle's purposes:

(E) Shelters for belongings are roofed.
Houses are shelters for belongings.

Houses are roofed.

'Why (i.e. with what purpose) are houses roofed?'—'In order to keep things safe.' Thus the middle term gives the final explanation of the conclusion; and at the same time, it expresses (part of) the essence of *house*—houses are, in Aristotle's view, necessarily shelters (*An A* 1, 403^b3–6; *Met Z* 17, 1041^a26–30).

94^b23: This paragraph presents two complementary theses about the temporal relations between the terms of efficient and final explanations. Suppose that C is A because of B; then (a) if the "because" is efficient, B is 'first'—i.e. (presumably) the temporal order is B, C, A; and (b) if the "because" is final, B is last and C first—i.e. the temporal order is C, A, B. There is a minor difficulty in (a): Aristotle should surely have given the order as C, B, A. But the major difficulty with both (a) and (b) is this: if the explanations are to be given demonstratively, in arguments of the sort that have just been discussed, then all three terms in each case will be simultaneous; for if A holds of C of necessity then a thing cannot be C *before* it is A. Here, at least, Aristotle confuses his official analytic conception of explanation with the ordinary notion of explanation which allows it to link events that are separated in time. This confusion (strongly underlined by Robin) leads directly to the argument of the next few chapters.

If we ignore the confusion, and extract (a) and (b) from their syllogistic contexts, we get:

(a') If **a**'s being F causes **a**'s being G, then **a** is F before **a** is G;
(b') If **a**'s being G is the purpose of **a**'s being F, then **a** is G after **a** is F.

Both (a') and (b') are, I think, false: substitute "sitting in the sun" for "being F" and "warm" for "G". ((a') should not be confused with the thesis that if an event E' causes E, then E' occurs before E.) Aristotle may have thought that efficient and final explanations were complementary to one another in the sense that F efficiently explains G if and only if G finally explains F. But it is evident that there may be efficient explanations where no final explanations are appropriate; and it does not seem to be the case that if **a** is *F* in order to be *G*, then **a**'s being *F* must *bring about* **a**'s being *G*.

94^b27: Aristotle offers two cases where two different types of explanation are equally appropriate. The first case asks why something 'holds', i.e. why a certain (type of) state of affairs obtains. The second case, which Aristotle appears to regard as less straightforward, asks why something 'occurs', i.e. why a certain (type of) event occurs. The second example is clear, but implausible: Why does it thunder?—both because the extinction of fire in the clouds necessitates thunder, and in order to terrify the damned. The first example is more plausible but less plain. The question is: Why does light pass through the lantern? And the two answers seem to be: (*a*) because light is composed of fine particles which can pass through the pores of the horn sides of the lantern; and (*b*) in order to prevent our stumbling. Neither answer is felicitous: (*a*)—which Aristotle in fact rejects: *GC A* 8, 326^b7–21—seems to explain *how* light can pass through the lantern, and gives at most a necessary and not a necessitating condition for the transition of light. (*b*) fits some such question as: Why do people carry lanterns? and is quite inappropriate to the question Aristotle has framed. (There can hardly be a reference to the teleological workings of nature, since the lantern is not a natural object.) There are many better examples in Aristotle's biological writings, e.g.: Why do stags shed their antlers? (*a*) In order that the stag may have less weight to carry about; and also (*b*) because their weight is so great that of necessity they fall off (*PA Γ* 2, 663^b10–14). Here (*a*) rests on the teleological interpretation of natural events. Aristotle explicitly says that examples of the sort he wants are especially common among natural products and processes (94^b35; cf. e.g. *GA B* 2, 743^b16–18). *PA* provides numerous examples of this sort of thing (see KULLMANN (1974), 329–38): that a certain type of animal has a certain feature is explained both by the fact that the matter of the animal necessitates the feature and by the fact that having the feature is good for the animal.

This passage is one of the earliest notes on the problem of the compatibility of different types of explanation. At *Phys B* 3, 195^a5, Aristotle says that "it happens that . . . there are many explanations of the same thing, non-incidentally" (= *Met Δ* 2, 1013^b5; cf. *H* 4, 1044^a33). With the relaxed sense of "explanation" that is current in the *Physics* this assertion holds no particular difficulty. In *APst*, however, one of the two purportedly compatible types of explanation is a necessitating condition; and if *Q* is necessitated by *R*, it is hard to see how it can also be 'explained' in terms of some purpose *P*. Suppose that the stag's antlers *must* fall off, because of their weight. Then it may, of course, also be true that their falling off is good for the stag; but it can hardly be true that they fall off *because* this is good for the stag, or that they fall of *in order to* benefit the stag.

In *Phys* and *PA* Aristotle looked more closely at the problem of conjoint teleological and necessitating explanation; and he answered the sort of difficulty I have just outlined by introducing the notion of 'hypothetical' necessity. This is a major retreat; for a condition is hypothetically necessary if it is a necessary condition, not if it is a necessitating condition; and reconciling hypothetical necessity with teleology does not reconcile necessitation and teleology. (See on all this Balme, 76–84; KULLMANN (1974), 329–38; COOPER (1987).)

94^{b}37: "There are two types of necessity": cf. *Met E* 2, 1026^{b}28–9; *Rhet A* 10, 1368^{b}35–7; and in general *Met Δ* 5. For the instance of the stone cf. *EN B* 1, 1103^{a}20 (for the natural movements of the four elements see, e.g., *Phys Δ* 8, 214^{b}13–16; *Cael Δ* 6). Force is discussed at *Met Δ* 5, 1015^{a}26–33; *EN Γ* 1, 1110^{a}1–4. Aristotle has no general discussion of natural necessity; his main accounts of the part played by necessity in nature turn on 'hypothetical' necessity (*Phys B* 9; *PA A* 1, 642^{a}2–^{b}4), which he sharply distinguishes from the two sorts of necessity mentioned in our passage: "One might perhaps puzzle over what sort of necessity in meant by those who talk of things happening from necessity; for it can be neither of the two sorts distinguished in our philosophical works" (642^{a}4–6; the reference is probably to our passage). See further Sorabji.

95^{a}3: "Among the products of thought . . .": i.e. 'among those types of thing which are normally produced as a result of planning and intention'. (See also *Met Z* 9.) Aristotle has just said that among natural objects, some are produced both by necessity and purposefully; he now adds that among artificial objects, some are produced by necessity, some by chance, and some purposefully. The two assertions are not exactly parallel: Aristotle does not say that in the case of artefacts one and the same thing may have both a necessitating and a final explanation. On chance see *Phys B* 4–6.

95^{a}6: "It is especially among things . . .": one plausible paraphrase of this tortuous sentence goes: 'Paradigmatically, *X* occurs for some purpose if (i) *X* could have failed to occur; (ii) *X* did not occur by chance; and (iii) the result of *X*'s occurrence is good.' In the *standard* case, a purposeful act is neither necessary nor chance; and it is beneficial. (The third condition seems odd; and passages such as *EN A* 1, 1094^{a}1–2, help only in cases of agency and do not cover natural purposes.) The end of the chapter thus corrects an impression given by the immediately preceding argument: necessity and purpose are, indeed, compatible; but standardly purpose is found in the absence of necessity.

CHAPTER 12

This chapter (on which see WIELAND (1972)) continues the discussion of explanation. Aristotle persists in using the terminology of syllogistic, and the variables *A, B, C*, . . . remain term-variables; in many of the cases he describes, event-variables would be more appropriate. It is hard to find a single consistent representation for everything Aristotle says. Interpretation is eased by the introduction of two conventions. First, we need copula variables, ϕ, ψ, ..., which have as substituends words such as "is", "was", "is coming to be", "has come to be" etc. which can be fitted into the gap in "a . . . A". Secondly, it is useful to allow the device of a dummy subject, "there", alongside genuine subjects such as "Socrates", "men". Thus "Socrates is wise", "All men come to be grey", and "There came to be clouds" all exemplify the formula "a ϕ A".

95^{a}10: Suppose that:

(1) **a** is A because **b** is B

is true; then, Aristotle asserts, if **a** is coming to be A, **a** is coming to be A because **b** is coming to be B; and similarly for "has come to be", and "will be". (Aristotle does not mention "was" and "will come to be": perhaps he—mistakenly—supposes that they are synonymous with "has come to be" and "will be".) In general:

(2) $(\exists\phi)(a \; \phi \; A \text{ because } b \; \phi \; B) \to (\forall\phi)(a \; \phi \; A \to a \; \phi \; A \text{ because } b \; \phi \; B)$.

In Aristotle's second illustration at 95^{a}16–21, **a** ϕ A becomes "there is ice (e.g. on the pond)". The initial question: What is ice? allows the transformation of "there is ice (on the pond)" into "(the pond's) water is solidified" (cf. *Met H* 2, 1042^{b}27; 1043^{a}10); and this transformation eases the syllogistic treatment of the example.

95^{a}22: Ross says that both illustrations of (2) take a middle term that is an efficient as well as a formal explanation. Strictly construed, the middle terms are not efficient explanations, but they are formal explanations. Nevertheless, thesis (2) is not limited to formal explanation; nor does it entail that every *explanans* must be contemporaneous with its *explanandum*. But both illustrations of (2) gave contemporaneous *explanantia* and *explananda*; and Aristotle now asks whether this was accidental, i.e. whether:

(3) $(\exists t)(\exists t')(t \neq t' \; \& \; a \; \phi \; A \text{ at } t \text{ because } b \; \psi \; B \text{ at } t')$

can have true instantiations. (In fact, Aristotle appears to presuppose that in any true instance of (3)—or indeed of (1) or (2)—**a** and **b** will be identical. In other words, the schema°underlying his discussion is:

(4) **a** ϕ A because **a** ψ B.

This presupposition is equivalent to the thought that explanation is essentially something which links one *term* to another *term*.)

95^{a}22: "an item which is explanatory in this way . . .": i.e. 'explanations of the same type as the preceding illustration'—formal explanations.

95^{a}24: "Can it be that in continuous time, as we think": i.e. 'Given that time is, as we think, continuous, can it be that . . .' or 'Given that time is continuous, can it be, as we think, that . . .' The point of the remark emerges later in the chapter. Aristotle argues for the continuity of time at *Phys Δ* 10, 219^{a}10–14; what he means is that for any two instants t_1 and t_2, where t_2 is later than t_1, there is an instant t_3 later than t_1 and earlier than t_2 (cf. e.g. *Phys Z* 3, 234^{a}8; Bonitz, 728^{a}37–45).

95ᵃ27:   Aristotle does not answer the question he has just posed; rather, he assumes that there are such non-contemporaneous pairs of *explanans* and *explanandum* and asks to what extent we can have knowledge of them. First he considers past pairs such as "Socrates died at noon because he drank a cup at hemlock at 10" (here "the time . . . is determined": 95ᵃ32, i.e. the gap between *explanans* and *explanandum* is of a specified duration). He argues that we can infer "Socrates drank a cup of hemlock" from "Socrates died", but we cannot infer "Socrates died" from "Socrates drank a cup of hemlock". His argument for the second point is sound: there are times—e.g. 11 o'clock—at which it is true to say "Socrates drank a cup of hemlock" but false to say "Socrates died"; hence the former does not entail the latter.

It is, however, equally clear that we cannot infer "Socrates drank hemlock" from "Socrates died". Thus when Aristotle says "deductions start from what has come about later" (95ᵃ28), he does not mean that we can *always* infer from *explanandum* to *explanans*, but only that we can *sometimes* do so; and the favourable cases, it is reasonable to think, are those in which there is a formal connection between *explanans* and *explanandum*. Consider: "Socrates died of hemlock because he drank a cup of hemlock". Here it seems that we can infer from *explanandum* to *explanans*, but not vice versa—and for precisely the reason Aristotle gives. (The inference requires that "the time is indeterminate".)

95ᵃ28:   "although the principle . . .": presumably (if the text is right): 'but here it is the earlier event which is in fact the originative source of the later'.

95ᵃ35:   "Nor can you argue . . .": Mure and Ross punctuate lightly before "nor": 'And the same account also goes for what will be the case, i.e. one cannot infer that since this has come about this will be.' But Aristotle does not proceed to give "the same account"; and I have therefore reverted to the older punctuation. Aristotle's *first argument* against the inference from "Socrates has drunk hemlock" to "Socrates will die" turns on the principle that "the middle term must be of the same type (*homogonon*)" as each of the extremes. The deduction, if it is to exhibit a middle term at all, must contain an inference of the form:

(5) If **a** φ *A*, then **a** ψ *B*.
(6) If **a** ψ *B*, then **a** χ *C*.
(7) If **a** φ *A*, then **a** χ *C*.

From (5) Aristotle in effect infers that φ = ψ, and from (6) that ψ = χ; hence φ = χ. But by hypothesis φ ≠ χ. Aristotle gives no argument for these inferences; they certainly do not follow from (3); and they appear to be invalid.

Aristotle's *second argument* (95ᵃ39–ᵇ1) is an application of the sound argument of 95ᵃ31–5. Aristotle has already said (95ᵃ35) that the argument shows the invalidity of inferring from "Socrates will drink hemlock" to "Socrates will die". Both applications of the good argument are bad.

It seems merely false to say that from "Socrates will drink (has drunk) a lethal dose of hemlock" we cannot infer "Socrates will die of hemlock". And Aristotle's argument, which worked for the past, does not work for the future; for at any point after Socrates' taking the lethal dose we *can* truly say "Socrates will die". Has Aristotle got an answer to this? It would be both implausible and irrelevant to urge, sceptically, that we cannot *know* if the dose is lethal until we know that Socrates has actually died from it. It is true but irrelevant that if Socrates has taken a lethal dose and is not yet dead we cannot now truly say that he *is* dead (Ross). In certain passages Aristotle says, or appears to say, that if at *t* it is true to say that **a** is *A*, it does not follow that at all times before *t* it was true to say that **a** would be *A* (see *Met E* 3; *Int* 9; *GC B* 11). Thus we can truly say at noon that Socrates is dead of hemlock; but we could not truly have said at 11 o'clock that Socrates would die of hemlock at noon. The three chapters I have referred to are, however, notoriously hard. And in any case their thesis is hardly applicable to the particular cases with which we are concerned; for here we are not interested in saying "**a** will be *A*" until after the occurrence of the cause of **a**'s being *A*, i.e. until it is (on any account) determinately true that **a** will be *A*.

95ᵇ1: Aristotle reserves a thorough discussion of the issues broached in this section to the *Physics* (see *Δ* 10–14; *Z*); unsurprisingly the section as it stands is opaque and unsatisfactory.

Ross says that Aristotle here turns from epistemology to metaphysics. Yet the question of what holds events together (*sunechei*) is plainly akin to the question of why time is continuous (*suneches*: 95ᵃ24); and the section can plausibly be connected to its predecessor if we imagine the following objection to its predecessor's arguments: 'Suppose that time is not continuous: then in some cases at least it *will* be legitimate to infer "**a** is *A* at t_2" from "**b** is *B* at t_1', where t_2 is after t_1; for if t_1 is next to t_2 there will be no time at which one can truly say the latter but not the former.'

"The now is what holds time together, as we said [sc. at 220ᵃ5]; for it holds together past and future time, and is a limit of time; for it is the beginning of the one and the end of the other" (*Phys Δ* 12, 222ᵃ10–12). Our passage contains no hint of this answer to the metaphysical question; nor indeed is it clear that Aristotle offers any answer to it at all. Rather, his train of thought seems to run like this: 'What holds time together? i.e. what attaches one instant to the next?—Well, time isn't held together in *this* sense; for it is not the case that every instant is next to another instant.' (Aristotle proceeds to deny the contiguity of *events* not of instants; but the two denials are equivalent on the plausible and Aristotelian view that every point of time is occupied by an event (*Phys Δ* 11, 219ᵃ1).)

X is next to (*echomenon*) *Y* if it is consecutive upon *Y* and touches it (*Phys E* 3, 227ᵃ6); *X* is consecutive upon *Y* if there is no third thing, *Z*, of the same sort as *X* and *Y*, in between *X* and *Y* (227ᵃ1); and *X* touches *Y* if the extreme points of *X* and *Y* are 'together' (227ᵃ7). But, Aristotle argues, past events, like points (or instants) have no parts and hence cannot be next to one another. Why does Aristotle assume that past happenings are thus instantaneous? Some, perhaps, like Plato's birth or Alexander's death, may have temporal location but no duration; but others, like Plato's writing of the *Republic* or Alexander's expedition to India, surely have duration. Why, then, should we not suppose that two period-events, A and B, are next to one another? i.e. that the last moment of A, t_a, is identical with the first moment of B, t_b? Aristotle's answer in the *Physics* (Z 5–6) is that no event—or at least no change—has a first moment: for any instant t in B there is a prior moment t' which is also in B. But Aristotle's opponent may still maintain that A and B can be next to one another in a slightly weaker sense: t_a, he may say, is the last moment of A and is not a moment of B; but any later moment t_e, however close to t_a, is a moment of B. And if that is so it will *not* be possible to find a time between A and B in which the statement that B is occurring is false.

Although Aristotle says that present events cannot be next to past events "for the same reason" (95^{b}7), he compares present events not to points but rather to lines. The reason is the same only generically: an indivisible (a point) cannot be next to anything at all, whether another indivisible (a point) or a divisible (a line). Thus a past point-event cannot be next to a present period-event; either it is included in the present event or else there are infinitely many point-events between it and the present. Why does Aristotle assume that present events are all period-events? And how can he reconcile this with the existence of past point-events, given that every past event was once present? Perhaps he was misled by the terms he used: the present participle *ginomenon* ("what is coming about") naturally suggests a continuing process; the past participles *gegonos*, *genomenon*, *gegenēmenon*, are more readily taken to denote what Ross calls "completions of change", or point-events.

Why do "infinitely many items which have come about inhere in what is coming about"? An answer can be extracted from *Phys Z* 6, 236^{b}32–237^{a}17: let AB represent the present period-event of $\mathbf{a}$'s ϕ-ing, and let C be an arbitrary point on AB—the present moment. At C it is true to say in respect of every point D on AC that $\mathbf{a}$ was ϕ-ing at D. Since there are infinitely many such points, the present event AB contains infinitely many past events.

It is tempting to take the presentness of AB literally, and to find in it the notion of the 'specious present'; but it is more likely that AB represents any period-event which is not yet completed.

95^{b}13:   Aristotle now explains how the inferences which 95^{a}22–^{b}1 found legitimate should be formally presented.

95^{b}13:   "when events come about consecutively": the previous section has implicitly denied that any events can come about consecutively (*ephexēs*) in the technical sense of the term (*Phys E* 2, 236^{b}34–237^{a}6; see above). "Consecutively" is presumably being used loosely to

[""]

mean "not at the same time": i.e. 'in the case of explanations where *explanans* and *explanandum* are not contemporaneous'.

95^{b}15: "Here too . . .": the sentence probably states what it is that must be assumed in consecutive cases. "Here too": i.e. 'as well as in the cases exemplified at 95^{a}14–21'. "The middle term and the first term must be immediate": probably 'both premisses are immediate' (i.e. "the middle" and "the first" stand for "the premiss in which the middle is predicate", and "the premiss in which the first is predicate"), rather than 'the first premiss is immediate' (i.e. "the middle and the first" stands for "the premiss predicating the first of the middle").

95^{b}17: "C is the principle . . .": i.e. 'C is the point from which our knowledge starts' (contrast 95^{a}28, where "principle" means "originative explanation"). *Phys* Δ 11, 219^{b}11, is cited by the commentators to explain how "the present . . . is the principle of time". But the discussion in *Phys* Δ 11 (which does not use the phrase "principle of time") has no bearing on our passage. Aristotle is making an epistemological point: 'Our knowledge of events must be grounded on knowledge of the present.'

95^{b}20: "and C is the explanation . . .": the commentators suppose that "explanation" here means *causa cognoscendi*—C explains how we know, or why we believe, that A occurred; but C cannot explain A itself, since C is later than A. But the text does not suggest that "explanation" has an unusual reference here; rather, C does explain some fact in the world—not A, however, but the connection between D and A: 'What explains the fact that D requires A?—C, because D requires C and C A.'

95^{b}23: "because of the infinity . . .": i.e. 'because between any two past events there is a third' (as 95^{b}1–12 has argued). From the proposition that events are not consecutive, it does not follow that there are no true immediate propositions of the form (5). An event E_3 may occur between E_1 and E_2 without forming any sort of causal link between them. Aristotle assumes without argument that if a proposition of the form (5) is immediate, then the events denoted by its antecedent and its consequent must be contiguous; and his next sentence, "However that may be . . .", offers the absurd compromise that if neither premiss can be immediate, then at least the *first* premiss must be.

95^{b}24: "However that may be . . .": i.e. 'The first premiss must both be immediate and contain in its antecedent whichever of the three terms in the inference is nearest to the present moment' (where "first from the present moment" means "nearest in time to now"). Or: 'The first premiss must be immediate, i.e. it must connect X with Y where X is a present event and Y is causally contiguous to X' (where "first from the present moment" means "non-mediately connected with the present event"). The first paraphrase is grammatically harder; the second commits Aristotle to the view that all causal inferences must start from a present event.

95^{b}30: "the division is infinite": i.e. 'there are infinitely many points at which the time-slice $D-A$ can be cut'; for this use of "division" (here, *tomē*) cf. *Phys Z* 6, 237^{a}9; Θ 8, 262^{b}20.

95^{b}31: The cases sketched in the two preceding sections are now illustrated by a favourite example of Aristotle's (Bonitz, 324^{a}55–61).

95^{b}38: The last two sections of *B* 12 are appendixes. The first takes up again the question of circular arguments, which have already been discussed in *A* 3 (the reference at 96^{a}1 is probably to *A* 3, 73^{a}6–20). The cyclical nature of the phenomena of the physical world impressed Aristotle. The *locus classicus* for this is *GC B* 11: "If what moves always in a circle moves something, necessarily the motion of this too will be circular—e.g. since the upper locomotion is circular, the sun moves thus; and if that is the case, because of this the seasons come about in a circle and revolve; and if these come about in this way, the things under them again will do so" (338^{b}1–5; cf. Bonitz, 414^{a}6–14). The present passage indicates, I think, that Aristotle toyed with the idea of representing the natural cycles of *GC B* 11 by means of circular demonstrations: the reciprocations of nature would be mirrored in the reciprocal implications of logic. If that is so, then one upholder of the theory of circular proof was the young Aristotle (see p. 104; BARNES (1976), 290–2).

Detailed interpretation of the present appendix is difficult; I offer the following paraphrase (which involves a new punctuation of the text) without great confidence: 'Suppose we have an argument AaB, $BaC \vdash AaC$, and that this explains a circular generation. Now we shall also have CaA; for the conclusion converts—for that "is what being circular is". Hence in the case of circular generation the premisses convert too, as *A* 3 proved; i.e. middle and extremes "follow one another"—BaA and AaB, BaC and CaB.' (The commentators give different accounts.)

In the concrete example which Aristotle offers, the appearance of circularity is falsely imposed by the vagueness of the premisses. To say that the conclusion converts is to say that if it rains then there is an exhalation of steam, and if there is an exhalation of steam then it rains. But this is true only if the connective "if ... then ..." is taken in a temporal sense, or if temporal tags are grafted onto the argument ('If it rains at t then there are exhalations at t_1; and if there are exhalations at t_1 then it rains at t_2'). It is reasonable to talk of cyclical events in such cases; but they cannot be expressed by means of 'circular' inferences of the sort Aristotle pictures. There is perhaps an inkling of this in *GC B* 11: discussing circular generation Aristotle concludes that "in cases in which the changing substance is not imperishable but perishable, it is necessary for them to revolve in kind but not in number. Whence if water comes from air and air from water, these are the same in form but not in number" (338^{b}16–18). The rain at t is "the same in form but not in number" as the rain at t_2, i.e. it is a different occurrence of the same type of event. *GC* does not attempt any formalization of such circularities; and the formalization is, I think, beyond the powers of syllogistic.

96ᵃ8: On the substance of this second Appendix see *A* 30, 87ᵇ20, and notes. There Aristotle argued that 'for the most part' premisses entail 'for the most part' conclusions; here he argues for the converse, that 'for the most part' conclusions require 'for the most part' premisses. His words seem at first blush to suggest that in order to infer a 'for the most part' conclusion *both* premisses must be 'for the most part'. But his argument only supports the position that at least one premiss must be 'for the most part'; and this is what he explicitly holds at *APr A* 27, 43ᵇ33–5: "In the case of for the most part problems, the deduction too must proceed from propositions which—either all or some of them—are for the most part." The argument also shows that Aristotle held that *For the most part Cs are A* entails *not-(AaC)* (cf. *Top B* 5, 112ᵇ5–7). We might think that *For the most part Cs are A* is entailed by *AaC*; and hence (since *AaC* can be consistently interpreted) that it does not entail *not-(AaC)*. Aristotle, I suspect, was influenced by the fact that anyone who says *For the most part Cs are A* may be taken to imply *not-AaC*; and he interpreted this 'conversational implicature' as an entailment.

However that may be, what are we to make of Aristotle's claim at 96ᵃ8? In full generality, the claim is this: if a conclusion of the form "For the most part, *P*" follows from a set of premisses, $Q_1, Q_2, \ldots, Q_n$, then at least one of the Q_is must have the form "For the most part, *P*". In *APr A* 27 Aristotle is doubtless thinking of a restricted version of the claim—a version restricted to syllogistical inferences. The claim may well sound plausible; but until we find a coherent interpretation of "for the most part", we shall not be able to assess it—and we may be sure that Aristotle himself was not in a position to prove or disprove it.

CHAPTER 13

B 13 attempts to provide recipes for the discovery of definitions; this task is contrasted with that of *B* 3–10, which is alluded to at 96ᵃ20. There the main question was to what extent, if at all, essences can be exhibited in demonstrations; here Aristotle asks how we can get hold of such potential exhibits in the first place.

Ross thinks that *B* 13 attempts the *same* task as *B* 8: what *B* 8 did for 'causal' definitions, *B* 13 will do for the 'immediate' essences referred to in *B* 9. There is no hint of this in the text, and the example of *man* at *B* 8, 93ᵃ24, is just the sort of thing Aristotle is primarily thinking about in *B* 13. Other scholars say that *B* 13 is concerned solely with the definition of substances: that is refuted by 96ᵇ20, and by several of the examples discussed in the chapter.

96ᵃ20: "how what something is can be elucidated in the terms (*horoi*)": i.e. 'to what extent essences can be exhibited through the terms of a demonstration'. *Horoi* is often rendered "definitions" here; but the rendering has nothing to recommend it.

96ᵃ24: If we want to define a term *S* we must look first for predicates $A_1, A_2, \ldots$, satisfying three conditions: (i) every *S* is A_i; (ii) for some *S'* distinct from S, every S' is A_i; and (iii) for all S' distinct from S, if every S' is A_i then S and S' belong to the same kind (are species of the same genus). Notice that this procedure presupposes both that S is a species, and that we have already identified its genus or kind. Aristotle's illustration is complicated by the fact that he first takes a predicate, *existing*, which satisfies (i) and (ii) but not (iii), and only then gives one, *odd*, which satisfies (i), (ii), and (iii).

The essence of S, we can now say (96ᵃ32), is a conjunction, ϕ, of predicates $A_1, A_2, \ldots, A_n$, where, first, each A_i satisfies (i)–(iii), and secondly, $Sa\phi$.

So far, the recipe does not ensure that S has a unique essence: choose B distinct from each A_i in ϕ but satisfying (i)–(iii); then the conjunction ϕ & B will satisfy all the requirements so far placed on essences. Aristotle's answer to this is implicit in his use of the word "first" at 96ᵃ33: we are to cease collecting A_is at the *first* conjunction which has the specified properties. Since B was picked after ϕ had been established, ϕ & B is not the essence of S. But suppose that we have picked A_1, $A_2, \ldots, A_{n-1}$ (call it ϕ'); and that ϕ' & A_n (= ϕ) and ϕ' & B both have the specified properties: how can we choose between these two alternative essences? We can do so only if "first" refers not to the order of our selecting the A_is but rather to some objective ordering of them; one of the main efforts of the rest of the chapter is to work out how such an objective ordering can be achieved.

96ᵃ36: "prime (in both senses . . .)": i.e. being neither the product nor the sum of two integers. Often, though not invariably, Aristotle supposes that one is not a number (e.g. *Met N* 1, 1088ᵃ6–8; cf. Heath (2), 83–4); hence three is not the sum of two integers. Since the only numbers prime in this latter way are 2 and 3, *number*, *odd*, and *prime in this sense* are sufficient to define *three*. If we read "and" in "prime and prime in *this* sense" (96ᵃ38) as "i.e.", we get precisely these three notions as definitive of *three*; 96ᵃ36 then has to be taken as listing attributes that hold, but may not be definitive, of *three*.

96ᵇ1: We may still wonder whether ϕ is the *essence* of S. 96ᵇ1–6 makes explicit the condition implicit in "always" at 96ᵃ24: the A_is, if they are to be essential ("in what a thing is") must be necessary predicates of S. Condition (i) should be rewritten as: (i') necessarily every S is A_i. Similar modifications must be made to (ii) and (iii). (At 96ᵇ2 I translate the MS text, which makes Aristotle's parenthesis otiose; Ross's emendation removes this minor inelegance.)

There follows (96ᵇ6) an argument for the essential status of ϕ: 'If ϕ is not the essence of S, it is a kind or genus of S; if G is a genus of S then it is possible that G belongs to something which is not S (cf. e.g. *Top A* 5, 102ᵃ31); but necessarily—by construction—if **a** is ϕ then **a** is an S (". . . it holds of nothing other than atomic (i.e. individual) triplets"). Hence ϕ is the essence of S'.

Aristotle has no explicit argument for his first premiss; and we might wonder how he excludes the possibility that ϕ is a *property* of S (*idion*:

see *A* 3, 73ᵃ7 note). The commentators deal with this by assuming that φ is predicated 'in what *S* is', i.e. that φ is either a part or the whole of the essence of *S*. The text does not state this assumption; and if Aristotle is making it, it needs justification: the whole purpose of the chapter is to tell us how to hunt down what is predicated in *S*'s essence. Arguments which depend on the assumption that we have already done this are not very helpful.

Aristotle's answer is, I think, implicit in the word "last" at 96ᵇ12: he is assuming that the A_is that satisfy (i)–(iii) are arranged in an ordered set ψ, $\langle A_1, A_2, \ldots, A_n, \ldots, A_m \rangle$. Let ϕ_i be the ordered set $\langle A_1, A_2, \ldots A_i \rangle$. Then ϕ_n, according to 96ᵃ33, gives the essence of *S* if $Sa\phi_n$ and for no $j < n\ Sa\phi_j$. ϕ_n is now (96ᵇ12) called "the last such predication to hold of the atoms": if we run back through the ϕ_is starting at ϕ_m, ϕ_n will be the last set which fails to satisfy (ii).

Fairly clearly, the ordering relation for ψ is that of subsumption: i.e. $(\forall_i)\ (A_i a A_{i+1})$. Given this ordering for ψ, then if ϕ_n is not the essence of *S* and if not-$(Sa\phi_{n-1})$, ϕ_n is a genus of *S*. If this does something to explain Aristotle's argument, if does not justify it; for he gives no argument for the assumption that ψ can be ordered by subsumption— and indeed it clearly cannot be.

96ᵇ15: This section is exceedingly difficult; even its overall purpose is obscure. Aristotle is offering advice to anyone "dealing with some whole". The traditional interpretation takes this phrase to designate the attempt to define a term which is intermediate between *infima species* and *summum genus*. Pacius thought that Aristotle was discussing the definition of a particular type of *infima species*. Waitz and Ross think that Aristotle is providing general guidance on how to approach a subject (e.g. geometry) which one wants to treat demonstratively. If this last suggestion is right, then the section is at best loosely connected with the rest of *B* 13.

The section divides into two parts, 96ᵇ15–21 and 96ᵇ21–5; I shall first take the parts separately.

It is natural to take "what is atomic in form" (96ᵇ16) to designate *infimae species* (cf. Bonitz, 120ᵃ58–ᵇ4). Thus when 'dealing with a whole' we are enjoined to determine the *infimae species* of the kind we are interested in; to define these *infimae species*; and to find their kind and infer their attributes.

The third injunction requires three glosses. First, "getting what the kind is" (96ᵇ19): i.e. 'finding out into what genus, i.e. under what category, *S* falls'. But why should this form part of our study? Does Aristotle imply that unless we know the category of *S* we cannot discover its properties? Secondly, the "proper attributes" (96ᵇ20) of the chosen *infima species* are probably the 'in itself incidentals' which it is the task of demonstrations to establish. (*An A* 1, 402ᵃ15 refers to these as "incidental properties" and says at 402ᵇ16–403ᵃ1 that their study is useful in the search for essences; but it is hard to find a close connection between that passage and ours.) Thirdly, what are "the primitive common items" (96^{b}20)? Hardly the most common predicates of all, the categories. Ross thinks of the predicates common to all species of the kind in question; but this allows no sense to the word "primitive" (*prōtos*). Reference to the use of "first" (*prōtos*) at 96^{a}33 suggests rather that "the primitive common items" are the members of ϕ_n; the 'in itself incidentals' of S are to be inferred from its essence. On the other hand, comparison with A 10, 76^{b}10, suggests the common axioms: we should infer the attributes of S by way of the common axioms—first ascertaining the kind of S in order to ensure the right instantiation of those axioms. This suggestion is, I think, the most appealing; but it gives no clear sense to "primitive".

I turn to 96^{b}21–5. Comparison with A 28, 87^{a}38–9, encourages us to construe "the items compounded from the atoms" (96^{b}21) as "the derived terms", and to take "the atoms" (96^{b}21) and "the simples" (96^{b}23) to designate primitive terms. "The characteristics" (96^{b}21, 24) then designates the predicates proper to the science in question. "The definitions" (96^{b}22) will be the definitions of the derived terms.

Thus: 'If you start from the definitions of the derived terms and a knowledge of the attributes of the primitives, then you will be able to work out the attributes of the derived terms; for the definitions and the attributions of primitives act as principles, and attributes hold of derived terms in virtue of their holding of primitives.' For example, in geometry if we start from the definition of *isosceles* as *triangle with two equal sides* and if we know that triangles have 2 R, then we shall easily demonstrate that the isosceles has 2 R.

96^{b}16–25 as a whole thus yields the following argument: 'First pick out the atoms, and prove their attributes; for the attributes of non-atoms will be deducible from these; for attributes hold of non-atoms in virtue of holding of atoms.' The argument seems neat; but it equivocates on the term "atom": at its first occurrence it means "*infima species*"; at its second, "primitive term"; at its third and fourth, "primary subject of predication". It is easy to see that these senses do not coincide.

"Atom" cannot be read univocally as "*infima species*": it is hard to refer "the items compounded from the atoms" to the higher genera; it is impossible to suppose that attributes "hold of the other things in virtue of" their holding of an *infima species*.

Can "atom" be read univocally as "primitive term"? The suggestion explains Aristotle's use of "the primitives" at 96^{b}16; but it does not fit the arithmetical examples (*triad* and *pair* are not primitive terms), nor is it clear why Aristotle should refer to the primitives as "atomic in form".

Evidently, "atom" cannot be read univocally as "primary subject of predication".

Pacius offers a compromise solution: *ta atoma tōi eidei ta prōta* (96^{b}16: "what is atomic in form—the primitives") is to be translated as "the primary *infimae species*"; and that is glossed as 'those *infimae species* from which the remaining ones are constructed' (as the integers are constructed from the numbers 2 and 3, or as plane figures are constructible from triangles). Thus "atom" designates univocally this special type of *infima species*. Against this ingenious interpretation it must be said, first, that Aristotle gives no indication that what he has to say is limited to those 'wholes' whose *infimae species* form ordered series of the sort Pacius requires; on the contrary, he gives every appearance of making an entirely general point. And secondly, Pacius must ascribe a patently false view to Aristotle—viz. that the properties of non-primary *infimae species* are all properties of primary *infimae species* (Pacius actually says that "the quintuplet has the properties of the pair and the triplet from which it is compounded").

If 96^{b}16–25 has a coherent interpretation, it remains to be found.

96^{b}25:   Aristotle now returns to the topic of 'division' which he has criticized in *B* 5: and he enlarges upon the hints of 91^{b}28–35 that division may help in the discovery of definitions, even though it can have no probative force. The pursuit for which divisions will be useful is either the one described in 96^{b}16–25 or else the "hunt" which is the general subject of *B* 13. They will be useful "for deducing" only in a weak sense of "deduce"—*sullogizesthai* here has its original meaning of "compute" or "work out".

96^{b}30:   "But it makes a difference . . .": sometimes permuting adjectives makes a difference to the sense of a phrase—e.g. *yam* might be defined as *American sweet potato* but not as *sweet American potato*. But such differences are rare, and are not exemplified by Aristotle's illustration. Rather, Aristotle has in mind his thesis that essences are somehow unitary ("*animal tame* constitutes a single item": 96^{b}33).

A definitional formula for *S* has the form:

(1) $G\ D_1\ D_2 \ldots D_n,$

where *G* is the ultimate genus of *S* and the D_is are *differentiae*. Now (1) represents a unity composed of two elements, a genus and a difference; this can be shown by bracketing, thus:

(2) $(G\ D_1\ D_2 \ldots D_{n-1})D_n.$

The bracketed portion of (2) must again represent a unity of two elements; and so on. Thus (1) must be a nested set of genera and differences, thus:

(3) $((\ldots ((G\ D_1)\ D_2) \ldots)D_{n-1})D_n.$

Not every ordering of the D_is will be such that every pair of brackets in (3) encloses a unity. Aristotle appears to assume that only one such ordering will satisfy this requirement; and he thinks that division enables us to secure that ordering.

Aristotle offers no argument in support of this conclusion. The commentators in effect identify (3) with the set ϕ_n. Thus they take the ordering principle for (3) to be subsumption; and they suppose that (X, Y) expresses a unity only if XaY. Finally they observe that division will ensure that (3) is ordered by the subsumption relation.

The connection between unity and subsumption is made explicit in *Met Z* 12; and it is tacitly supposed later in our present chapter. None the less, it sits uneasily on the argument here; for Aristotle's illustration—*tame two-footed animal*—fails to exhibit the required subsumption. (Not all birds are tame: *HA E* 13, 544^{a}29; and, more generally, note the pertinent doubts at *Top Z* 6, 144^{b}12–30.)

96^{b}31: "e.g. whether you say *animal tame two-footed* . . .": I have followed the Greek closely here, preserving the word-order. *Animal tame two-footed* gives the acceptable bracketing (*animal tame*) *two-footed*. *Two-footed animal tame* must therefore be unacceptable. *Two-footed animal* surely constitutes as much of a 'unity' as *tame animal*: presumably "*two-footed animal*" is unacceptable because it does not exhibit the subsumption relation (not all animals are two-footed).

96^{b}35: "then you must make a division . . .": i.e. 'when one postulates the elements of the definition one must do so on the basis of a division'. The Greek permits three further interpretations, viz.: 'one must, when making divisions, postulate 〈rather than try to prove〉'; 'it follows that, when making divisions, one postulates 〈rather than proves〉'; 'it follows that one postulates on the basis of division'. Ross argues cogently for the version I have adopted.

96^{b}35: Aristotle's argument assumes that only one division of a kind divides it exhaustively; but the examples he has already used prove this to be false: both *tame/wild* and *terrestrial/aquatic/aerial* exhaustively divide *animal*. Thus the instruction to 'take the first difference' is not uniquely satisfiable; hence the divisional procedure cannot guarantee that "you omit nothing in what the thing is" (96^{b}35).

In *Met Z* 12 Aristotle argues that, in the strict sense, the definition of *S* consists just of *G* and D_n, the last difference; if that were so, then it would not of course matter whether any differences were omitted in the definitional procedure.

97^{a}6: "Eudemus says that in the opinion of Speusippus it is impossible to define anything that there is without knowing everything that there is" (Speusippus, frag. 31^b Lang = 63a Tarán—see further frags. 31^{c-c} Lang = 63b–e Tarán; Cherniss, 59–63; TARÁN (1981), 388–92). Speusippus did not infer that definition was impossible; rather he engaged in a heroic pursuit of omniscience. Aristotle first sets out the Speusippan argument (97^{a}6–11), then offers two objections (97^{a}11–14, 14–22).

Speusippus' argument is drawn up against any sort of definition, and not specifically against divisional definition; Aristotle deals with it here because he can find objections based on the properties of divisions. It is not clear from our texts exactly how Speusippus' argument should be set out.

First, the references in the key sentence ("Yet some people say . . .

differences": 97ᵃ8) are obscure. I paraphrase: 'But (i) you cannot know how X differs from Y without knowing Y; and (ii) if you do not know how Y differs from other things, you do not know Y.' Secondly, "knowing X" might, I think, mean either (A) "knowing what X is" or (B) "being able to recognize Xs". These two interpretations generate two arguments for two different conclusions. Thirdly, the two arguments each require one premiss which is not found in the text.

In *Argument A*, (i) becomes (6), (ii) becomes (5), and (4) must be supplied; thus:

(4) Anyone who has defined X knows what X is;
(5) Anyone who knows what X is knows, for every Y, how, if at all, X differs from Y;
(6) Anyone who knows how, if at all, X differs from Y knows what Y is.

Hence:

(7) Anyone who has defined anything knows what everything is.

In *Argument B*, (i) becomes (10), (ii) becomes (9), and (8) is supplied; thus:

(8) Anyone who has defined X is able to recognize Xs;
(9) Anyone who is able to recognize Xs knows, for every Y, whether or not Xs differ from Ys;
(10) Anyone who knows whether or not Xs differ from Ys is able to recognize Ys.

Hence:

(11) Anyone who has defined anything is able to recognize everything.

Speusippus supported his second premiss—i.e. either (5) or (9)—by observing that X is non-identical with Y if it differs from Y, and identical with Y if it does not differ from Y. Perhaps he meant that if you can recognize Xs (or know what Xs are), and X and Y are not the same, then you can pick out Xs from Ys—you know that (or how) X differs from Y.

In his *first objection* Aristotle argues that the proposition used to support (5) or (9) is false: not all differences ground non-identity; S and S' may both belong to G, and thus be the same in kind, while having many different attributes. Not all differences are essential ("in respect of their essence": 97ᵃ13), and only essential differences need be known by a definer (but contrast *Top A* 18, 108ᵇ2–4). Dogs differ from cats, but they do not differ *qua* animal; thus you may know what an animal is without knowing how dogs differ from cats. (And you may know what an animal is without knowing anything at all about tapirs or pangolins.)

Aristotle's *second objection* turns on divisional procedure: 'You will get a definition of X given two assumptions—and neither assumption involves you in omniscience.' The first assumption is that every species of G is either D_1 or D^*_1, where D^*_i is the opposite of D_i. Evidently this does not involve us in omniscience. The second assumption is that S is D_1. And we can clearly know this whether or not we know anything else that is D_1 or D^*_1: I can know that men are two-legged without knowing either that birds are two-legged or that cows are four-legged. The same assumptions hold for the genus $(G\ D_1)$—that every S in $(G\ D_1)$ is either D_2 or D^*_2, and that S is D_2. And thus one proceeds along (3), never needing to know anything about any species other than S.

As it stands, Aristotle's objection will only work against a Speusippan who is prepared to countenance divisional definitions; but his central point is not limited to divisional contexts and is effective against any Speusippan theorist: I can know that S is D_1 without knowing of any S' whether it is D_1 or D^*_1. Speusippus' second premiss—(5) or (9)—is simply false.

97ᵃ20: "The claim that everything falls into the division...": i.e. 'Every S in G is either D_1 or D^*_1, if D_1 is to constitute a genuine *differentia* of G' (cf. 96ᵇ35–97ᵃ6). This is not a 'postulate' because it does not propound anything that a (Speusippan) interlocutor would not already believe (A 10, 76ᵇ23–34).

97ᵃ23: This section contains Aristotle's considered statement of the method of divisional definition; the divider will get a correct definition provided that (a) he collects essential predicates of S; (b) he arranges these in their proper order; and (c) he ensures that none are omitted (cf. B 5, 91ᵇ28–32). Though Aristotle presents this as a partial vindication of the divisional method, it can hardly serve as such: proviso (a), even in Aristotle's description, has no connection with division; and (b) and (c) do not require the setting-up of a formal division.

(a) 97ᵃ26–8: By "the ability to establish things through the kind" Aristotle apparently means the capacity to use the *topoi* or recipes which he sets out and discusses in *Top Δ*: the recipes allow us to test whether or not G is a kind under which a sort S falls. Aristotle states that the same recipes will serve for *differentiae* (cf. *Top A* 4, 101ᵇ17–19), so that all the essential predicates of S will be discoverable by these means. The recipes for 'deducing' incidentals (i.e. contingent attributes of S) are offered in *Top Γ*. In *Top Z* Aristotle offers a series of *topoi* for the establishment of definitions; it is strange that he does not refer to these here.

(b) 97ᵃ28–34: By procedure (a) we have collected the A_is which are to be conjoined into ϕ_n, the defining set of S. In order to get the A_is in their correct order, we must first select that A_j from ϕ_n such that $(\forall i)\ (A_j\ aA_i)$ & not-$(\forall i)\ (A_i\ aA_j)$ [did Aristotle mean: ... & not-$(\exists i)\ (A_i\ aA_j)$?]. A_j is the first element in the definition of S. Let $\phi_n - A_j$ be ϕ_j: now carry out the same procedure on ϕ_j: the element selected from ϕ_j will be the second element of the definition of S. Carry on in this way until all of ϕ_n is exhausted.

This procedure assumes that at every stage there is a unique A_i satisfying the selection requirements. If there is ever more than one such A_i, then perhaps some arbitrary ordering procedure could be harmlessly superadded; but if there is *no* such A_i then the procedure breaks down. The assumption that there is always at least one such A_i is equivalent to the assumption that (3) can always be ordered by subsumption. The falsity of this assumption has already been seen.

(c) 97^{a}35–^{b}6: The last paragraph is not one of Aristotle's clearest; I offer the following paraphrase: 'That ϕ_n is a complete definition of S is seen as follows: the defining process begins by taking the first A_i, viz. A_1, and, noting that every S in A_1 is either A_2 or A^*_2, by grasping that S is A_2; then it treats this new whole—viz. $(A_1\ A_2)$—in the same way to elicit A_3. When the final whole is reached—(. . . $((A_1\ A_2)$ . . .$)A_n)$ (call it A_s)—it is clear that there is no further divisional pair A_{n+1}/A^*_{n+1} such that every S in A_s is either A_{n+1} or A^*_{n+1}—or rather that, whether or not there is such a pair, at any rate no A_s belongs to a different sort from any S. Now A_s cannot contain anything *not* in the definition of S, since the A_is were selected as essential predicates. Nor can there be any item A^* which is not in A_s but is in the definition of S. For A^* would have to be either the kind or the difference of S; it cannot be the kind of S, since A_1—or rather (. . . $((A_1\ A_2)$ . . .$)A_{n-1})$—is that; and it cannot be a difference because A_s has no, or no relevant, differences.'

Aristotle's argument is sound; but again only on the undefended and indefensible assumption that all the definitional elements of S can be uniquely arranged in a descending order.

97^{a}38: "—or rather . . .": "or" is corrective; any differences there may be within A_s will not be *specific* differences between S and some other species in A_s.

97^{b}2: "it would have to be either a kind . . .": an improved version of the argument at 96^{b}6–10.

97^{b}7: The illustration at 97^{b}15–25 (cf. *EN* $\varDelta$ 7–9; *EE* $\varGamma$ 5) illuminates the abstract prescription of 97^{b}7–15. Aristotle does not say whether this method of hunting definitions is alternative or complementary to the method of division.

Aristotle thinks that we acquire general concepts by a process of abstraction (cf. *Phys A* 1; *APst B* 19); he now suggests that we can define those concepts by, so to speak, justifying our acquisition of them.

Suppose we have to define S. We first take the *infimae species* of S—say S_1, S_2, S_3—and consider the sets of individuals $\{\mathbf{a}_1, \mathbf{a}_2 \ldots\}$ in S_1, $\{\mathbf{b}_1, \mathbf{b}_2 \ldots\}$ in S_2 and $\{\mathbf{c}_1, \mathbf{c}_2 \ldots\}$ in S_3. The $\mathbf{a}_i$s are all "similar and undifferentiated" (97^{b}7) since they belong to the same *infima species*. Next, we collect the attributes common to all the $\mathbf{a}_i$s—the set $\phi_\mathbf{a}$—and similarly for the $\mathbf{b}_i$s and the $\mathbf{c}_i$s. Finally, ϕ_s is formed by selecting all and only the common members of $\phi_\mathbf{a}$, $\phi_\mathbf{b}$, and $\phi_\mathbf{c}$ (ϕ_s is the intersection of $\phi_\mathbf{a}$ and $\phi_\mathbf{b}$ and $\phi_\mathbf{c}$): is ϕ_s is non-empty, then its members conjunctively constitute the definition of S; if ϕ_s is empty, S is ambiguous (it will have three senses if $\phi_\mathbf{a}$, $\phi_\mathbf{b}$, and $\phi_\mathbf{c}$ have no overlap at all, and two senses if any pair of $\phi_\mathbf{a}$, $\phi_\mathbf{b}$, and $\phi_\mathbf{c}$ have a non-empty intersection).

There are three standing objections to any such abstractionist account of the definition of general terms. First, it seems clear that the abstractionist will often collect far too many attributes in ϕ_s: there are many predicates non-essential to men and yet shared by all men (e.g. "having hairless palms", "being red-blooded", "being less than 10 feet tall"). The abstractionist will wrongly put these into his definition.

Secondly, abstractionism is likely to produce a non-empty ϕ_s in cases of ambiguous S: if S is *mole*, ϕ_s will contain at least *physical object*, and this will then count as the definition of *mole*. The procedure will not allow us to distinguish between the animal and the artefact.

Thirdly, abstractions cannot account for those general terms whose instances do not have any set of features in common. The stock example is the term *game*: the word "game", it is said, is not ambiguous; yet there are no features which *all* games—tennis, poker, polo, solitaire—have in common: rather, games are united by a looser 'family resemblance'.

Aristotle has at least a partial answer to these criticisms; it is implicit in his requirement that we find the features which belong to magnanimous men *as such* (97^{b}17)—i.e. the features each has in virtue of being a magnanimous man. All other features, whether peculiar to individual Ss or common to all our initial set, can be disregarded. This amounts to the stipulation that ϕ_a is constituted by those predicates which are common to every a_i and which belong to a_i in virtue of the fact that a_i is an S. This saps, but does not entirely destroy, the force of the first objection: it ensures that ϕ_s will not contain any accidental features of S; but it does not exclude non-definitive necessary features of S from ϕ_s.

The further stipulation—not explicit in Aristotle but obvious enough (see 96^{a}32)—that the conjuncts of ϕ_s should together entail S, is sufficient to overcome the second objection. And the third objection seems to me to have no power.

Aristotle's 'abstractionism' is, I think, less objectionable than it seemed at first sight: that is so at least in part because abstraction, on closer examination, plays no very serious part in it.

97^{b}25: The last section of *B* 13 contains four notes only loosely interconnected.

(*a*) 97^{b}25: "Every definition is ... universal": i.e. 'every *definiens* holds universally of its *definiendum*'. The doctor is not prescribing medicines to make eyes healthy but determining or defining what state of an eye—or of a particular sort of eye (e.g. a human eye)—is a healthy state. The commentators attach this note to the preceding section: since the two putative *definientia* of *magnanimity* do not belong to all cases of magnanimity, the term "magnanimous" must cover two *definienda*.

(*b*) 97^{b}28: "the particulars" and "undifferentiated items" are *infimae species*, not individuals. The more general a term, the more easily its homonymy will escape our notice, because (presumably) we are likely to have to consider more cases of the more general term before we hit upon its homonymy.

(c) *97ᵇ31*: On clarity in definition see *Top Z* 2, where homonymy and metaphor appear as the first two sources of obscurity. "The particulars which you have mentioned" (97ᵇ33) are individuals of the kind stated or laid down for definition. For the examples of similarity and sharpness see *B* 17, 99ᵃ11–15; *Top A* 15, 106ᵃ12–20.

(d) *97ᵇ37*: For similar judgements on metaphor see e.g. *Top Δ* 3, 123ᵃ33–7; *I* 17, 176ᵇ14–25; *Metr B* 3, 357ᵃ24–32. On metaphor in general: *Rhet Γ* 2, 10–11; *Poet* 21, 1457ᵇ6–33.

CHAPTER 14

"The things about which deductions are, are the problems" (*Top A* 4, 101ᵇ16). To set a problem is to pose a question of the form: "Is *P* the case or not?"; and to answer a problem is to provide a deduction concluding either to *P* or to not-*P* (*Top A* 4, 101ᵇ15–36; 11, 104ᵇ1–5). To "get to grips with" a problem (98ᵃ1) is probably to acquire premisses appropriate to its solution (cf. *APr A* 27, 43ᵇ1). The method Aristotle offers is a good way of tackling problems just in so far as it leads to their easy solution. (See LENNOX (1987), 97–9.)

The method consists in the construction (by division) of a tree of the genus and species of the subject under study, and in the assembly (by reference to the anatomies) of all those predicates holding universally of the genus or of its species. With this machinery our problems can be solved demonstratively: we want to know if *S* is *P* or not. *S* is shown to be *P* provided that *P* is among the predicates assembled against some species *S'* which is above *S* in the relevant tree. In such a case a deduction is forthcoming; and the machinery ensures that the deduction is demonstrative, thus answering the question *why S is P*.

APr A 27, 43ᵇ1–40, describes a more elaborate machinery for tackling problems; the elaborations are due to the fact that non-demonstrative deductions are acceptable in the context of the chapter.

98ᵃ2: ". . . the anatomies and the divisions": the use of the divisions is straightforward (Aristotle himself compiled several books of 'divisions' —Bonitz, 104ᵃ21–33—and such compilation was a common practice in the Academy). The 'anatomies' are less clear. Aristotle wrote *Anatomies*, which seem to have been detailed anatomical descriptions of animals based on dissection (Bonitz, 104ᵃ3–17). Since Pacius, however, the commentators have felt the need to find a different sort of 'anatomies' in our passage, and they have supposed that Aristotle is referring to some logical exercises about which we know nothing. Such a supposition requires us to take "anatomies" in a singular sense; and the reasons advanced in its favour (and collected by Ross) seem very feeble. I prefer to refer "anatomies" to the *Anatomies* (cf. esp. *PA Γ* 14, 674ᵇ17~98ᵃ17).

98ᵃ10: "*C, D, E,* individual animals": i.e. 'individual *species of* animal'.

98ᵃ13: Cf. *A* 5, 74ᵃ17–25; *APr A* 35.—Aristotle follows his own advice and regularly attends to 'anonymous' characteristics—i.e. characteristics only describable by periphrasis. The illustration goes like this: 'Why do cows have a third stomach?—Because they have no top incisors (and hence need some other aid to digestion).—And why do they have no top incisors?—Because they have horns (which use up all the tough tooth-material available to them)' (*PA* Γ 14, 674ᵃ22–ᵇ17; cf. 2, 663ᵇ31–664ᵃ3). See further BALME (1987), 86–8; GOTTHELF (1987), 178–85; LENNOX (1987), 114–18.

98ᵃ13: "At present we argue . . .": I take Aristotle to be referring to the ways of contemporary biologists, who limit themselves to attributes expressible by a single common term. The orthodox but less plausible reading translates: "At present we are speaking . . ."; and glosses: 'In the last section we were speaking . . .'.

98ᵃ20: Analogies are a profound feature of Aristotle's biology; for the present illustration see Bonitz, 535ᵃ43–51 (and for the squid's pounce: *HA* Δ 1, 524ᵇ22–8; for the 'spine', here used specifically of the bone-structure of fish: Bonitz, 23ᵇ51–24ᵃ14; on bones: *PA* *B* 9). 'Why does X's flesh remain rigid?—Because X has a pounce (where X is "squid") or a spine (where X is "fish") or bones (where X is, e.g., "man")'. (Cf. *PA* *B* 8, 654ᵃ19–26; *HA* Δ 7, 532ᵃ31–ᵇ3.)

Aristotelian analogies are almost invariably functional; why then can we not "take any one identical thing which ⟨all the analogous parts⟩ should be called" (98ᵃ21)? If the parts all fulfil some function F, then the "one identical thing" can be named by the term "substance fulfilling function F". Aristotle would argue that this term does not pick out any 'nature'; it is a purely formal description and (necessarily) does not specify the stuff or shape of the substance concerned; but a 'nature' needs material as well as formal specification.

CHAPTER 15

Aristotle means to describe two ways in which a pair of problems may be connected, but he does not express his meaning very clearly. Suppose two problems, *Is S P or not?* and *Is S' P' or not?* These may be connected first (98ᵃ24–9) if *S is P* and *S' is P'* are both demonstrated through a middle term M or through middle terms M and M' which are forms of some kind K; or secondly (98ᵃ29–34) if $S = S'$ and P' is the middle term in the proof of S is P.

On 'reciprocity', *antiperistasis*, see Ross; on reflection, *anaklasis*, see e.g. *Metr B* 9, 370ᵃ16–25. For echoes, [*Probl*] *IA* 8; mirrors, e.g., *Sens* 2, 438ᵃ5–10; rainbows, *A* 13, 79ᵃ11, notes: in these three cases the middle term will be the same in kind but different in form, either as holding of different things (reflection of sound in the first case, of light in the latter two) or as holding in a different way (light is bent in one way by rain-drops, in another by mirrors). Aristotle wrote a book on the *Flooding of the Nile*, of which we have a Latin epitome (frags. 246–8 R³); the problem was a standing one for Greek scientists.

CHAPTER 16

The language of *B* 16 suggests at first that Aristotle is reopening the questions already answered in *B* 12 about the temporal relations between *explanans* and *explanandum*. But the argument of the chapter shows that the temporal language is being used in a logical sense: the problem of the chapter is, in short, to determine whether an *explanans* constitutes both a necessary and a sufficient condition for its *explanandum*.

98ª35:   Thus suppose that *C* is *A* because of *B*; i.e. that *AaC*, through a middle term *B*. Then, Aristotle asks, is it the case (i) that *BaA*, and (ii) that *AaB*? It is evident from the whole of *APst* that the answer to (ii) is affirmative; Aristotle here suggests that the answer to (i) might be affirmative as well—for if *B* does *not* always hold when *A* holds, there must be some other explanation of *A*'s holding; so that *B* is not after all the correct explanation ($98^{b}2$). It is this latter suggestion which is the controversial one, and which the rest of the chapter takes up. There are three arguments.

98ᵇ4:   *Argument (A)*, that it cannot be the case that *BaA*: 'If we had both *AaB* and *BaA* we should be able to demonstrate both *AaC* and *BaC*; but that, as *A* 3 showed, is not possible' ($98^{b}4$–16). To this objection Aristotle replies, in the manner of *A* 13: 'There would, indeed, be both a syllogism concluding to *AaC* and one concluding to *BaC*; but only the former would be a genuine demonstration of the reasoned fact—the latter is either no demonstration at all or else (as *B* 16 actually has it) only a demonstration of the fact' ($98^{b}16$–24). The illustrations and the argument run closely parallel to those of *A* 13; but *B* 16 adds one important point, won by the discussions of *B* 3–12: "an explanation is prior to what it is explanatory of" ($98^{b}17$) and the priority is definitional ($98^{b}22$). Thus the argument through *B* to *AaC* is the proper demonstration provided only that *B* is an element in the definition of *A*, and not vice versa.

98ᵇ25:   *Argument (B)*, that it need not be the case that *BaA*. In Aristotle's terminology, "*B* is explanatory of *A*" is elliptical for "*B* is explanatory of *A* for *C*"—i.e. "*B* explains why *C* is *A*". Thus there are 'several explanations of one thing' if there are distinct terms *B*, *C*, such that *B* explains why *D* is *A*, and *C* explains why *E* is *A*. If we have *AaB*, *AaC*, *BaD*, *CaE*, and if both *AaB* and *AaC* are immediate, then (granted certain other obvious assumptions) both *B* and *C* will be explanatory of the same thing, viz. *A*. For possible illustrations see *A* 13, 78ª14–21; *A* 29.

98ᵇ29:   "Hence when the explanation holds . . .": i.e. 'If *B* is explanatory of *A* for anything, then if *B* holds of *X*, *A* holds of *X*; but if *A* holds of *X*, and *B* is explanatory of *A* for something, it does not follow that *B* holds of *X*—there must be *some Y* explanatory of *A* for *X*, but it need not be *B*.'

98ᵇ32: *Argument* (C), that *BaA* must hold. The editors take (C) to give Aristotle's 'real' answer. But the section is as tentatively expressed as its predecessor; argument (C) is by no means conclusive; and the question of *B* 16 continues into *B* 17. Plainly *B* 16 is aporematic, and Aristotle's considered view is not to be sought inside it.

The argument is obscure; and both syntax and sense are in parts uncertain. The following comments are tentative. By "problems are always universal" I take Aristotle to mean that the conclusion of any explanatory demonstration will always be of the form *AaC*; and by "the explanation is some whole" he means that the premisses will have the form *AaB* and *BaC*. In that case, "what it is explanatory of must be universal". What does this dark phrase signify? The illustrative example should help. "Shedding leaves" is substituted for *A*, and the whole to which it is "determined" is evidently *C*. *A* "holds of these items universally", i.e. *AaC*. In addition, *A* "is determined to" *C*, even if *C* "has forms". Here I suppose that Aristotle is harking back to his previous example, where we had both *AaD* and *AaE*: if this is so, he now suggests, then *D* and *E* will be forms or species of *C*, so that *A* will be *limited to* *C*; thus *A* is 'determined to' *C* inasmuch as *CaA*. Now given *CaA* and *BaC*, we may infer that *BaA*, so that "the middle term and what it is explanatory of . . . must convert".

The argument, thus reconstructed, is valid (some reconstructions present Aristotle with an evidently invalid argument); but it lacks probative force. For Aristotle does not explain why *A* must be determined to *C* in this fashion: why, we must ask, should *D* and *E* be species of *C*?

98ᵇ36–8 perhaps suggest a different line of thought. Suppose that trees in general shed their leaves because of solidification. Then (1) "if a tree . . .": i.e. if, e.g., oaks shed their leaves, then their moisture solidifies; and (2) "if solidification . . .": i.e. if the moisture of, e.g., oaks solidifies, then oaks shed their leaves. Aristotle is not thinking of leaf-shedding in general, but of the leaf-shedding *of trees*; and consequently he is not interested in solidification in general, but in solidification *in trees*. Perhaps, then, this is the sense in which *A* is "determined to" *C*; and if we assume that our terms are limited in this way (or, in a modern jargon, that the universe of discourse is limited to, e.g., trees), then *A* and *B* will convert: given that we are talking exclusively about trees, then every leaf-dropper is a solidifier and vice versa.

CHAPTER 17

99ᵃ1: Suppose that we have two arguments, (*a*) *AaB*, *BaC* ⊢ *AaC*, and (*b*) *AaD*, *DaE* ⊢ *AaE*; each is claimed to be an explanatory demonstration. Aristotle considers briefly several cases (six, in all probability) in which this claim might be made.

(i) Both (*a*) and (*b*) are full demonstrations (99ᵃ2). Then in (*a*) *B* is 'the account' of *A*, and in (*b*) *D* is 'the account' of *A*. A single term cannot have two accounts; hence if B and D are distinct, (a) and (b) are not both explanatory demonstrations.

APst, however, does not commit Aristotle to the view that the middle term in a demonstration must express the whole definition of the major; the most it requires is that the middle should express part of the definition of the major (and it probably does not require even this). But then it is clearly a possibility that both B and D should represent parts of the definition of A, and hence that (a) and (b) should both be explanatory.

(ii) Either AaC or AaE is shown "in virtue of a sign" (99ᵃ3) (see *APr* B 27 for sign arguments). Aristotle implies (99ᵃ4) that in this case it *is* possible for both (a) and (b) to be explanatory deductions; but sign arguments infer cause from effect, so that if either (a) or (b) is a sign argument it is not an explanatory deduction.

(iii) Either AaC or AaE is proved incidentally (99ᵃ3). "But such things are not thought to count as problems" (99ᵃ6). If a genuine problem has as its solution the conclusion that the moon is eclipsed (AaC), then we might "inquire incidentally . . . about what it is explanatory of" (99ᵃ5) by asking whether BaC (where B is any incidental attribute of eclipses, e.g. that of terrifying the superstitious); and we might inquire incidentally "about what it is explanatory for" by asking whether AaE (where E is any incidental attribute of the moon, e.g. being the home of Artemis). Only the latter case is strictly relevant here. AaE does not give rise to a 'problem' because it is an incidental connection, and such connections have no explanation. Hence, given (iii), (a) and (b) are not both explanatory demonstrations.

At 99ᵃ6 the word "otherwise" (*ei . . . mē*) is generally expanded into: 'If they *are* treated as problems . . .'; in that case what I list as (iv) and (v) are in fact two examples of (iii). But Ross argues plausibly that "otherwise" is parallel to "if the conclusions have been demonstrated . . ." (99ᵃ2) and "if they have not . . ." (99ᵃ4); thus it introduces a further pair of cases, parallel and not subordinate to (iii).

(iv) "if they are in a kind . . .": i.e. 'If C and E are both species of some kind G, then B and D will both be species of some kind G'; ⟨and in that case neither (a) nor (b) will be properly explanatory. Explanation must come from a deduction with G' as its middle term⟩.' The case is illustrated at 99ᵃ8–11. (For the illustration cf. A 5, 74ᵃ18, notes.) The major premiss of the argument was implicit in the reasoning of B 16, 98ᵇ34; again, Aristotle offers nothing in its support.

(v) "if the items are homonymous . . .": i.e. 'If C and E are homonymous in (a) and (b), both bearing the 'name' A, but in a different sense, then B and D are homonymous in (a) and (b), for the same reason.' Hence both (a) and (b) may be demonstrative, but uninterestingly so; for, given (v), they do not supply genuine instances of different explanations for some *one* feature.

Case (v) is illustrated at 99ᵃ11–15. The account of similar figures is the same as that found at Euclid, vi def. 1; the account of similar colours is singular: it presumably means that X and Y are similar in

colour if they are perceptually indistinguishable in respect of colour.
(vi) 99^{a}15: if C and E are "the same by analogy" then so too are B
and D (cf. B 14, 98^{a}20–3). Aristotle implies, I think, that here (a) and
(b) do not offer *different* explanations for the same thing; but he seems
to concede all that an opponent could want: in any pair of cases (a) and
(b), there will of course be an *analogy* between B and D (for by
construction each explains the occurrence of some one term A); yet for
all that, B and D may be, in a clear sense, different terms.

99^{a}16:   This section enlarges upon the argument of B 16, 98^{b}32–8.
Suppose n arguments of the form: $AaB, BaC_1 \vdash AaC_1$; $AaB, BaC_2 \vdash$
AaC_2; . . . ; $AaB, BaC_n \vdash AaC_n$. Then "if the items are taken severally",
A "extends further" than each; i.e. $(\forall i)\ (AaC_i \rightarrow (\exists j)\ (i \neq j\ \&\ AaC_j)$.
"But if they are taken all together it extends equally"; i.e. if C is the
disjunction of all the C_is, then $AaC\ \&\ CaA$. "Similarly for the middle
term": i.e. the same argument goes through if A is replaced by B. (For
the mathematical illustration see A 24, 86^{a}1; and with the argument in
general cf. *APr B* 23, 68^{b}18–29.)
If we suppose that B is the primitive middle term (99^{a}25), i.e. that
AaB is immediate, then B gives the definition of A. Working from the
other direction, we can find some term D such that DaC_i is immediate
for every C_i (99^{a}26). Finally, there may be one or more middle terms
between B and D (99^{a}27). (The illustration is familiar from B 16; "the
connection of the seed" (99^{a}29) is said to mean "the joint between leaf
and stem".)
The argument in this section makes some little advance over 98^{b}32–8.
It is true that Aristotle gives us no new reason for thinking that A will be
coextensive with—i.e. will convert with—all the C_is taken together. The
C_is are supposed to comprise all the species of some genus (e.g. the
genus of trees); and A is doubtless intended to be 'determined to' this
genus. But, again, there is no argument to show that it *must* be so
determined. We do, however, get a new reason for holding that the first
premiss, AaB, in an explanatory demonstration must convert, i.e. that
BaA must also hold. For B is said to be the definition of A, and
a *definiens* must have the same extension as its *definiendum*. More
precisely, Aristotle claims that the primary major premiss in any demonstrative chain must be a definition and hence must convert. ('Why may
not B simply be *part* of the definition of A, the part which, so to speak,
explains why A holds of C?'—Well, if D is the definition of A, and B is a
part of D, then we shall be able to derive AaB from AaD and DaB, so
that AaB will not be a primitive proposition.)

99^{a}30:   This section ends (99^{b}4–7) with a clear answer to Aristotle's
question: there cannot be different explanations of the same attribute for
different *individuals* of the same species; but there *can* be different
explanations of the same attribute for different *types* of thing. And
Aristotle's example (for which see *Long Vit* 4–6; *PA Δ* 2, 677^{a}30–^{b}1;

APr A 23, 68ᵇ15–29) makes it unequivocally clear that in some cases at least the answers to the questions: Why is *C A*? and: Why is *E A*? may be different.

The argument which leads to this conclusion is, however, uncertain. It begins by promising a 'schematic' presentation of the interrelation between *explanans* and *explanandum*. "Schematically" translates *epi tōn schēmatōn*, literally "in the case of the figures". We would naturally suppose this to mean "considered syllogistically"; but the consideration that follows is not syllogistic, and we must, I suppose, follow the traditional explanation of the phrase which refers the 'figures' to the letters used in setting out the examples. The two examples 'schematically' treated, moreover, do not illustrate the interrelations sketched in the preceding section (99ᵃ16–29); rather, they hark back to *B* 16, 98ᵇ25–31, with which the preceding section is at odds.

Ross notes the connection with 98ᵇ25–31; but he thinks that he can reconcile the doctrine of 98ᵇ25–31 with that of 99ᵃ16–29: Aristotle, he thinks, "*is taking for granted* two syllogisms which connect *B* and *C* respectively with *A* through a middle term definitory of *A*". Thus a complete demonstrative chain for, say, *AaD*, will begin with some premiss *AaF* where *F* is a definition of *A*; but lower down in the chain, the middle term will not be definitive and the premisses will not convert. And it is one of these lower, non-definitive, middle terms, say *B*, which is, properly speaking, explanatory of *AaD*.

This account is, I think, self-consistent and consistent with the letter of the text; moreover, it effects a pleasant syncretism between the divergent views of the earlier parts of *B* 17 and *B* 16. But it is somewhat contrived; and the text gives no hint of it: I suspect there is no reconciliation.

99ᵃ34: "I call universal . . .": this use of *katholou* and the complementary use of "primitive universal" are unique.

99ᵃ36: ". . . *A* must extend alongside further than *B*: if it does not, why will *B* be explanatory rather than *A*?" (99ᵃ36–7): i.e. 'We must have *AaB* but not *BaA*. For suppose *AaB* & *BaA*: then we should have no reason to choose between *AaB*, *BaC* ⊢ *AaC* and *BaA*, *AaC* ⊢ *BaC* as our explanatory demonstration.' Could Aristotle have written this, without gloss or apology, immediately after writing 99ᵃ21 (which says that *AaB must* convert) and 98ᵇ19–24 (which explains how we should discriminate between the two candidate demonstrations)?

99ᵃ38: If for every *i* AaE_i, then "all of them together will be some one thing different from *B*"; i.e. for some *C* distinct from *B* we shall have *CaE*. Aristotle gives a reason for this; and then, in the parenthetical sentences, he indicates that he is not yet clear about the matter. "If not . . .": i.e. 'unless there is such a *C* you will not be able to say that *AaE* whereas not-*EaA*'. We are evidently still assuming that *AaD*, where *D* is distinct from *E*: hence not-*EaA*. Perhaps the thought is this: since *E* is distinct from *A*, there must be some reason why *AaE*, and unless you can grasp that reason, *C*, then you cannot properly affirm that *AaE*.

"Why will there not be . . .": i.e. 'given that we have B in the case of the D_is, it is only reasonable to suppose that we shall have C in the case of the E_is'. This sentence is introduced by the word *gar* ("for"); but it is not clear whether Aristotle intends it to offer an explanation of the immediately preceding sentence, or rather to provide a second reason for the general thesis of the paragraph.

However that may be, the parenthesis at 99^b2-3 shows that Aristotle was aware of the weakness of the preceding lines. The general frailty of this section, and the fact that it fits ill into its context, lead to the suspicion that, despite superficial appearances, it does not give Aristotle's last word on the issue raised in *B* 16. In that case, we do not have Aristotle's last word.

CHAPTER 18

This chapter considers *ex professo* a question which we have already met with incidentally (above, p. 155) and which the end of *B* 17 has tacitly posed again (and tacitly answered). Suppose we have a conclusion AaD mediated by n middle terms, $B_1, B_2, \ldots, B_n$ (AaB_1, B_naD, and each B_iaB_{i+1} are immediate). Thus there are n candidate demonstrations of AaD: which is the truly explanatory demonstration? which B_i is explanatory of A for D? Aristotle takes the simplest case, in which $n = 2$ ($B_1 = B$, $B_2 = C$); and he answers that C is explanatory. His argument for this answer is poor: 'Since C certainly explains BaD, it explains AaD.' Pacius observes that if you at first cite only B in explanation of AaD you will be obliged eventually to cite C if you are to give a full explanation; if this is true, it works equally well with B and C reversed. It is indeed surprising that Aristotle himself did not notice this point, and that he never questioned the tacit presupposition of *B* 18 that just one of B and C must be 'the' explanation of AaD. For, given Aristotle's notion of explanation, it seems very plausible to suggest that AaD is explained by reference to *all* the propositions used in its demonstration, or at least by reference to all the first principles on which its demonstration depends— and in either case *all* the terms which mediate AaD will be equally involved in its explanation.

99^b7: "If the explanations do not at once arrive at what is atomic": i.e. 'if the first middle term between A and D does not yield a pair of immediate propositions AaX, XaD'. Thus Mure and Ross; earlier editors attach the sentence to the end of *B* 17, and read "what is atomic" as "what is individual"; this gives a good sense, but it makes the end of *B* 17 somewhat prolix and the beginning of *B* 18 somewhat abrupt.

99^b9: "the one which is primitive in the direction of the universal . . .": i.e. B, which is immediately connected to A, the most general term in the series.

99^b11: "the one nearest to what it is explanatory for": the explanatory term is explanatory of *A for D*; and the 'nearest' term to *D*, i.e. the term immediately connected to *D*, is *C*. Thus "the nearest . . ." denotes *C*.

99^{b}12: "this term explains why the primitive term falls under the universal": "this term" refers to *C*, "the primitive term" to *D*, and "the universal" to *B* (as the next clause makes clear).

This is, I think, the appropriate place to discuss a doctrine about which I have so far said nothing; I mean the doctrine of the Commensurate Universal. In its most extreme form this doctrine states that the premisses of a demonstration must be 'universal' in the strong sense of being about 'commensurate' universals—in short, that they must convert. (If *AaB* and *BaA*, then *A* and *B* are commensurate, or coextensive.) See e.g. KULLMANN (1974), 183.

The terminology of the doctrine is not Aristotelian. Some think that Aristotle's phrase for the commensurate universal is "primitive universal" (see *B* 17, 99^{a}34—*A* 4, 74^{a}3, and *B* 19, 100^{a}16, connect "primitive" and "universal" in quite different ways); but this is plainly wrong (*pace* INWOOD (1979)).

The doctrine is not explicit in Aristotle. Some have found it at *A* 4, 74^{a}3, where what holds universally of *B* is contrasted with what extends "further than *B*". Others have found the doctrine at *B* 17, 99^{a}16–29; but there (see p. 255) Aristotle allows immediate premises which are noncommensurate (the *DaC$_{i}$*s).

Is the doctrine implicit in Aristotle? Four arguments have suggested that it is. First, the premisses of demonstrations are definitions, and definitions all convert (cf. *A* 12, 78^{a}12).—But Aristotle does not, I think, really believe that all the premisses of every demonstration are full definitions (though see p. 107). Secondly, I2-predications convert, and every demonstration consists of I2-predications.—But it is not quite clear that every I2-predication must convert (see p. 113); and even if Aristotle does sometimes assume that every demonstration must contain at least one I2-predication, he neither justifies this assumption nor makes the stronger assumption that every demonstration must consist solely of I2-predications.

Thirdly, there is an argument of Zabarella's: ". . . no predicate can belong to its subject primitively unless it is coextensive with it; for if it extends further and belongs in another subject too, then it will not belong in that primitively, but in some other prior to it—viz. the common kind which embraces these two subjects."—Zabarella assumes that if *AaB* and *AaC*, then for some *D* prior to *B* and *C*, *AaD*. But Aristotle argues against this principle at *A* 23, 84^{b}3–18; he implies its falsity at *A* 3, 73^{a}17; and he countenances its negation at *B* 16, 98^{b}26–8 (cf. *APr B* 21, 66^{b}20). Finally, there is the position discussed in *B* 16–17, that explanatory middle terms must convert.—But in so far as *B* 16–17 reach any conclusion, it is against rather than for this position.

There is, in any case, excellent evidence that Aristotle did not adhere to the doctrine of the commensurate universal: he says explicitly once, and he implies more than once, that convertible propositions are not the rule in demonstrations (*A* 3, 73^{a}18; cf. *A* 12, 78^{a}6–12; *A* 13, 78^{a}29, ^{b}11). What should Aristotle have said about the doctrine? Some of the principles of every demonstrative science are definitions; and definitions convert: hence some premisses of some demonstrations will deal with commensurate universals. But there is, as far as I can see, no reason for Aristotle to adopt anything stronger than this rather humdrum thesis.

CHAPTER 19

The subject of this celebrated chapter is our apprehension of first principles. Aristotle's view on this topic has already been intimated in *APst* (cf. *A* 2, 71^{b}16; 3, 72^{b}18–25) and it is worked out, in a fashion closely parallel to that of *B* 19, in the first chapter of the *Metaphysics*. The source of *B* 19 is to be found in Plato: "Is it the blood with which we think, or air, or fire? Or none of these but rather the brain, which supplies the senses of hearing and seeing and smelling—and from these memory and opinion might come about, and from memory and opinion, when they come to rest, understanding comes about in the same way?" (*Phaedo* 96^b; cf. *Phaedrus*, 249^b). Socrates is reporting his early cogitations on natural science; and it is probable that the theory he describes here was advanced by some earlier thinker.

B 19 raises numerous problems, of general and of detailed interpretation. It is well to begin by stating three puzzles which affect the chapter as a whole. First, *B* 19 is Janus-faced, looking in one direction towards empiricism, and in the other towards rationalism. The principles are apprehended by 'induction' (*epagōgē*) in an honest empiricist way; but they are also grasped by *nous*, or 'intuition' as it is normally translated, in the easy rationalist fashion. It is a classic problem in Aristotelian scholarship to explain or reconcile these two apparently opposing aspects of Aristotle's thought. (There is an excellent statement of the problem in Le Blond (1), 131–40; cf. 274, 371 n. 2; and Lee, 118–24.)

Secondly, the opening section of *B* 19 pretends to broach a new subject, the apprehension of the principles. Yet a major portion of Book *B* has, it seems, been devoted to just this topic: definitions are principles, and a chief aim of the book has been to explain how we may come to grasp definitions. Does *B* 19 belong to a different stratum of Aristotle's thought? Or are the two attempts to account for our apprehension of the principles complementary?

Thirdly, most commentators have found a deep-seated ambiguity in *B* 19: its 'principles' vacillate between primitive propositions and primitive terms. On the one hand, if Aristotle means to talk about the principles of demonstrations, he should be speaking of propositions; on the other hand, much of the language of *B* 19 suggests that he is speaking of concept-acquisition. Was Aristotle guilty of a gross confusion? Or is there some way out? (There is a clear statement of this puzzle in Solmsen, 95–101.)

I shall return briefly to these three puzzles at the end of my comments. The chapter begins with a short preamble (99^{b}15–19), which indicates that the official goal of the *Analytics*, announced at *APr A* 1, 24^{a}10–11, has been achieved, and which then poses a further and supplementary object of study. The body of the chapter then divides into three parts: first, Aristotle states the two questions he wants to discuss (99^{b}20–6); then follows a long answer to what I shall call the first question (99^{b}26–100^{b}5); and finally there is a short answer to the second question (100^{b}5–17).

99^{b}20: The two questions about our apprehension of the principles are stated at 99^{b}18, and elaborated in 99^{b}22–6. The *first question* about the principles asks "how they become familiar". The *second question* asks "what is the state which gets to know them". Both questions presuppose that we do know the principles: Aristotle refers back (99^{b}21) to *A* 2, 72^{b}25–^{b}4, where he argued that if we have demonstrative knowledge, then we know the principles; he takes it as evident that we do have demonstrative knowledge.

The second question is reformulated at 99^{b}22–4 in a somewhat negligent manner. I paraphrase as follows: 'Is knowledge of the principles the same sort of knowledge as knowledge of the theorems? i.e. do we have understanding of the principles as we do of the theorems, or is there rather some other sort of knowledge of the principles?'

The first question is restated at 99^{b}25 in terms of the phrase "the states present in us". "State" translates *hexis*, the verbal noun from *echein* ("have"). Aristotle regularly uses the word of mental dispositions, especially of cognitive and virtuous ones (Bonitz, 261^{a}13–24). There is a temptation to slide from "disposition" to "faculty"; to observe the apparent appropriateness of the term "faculty" for *hexis* at 99^{b}18; and to conclude that *hexis* means "faculty" throughout *B* 19. If that is so, the first question comes to ask whether the faculty by which we apprehend the principles is innate or not. The question is indubitably Aristotelian; for the faculty turns out to be *nous*, and the problem of the origins of *nous* is debated (with notorious obscurity) at *GA B* 3 (cf. *An A* 4, 408^{b}18–19).

Nevertheless, this is not Aristotle's question in *B* 19. First, he talks of states (*hexeis*: plural) and not of a single state or faculty; secondly, the initial formulation of the question at 99^{b}18 hardly suggests inquiry into the origins of a faculty; and thirdly, Aristotle's answer simply cannot be accommodated to this question. Thus 'states', in the first question at least, are 'havings' or graspings: "the states are present in us" (99^{b}25) means ."the graspings are in us", i.e. "we already grasp ⟨the principles⟩", i.e. "we already know ⟨the principles⟩". In reading the translation it may help to bear in mind that the Greek for "state" is cognate with the Greek for "grasp" or "possess"; English does not allow this connection to appear.

Are there 'states' "present in us" (*enousai*)? *Eneinai*, "be (present) in", does not *mean* "be innate in" (cf. e.g. *A* 10, 76^{b}30: *sumphutos* (e.g.

Met A 9, 993^{a}1) is Aristotle's word for "innate"). Similarly, at 99^{b}26 and 31 *echein* ("possess") does not *mean* "possess innately". (*Echein* is the converse relation to *eneinai*; cf. *EN H* 3, 1147^{a}34.) Nevertheless, when Aristotle asks if the states are 'present in us' he certainly means to ask whether or not they are innate: the contrast with "come about in us" (99^{b}25) is enough to show this; and it is confirmed by passages in the *Phaedo* and *Meno* where Plato discusses innate knowledge under the heading of knowledge that is "present in us" (cf. *Phaedo* 73^a; *Meno* 85^c).

The first question thus runs: 'Do we have innate knowledge of the principles, or is our knowledge acquired? And if it is acquired, how is it acquired?'

99^{b}26: *The First Question Answered*: The dilemma with which Aristotle's discussion opens is stated again, in a slightly different context, at *Met A* 9, 992^{b}24–993^{a}2.

If we suppose that knowledge of principles is *innate* (99^{b}26–7), then we have knowledge which is more exact than that given by demonstration (for the reasons cited at *A* 2, 72^{a}25–^{b}4) and yet this knowledge remains entirely unobserved. ("If it is in fact connate, it is wonderful how we should have the strongest sort of understanding (*epistēmē*) without its being noticed": *Met A* 9, 993^{a}1.) The commentators all take Aristotle to mean that we could not have such knowledge without noticing it *ourselves*; and it is true that Aristotle supposes knowledge, like perception, to be a self-conscious state (cf. *Met A* 9, 1074^{b}35–6); but the text, both in *APst* and in *Met A* 9, is more likely to mean: "it could not escape *others'* notice that we have such knowledge". Aristotle is making the correct and pertinent point that infants evidently do not have the strong abstract knowledge which the innate hypothesis ascribes to them.

Aristotle accepts this argument as conclusive. The standard reaction to it—present already in Plato (*Meno* 86^{a}6; *Phaedo* 73^{c}6)—is to say that the knowledge is present in infants but does not emerge without the operation of some external stimulation. Aristotle would doubtless have adopted Locke's answer to this reaction: it reduces innatism to the uncontroversial hypothesis that human infants have certain innate cognitive *capacities* the exercise of which waits upon experience.

If, then, we suppose that knowledge of the principles is *acquired* (99^{b}27–34), we should infer, by the general principle enunciated in *A* 1, that it is derived from some pre-existing knowledge: we cannot acquire knowledge of the principles if we "are ignorant and possess no state at all" (99^{b}32). Thus, Aristotle concludes, we must have (sc. innately) some 'capacity' or faculty from whose deliverances we can derive our knowledge of the principles; and the deliverances of that faculty must of course be less exact than our knowledge of the principles themselves—for otherwise the argument of 99^{b}26–7 could be deployed again.

Aristotle's argument here is not good: if he is to apply the general principle of *A* 1, then he must conclude that we have some innate *items of knowledge*; and these items, by *A* 2, will be more exact than our resulting knowledge of the principles. Aristotle's conclusion, that we have an innate cognitive *capacity*, has nothing to do with the principle of *A* 1. The fact is that *A* 1, which deals with the 'intellectual learning' of derived propositions, is inapplicable in *B* 19, which is concerned with a non-intellectual acquisition of underivable principles. Our knowledge of the principles does not depend upon any other knowledge at all; and that is merely to say that knowledge of principles is not deduced knowledge. (But see BOLTON (1991), 5 n. 4.) But Aristotle's argument is readily repaired: he need only say that our knowledge of the principles, if it is acquired, must depend upon the exercise of some capacity or other. Aristotle does not have an argument for this assertion: why, it might be asked, should not the principles be put into our minds by chance or divine providence? Aristotle might have maintained that the facts were against this view: our acquisition of the principles does not seem to be a haphazard affair, but to proceed in a regular and intelligible fashion. He might also have argued that the haphazard acquisition of a belief is not enough to support a *knowledge* of the principles: knowledge must be connected with its object; it cannot result from the chance entertainment of a proposition. Thus what is wanted is a causal account of the acquisition of the principles—an account which will link our knowledge of them with the facts they state.

99^{b}34: There is such a capacity, innate in all animals, viz. perception. (It is a definitional truth, in Aristotle's view, that animals can perceive (e.g. *An B* 2, 413^{b}1–4; Bonitz, 19^{b}42–7).) To justify the claim that perception can yield knowledge of the principles, Aristotle needs to give an account of the cognitive path from perception to comprehension; this account makes up the rest of his answer to the first question.

At 100^{a}3–9 four stages along the path are distinguished: understanding is based upon experience, experience upon memory, and memory upon perception. This tallies closely with *Met A* 1, 980^{a}27–981^{a}3. At 99^{b}34–100^{a}3, however, only three stages appear: perception breeds memory, memory leads to an 'account'. Most commentators elicit a fourth stage from 99^{b}39, but that is implausible (see below). Pacius supposes that 99^{b}34–100^{a}3 does not prefigure 100^{a}3–9 but rather distinguishes three types of creature, only the highest of which can undergo the cognitive development that 100^{a}3–9 describes. This ingenious suggestion cannot be squared with the developmental language of 100^{a}2–3. Thus it seems best to take 100^{a}3–9 as correcting and amplifying 99^{b}34–100^{a}3; the three-stage account is expanded to four stages. (At 100^{a}3 the particle *men oun* ("Thus") should perhaps be translated "or rather".)

Stage (A) is perception. Aristotle frequently says that perception *krinei* or is *kritikos* (e.g. *An B* 6, 418^{a}14–16; 11, 424^{a}5–10; *Γ* 2, 426^{b}8–14). *Krinein* may mean either "judge" or "discriminate", and to say that perception is *kritikē* is to say either that perception makes judgements or that it can discriminate. It has been disputed which of these two things

Aristotle means to say. On the whole, it seems more probable that he had discrimination rather than judgement in mind; and I have therefore translated *kritikos* at 99^{b}35 by "discriminatory". The point is not entirely trifling: if *kritikos* is taken here to mean "judgemental", and if a capacity to judge presupposes some conceptual mastery, then Stage (A) will already involve the possession of concepts, and the four-stage account cannot coherently function as an account of concept-acquisition.

Stage (B) deals with the ability to retain a percept, i.e. with (a type of) memory. This stage raises several questions. First, Aristotle occasionally talks of memory in terms of something's 'remaining' in the mind (*Mem* 1, 450^{b}10–11; cf. *Crat* 437^b; [*Def*] 415^a—the English "retention" suggests something less passive than the Greek *monē*, which is literally a 'remaining'); but what 'remains' is properly not a percept or sense-impression but a 'phantasm' or mental image, which is as it were the trace or imprint of a percept (e.g. *Mem* 1, 450^{a}25–^{b}11), and memory requires in addition to this retention the ability to resurrect these imprints (cf. *Mem* 2, 452^{a}10–11).

Secondly, at *Met A* 1, 980^{a}29, and again at *Mem* 1, 450^{a}15–21, Aristotle asserts that some animals do and others do not have memory (cf. 99^{b}36). *Mem* specifies that the memory-less creatures are those which do not perceive time. The zoological works do not take up the point or attempt to identify the animals in question.

Finally, there is a textual crux at 99^{b}39, which seriously affects the sense of the passage. The MSS begin the sentence with the words *en hois d'enestin aisthanomenois* ... (one MS has the trivial variant *estin* for *enestin*): "some animals can, while perceiving, ...". The present participle, *aisthanomenois*, is puzzling, since Stage (B) is concerned with what some animals can do when they are *not* or *no longer* perceiving. Trendelenburg inserted a negative participle, *mē*, before the participle: "some animals can, while not perceiving, ..."; Ueberweg proposed the past participle, *aisthomenois*, in place of the present participle: "some animals can, after they have perceived, ...". One or other of these emendations should probably be accepted, and I have followed Ueberweg and the OCT. (Other remedies are possible; but the general sense is not really in doubt.)

In the OCT, the sentence continues thus: ... *echein eti en tēi psuchēi*. This reading is found in only one MS (the OCT's critical apparatus is inaccurate). Four MSS offer *hen ti* in place of *en tēi*. The majority reading gives the following sense: "some animals can ... still hold some single item in their soul". This 'single item' might be identified with the "single experience" which is generated by many memories of the same thing (100^{a}5); so that 99^{b}34–100^{a}3 will after all describe four, and not three, stages on the road to understanding. But "holding some single item" is a poor way of describing experience inasmuch as experience is distinguished from knowledge by the fact that it grasps the constituents of a unity but not the unity itself; and, further, 100^{a}2 generates Stage (D) directly from Stage (B) without mentioning any intermediate grasping of 'some single item'. Thus it is unlikely that Stage (C) should be read into 99^{b}39; and in that case it seems best to follow the OCT and read *en têi* rather than *hen ti*.

Stage (C) is 'experience' (*empeiria*); it is only spelled out in the amplified account of 100^{a}3–9. What is experience? And does the experienced man formulate any sort of universal proposition? Experience depends on the presence of many memories of the same thing (*Met A* 1, 980^{b}29). We might, then, imagine the experienced man saying something like: "All the *B*s I've ever come across have been *A*" (cf. *A* 1, 71^{a}34, for this form of expression); and the depth of his experience is determined by the number of *B*s he has witnessed. He differs from the man of knowledge in that his universal judgement is limited to past, observed, cases of *A*'s holding of *B*. On the other hand, *Met A* 1, 981^{a}5–9, suggests that the man of experience simply remembers many propositions of the form "This *B* is *A*" ("Socrates was cured of fever by taking hellebore"), and does not formulate any general proposition. The distinction between these two ways of taking "experience" is not perhaps very great: each seems to provide a perfectly reasonable account of what it is to rely on experience.

Stage (D) contains some puzzles. First, the reference to an 'account' (i.e. a definition) at 100^{a}2, and the language of 100^{a}6–8, suggest concept-acquisition. On the other hand, the distinction between skill and understanding (100^{a}8) is readily explained propositionally: the propositions of understanding simply state facts; those of skill also give instructions for acting or producing (cf. *EN Z* 4, 1140^{a}10–13).

This account comes "from experience, or from all the universal which has come to rest in the soul" (100^{a}6). 'Resting' here amounts to no more than presence (the phrase comes from *Phaedo* 96^b—*Int* 3, 16^{b}20, and *Phys H* 3, 247^{b}10, have nothing to do with the case). And the connective "or" is presumably epexegetic—"i.e." (cf. Le Blond (1), 129 n. 1). What, then, is "all the universal"? The parallel in *Met A* 1 runs: "Skill comes about when from the many thoughts of experience a single universal belief about similar things comes about" (981^{a}5–7). The jump to "universal belief" is presumably inductive. The passage plainly deals with propositional knowledge. It refers to *many* thoughts, where our passage refers to *all* the universal. We might gloss "all the universal" in terms of 'perfect' induction: proper knowledge that every *B* is *A* only comes about when *all* the relevant particular propositions are known (cf. *APr B* 23, 68^{b}27–9). But it is hard to believe that Aristotle ever supposed 'experience' to be capable of providing the materials for a 'perfect' induction. Perhaps, then, Aristotle is thinking primarily of concept-acquisition: we understand a notion, *A*, when 'all' *A* rests in our minds; and that, presumably, will occur either when the successive impressions of particular *A*s have etched a complete image in our minds, or else when we have enough concurrent images of *A*s to extract all and only the essential attributes of *A*. ("All the universal" is identified as "the one apart from the many": this phrase regularly denotes 'separate',

Platonic universals (cf. *A* 11, 77^a5, notes); but it does not always do so (see Cherniss, 77 n. 56) and quite evidently it does not do so here.)

The 'account' of 100^a1 becomes at 100^a8 "a principle of . . . understanding" (for the phrase see *A* 3, 72^b24, notes). Aristotle is doubtless thinking primarily of a 'principle of understanding', or comprehension, of the principles. But nothing in the four-stage account restricts it to principles: we might, then, take *B* 19 as a general description of the acquisition of universal knowledge—and the parallel in *Met A* 1 talks in general of "skill and understanding". Suppose, then, that *P* is a principle and *Q* is not, but that **a** acquires knowledge both of *P* and of *Q* by the process described in *B* 19. Now by *A* 2 **a**'s knowledge of *P* must be superior to his knowledge of *Q*; and so a single process may lead to knowledge of different worth when applied to different objects. That is, I think, a trifle paradoxical: the paradox does not arise if Aristotle is thinking only of concept-acquisition.

100^a10: This paragraph sums up the answer to the first question, pointing out that it satisfies the two conditions laid down at 99^b32–4.

100^a10: "inhere in us in a determinate form (*aphōrismenai*)": i.e. 'are innately present in us in an actualized state'; cf. Bonitz, 129^a30–4.

100^a12: "as in a battle . . .": the metaphor is repeated, in a slightly different context, at [*Probl*] *IZ* 7, 917^a28–32; *KZ* 8, 941^a9–13. At 100^a13 the MSS read *archēn*. The commentators take this to mean "until they come to a starting-point", and suppose an Aristotelian pun (since *archē* also means "first principle"). But the pun is frigid, and I cannot imagine what 'starting-point' the routed soldiers might come to. The phrase ought to mean something like "until they reach a certain strength". I doubt if the received text can bear this meaning; and I continue, with a parent's partiality, to favour the emendation *alkēn*. (The word *alkē* is Aristotelian; and the phrase *eis alkēn elthein* is found at Euripides, *Phoen* 421.)

100^a14: ". . . what we have just said": "just" translates *palai*, a word which may also mean "some time ago". Waitz, taking it in the latter sense, refers to *B* 13, 97^b7–25; but it is hard to see how the present passage could have been offered as a clearer version of that earlier text, and I take Aristotle to be referring to what he has just said—perhaps, in particular, to 100^a3–9 (see BRUNSCHWIG (1981), 84–6). However that may be, Aristotle is trying to explain how we apprehend the highest universals (cf. in general *Phys A* 1): we are to proceed, by successive 'stands', from low universals such as *man* ("such-and-such an animal": 100^b2) up through *animal*, until we reach "something partless and universal" (100^b2) i.e. the appropriate category (in the illustrative case, substance). The categories are *amerē* in that they have no logical 'parts' (cf. e.g. *Met Δ* 25, 1023^b24): "the so-called kinds are universal and indivisible (for there is no account of them)" (*Met Δ* 3, 1014^b9–10). They are "the universals" *par excellence* in that they are the highest universals.

Several points of detail require notice:

100ᵃ16: "one of the undifferentiated items": i.e. an *infima species* (cf. *B* 13, 97ᵇ31)—not an individual, for the 'stand' of a single individual cannot yield anything universal (see 100ᵃ5–8). (I here follow the orthodox interpretation. It has recently been suggested that the *adiaphora* here are "unities composed of (as yet) undifferentiated things"; these unarticulated unities, which are the same as "all the universal" (100ᵃ6), are then identified with the 'confused' universals from which we are said to start out at *Phys A* 1, 183ᵃ22–4. See BOLTON (1991), 6–9.)

100ᵃ16: "there is a primitive universal in the soul": if this translation is correct, a 'primitive' universal must be the same as an *infima species*. The text might perhaps better be rendered: "then for the first time there is a universal in the soul".

100ᵃ17: "for although you perceive...": This remark attempts to cope with an objection that has been in the air since 99ᵇ35: the process Aristotle describes produces universals; but it starts from perception and perception is of particulars—how, then, can the gap between particulars and universals be jumped? Aristotle's answer is that perception in fact gives us universals from the start (cf. *A* 31, 87ᵇ29, notes). He means that we perceive things *as As*; and that this, so to speak, lodges the universal, *A*, in our minds from the start—although we shall not, of course, have an explicit or articulated understanding of *A* until we have advanced to Stage (D). (It should be noted that this account is intended to hold for *all* perceivers: it is not peculiar to human perception, nor does it involve the intellect in any way. Even a fly sees an *F*.)

Aristotle's illustration is in some ways unfortunate. It is essential for him to pick an *infima species*, like *man*; for his task is to show how we climb the Porphyrean tree from *infima species* to *summum genus*. Yet it is not clear how we are to apprehend *man* in the first place. Aristotle's theory of perception divides the objects of perception into two classes, essential and incidental (cf. *An B* 6). Essential objects are either proper to a given sense (e.g. colours to sight, sounds to hearing) or common (e.g. motion, shape, size). Incidental objects cover everything else; if *X* is an incidental object of perception, then I perceive *X* only if there is some essential object *Y* such that I perceive *Y* and *Y* is *X*. Individuals are the prime examples of incidental objects (*An B* 6, 418ᵃ21; *Γ* 1, 425ᵃ25). There is very little evidence for *man*, but what there is makes it an incidental object (*An Γ* 6, 430ᵇ29); and it is in any case hard to see how *man* could be either a proper or a common sensible. *Man*, then, is not directly implanted in our minds by the senses, as Aristotle's words in *B* 19 suggest; but in that case we need an account, which Aristotle nowhere gives, of how such concepts as *man* are derived from the data of perception.

100ᵇ1: "Next, a stand is made among these items": just as the different impressions of the 'primitive' universal rallied until that universal made a stand, so now the different 'primitive' universals will rally until the secondary universal can make a stand. Thus *man, horse, lion*, etc. will give rise to *land animal*. Presumably some process of abstraction is required to move from the several primitives to the single secondary universal.

100^b4: "we must get to know the primitives by induction": the 'primitives' here are principles rather than the 'primitive' universals of 100^a16 (cf. *EN Z* 3, 1139^b30-1). Ross supposes that these 'primitives' are axioms, i.e. propositional principles; and he thinks that 100^b3-5 contains the following argument: '⟨We have just seen that⟩ perception . . . instils the universal ⟨concepts by induction⟩; thus it is clear, ⟨by analogy⟩, that we get to know the primitive ⟨propositions⟩ by induction.' It is, I think, difficult to extract this from the text; if only because Aristotle never in *B* 19 makes explicit the distinction between primitive concepts and primitive propositions.

It is possible to make sense of 100^b3-5 by construing the 'primitives' as terms—specifically, as terms for the *summa genera*. Thus: 'We come to understand topmost terms by induction; for ⟨first, the movement upward from first to higher universals is, as we have just seen, plainly inductive; and secondly,⟩ the acquisition of the first, lowest, universals is inductively based.' Here "induction" is used, in a weak sense, to refer to any cognitive progress from the less to the more general; and perception "instils universals" by induction simply because our first grasp of the universal *A* depends on our having perceived a quantity of individual *A*s. Thus construed, 100^b3-5 says no more than that concept acquisition proceeds from the less to the more general. (For induction as the way to the principles see also e.g. *Phys A* 2, 185^a13; *Met E* 1, 1025^b10-18; *EN A* 7, 1098^b3-5.)

100^b5: *The Second Question Answered*: What is the state, or *hexis*, that grasps the principles? Aristotle answers that it is *nous* or comprehension. Thus:

(1) If *P* is a principle and **a** apprehends *P*, then **a** comprehends *P*.

There is a parallel argument in *EN Z* 6; and (1) has been anticipated at *A* 23, 85^a1; 24, 86^a29; and 33, 88^b35.

The commentators translate *nous* by "intuition". The word "intuition" is a term of art; when it has a determinate sense (and does not merely stand for knowing we know not how), it implies a sort of mental 'vision': intuition is mental sight; intuited truths are just 'seen' to be true; intuiting that *P* is coming to know that *P* without any ratiocination and without using sense-perception—it is 'seeing' that *P*. The term "intuition" has a hallowed connection with *B* 19; indeed, the classical distinction between 'intuitive' and 'demonstrative' knowledge, which is common property to rationalists and empiricists, derives ultimately from this chapter.

Tradition apart, does anything speak in favour of translating *nous* by "intuition"? The best argument I can provide is this: in *EN Z* 11, Aristotle says that "*nous* deals with what is ultimate in both directions;

for *nous*, and not reason (*logos*), deals with both the primitive definitions and the ultimate items". And he adds that "one needs to have
perception of the latter, and that is *nous*" (1143ᵃ35–ᵇ5). The *nous* which
deals with individuals, in particular mathematical individuals (cf. *A* 12,
77ᵇ31, notes), is, or is like, perception; and this *nous* is identified in *EN*
with the *nous* which deals with definitions or first principles, and hence
with the *nous* of *B* 19: therefore, the *nous* of *B* 19 is a sort of perception;
and if that is so, we can hardly jib at the translation "intuition".

Given this translation, we can now see that in *B* 19 Aristotle recognizes, at least tacitly, the notorious frailty of induction: induction,
according to *B* 19, cannot by itself get us to the principles; there is a
chasm which induction will not leap—we must fly over it on the back of
intuition. The principles, in short, are apprehended by induction plus
intuition, or by 'intuitive induction'.

This, I suppose, is the orthodox view of *B* 19. (For a recent defence of
the 'intuitionist' interpretation of *B* 19 see IRWIN (1988), 134–6, 531–2;
contra BOLTON (1991), 15–17.) Some scholars find it artificial in its
reconciliation of the inductive and the intuitive elements in Aristotle's
account; they prefer to accept it as a sad truth that Aristotle entertained
two mutually inconsistent theories about our knowledge of the principles,
and could not decide between them.

There is a powerful objection to the orthodox view which tells equally
against this reaction to it: both the orthodoxy and its enemies assume
that *nous* and induction are elements in the answer to a single question.
But this assumption is false: Aristotle carefully distinguishes his first
question from his second; and he clearly indicates that induction figures
in the answer to the first, *nous* in the answer to the second. If the
questions are genuinely distinct, their answers cannot conflict in the way
the unorthodox fear, nor need they be reconciled after the fashion of the
orthodoxy.

We may go a little further. It is Aristotle's first question, not his
second, which asks about the process or method by which we gain
knowledge of the principles; and the method is, in a word, inductive.
Nous, which answers the second question, is not intended to pick out
some faculty or method of acquiring knowledge: *nous*, the state or
disposition, stands to induction as understanding (*epistēmē*) stands to
demonstration. Understanding is not a means of acquiring knowledge.
Nor, then, is *nous*.

If this argument is sound, then "intuition" will not do as a translation
for *nous*; for intuition is precisely a faculty or means of gaining knowledge. Hence in my translation I abandon "intuition" and use instead the
colourless word "comprehension". Aristotle's use of *nous* and its cognates is vast and various (Bonitz, 486ᵇ37–487ᵇ20; 491ᵃ18–ᵇ34): nothing
in it imposes a translation like "intuition" or opposes "comprehension".
There remains the argument based on *EN Z* 11: I think that this does
have some force, and that Aristotle's thoughts about the role of *nous*
were not as clear as I have pretended; but the argument in *Z* 11 is

difficult in itself, and without parallel elsewhere; and the identification of *nous* of the principles with quasi-perceptual *nous* is probably denied implicitly at *A* 33, 88^{b}36 (see note). In any case, the evidence provided by the structure of *B* 19 is stronger than an argument culled from an aside in *EN*. (See further Wieland, 62–9; Kosman; Lesher.)

What, then, is the significance of Aristotle's second question, and of his answer to it? The substantive points about our knowledge of principles have already been made; they are that (*a*) we cannot demonstrate the principles, but (*b*) the principles can be known. The first question is the obvious one: how can (*b*) be true, given (*a*). What other question remains? Only, I think, a terminological one: If **a** knows that *P* and *P* is a theorem, then it is proper to say that **a** *understands* that *P*: if **a** knows that *P* and *P* is an axiom, what is the *mot juste* for his knowledge? It is worth asking the question, since it is useful to have different terms to designate the different types of knowledge required for axioms and for theorems. But nothing important hangs on the answer; and though Aristotle had reasons for choosing *nous*, an invented term might have had greater advantages.

Did Aristotle recognize the comparative triviality of his second question? He does not spend much time on it here. Elsewhere, in *A* 3 (see notes) he is happy enough to say that we understand (*epistasthai*) the principles: what matters is not that *nous* rather than *epistēmē* is their mode of apprehension, but that they are not susceptible to *demonstrative epistēmē*.

None the less, Aristotle does argue for (1), his answer to the second question. The argument falls into two parts, the first occupying 100^{b}5–12, the second occupying 100^{b}12–17.

The first part makes use of four premisses:

(2) If **a** apprehends that *P*, then either **a** understands that *P* or **a** comprehends that *P*.

(I use "**a** apprehends that *P*" to mean "**a** stands in some propositional attitude ϕ to *P*, such that ($\forall y$) (necessarily, if *y* ϕs that *P*, then *P*).")

(3) If *P* is truer and more exact than *Q* and **a** understands that *Q* and **a** apprehends that *P*, then **a** comprehends that *P*.

(This, I take it, is the force of saying that only comprehension is truer and more exact than understanding.)

(4) If *P* is a principle and *Q* a theorem, then *P* is more familiar than *Q*.

(Cf. *A* 2, 72^{a}25–^{b}4.)

(5) If **a** understands that *P*, then **a** has an account of *P*.

(Cf. *EN Z* 6, 1140^{b}33—to 'have an account of *P*' is presumably to give, or be able to give, a deductive argument for *P*.)

As an intermediate conclusion Aristotle offers:

(6) If *P* is a principle, **a** does not understand that *P*.

From (2)–(5) we are to infer (1) via (6). The argument is enthymematic, and can be filled out in more than one way. First, we might add the further premiss:

(7) If **a** has an account of P, then P is not a principle.

This, of course, is a truism. From (5) and (7) we can infer (6); and (2) and (6) together entail (1). It is this argument, or something very similar to it, which *EN Z* 6 uses in proof of (1). Thus construed, the argument is not, strictly speaking, sound; for (2) is false (cf. *EN Z* 6, 1141^{a}5). But the point of the argument is plain enough, and plausible: *nous* is regularly used of non-ratiocinative knowledge, and hence is appropriate for knowledge of the principles.

The second way of filling out Aristotle's argument requires some premiss linking familiarity with truth and exactness; then (1) will follow from (3) and (4). Again, the argument will not be sound, but it will serve to express a reasonable point: the principles, being the source of truth and exactness for the theorems, are (by the thesis of *A* 2, 72^{a}29) more true and more exact than them—hence *nous*, which is often used of an exalted grade of apprehension (see esp. *Phil* 59^d), is appropriate.

I turn to 100^{b}12–17. The main premiss here, founded on a weak analogy, is that "understanding is not a principle of understanding". I take this to amount to:

(8) If **a**'s apprehension that P is an ultimate ground for his understanding that Q, then **a** does not understand that P.

From (2) and (8) there follows:

(9) If **a** apprehends that P, and **a**'s apprehension that P is an ultimate ground for his understanding that Q, then **a** comprehends that P.

And (9), together with the truistic:

(10) If P is a principle, **a**'s apprehension that P is an ultimate ground for his understanding that Q

entails (1).

'And in this way the principle of understanding, *nous*, apprehends the principles of a science; and understanding as a whole apprehends the body of the science as a whole.' Aristotle's conclusion, like his exordium, is aphoristic. I do not think that we are expected to pay philosophical attention to it—nor, for that matter, to the second question as a whole. *Nous* has no philosophical importance in *APst*.

I return, finally, to the three general puzzles about *B* 19 which I posed at the beginning of my comments on the chapter.

First, the Janus character of *B* 19 has proved illusory: the answer Aristotle gives to the first question is whole-heartedly empiricist; and only a failure to distinguish between the two questions of *B* 19 will permit a rationalistic interpretation. *Nous* is an answer to the second question, not a rival, rationalistic, answer to the first: 'intuition' as a mode of discovery is absent from *APst*.

Secondly, the relation between *B* 19 and the earlier parts of Book *B* remains obscure; unless we accept Waitz's account of 100ᵃ14, we shall find no recognition in *B* 19 of any earlier discussion of how we might acquire knowledge of the principles. My own guess, for what it is worth, is that *B* 19 began life as an independent essay on the subject; and was at some later stage tacked on to the discussions of *B* 1–18. (The preamble to the chapter supports this guess.) But *B* 19 does not contradict the preceding parts of *B*; and it may be more attractive to see in it a generalization of the thesis implicit in earlier chapters: *B* 19 states formally and in abstract terms what *B* 13, say, had informally implied and concretely illustrated. (BRUNSCHWIG (1981), 81–96, has urged that "we cannot hold that the problem of knowledge of the principles has been examined before it is officially introduced in *B* 19"; for *B* 3–18 do not formally discuss the question 'How can we know the principles?'—rather, they continue the discussion of demonstration and concern themselves with the question 'To what extent, if at all, can demonstration deal with essences?' This account of *B* 3–18 seems to be, as it were, true *de jure*: *de facto*, however, it remains the case that the chapters contain a quantity of material directly relevant to the question 'How can we know the principles?' Note that the ancient commentators, from Theophrastus onwards (frag. 36 Graeser; cf. MORAUX (1979), 81–9), puzzled over the relationship between the two books of *APst*: what is *B* about? and how does it connect to *A*?)

Finally, in my detailed comments on the first question I have tried to indicate how the text lies with regard to a propositional or a conceptual account of the principles. Aristotle's answer can be told in either way. Thus propositionally, we have the following four stages: (P1) **a** sees that this swan is white; (P2) **a** remembers that this swan is white; (P3) **a** grasps that this swan and that swan and . . . and the other swan is white; (P4) **a** understands that all swans are white. Conceptually, the sequence is: (C1) **a** sees a swan; (C2) **a** retains a memory image of a swan; (C3) **a** has retained many such images of swans; (C4) **a** has the notion of *swan*.

Some parts of the text tell strongly for one story, some for the other; and I feel obliged to concede that Aristotle did not realize that he was vacillating between two stories. This conclusion can perhaps be made more palatable by a pair of considerations: first, at stage (C4) **a** 'has the notion of *swan*' in a strong sense—he has an 'account' or definition of what it is to be a swan. Thus the conceptual sequence terminates in something which either is a propositional principle or at least immediately yields one. Secondly, Aristotle had a persistent tendency to treat definitions as the paradigm—or even as the sole—case of propositional principles (above, p. 107). Thus he might have imagined that the distinction between (P1)–(P4) and (C1)–(C4) was a trifling pedantry: the ascent to (C4) yields any interesting results which might be extracted from (P4); and it offers the further advantage of accounting for our conceptual equipment. (See further KAHN (1981), 387–97.)

REFERENCES

The most useful commentaries on *APst* are those of:
J. Philoponus, *In Aristotelis Analytica Posteriora Commentaria*, ed.
M. Wallies, Commentaria in Aristotelem Graeca, xiii. 3 (Berlin, 1909)
J. Zabarella, *In duos Aristotelis libros Posteriorum Analyticorum Commentaria* (Venice, 1582)
J. Pacius, *In Aristotelis Organon commentarius analyticus* (Frankfurt, 1597)
T. Waitz, *Aristotelis Organon* (Leipzig, 1844–6)
W. D. Ross, *Aristotle's Prior and Posterior Analytics* (Oxford, 1949).

In addition, the mathematical passages are all analysed in:
T. L. Heath (2), *Mathematics in Aristotle* (Oxford, 1949)
and the passages bearing on Plato and the Academy are discussed in:
H. F. Cherniss, *Aristotle's Criticism of Plato and the Academy* (Baltimore, 1944).

There are helpful footnotes to G. R. G. Mure's version of *APst* in volume i of the 'Oxford Translation' (Oxford, 1928). And there is invaluable comparative material in:
H. Bonitz, *Index Aristotelicus* (Berlin, 1870).

Several articles bearing on *APst* are included in:
J. Barnes, M. Schofield, R. Sorabji (eds.), *Aristotle—I: Science* (London, 1975).

Among books, see especially:
J. M. Le Blond (1), *Logique et méthode chez Aristote* (Paris, 1939)
S. Mansion, *Le Jugement d' existence chez Aristote* (Louvain, 1976²)
W. Wieland, *Die aristotelische Physik* (Göttingen, 1970²).

On the object and aim of Book *A* see:
H. Scholz, "Die Axiomatik der Alten", *Blätter für deutsche Philosophie*, 4 (1930–1), 259–78 (repr., in translation, in Barnes, Schofield, and Sorabji)
J. Barnes, "Aristotle's Theory of Demonstration", *Phronesis*, 14 (1969), 123–52 (repr. in Barnes, Schofield, and Sorabji)
J. Jope, "Subordinate Demonstrative Science in the Sixth Book of Aristotle's *Physics*", *Classical Quarterly*, 22 (1972), 278–92.

On the connection between Book *A* and Greek mathematics see:
T. L. Heath (1), *The Thirteen Books of Euclid's Elements* (Cambridge, 1925²)
H. D. P. Lee, "Geometrical Method and Aristotle's Account of First Principles", *Classical Quarterly*, 29 (1935), 113–24.

273

Definition, the main subject of Book *B*, is treated in:

J. M. Le Blond (2), "La Définition chez Aristote", *Gregorianum*, 20 (1939), 351–80 (repr., in translation, in vol. iii of Barnes, Schofield, and Sorabji)

R. Sorabji, "Aristotle and Oxford Philosophy", *American Philosophical Quarterly*, 6 (1969), 127–35.

The chronology of the *Analytics* (and much else) is discussed in:

F. Solmsen, *Die Entwicklung der aristotelischen Logik und Rhetorik* (Berlin, 1929).

Solmsen and Ross engaged in a long controversy (see *Philosophical Review* for 1949 and 1951, and the introduction to Ross's edition of the *Analytics*); there is a clear account of the matter by:

A. Mansion, "L'Origine du syllogisme et la théorie de la science chez Aristote", in S. Mansion (ed.), *Aristote et les problèmes de méthode* (Louvain, 1961).

On Aristotle's syllogistic see especially:

G. Patzig, *Aristotle's Theory of the Syllogism* (Dordrecht, 1969), which contains ample references to the rest of the vast literature. The terminology of syllogistic, and of the *Analytics* in general, is analysed in:

B. Einarson, "On Certain Mathematical Terms in Aristotle's Logic", *American Journal of Philology*, 57 (1936), 33–54 and 151–72.

Among studies bearing on more particular aspects of *APst* I refer to the following:

L. A. Kosman, "Understanding, Explanation and Insight in the *Posterior Analytics*", in E. N. Lee, A. P. D. Mourelatos, and R. M. Rorty (eds.), *Exegesis and Argument, Phronesis* supp. vol. 1 (Assen, 1973) —relevant mainly to *A* 2 and *B* 19. On *A* 2 see also:

J. Lyons, *Structural Semantics*, Publications of the Philological Society, xx (Oxford, 1963).

On *A* 3 see:

G. R. Morrow, "Plato and the Mathematicians: An Interpretation of Socrates' Dream in the *Theaetetus*", *Philosophical Review*, 79 (1970), 309–33.

On the various issues raised by *A* 4 see, in addition to Sorabji's article:

K. J. J. Hintikka (1), "Necessity, Universality and Time in Aristotle", *Ajatus*, 30 (1957), 65–90 (repr. in vol. iii of Barnes, Schofield, and Sorabji)

K. J. J. Hintikka (3), *Time and Necessity* (Oxford, 1973)

C. A. Kirwan (ed.), *Aristotle's* Metaphysics *Books Γ, Δ, E*, Clarendon Aristotle series (Oxford, 1971).

Hintikka's work bears also on *A* 6 and *A* 8; and on *A* 10 see:

K. J. J. Hintikka (2), "On the Ingredients of an Aristotelian Science", *Nous*, 6 (1972), 55–69.

A 11 is treated by:
I. Husik, "Aristotle on the Law of Contradiction and the Basis of the Syllogism", *Mind*, 15 (1906), 215–22 (repr. in I. Husik, *Philosophical Essays* (Oxford, 1952)).

On *A* 13 see:
B. A. Brody, "Towards an Aristotelian Theory of Scientific Explanation", *Philosophy of Science*, 39 (1972), 20–31.

Some of the problems in *A* 19–22 are eased by:
R. Demos, "The Structure of Substance according to Aristotle", *Philosophy and Phenomenological Research*, 5 (1944–5), 255–68.
D. W. Hamlyn, "Aristotle on Predication", *Phronesis*, 6 (1961), 110–25.
J. L. Ackrill (ed.), *Aristotle's* Categories *and* de Interpretatione, Clarendon Aristotle series (Oxford, 1963).

On *B* 1–2, and in general on the verb *einai* in *APst* see:
C. H. Kahn, *The Verb* Be *in Ancient Greek, Foundations of Language* supp. vol. 16 (Dordrecht, 1973).

Some of the issues in *B* 11 are discussed in:
W. W. Fortenbaugh, "Nicomachean Ethics, I, 1096^{b}26–9", *Phronesis*, 11 (1966), 185–94
M. Mignucci, "Di un Passo Controverso degli "Analitici Secondi" di Aristotele", in *Scritti in Onore di Carlo Giacon* (Padua, 1972)
D. M. Balme (ed.), *Aristotle's* de Partibus Animalium *I and* de Generatione Animalium *I*, Clarendon Aristotle series (Oxford, 1972).

On *B* 12 see Demos's paper, and especially:
L. Robin, "Sur la conception aristotélicienne de la causalité", *Archiv für Geschichte der Philosophie*, 23 (1910), 1–28 and 184–210.

On *B* 19, in addition to Kosman's paper, see:
J. H. Lesher, "The Meaning of *ΝΟΥΣ* in the Posterior Analytics", *Phronesis*, 18 (1973), 44–68.

SUPPLEMENTARY REFERENCES

ACKRILL, J. L. (1981), "Aristotle's Theory of Definition: Some Questions on *Posterior Analytics*, II. 8–10", in BERTI (1981).
ALBERTI, ANTONINA (ed.) (1990), *Logica, mente e persona* (Florence).
BALME, D. M. (1987), "Aristotle's Use of Division and Differentiae", in GOTTHELF and LENNOX (1987).
BARNES, JONATHAN (1976), "Aristotle, Menaechmus, and Circular Proof", *Classical Quarterly*, 26: 278–92.
—— (1981), "Proof and the Syllogism", in BERTI (1981).
—— (1982), "Sheep have Four Legs", in *Proceedings of the World Congress on Aristotle*, iii (Athens).
—— (1985), "Aristotelian Arithmetic", *Revue de la philosophie ancienne*, 3: 97–133.
—— (1990a), *The Toils of Scepticism* (Cambridge).
—— (1990b), "Logical Form and Logical Matter", in ALBERTI (1990).
BARNES, JONATHAN, BOBZIEN, SUSANNE, FLANNERY, KEVIN, and IERODIAKONOU, KATERINA (1991), *Alexander of Aphrodisias: On Aristotle, Prior Analytics, I. 1–7* (London).
BERTI, ENRICO (ed.) (1981), *Aristotle on Science: The* Posterior Analytics (Padua).
BOLTON, ROBERT (1976), "Essentialism and Semantic Theory in Aristotle", *Philosophical Review*, 85: 514–44.
—— (1987), "Definition and Scientific Method in Aristotle's *Posterior Analytics* and *Generation of Animals*", in GOTTHELF and LENNOX (1987).
—— (1991), "Aristotle's Method in Natural Science: *Physics*, I", in JUDSON (1991b).
BRUNSCHWIG, JACQUES (1981), "L'Objet et la structure des *Seconds Analytiques* d'après Aristote", in BERTI (1981).
BURNYEAT, M. F. (1981), "Aristotle on Understanding Knowledge", in BERTI (1981).
CAUJOLLE-ZASLAWSKY, F. (1990), "Étude préparatoire à une interprétation du sens aristotélicien d'ἐπαγωγή", in DEVEREUX and PELLEGRIN (1990).
CHARLES, DAVID (1990), "Aristotle on Meaning, Natural Kinds and Natural History", in DEVEREUX and PELLEGRIN (1990).
COOPER, JOHN M. (1987), "Hypothetical Necessity and Natural Teleology", in GOTTHELF and LENNOX (1987).
CORCORAN, JOHN (ed.) (1974), *Ancient Logic and its Modern Interpretations* (Dordrecht).
DE GANDT, FRANÇOIS (1975–6), "La *mathésis* d'Aristote: Introduction aux *Analytiques Seconds*", *Revue des sciences philosophiques et théologiques*, 59: 564–600; 60: 37–84.

DEMOSS, DAVID, and DEVEREUX, DANIEL (1988), "Essence, Existence, and Nominal Definition in Aristotle's *Post. Analytics*, II. 8–10", *Phronesis*, 32: 133–54.

DESLAURIERS, MARGUERITE (1990), "Aristotle's Four Types of Definition", *Apeiron*, 23: 1–26.

DEVEREUX, DANIEL, and PELLEGRIN, PIERRE (eds.) (1990), *Biologie, Logique et Métaphysique chez Aristote* (Paris).

DÖRING, KLAUS (1972), *Die Megariker* (Amsterdam).

EBERT, THEODOR (1980), Review of MIGNUCCI (1975) and Barnes, *Aristotle: Posterior Analytics*, *Archiv für Geschichte der Philosophie*, 62: 85–91.

EVERSON, STEPHEN (ed.) (1990), *Epistemology: Companions to Ancient Thought, I* (Cambridge).

FEREJOHN, MICHAEL T. (1981), "Aristotle on Necessary Truth and Logical Priority", *American Philosophical Quarterly*, 18: 285–93.

—— (1988), "Meno's Paradox and *de re* Knowledge in Aristotle's Theory of Demonstration", *History of Philosophy Quarterly*, 5: 99–117.

—— (1991), *The Origins of Aristotelian Science* (New Haven, Conn.).

FREELAND, CYNTHIA A. (1991), "Accidental Causes and Real Explanations", in JUDSON (1991*b*).

GOMEZ-LOBO, ALFONSO (1978), "Aristotle's First Philosophy and the Principles of Particular Sciences", *Zeitschrift für philosophische Forschung*, 32: 183–94.

—— (1980), "The So-called Question of Existence in Aristotle, *An. Post.* 2. 1–2", *Review of Metaphysics*, 34: 71–89.

—— (1981), "Definitions in Aristotle's *Posterior Analytics*", in O'MEARA (1981).

GOTTHELF, ALLAN (1987), "First Principles in Aristotle's *Parts of Animals*", in GOTTHELF and LENNOX (1987).

—— and LENNOX, JAMES (eds.) (1987), *Philosophical Issues in Aristotle's Biology* (Cambridge).

GRAESER, ANDREAS (ed.) (1987), *Mathematics and Metaphysics in Aristotle*, Berner Reihe philosophischer Studien, vi (Bern/Stuttgart).

GRANGER, GILLES-GASTON (1976), *La Théorie aristotélicienne de la science* (Paris).

GRANGER, HERBERT (1981), "The Differentia and the *Per Se* Accident in Aristotle", *Archiv für Geschichte der Philosophie*, 66: 118–29.

GUARIGLIA, OSVALDO N. (1985), "Die Definition und die Kausalerklärung bei Aristoteles", in MENNE and OEFFENBERGER (1985).

HADGOPOULOS, DEMETRIUS J. (1977), "διὰ μέσων or δι' ἀμέσων?—*Posterior Analytics*, II, viii, 93a36", *Apeiron*, 11: 32–9.

INWOOD, BRAD (1979), "A Note on Commensurate Universals in the *Posterior Analytics*", *Phronesis*, 24: 320–9.

IRWIN, T. H. (1988), *Aristotle's First Principles* (Oxford).

JUDSON, LINDSAY (1991*a*), "Chance and 'Always or For the Most Part' in Aristotle", in JUDSON (1991*b*).

JUDSON, LINDSAY (ed.) (1991*b*), *Aristotle's* Physics (Oxford).

KAHN, CHARLES H. (1981), "The Role of *nous* in the Cognition of First Principles in *Posterior Analytics*, II. 19", in BERTI (1981).

KRETZMANN, NORMAN (ed.) (1982), *Infinity and Continuity in Ancient and Mediaeval Thought* (Ithaca, NY).

KULLMANN, WOLFGANG (1974), *Wissenschaft und Methode: Interpretationen zur aristotelischen Theorie der Naturwissenschaft* (Berlin).

—— (1981), "Die Funktion der mathematischen Beispiele in Aristoteles' *Analytica Posteriora*", in BERTI (1981).

KUNG, JOAN (1982), "Aristotle's *de Motu Animalium* and the Separability of the Sciences", *Journal of the History of Philosophy*, 20: 65–76.

LANDOR, BLAKE (1981), "Definitions and Hypotheses in *Posterior Analytics*, 72^{a}19–25 and 76^{b}35–77^{a}4", *Phronesis*, 26: 308–18.

—— (1985), "Aristotle on Demonstrating Essence", *Apeiron*, 19: 116–32.

LEAR, JONATHAN (1980), *Aristotle and Logical Theory* (Cambridge).

LENNOX, JAMES (1987), "Divide and Explain: the *Posterior Analytics* in Practice", in GOTTHELF and LENNOX (1987).

LLOYD, G. E. R. (1961), "The Development of Aristotle's Theory of the Classification of Animals", *Phronesis*, 6: 59–81 (repr. with additions in LLOYD (1991)).

—— (1990), "Aristotle's Zoology and his Metaphysics: the status quaestionis", in DEVEREUX and PELLEGRIN (1990) (repr. in LLOYD (1991)).

—— (1991), *Methods and Problems in Greek Science* (Cambridge).

MCKIRAHAN, RICHARD D. (1983), "Aristotelian Epagoge in *Prior Analytics*, 2. 21 and *Posterior Analytics*, I. I", *Journal of the History of Philosophy*, 21: 1–13.

MANSION, SUZANNE (1984), "'Plus connu en soi', 'Plus connu pour nous': une distinction épistémologique importante chez Aristote", in S. MANSION, *Études Aristotéliciennes* (Louvain-la-Neuve).

MENNE, A., and OEFFENBERGER, N. (eds.) (1982, 1985, 1988, 1990), *Zur modernen Deutung der aristotelischen Logik*, i–iv (Hildesheim).

MIGNUCCI, MARIO (1975), *L'Argomentazione dimostrativa in Aristotele* (Padua).

—— (1981), "Ὡς ἐπὶ τὸ πολύ et nécessaire dans la conception aristotélicienne de la science", in BERTI (1981) (repr. in MENNE and OEFFENBERGER (1988)).

—— (1987), "Aristotle's Arithmetic", in GRAESER (1987).

MORAUX, P. (1979), *Le Commentaire d'Alexandre d'Aphrodisie aux "Seconds Analytiques" d'Aristote*, Peripatoi, xiii (Berlin).

MORAVCSIK, JULIUS M. E. (1974), "Aristotle on Adequate Explanations", *Synthèse*, 28: 3–27.

—— (1975), "Aitia as Generative Factor in Aristotle's Philosophy", *Dialogue*, 14: 622–38.

MUELLER, IAN (1974), "Greek Mathematics and Greek Logic", in CORCORAN (1974).

—— (1982), "Aristotle and the Quadrature of the Circle", in KRETZMANN (1982).

NOVAK, JOSEPH A. (1978), "A Geometrical Syllogism: *Posterior Analytics*, II. 11", *Apeiron*, 12: 26–33.

NUSSBAUM, MARTHA C. (1985), *Aristotle's* de Motu Animalium (first edn. 1978; Princeton, NJ).

O'MEARA, D. J. (ed.) (1981), *Studies in Aristotle*, Studies in Philosophy and the History of Philosophy, ix (Washington, DC).

PATZIG, GÜNTHER (1981), "Erkenntnisgründe, Realgründe und Erklärungen (zu *Anal. Post. A* 13)", in BERTI (1981).

PELLEGRIN, PIERRE (1981), "Division et syllogisme chez Aristote", *Revue philosophique de la France et de l'étranger*, 171: 169–87.

SCANLAN, MICHAEL (1982), "On Finding Compactness in Aristotle", *History and Philosophy of Logic*, 4: 1–8.

SMITH, ROBIN (1982a), "The Relationship of Aristotle's Two *Analytics*", *Classical Quarterly*, 32: 327–35.

—— (1982b), "The Syllogism in *Posterior Analytics* I", *Archiv für Geschichte der Philosophie*, 64: 113–35.

—— (1986), "Immediate Propositions and Aristotle's Proof Theory", *Ancient Philosophy*, 6: 47–68.

—— (1989), *Aristotle: Prior Analytics* (Indianapolis).

SORABJI, RICHARD (1980), *Necessity, Cause and Blame* (London).

—— (1981), "Definitions: Why Necessary and in What Way?", in BERTI (1981).

STRIKER, GISELA (1977), Review of Barnes, *Aristotle's Posterior Analytics*, *Zeitschrift für philosophische Forschung*, 31: 316–20.

TARÁN, LEONARDO (1981), *Speusippus of Athens*, Philosophia Antiqua, xxxix (Leiden).

TAYLOR, C. C. W. (1990), "Aristotle's Epistemology", in EVERSON (1990).

TILES, J. E. (1983), "Why the Triangle has Two Right Angles Kath' Hauto", *Phronesis*, 27: 1–16.

VAN FRAASSEN, BAS C. (1980), "A Re-examination of Aristotle's Philosophy of Science", *Dialogue*, 19: 20–45.

VERDENIUS, W. J. (1981), "Notes on Some Passages in Book I", in BERTI (1981).

VON FRITZ, KURT (1955), "Die ARXAI in der griechischen Mathematik", *Archiv für Begriffsgeschichte*, 1: 12–103 (repr. in VON FRITZ (1971)).

—— (1971), *Grundprobleme der Geschichte der antiken Wissenschaft* (Berlin).

WIANS, WILLIAM (1989), "Aristotle, Demonstration, and Teaching", *Ancient Philosophy*, 9: 245–53.

WIELAND, WOLFGANG (1972), "Zeitliche Kausalstrukturen in der aristotelischen Logik", *Archiv für Geschichte der Philosophie*, 54: 229–37 (repr. in MENNE and OEFFENBERGER (1988)).

WILLIAMS, MARK F. (1984), *Studies in the Manuscript Tradition of Aristotle's Analytica*, Beiträge zur klassischen Philologie, clxi (Königstein).

GLOSSARIES

The glossaries list technical and semi-technical terms, and a few others besides. For the most part, the equivalences which they give hold only for the most part.

I Greek–English

Note that compound verbs are usually entered under their simple form.

ἀγνοεῖν etc.	be ignorant of (see p. 151)
ἀγχίνοια	acumen
αἰσθάνεσθαι	perceive
αἴσθημα	percept
αἴσθησις	perception
αἰσθητικός	empirical (79^a2)
αἰτεῖσθαι	postulate (see p. 141)
αἴτημα	postulate
αἰτία	explanation (see p. 89)
αἰτιατός	explanandum (76^a20: explainable)
αἴτιος	explanatory
ἀκολουθεῖν	follow
παρακολουθεῖν etc.	be interrelated with
ἄκρα	extreme terms
ἀκριβής etc.	exact (see p. 189)
ἀληθής etc.	true
ἄμεσος	immediate (see p. 94)
ἀμφισβητεῖν	dispute
ἀνάγειν	lead back; refer
ἀναγωγή	reduction
ἀναγκαῖος etc.	necessary
ἀναιρεῖν	reject
ἀναλογία	analogy
ἀνάλυσις	analysis
ἀντικεῖσθαι etc.	be opposed, opposite to
ἀντιστρέφειν etc.	convert (see pp. 109, 153, 166)
ἀξιοῦν	claim
ἀξίωμα	axiom (see p. 99)
ἀπατᾶσθαι etc.	err
ἄπειρος	infinite
ἁπλοῦς	simple
ἁπλῶς	*simpliciter* (see p. 87)
ἀποδιδόναι	elucidate (78^b22: set out)
ἀπορία etc.	puzzle
ἀπόφανσις	statement

ἀρχή etc.	principle; beginning; start (see p. 238)
ἄτομος	atomic (see p. 163)
ἀφαιρεῖν etc.	remove (81ᵇ3: abstraction)
γένος	kind
γίγνεσθαι	become; come about; occur
παραγίγνεσθαι	be acquired
γίγνωσκειν etc.	know (see p. 82)
γνωστικός	cognitive
γνωρίζειν	get to know (acquire knowledge, become known)
γνώριμος	familiar (see p. 95)
γνωρισμός	recognition
δεικνύναι etc.	prove
δεικτικός	probative (see p. 183)
ἀποδεικνύναι etc.	demonstrate
ἀναπόδεικτος	indemonstrable (see p. 94)
ἐπιδεικνύναι	show
δῆλος	plain
δηλοῦν	show
διαιρεῖν etc.	divide
διαλέγεσθαι	argue (92ᵇ32: talk)
διαλεκτικός	dialectical
διαλεκτική	dialectic
διάνοια	thought
διανοητικός	intellectual
διάστημα	interval
τὸ διὰ τί	the reason why
διαφορά etc.	difference
τὸ διότι	the reason why
δόξα etc.	opinion
δύναμις	capacity
δυνάμει	potentially
εἰδέναι	know (see p. 82)
προειδέναι	know already
εἶδος	form
εἶναι	be (the case); exist; hold; occur (see p. 84)
ἐκ	from (see pp. 81, 139)
ἐκλέγειν	excerpt
ἐλέγχειν	refute
ἐμβάλλεσθαι	interpolate
ἐμπίπτειν	fall
παρεμπίπτειν	fall in between
ἐναντίος	contrary
ὑπεναντίος	not in accordance with
ἔνδοξος	reputable (see p. 126)
ἕνεκα τίνος etc.	with what purpose
ἔνστασις	objection

ἐπαγωγή etc.	induction (see p. 83)
ἕπεσθαι	follow
ἐπίστασθαι	understand (see p. 82)
ἐπιστήμη	understanding; science
ἐπιστημονικός	scientific
ἐπιστητός	understandable
ἐρωτᾶν	ask (see p. 83)
ἐρώτημα	question
ἔσχατος	last
ἐφαρμόττειν	attach to (see p. 195)
ἐφεξῆς	consecutively
ἔχειν	have; grasp; possess; contain
ἐχόμενος	next to (90ᵇ1: neighbouring)
ἕξις	state (see p. 260)
ζητεῖν etc.	seek
ἦ	as
θέσις etc.	(see τιθέναι etc.)
θεωρεῖν etc.	study (88ᵃ3: observe)
θηρεύειν etc.	hunt
ἴδιος	proper (see p. 110)
ἵστασθαι	come to a stop; make a stand
καθ᾽ αὑτό	in itself (see p. 111)
καθ᾽ ἕκαστον	particular (see p. 83) (99ᵃ18: severally)
καθόλου	universal(ly) (see pp. 111, 256) (95ᵇ12: general)
καταπυκνοῦσθαι	thicken
κατασκευάζειν	establish
κατηγορεῖν etc.	predicate (see p. 117)
κατηγορικός	positive
κινεῖν etc.	change; move
κοινός	common (see p. 99)
κύριος	important for (76ᵃ18: sovereign)
κυρίως	properly
κύκλος etc.	circle
λαμβάνειν	get; take; assume
ἐκλαμβάνειν	extract
μεταλαμβάνειν	take instead (se p. 230)
προσλαμβάνειν	assume in addition
ὑπολαμβάνειν etc.	believe
λανθάνειν	escape notice
λέγειν	say; argue; call; mean; state; speak about; describe
λογισμός	calculation
λόγος	account; argument; ratio
λογικός	general (see pp. 173, 218)
μανθάνειν etc.	learn
μάθημα	mathematics (see p. 152)

μαθηματικός	mathematical
μέσον	middle term
μεταβαίνειν	cross
μεταβάλλειν	alter
νοεῖν etc.	think
νοῦς	comprehension (see p. 267)
οἰκεῖος	appropriate
οἷον	e.g.; i.e.
ὁμώνυμος etc.	homonymous
ὄνομα	name
ὅπερ	just what is (see p. 176)
ὁρίζειν etc.	define
διορίζειν	define
ὅρος	term; definition
τὸ ὅτι	the fact
οὐσία	substance; essence (see p. 177)
πάθημα	attribute
πάθος	attribute
παρά	apart from (see p. 144)
περαίνειν	bound
πεπερασμένος etc.	finite
πέρας	limit
πιστεύειν etc.	be convinced of
πρᾶγμα	object
πρόβλημα	problem (see p. 250)
πρότασις	proposition (see p. 97)
πρότερος	prior; former; earlier; before; already (see p. 95)
πρῶτος	first; primitive; prime
πτῶσις	aspect (see p. 224)
σημαίνειν	mean
σημεῖον	evidence
σκοπεῖν etc.	inquire
στέρησις etc.	privation
στοιχεῖον	element
συγγενής	of a kind
συλλογίζεσθαι etc.	deduce (see pp. 83, 244)
ἀσυλλόγιστος	non-deductive
συμβεβηκός	incidental (see p. 89)
συμπέρασμα	conclusion
συνεχής	continuous
συνιέναι	grasp (only at: 71ᵃ7, ᵃ12, ᵇ32; 76ᵇ37)
συστοιχία	chain (see p. 163)
σχῆμα	figure
σῴζειν	preserve (see p. 127)
τελευταῖος	ultimate
τὸ τί ἐστι	what something is (see p. 174)

τὸ τί ἦν εἶναι	what it is to be something (see p. 174)
τιθέναι	posit; position
θέσις	posit; position ($75^{b}32$; $94^{a}2$: arrangement)
μετατιθέναι	transpose
πρόσθεσις	additional posit
ὑποτιθέναι	suppose
ὑπόθεσις	supposition (see p. 100)
ὑπάρχειν	hold (of); occur
ἐνυπάρχειν	inhere in
ὑποκείμενον	underlying subject
φάναι	say; assert
ἀντίφασις	contradictory pair
ἀποφάναι etc.	deny
ἀπόφασις	negation
καταφάναι etc.	affirm
φανερός	clear
φάσκειν	say; declare
φθείρειν etc.	perish (see p. 127)
φύσις	nature; natural object
φυσική	natural science
χῶρις	separately
ψευδής etc.	false
ψυχή	soul
ὡς ἐπὶ τὸ πολύ	for the most part (see p. 192)

II English–Greek

abstraction	ἀφαίρεσις
account (n.)	λόγος
acquire knowledge	γνωρίζειν
acumen	ἀγχίνοια
affirm	καταφάναι
alter	μεταβάλλειν
analogy	ἀναλογία
analysis	ἀνάλυσις
apart from	παρά (see p. 144)
appropriate (adj.)	οἰκεῖος
argue	διαλέγεσθαι
argument	λόγος
as	ᾗ
ask	ἐρωτᾶν (see p. 83)
aspect	πτῶσις (see p. 224)
assert	φάναι
assume	λαμβάνειν
assume in addition	προσλαμβάνειν
atomic	ἄτομος (see p. 163)

attach to	ἐφαρμόττειν (see p. 195)
attribute (n.)	πάθημα, πάθος
beginning	ἀρχή
believe	ὑπολαμβάνειν
bound (vb.)	περαίνειν
calculation	λογισμός
capacity	δύναμις
chain	συστοιχία (see p. 163)
claim (vb.)	ἀξιοῦν
clear (adj.)	φανερός
cognitive	γνωστικός
common	κοινός
comprehension	νοῦς (see p. 267)
conclusion	συμπέρασμα
consecutively	ἐφεξῆς
continuous	συνεχής
contradictory pair	ἀντίφασις
contrary	ἐναντίος
convert	ἀντιστρέφειν (see pp. 109, 153, 166)
convinced of, be	πιστεύειν
cross (vb.)	μεταβαίνειν
declare	φάσκειν
deduce	συλλογίζεσθαι
deduction	συλλογισμός (see p. 83)
define	ὁρίζειν, διορίζειν
definition	ὅρος
demonstrate	ἀποδεικνύναι
dialectic	διαλεκτική
difference	διαφορά
dispute (vb.)	ἀμφισβητεῖν
divide	διαιρεῖν
division	διαίρεσις
e.g.	οἷον
element	στοιχεῖον
elucidate	ἀποδιδόναι
empirical	αἰσθητικός
err	ἀπατᾶσθαι
escape notice	λανθάνειν
essence	οὐσία
establish	κατασκευάζειν
evidence	σημεῖον
exact (adj.)	ἀκριβής (see p. 189)
excerpt (vb.)	ἐκλέγειν
explanandum	αἰτιατός
explanation	αἰτία (see p. 89)
explanatory	αἴτιος

286

extract (vb.)	ἐκλαμβάνειν
extreme terms	ἄκρα
fact, the	τὸ ὅτι
fall	ἐμπίπτειν
false	ψευδής
familiar	γνώριμος (see p. 95)
figure	σχῆμα
finite	πεπερασμένος
follow	ἕπεσθαι, ἀκολουθεῖν
form	εἶδος
general (adj.)	λογικός (see pp. 173, 218)
get to know	γνωρίζειν
grasp (vb.)	ἔχειν, συνιέναι
hold (of)	ὑπάρχειν
homonymous	ὁμώνυμος
hunt (vb.)	θηρεύειν
i.e.	οἷον
ignorance	ἄγνοια (see p. 151)
immediate	ἄμεσος (see p. 94)
important	κύριος
incidental	συμβεβηκός (see p. 89)
indemonstrable	ἀναπόδεικτος (see p. 94)
induction	ἐπαγωγή (see p. 83)
infinite	ἄπειρος
inhere in	ἐνυπάρχειν
in itself	καθ' αὑτό (see p. 111)
inquire	σκοπεῖν
intellectual	διανοητικός
interpolate	ἐμβάλλεσθαι
interval	διάστημα
just what is	ὅπερ (see p. 176)
kind (n.)	γένος
kind, of a	συγγενής
know	γίγνωσκειν, εἰδέναι (see p. 82)
knowledge	γνῶσις
last (adj.)	ἔσχατος
learn	μανθάνειν
limit (n.)	πέρας
mathematics	μάθημα (see p. 152)
mean (vb.)	σημαίνειν
middle term	μέσον
most part, for the	ὡς ἐπὶ τὸ πολύ (see p. 192)
name (n.)	ὄνομα
nature	φύσις

287

natural object	φύσις
natural science	φυσική
negation	ἀπόφασις
next to	ἐχόμενος
non-deductive	ἀσυλλόγιστος
object (n.)	πρᾶγμα
objection	ἔνστασις
opinion	δόξα
opposite	ἀντικείμενος
particular	καθ᾿ ἕκαστον (see p. 83)
perceive	αἰσθάνεσθαι
percept	αἴσθημα
perception	αἴσθησις
perish	φθείρειν
plain	δῆλος
posit (n.)	θέσις
posit (vb.)	τιθέναι
positive	κατηγορικός
postulate (vb.)	αἰτεῖσθαι
postulate (n.)	αἴτημα
potentially	δυνάμει
predicate (vb.)	κατηγορεῖν
preserve	σῴζειν
prime	πρῶτος
primitive	πρῶτος
principle	ἀρχή
prior	πρότερος
privation	στέρησις
probative	δεικτικός
problem	πρόβλημα (see p. 250)
proper	ἴδιος (see p. 110)
properly	κυρίως
prove	δεικνύναι
purpose, with what	ἕνεκα τίνος
puzzle (n.)	ἀπορία
question (n.)	ἐρώτημα
ratio	λόγος
reason why, the	τὸ διὰ τί, τὸ διότι
recognition	γνωρισμός
reduction	ἀναγωγή
refer	ἀνάγειν
reject	ἀναιρεῖν
remove	ἀφαιρεῖν
reputable	ἔνδοξος
science	ἐπιστήμη

GLOSSARIES

scientific	ἐπιστημονικός
seek	ζητεῖν
separately	χῶρις
show	δηλοῦν, ἐπιδεικνύναι
simple	ἁπλοῦς
simpliciter	ἁπλῶς (see p. 87)
soul	ψυχή
sovereign (adj.)	κύριος
start	ἀρχή
state (n.)	ἕξις (see p. 260)
statement	ἀπόφανσις
study	θεωρεῖν
substance	οὐσία
suppose	ὑποτιθέναι
supposition	ὑπόθεσις
term	ὅρος
thicken	καταπυκνοῦσθαι
think	νοεῖν
thought	διάνοια
transpose	μετατιθέναι
true	ἀληθής
ultimate	τελευταῖος
underlying subject	ὑποκείμενον
understand	ἐπίστασθαι (see p. 82)
understanding	ἐπιστήμη
universal	καθόλου (see pp. 111, 256)
what it is to be something	τὸ τί ἦν εἶναι (see p. 174)
what something is	τὸ τί ἐστι (see p. 174)

INDEX OF NAMES[1]

---

[1] Modern scholars are not indexed.

INDEX OF PASSAGES[2]

ARISTOTLE
An B 2, 413^{a}10–20: 216
  12, 424^{a}21–4: 193
  Γ 8, 432^{b}3–6: 168
APr A 1, 24^{a}10–11: xx–xxi
  24^{a}22–5: 98
  24^{b}18–20: 82–3
  24^{b}28–30: 111
  27, 43^{b}33–5: 240
  31, 46^{a}32–7: 210
  B 2, 54^{a}4–6: 165
  5, 57^{b}18–21: 105–6
  21, 67^{a}12–26: 85–8
  26, 69^{a}37–^{b}1: 152
EN Z 3, 1139^{b}18–21: 91
  11, 1143^{a}35–^{b}5: 267–8
GA B 8, 747^{b}27–30: 173
GC B 11, 338^{b}1–5: 239
  338^{b}16–18: 239
HA A 6, 491^{a}9–14: xix–xx
Int 3, 16^{b}19–22: 142
Met A 1, 981^{a}5–7: 264
  9, 993^{a}1: 261
  α 1, 993^{b}23–6: 101
  3, 995^{b}15–16: 190
  B 2, 997^{b}35–998^{a}4: 142
  4, 999^{a}26–9: 186
  Γ 4, 1005^{a}19–22: 148
  Δ 3, 1014^{b}9–10: 265
  4, 1015^{a}11–13: 184
  18, 1022^{a}19–20: 117
  25, 1023^{b}23: 190
  30, 1025^{a}30–2: 113
  Z 4, 1030^{a}7–9: 217

  5, 1030^{b}18–26: 113
  Δ 4, 1070^{b}22: 229
PA A 1, 642^{a}4–6: 235
Phys B 3, 195^{a}5: 232
  Δ 12, 222^{a}10–12: 236
Top A 1, 100^{a}18–20: 148
  100^{a}27–9: 94
  105^{a}5–17: 150
  4, 101^{b}16: 250
  B 10, 115^{b}29–35: 87
  E 1, 129^{a}29–31: 173
  Z 4, 141^{b}29–34: 96
  H 3, 153^{a}11–15: 212
  Ι 11, 172^{a}15–21: 149

ARISTOXENUS
Elementa Harmonica B 33: 142

PAPPUS
Collectio ii. 634: 153

PLATO
Meno 80de: 88
  98^a: 90
Phaedo 96^b: 259
Theaet 189^e: 140

SEXTUS EMPIRICUS
adv Math viii. 23: 94–5

THEOPHRASTUS
frag 33 Graeser 99
  34   122

---

[2] The index lists texts, outside *APst*, which are either cited or discussed in the Commentary.

INDEX OF SUBJECTS[3]

abstraction:
  and concepts 248–9, 264, 266–7
  and mathematical objects 85, 168,
    190
  see also mathematics
acumen 202
alpha privative 151
  see also negatives
analogy 138–9, 251, 255
analysis 153–4
anatomy 250
anonymous characteristics 124, 251
appropriateness 93, 97, 126, 130,
    134–7, 166, 173
arithmetic 135, 158, 195–6, 197
  see also numbers
'as such' 118–19, 121–2, 135, 184
astronomy 158, 159, 160, 161
atomicity 163, 243, 257
axioms 99–100, 121, 131, 138–9,
    140–1, 143, 160, 240
  and dialectic 148
  finite xviii, 196
  relative to sciences 99–100
  see also principles; sciences

'be' 84, 100, 203, 218
  see also copula; existence
beauty 132
begging the question 87, 208, 210
belief 201–2
  see also opinion
biology xix–xx, 92, 122, 230, 232, 251

categories 176–7, 178–9, 196, 242,
    265, 266, 267
catoptrics 159, 161
causa cognoscendi 226, 238
cause 89–90, 156, 224, 231, 254
  see also definitions; explanation
certainty 102, 198
chains of terms 131, 163, 169, 191, 256
chance 191–2, 205–6, 233, 262
  not knowable 192

change 116, 175, 191
  no first moment of 237
chronology of A.'s works xv, xxi,
    103–4, 131, 149, 212, 214, 239,
    259, 271
circular proof 103–4, 105–6, 107–10,
    170, 239
common beliefs 91, 198
'common to all' 99–100, 136, 138
comprehension 102, 106–7, 187, 199,
    265, 267
concepts:
  acquisition of 97, 248, 259, 263,
    264–5, 267, 271
  and perception 186
  see also abstraction; terms
consecutiveness 211, 236–7, 237–8
  see also time
contingency 92, 127, 197, 228
  see also necessity
contradictory pairs 98, 98–9, 101, 118
contraries 118, 131–2, 141–2, 165,
    213–14
conversion 109–10, 153, 154, 156,
    166, 209, 210, 239, 255, 256,
    258–9
  laws of xvii
  see also definitions
conviction 102–3
copula 233–4, 235
  see also 'be'
counterpredication 110, 171, 177, 178
  see also conversion

deductions 82–3, 140, 212–13, 218,
    226, 227
  see also syllogisms
definitions:
  causal 224, 240
  and conversion 154, 209, 255, 258
  = *definiens* 100, 200, 208
  definition of 213, 223–4
  and demonstration 207–22, 254
  discovery of 240–9

---

[3] The index covers the Introduction and the Commentary: it does not cover
Aristotle's text. A little supplementary material may be found in the Glossaries.

CPSIA information can be obtained
at www.ICGtesting.com
Printed in the USA
BVHW082053040822
643840BV00015B/220